VIRTUAL LIVES

This book and others available at
www.treetongue.co.uk

VIRTUAL LIVES
The Animated Zodiac

Phoebe Wyss

Tree Tongue Publishing
www.treetongue.co.uk

Published by Tree Tongue
2 Chapel Down Cottages
Threshers
Crediton
Devon
EX17 3PB

ISBN 0-954-6099-8-0

CONTENTS

PREFACE

Suppose the universe as a whole is alive and conscious. Suppose it is an organism possessing an intelligent mind and a feeling soul. Then it would literally be a macrocosm of the human microcosm. People who accept James Lovelock's Gaia hypothesis see planet earth in this way. And there are scientists today who propose that consciousness is not exclusive to humankind, but is found in the cells of all living beings, and may be a basic property of the universe as a whole. So is it too far-fetched to assume that the universe has an inner life?

We speak of the universe as a thing, but what we experience is 'universing', a verb not a noun, an on-going process in which we are caught up. We participate with our bodies in the universe's material dimension, with our minds in its mental level, and in the universal soul with our psyches. Seen in this way, instead of being something separate and private, our inner life becomes a ripple in the inner life of the whole.

Since ancient times it has been known that the universe is both structured and free. Information on cosmic time cycles is contained in Neolithic earthworks, pyramids and stone circles. The Greeks acknowledged the non-random nature of the universe when they called it a 'cosmos', and Pythagoras is credited with discovering the sacred geometry that structures natural forms.

But this alive and intelligent universe is also free, and possesses infinite scope for creativity. And, although the process of 'universing' proceeds in an orderly fashion, modifications and mutations occur continuously. In a similar way, although human nature and human life are determined by structural principles on the implicate level of the psyche, we also possess free will.

The patterning of the inner life of the universe was a subject investigated by the great psychologist C.G.Jung. He used the term 'archetypes' for the facets of the universal psyche that have been personified as gods and goddesses in different cultures over the ages. To begin with Jung located the archetypes in the collective human unconscious, but in his later work he spoke of them as structural principles within the cosmic psyche itself.

Twelve primary archetypes have been recognised since ancient times by cultures all over the world, and represented by zodiac symbols. Although the animals chosen differ on different continents, their number has always remained twelve. They manifest on all levels of the scale of being - human, animal, plant, metal and mineral. An experience of astrology makes us aware of the determining role they play in our life. They not only structure the human personality, but they also provide a script for our individual and collective lives.

If it's true that there's a set of twelve foundational principles embedded in the universal psyche, this could explain how astrology works. What occurs at any particular time is a manifestation of the predominant archetypal forces of the moment. And, because they are built into our minds, the archetypes determine the way we see the world, and affect how we experience events. They also determine which genes will manifest to form our physical bodies, and which chemical processes will occur to create how we think, feel and act.

To readers unversed in astrology these ideas may sound wacky, until they have experienced their truth for themselves. So this book has been written to give people an awareness and understanding of the astrological archetypes by bringing them to life in an entertaining and humorous way. Through experiencing the lives of the twelve characters, readers will become aware of how the archetypes manifest in their own lives, and learn to recognise their signature in the lives of those around them. Thus the proof of the pudding will be in the eating.

We each have all twelve archetypes in us but in different proportions, which explains our individual differences. Your birth chart will show the proportions of your particular mix (see Appendix). The sun sign archetype usually predominates, which is why you are most likely to identify with the character in the book representing your zodiac sign. But there will be qualities that don't fit. In which case, if you know your rising sign, and read the corresponding story, the picture may be more complete.

You may recognise some of your other traits in the characters representing your moon sign, and the sign corresponding to the house of your sun. In my experience, at least four archetypes predominate in most of us, and are usually represented by these four factors - sun sign, rising sign, moon sign and sign corresponding to the sun house.

However there is another factor from your birthchart to pay attention to, when determining the main archetypes in your makeup. If you have one of the outer planets close to your sun (say within 10 degrees), or close to your ascendant (say 10 degrees, but below the ascendant in the first house) they will bring in their corresponding archetypes. Therefore Jupiter conjunctions add a dash of Sagittarius, Saturn conjunctions a dash of Capricorn, Uranus conjunctions a dash of Aquarius, Neptune conjunctions a dash of Pisces, whereas Pluto conjunctions add a dash of the Scorpio archetype. (For instructions on how to find your main archetypes see Appendix at end of book.)

The fact that we are all a mixture of archetypes explains why some people are untypical of their zodiac signs. In such cases other archetypes are strongly enough represented to eclipse their sun sign qualities. In *Virtual Lives*, however, all the characters are stereotypical - unlike in real life where no Aries will be so strongly an Aries as Zak, and no Cancer will be so extreme as Mab. This is because each character has been designed to be a pure example of one archetype only, instead of being a mixture as in real life.

So nothing in these stories is random. The type of birth of each character, their childhood and youth, the kind of jobs they choose, their relationship patterns and their life challenges are all typical of the archetype they represent. We must conclude that nothing in life is a coincidence. Our inner patterning attracts certain events and certain types of people into our sphere, and everything that happens is made meaningful in the context of the archetypes.

As you read this book from chapter to chapter, you are given direct experience of the contrasting ways the characters see the world. It is like putting on a different pair of glasses in each story. So you realise how different other people's viewpoints can be to your own, and afterwards you may understand those people you don't get on with much better. There are six men and six women characters in the book corresponding to the traditional division of the archetypes into male and female energy forms.

Although the personalities of the twelve characters are determined by the archetypes they represent, and the themes in their 'life scripts' are laid down by these archetypes, each character has moral choices to make. The stories have been given a narrative framework of a metaphysical nature, as laid out in the Prologue. And the Prologue is where the reader must always start in order to understand the context of what follows, and make sense of terms like 'interlife', 'incarnation group' and 'inner guide' when they appear in the narrative. And why is the book called *Virtual Lives*? That has been left to the reader to find out.

The characters are shown as learning and growing through their life experiences, because, as the universe is both structured and free, we are determined by our archetypal mix and yet we remain free agents. We are free to make life-enhancing decisions, learn from our bad experiences, deepen our understanding of ourselves and our lives, and recognise our life purpose.

You don't have to believe in astrology to read and enjoy *Virtual Lives*. Just be ready to meet the twelve characters with an open mind. Then, by comparing Zak, Nel, Bob and Mab etc to yourself and those close to you, you can come to your own conclusions about whether there's anything in astrology or not.

FOREWORD

Note on the Format of the Book

This book started out as an idea for a series of twelve radio plays. Twelve 'talking heads' would relate their life stories, and thereby embody the astrological archetypes. Thus the zodiac would be animated in the form of twelve archetypical characters living twelve archetypical lives from birth to death.

When I learned about podcasts, I decided this was the way to go. Thus these stories, read using different voices, will appear as a podcast on www.astrophoebe.com where a number of them can be downloaded free.

This has been mentioned at the outset because *Virtual Lives* should not be read as a novel. It is basically a series of plays in the docu-drama form that melds fiction with non-fiction. It documents how the astrological archetypes, as foundational principles of order in the cosmos, structure our individual lives and personalities, thereby increasing our awareness of them.

In addition it is a work of non-fiction in the self-help genre. The typical life lessons associated with each zodiac sign are clarified and discussed in the dialogues with the inner guide - a character called IG, who functions as life coach to all twelve. The lives are also given a metaphysical context in tune with the new emerging holistic spirituality centred on the evolution of consciousness.

So the intention behind *Virtual Lives* is to give listeners and readers an experience of the astrological archetypes in a form that is both entertaining and amusing. Much vain effort has been expended over the ages in trying to persuade doubters of the truth of astrology through rational argument, when they only need to consciously experience its amazing synchronicities for themselves.

Thus listeners and readers are led to draw parallels with their own lives and the lives of the people close to them. And a wider appreciation of astrology as a tool for understanding ourselves, each other and life in general may spread in the population.

I believe it's simplest to approach astrology through the twelve astrological archetypes, and the newcomer is given help in the Appendix and on the website with determining his or her own archetypal mix. Instructions are also given on how to obtain a birth chart free from the internet, and how to use it to identify your main archetypes. When newcomers have understood that they are determined by more than one astrological archetype - so they may be untypical of their sun sign - this can get rid of some preliminary objections to astrology.

Phoebe Wyss

PROLOGUE:
The Interlife

I always try to arrive in the group room well before the participants so I have time to prepare. I put the twelve reclining chairs in a circle with my own chair, the thirteenth, in the centre. Then I fix the freshly laundered cloths to the headrests. Each is embroidered with a different sign of the zodiac and, as I lay them out, I take care to keep the correct order, starting with Aries and finishing with Pisces.

Then I open the blinds. The group room is dome-shaped with glass walls stretching from floor to ceiling, so that, as the blinds fold back, the ink-black sky studded with stars appears around it. On the right is the sun, our own great star, and on the left the bright disc of the moon, and behind it I can see the earth, dazzling white and azure blue. Whether by coincidence or design, when seen from our location in space, the earth and the moon are exactly the same size. We have an hour to go before the eclipse.

The participants have begun to appear now. One moment the room is empty and the next it's full. I'm pleased to see that they're all wearing their medallions. They seem nervous, which is natural because there's a deep fear of birth in us all. It's always painful and often traumatic. So I put them at ease by tuning in to a Bach flute concerto, and piping it into our common mental space. Then when they've calmed down I begin.

'Hi everyone! You all know me - I'm IG, your life-coach and inner guide. The first thing is to find your chairs - it's a bit like a party game this. You move round the circle until you find a chair with the same zodiac symbol on its headrest as you carry on your medallion. When you've got a match, sit down!'

There's a lot of scuffling and telepathic chattering as they find their seats. The usual jokes are cracked about the Virgo - it's Meg this time - being sexually uptight, and everyone gives Sue, our Scorpio, a wide birth, feigning fear and horror when she crosses their path, which Sue, bless her, seems to relish. When they're all seated I launch into my introduction.

'Well now, you've all attended the preparation sessions for this your big day and know what to expect, so I'll be brief. As I explained in the first session, the law of synchronicity determines your choice of parents, so no one is ever born into the wrong family - remember that. And it also determines the events and circumstances of your birth.

Now some of you may be able to remember your birth last time round.... Hands up those who have past-birth memories!'

Most of the hands go up, but Zak, who's wearing the Aries medallion, shouts, 'Total blank! Sorry! Can't remember a sausage!'

'I can remember mine,' volunteers Les, who's sitting in the Libra chair, 'but it's all a bit hazy, because it was three hundred years ago.' He sounds apologetic, as if he'd like to do me the favour of remembering it better if he could.

'My last birth was amazing,' says Roy the Leo. 'My dear mother, who was an opera singer, went into labour on stage. She always maintained the contractions helped her reach the high notes, and my head popped out just as the final curtain came down.'

'It's all very well for you,' grumbles Sue the Scorpio. 'I want to forget my last birth, because it was a bloody nightmare. The cord got caught round my neck and I nearly strangled!'

'You poor thing!' Mab the Cancer is sympathetic, but there's a worried look on her face, and on some other faces, because Sue has expressed one of the deeper fears that haunt the incarnation groups.

'You're being morbid again,' says Pat to Sue. 'And that's not the right attitude to have when you're about to enter a womb, is it?' Pat the Capricorn is always very matter of fact.

The others are in agreement with her. 'Typical Scorpio!' they mutter.

'I protest!' chips in Jim the Aquarius. 'There's too much categorising going on here. We're not star signs, we're individuals!'

'Astrology is bunk,' Bob the Gemini says. 'It was just a coincidence that Sue picked the Scorpio medallion. She couldn't see what she was doing, because she was mentally blindfolded.'

'Ah! But nothing is random in the universe,' chips in Sid the Sagittarius. 'Events are governed by the law of synchronicity. Some of you haven't understood that yet, though it was explained to us in the first session.'

'Oh belt up and let's get on with incarnating!' shouts Zak impatiently.

'I can remember my last birth,' says Nel the Taurus, whose contributions always come a little late. 'And it wasn't very savoury I can tell you, nor was the life that followed it, so I think I deserve a better deal this time.'

'Well, you won't get it unless you've changed your patterns,' Sue says curtly. 'And that's unlikely knowing you. So you're probably going to have to live your last life all over again!'

Nel bridles at this, and, seeing one of their truculent arguments developing, Les as usual steps in.

'What do you think, Nel - are you the same person today that you were in your last life?' he asks.

'Definitely not! I've learned a thing or two in the meantime.'

'In which case your next life is bound to be better,' he says kindly. Les is evidently one of Nel's admirers, which I can understand as she's a blonde bombshell! But I mustn't get distracted.

'What I want to get across,' I say, 'is that there's no need to be afraid either of your birth or of what comes after, because you've prepared your life-scripts. It's why you joined an incarnation group in the first place, instead of tumbling blindly into rebirth like others do. So, whatever may befall you down below, you can rest assured that it has a purpose, and your life has an agenda.'

'Excuse me! I have a question.' Meg the Virgo has put up her hand. 'I attended every session and planned my incarnation very thoroughly, but if the amnesia is going to kick in, it will all be in vain. So why go to the bother of creating a script if we're going to forget it anyway?'

'Yes the amnesia, what about the amnesia?' chorus the others.

I sigh - then one more time. 'The forgetting is only on the surface,' I explain. 'Go deeper into yourself and you'll be able to contact that part of you that can remember your prenatal intentions.'

'But if that's the case,' objects Bob, 'what's the point of the amnesia in the first place? It doesn't make sense.'

'It's to protect you. If you could remember your past lives when you're incarnated, that would place an intolerable burden on your daily living. And if you remembered this beautiful place, where everyone is so free and happy, you wouldn't remain willingly on earth for three score years and ten. You'd all be trying to commit suicide, and we don't want that!'

'Because then nobody would become wise, and the human race wouldn't evolve.'

'You've got it, Sid! An incarnation is the best way to grow. Time on earth passes slowly, so you have a long lifetime in which to get to know all the facets of your self. And time is needed for your karmic stuff to come up and be eliminated. Of course some people get through their agendas quickly, and before you can say hey presto they're back up here again, while others are slowcoaches. Each person progresses at his own pace, and some need just a few lives down there, while others feel compelled to descend again and again.'

This last comment has dampened their spirits, so I quickly add, 'But, as members of an incarnation group working together with a life-coach, you are all on the fast track. So if there are no more questions....'

'I have a question,' interrupts Pat in a determined voice. 'I've planned my coming incarnation very carefully, but if the future is open, as you say it is, then there's nothing to stop things turning out quite differently, which I find most disconcerting.'

'Your life-script gives guidelines.' I reply. 'It doesn't carve your future on tablets of stone. That would be impossible, because the universe is in flux and, as a particle of the universe, you're in flux too, Pat. So my advice is stay open and be flexible.'

'Can I say something?' pipes up Mab. 'It's like this you see - I didn't put much effort into creating my script, and I slept through some of the sessions, but I still feel good about reincarnating. You see I trust that we're in the hands of Providence and, whether we know it or not, we're being taken care of.'

'That's what I believe too,' says Fay the Pisces, who up to now has been very quiet. 'We shouldn't think about things too much. We should just flow with the river, and let it carry us to the ocean.'

I sigh. There are always some participants in denial of their free will, who consequently don't plan their incarnations properly. And these are the ones who are most likely to end up where they don't want to be, and then blame me for it! Shall I have another quick go at getting across to them the contradictory concepts of free will and determinism?

'The will of the whole is free,' I begin, 'and, being part of the whole, in this sense you're also free. But, whether you can use your freedom or not, depends on your level of consciousness. The more unaware you are, the more blind, and the more blind you are, the more unfree.'

'We might think we're free,' interrupts Fay, 'but in fact we're determined by the stars. That's why there's always twelve people in an incarnation group, and why we've each been allotted to a different sign of the zodiac.'

Oh dear - another big subject that we don't have time for now! The eclipse will be starting any minute so I must be brief.

'The reason there are twelve of you,' I explain, 'is because the archetypal principles that form the primary matrix within the ground of being are twelve in number. They pre-exist all manifestations of form in matter, and structure the cosmos. Astrology, as you'll discover when you get round to studying it, reveals the patterns behind reality that result from the workings of this matrix .... Bother! I've lost them. Instead of listening they're chatting with each other telepathically.

'What I'm looking forward to most is being able to sleep in a real bed,' Mab is saying. 'I miss the nights up here. I've never got used to it not getting dark!'

4

'I'm looking forward to eating food again,' says Nel. 'As far as I'm concerned, there are two good things about being in a body - you can enjoy good food, and you can have proper sex. They almost make it worth while being born!'

'I prefer out of-the-body sex,' says Sue. 'It's more intense.'

'You would!' says Nel.

Sue gives her a dirty look.

'I must say I'm dreading having a body again. Bodies slow you down and they get in the way,' says Sid.

'That's a joke,' chips in Pat. 'You're the person who needs one the most. It'll do you good to be incarnated - bring you down to earth for a change!'

'Sid is right,' says Roy. 'It's a drag having to carry a body around with you all the time, especially when you're old and fat!'

'No one need get fat,' snaps Meg. 'If you discipline yourself to take exercise and watch your diet, you won't put on weight.'

'The trouble with bodies is they tie you down to a specific time and place, so you feel as if you're in prison,' complains Bob. 'And there's no escaping the force of gravity down there. It's like having weights on your feet!'

'And moving from one place to another can take hours or even days,' Sid adds, 'which makes travelling so laborious!'

'Everything's easier up here,' says Jim. 'We just think of where we want to be and we're teleported there instantly.'

'As soon as I'm born I'm going to have a fucking good scream!' exclaims Zak, who's getting frustrated.

'Me too,' chuckles Roy. 'That's one of the perks of being a baby - you can scream as much as you like and nobody can make you stop, unless you want to.'

'Relax,' I say. 'We're all set to go now - just a couple of last reminders. You joined the incarnation group with the intention of working on yourselves, and furthering your spiritual growth. But, once you're down there, and your mind is coupled again with the psyche and its layers of karmic contents, you'll have to make an on-going effort to stay alert. It's so easy to allow yourself to be taken over by the unconscious, and live like a robot. So, if growth is going to happen to you, don't forget to keep up your self-inquiry and, most important, stay in touch with me. If you go inside, you'll be able to hear my voice, and you'll find I'm always available to answer your questions.'

Glancing out of the window, I can see that the shadow of the moon has started eating into the earth. The total eclipse of the earth, that

5

everyone has been waiting for, has begun. I tell them to recline their chairs and close their eyes.

'Are you all sitting comfortably?' I ask.

'Yes!' they chorus. But then one of them - it's Bob of course - gets the giggles and starts to snort, which sets the others off. They're like a bunch of naughty kids larking about in class, I think. But, after I've piped some calming meditation music into their minds, they quieten down and just in time, because the moon has now covered the disc of the earth completely. The participants are lying motionless now, and the room feels as empty as if they've been spirited away, which in a sense they have.

The following narrative records the lives that each of the participants experiences. The stories are told in sequence using linear earth time, although in fact they all happen simultaneously. When my self is divided into twelve characters, my reality is also split, whereas in truth it is a one unified, twelve-sided whole.

Life 1
ZAK the ARIES

What are we waiting for? I know that ruddy music he's playing is meant to calm us down, but it's doing just the opposite - it's working me up! Just relax he says. Huh! He's asking the impossible. The harder I relax the more tense I get!

At last we've started. I can see planet earth out there in space, and it's getting gradually bigger so I must be travelling towards it, but much too slowly for my liking! Get a move on! I tap my fingers impatiently on the arm of my chair.

We're in the earth's atmosphere, and the descent has begun. All around me I see the colour red. It's a bright red like freshly shed blood, and I'm descending through it as if on a parachute. I seem to have arrived in some kind of war zone, because there are searchlights arching the sky, flares flashing and anti-aircraft flak whipping past. Then a bomb explodes just below my feet. I feel the force of the blast shaking up my molecules. This is the stuff! At last I'm seeing some action.

I surf the battle scene for a while, enjoying its virtual reality, while feeling as safe as a stem cell. Then the invisible but purposeful force that brought me here whisks me away. A brief sea crossing, and we're coming in to land. It's dark, but I can make out a small town below me. The windows of the houses are all blacked out and there's no street lighting.

I'm carried straight through the door of one the houses into the hall, and then we zoom in on the cupboard under the stairs. There's a woman in there with three kids, sheltering from the air raid. Her brats have been scrapping again and she's losing patience with them. It's a big relief when the all-clear signal comes, and they can crawl out - all except the woman who's lying on the cupboard floor moaning. She's in her ninth month, and the shock of the raid has brought on labour. So she sends her oldest boy to fetch the midwife, who fortunately lives very close by.

'Baby's coming!' the midwife announces, 'and coming quick, so we'd better make haste!'

At this my perspective switches and suddenly, without warning, I find myself inside the uterus of the woman in labour. Then it clicks! She's my mother and I'm the kid who's going to be born! After a long and tedious nine months, I've received the chemical signal indicating it's time to spring into action. So without delay I press my head with all my force into the exit's tight opening. Hurrah! I'm on my way out, and nothing is going to stop me now!

I'm proud of the fact that I make record time from the first contraction to the moment my head is born, soon to be followed by my shoulders and rest of my body. And there I lie on the bloodstained sheet - lobster red and howling.

This virtual reality experience is like having double vision. I both see the baby and I am the baby at the same time. Very weird I think, as I watch myself being cleaned up and given to mum to hold. I'm only an hour old, but I'm kicking so hard she can barely hold me. It's like, after being confined for so long, I'm bursting with pent-up energy, so I have to howl and kick with all my might.

'What's he yelling for, nurse? He don't stop.'

'Let him. Does 'em good. Clears out their lungs.'

A breast is stuck into my mouth. And I've worked up quite an appetite through the exertion of being born, so I'm hungry, but when I try to suck at it nothing comes out. And even when I pull more vigorously - still nothing. That makes me start yelling again, only to discover that it doesn't work - yelling while you're trying to drink is self-defeating. Mum gives an exhausted smile.

'There, there, little 'un! Don't get so upset. Just take it slowly, and you'll get your drink by and by,'

She turns to my brothers, who are standing beside the bed looking at me aghast.

'I dunno what's the matter with 'im, I really don't. You lot didn't create like that when you was born.'

If she could read my thoughts - which she can't - she'd know the reason. It's because I'm angry. There's nothing I hate more than being tiny, weak and dependent. It's the feeling of helplessness that I can't take. The date is April 1st 1944, April fool's day, and my name - Peter Stanley Ramsdale - is a joke too. But there's nothing I can do about anything any more, except scream the house down.

THE KID

The baby has vanished and a toddler has appeared. That's me at two with matted blonde curls and a pouting mouth. Cheeky devil! I can feel the weight of the full nappy hanging down between my legs. I've never learned to walk - only to run. And I've never learned to stop running without crashing into something.

It's 6am and I'm the first one up. Since I learned to scale the bars they can't confine me in my cot any longer. Up I go, swinging two sturdy legs over the top, and dropping down to the floor with a thump. Now I'm charging round the house leaving a trail of debris. I've become pretty unstoppable now I can move under my own steam, and nothing in the house is safe from my little hands, as I help myself to anything I want.

The only person in the family I take notice of is dad, who's home with us again now the war is over, and that's only because he clouts me, if I don't do what he says. But I always get my way with mum. If she tries to control me, I throw a temper tantrum and then she soon gives in. Okay, I know I'm a little devil, but I can be an angel too - so cute I make everyone smile. And when I give mum a big, slobbery kiss to say I'm sorry, her heart melts. I even look like an angel, albeit a tough one, with my bold blue eyes staring through my fringe of curls in scathing innocence.

I'm sitting at my desk in school. Miss Sedgewick has given us some beads and told us to count them. That's a zombie task if ever there was one, and I haven't any patience with it. I've no patience with anything at school except what I'm good at, which is sport. I'm easily the fastest runner in our class, and I can beat the fastest runner of the class above. But counting beads is boring, so I use my ruler instead to flick them at the necks of the children in front.

'Ouch! Who did that?'

'Ow! that really hurt!'

Miss Sedgewick comes waddling over to take the ruler away, rapping my knuckles with it sharply before confiscating it. Now total boredom sets in. How long still till playtime? The hands on the big wall-clock seem to be crawling slower and slower - in fact they've stopped. I'll burst if I have to sit here much longer! So I start hammering my foot against the leg of the desk in front, which I know will annoy Miss Sedgewick.

'Peter Ramsdale, stop that immediately, or there's a little boy I know who's going to miss his playtime!'

That shuts me up. Ting-a-ling - the bell at last! I'm up from my chair, and out of the door like greased lightning. Whooping and leaping, I race round and round the playground, every now and then intentionally barging into someone. I knock one small boy over. Sorry, but I have to be rough if I'm going to be respected as the dominant male round here. Playtime passes quickly and happily, what with wrestling with the boys and jumping out from behind the milk crates to scare the girls.

I've just turned thirteen, and I've come down to the chip shop to meet a gang of boys. There they are, slouching outside, all of them older than me - just a bunch of hooligans but heroes in my eyes. I have to pass a test to prove I've the balls to become a fully-fledged member of the gang. So we go to the piece of wasteland round the corner, and they form a circle around me. Then their leader produces a live rat, and says I have to bite its head off in one bite. That's my test. So I take the rat in my hand, and hold it close to my face. Its nose is quivering, and its little black eyes are bright and shiny.

'Go on then, bite!' they urge in voices shrill with excitement. 'Prove to us that you've got balls!'

I stand there for a moment, looking into the rat's eyes, and then, with a sudden swing of my arm, I fling it away as far as I can. As it flies over their heads, and disappears behind the fence, disappointment ripples round the circle.

'Cowardy, cowardy custard!' they jeer.

'It's you who's cowards!' I retort. 'Do you think it's a proof of balls to kill a tiny creature what doesn't stand a chance? Give me another test - go on!'

'Right mate, you asked for it! Come and fight me!'

He's a great, heavy bloke and much bigger than me.

'Alright!' I say but with a queasy feeling inside.

We square up facing each other. My right fist is clenched ready to hit him, and, as soon as he makes a move, I give it to him smack on the jaw. Then, before he knows what's what, I've punched him in the stomach too. He hits me on the side of my head, and it's such a whopper it knocks me flat. But I spring straight back up again, and so it goes on. Each time he knocks me down I jump up like a jack-in-the-box. The gang are on my side now, and are cheering me on.

'That's a plucky kid!' I hear one say.

We go on fighting until they've had their money's worth, and are compensated for their disappointment about the rat. Then the leader calls off the fight, and announces that I'm accepted as a gang member. Later on, while I'm walking home feeling proud of myself, I hear a voice inside my head that's speaking to me.

'That was well done, Zak - to throw the rat away.'

'Who the hell are you?'

'I'm IG, your inner guide. Don't you remember me - no? Then not to worry - it's the amnesia. I was watching you then, and saw you do what you felt was right, though it was risky and you felt scared.'

'But I didn't let them see it.'

'No, you hid your fear under a show of bravado. I've often noticed you doing that. And, when you're feeling scared, you rush in so you're the first to attack. That's another of your patterns.'

'Well I've learned a thing or two growing up with three brothers.'

'And what about your dad?'

'He's a brute. He'll give me a good hiding soon as look at me.'

'Yes, he seems to have it in for you. But it's your fault too for provoking him. Why do you always have to answer back?'

'Because I'm a cheeky devil.'

'It annoys him so much he gives you a thrashing.'

'Yeah. I don't care. I just let him get on with it and, when he's finished, I always slam the door when I leave the room. Once I slammed it so hard I broke the hinges. I got an extra belting for that.'

'It seems you need to get away quick afterwards.'

'Yeah, because otherwise I could lose it, and then I don't know what would happen.'

'It sounds as if you don't trust yourself. You're scared of your own anger, and your old man's as scared as you, which is why he thrashes you.'

'Him scared! He used to be a boxer when he was in the army!'

'It's just a suggestion. Think about it.'

'Me? I never think about things. I just do them.'

Two years later at fifteen I'm the leader of the pack, having won everyone's respect with my daredevil antics. It's a warm night in June and the gang have gathered on the scrubby patch of wasteland we've made our home. We've lit a bonfire and we're sitting round it, and Seamus has brought a quarter bottle of whisky to pass round. We're wondering what we could do for a lark. We dabble with illegality for kicks. Not that we do anything really criminal - it's just kids messing about. For example we'll set fire to a waste-paper bin, or put some rude graffiti up on a wall, or rip out a sign for a joke. I've never been caught, and I'm not worried about the police, because I know I can run faster than any cop round here.

When the whisky bottle's empty, someone suggests we break into the off-license to get another. I'm up for it. So me and two mates go round the back, where we manage to loosen the catch on one of the windows. But, when we start climbing in, the burglar alarm goes off, and sod's law has it that a police-car is passing at that very moment, which is how we get caught red-handed. So that night I arrive home escorted by a cop and - sod's law again - it's dad who opens the door.

'Can I have a word with you, sir?'

'What's 'e gone and done now?'

'Broken into an off-license.'

'We didn't pinch anything, honestly we didn't. We was just testing the security.'

'You watch your step, young man. I'm giving you a solemn warning. You're known to us down at the station as a trouble-maker and, unless you mend your ways, it'll be a criminal conviction for you more sooner than later!'

When he's gone it comes to a showdown between me and my dad. As I watch him rolling up his sleeves and reaching for the belt he always uses to wallop us, I yell,

'Fuck you! Fuck you! Not any more you don't. If you hit me with that I'll do you in!'

His face turns beetroot red, and his eyes are bulbous with rage.

'I'm going to teach you a lesson you'll never forget,' he shouts. 'I'm going to beat the living daylights out of you!'

Then he comes at me, but as he lunges I jump to one side. He comes at me again, and I duck. I manage to grab his wrist, and wrench the belt from his grasp, and throw it under the dresser. Then he starts punching me in the face, but I go for his legs, and bring him crashing down to the ground with me on top. Now we're locked together on the kitchen floor like two wrestlers amongst broken crockery and blood from my nose.

At this point mum appears shrieking at us to pack it in. And, when I've pinned dad down by the arms so that he's helpless, and proved I'm stronger than him, I do. I jump to my feet and walk out without saying a word, and I don't come back home again for a week. Things change after that. Dad stops molesting me, and he stops talking to me too. In fact he won't even look me in the face. It's as if, as far as he's concerned, I don't exist.

TWENTIES

Time flies by in virtual reality and before I know it I'm twenty-one, and I've grown into a handsome stud of a man, tall, broad-shouldered and athletic. I see myself sitting in the driving seat of my new car, a snazzy red MG with Annie in the passenger seat beside me. We're going to the flicks and we're late - Annie's fault of course!

The traffic is heavy in the town centre, and I'm going to need all my driving skills to get through and arrive in time. I put my foot down on the accelerator, and we're just getting up speed when the lights ahead change to red, and the Morris Minor in front stops suddenly, forcing me to brake. When we set off again the lady driver hugs the centre of the road. She's bent on torturing me, it seems, by keeping to the speed limit.

'Move over, you stupid old twat!' I yell.

But she's deaf and all, which forces me to perform a high-risk overtaking manoeuvre, whereby we narrowly miss a head-on collision with a car coming in the opposite direction. Annie lets out a squeal.

'Shut up, Annie!'

'You're a dangerous driver, you are!'

'Bollocks! You can rely on me. You know I've got quick reactions, and I've never had an accident in my whole life.'

'There's always a first time,' she says.

I forgive Annie's lack of trust in me because she's got such fantastic legs. My eye follows their line up from her high-heeled shoes to the hem of her skirt that's slipped half way up her thighs.

'Watch out!'

My attention switches back to the road in time to do an emergency stop, and we come to a halt, brakes screeching, before two children on a zebra crossing.

'See what I mean - quick reactions! I learned to brake like that when I was a runner for a drug dealer in the West End. I had to drive like a maniac then, because they'd beat me up if I came late!'

'Oh Pete! I didn't know you'd been involved in drugs!'

'Ha ha! Just one of my little business ventures! But don't worry, kid, I never touch them myself. Give me a double whisky any time.'

Annie is no one special - just one of the birds I take out when I want a date. But she's a good kid, and she worships the ground I tread on. If she had her way we'd be going steady, but she's got the wrong bloke for that!

My life appears to be one mad rush. I'm putting mountains of effort into my job, and at the same time I'm leading a maniacal social life. At work they see me as the whiz-kid, the high-flyer who's set to reach the top. I was given my own department last spring, which proves they've got the message. They know I have to be given a free rein. I can't deliver the goods with a boss breathing down my neck!

As I can manage on very little sleep, I'm out most nights partying into the small hours. Sometimes I don't go to bed at all, but drive from the party straight to the office, grabbing a cup of coffee on the way. Then I still have the energy to put in a full day's work before I finally crash out.

I left home when I left school at the age of sixteen. I had to get away from my dad. Home for me is now a rented apartment in West London, and I hardly ever see the family. My brothers avoid me - too scared of the old man I suppose - but mum sometimes gives me a call. She says he's washed his hands of me.

On Saturday afternoons you'll find me at the football stadium. I support the Lancers and they're playing at home today. I see myself on the terrace in the midst of a rocking, swaying crowd of supporters, wearing my green and white scarf and my woolly hat. We're into the second half and Jenkins has the ball. He's being tackled... but he's got through!

'Yeh! Go for it Jenkins! GO FOR IT! He's going to shoot. Ah! He's missed! He's fuckin' missed! Not again, I don't believe it! That was our chance to break even, and he fucked up - the twat!'

I was a soccer ace myself when I was at school, but now my game's squash. I prefer it because it's fast and one to one. Team sports are not my thing, as I like to rely on myself alone, but soccer will always be my best spectator sport. Bugger it! There goes the whistle and we've lost two-nil! I'm one of the first to start leaping over the seats. I always take the shortest route to the exit. You won't catch me queuing up with the mob. I'm cursing Jenkins and the ref as I go. When the Lancers lose I'm always in a foul mood, and I go straight home without speaking to anyone. When they win, of course, it's another matter. Then I'll join the fans in the pub for a celebration, and we'll make a night of it.

'So you've noticed a few things about yourself,' says that voice in my head, who self styles himself my inner guide. 'That's useful for your self-inquiry.'

'For my self bloody what?'

'Okay! Don't worry, Zak. It's only the amnesia. I just wondered why you're not going to the pub today.'

'Because I'm in a foul mood, that's why. When the Lancers lose, it totally spoils my day!'

'And why's that then? Have you ever asked yourself why you feel what you're feeling?'

'What the fuck for?'

'To understand yourself better, so you'll have more power over yourself, which will give you more power!'

'Okay wise guy, go ahead and show me how to do it.'

'Well, I see you identifying strongly with your team the Lancers, so that each match they play is like your personal battle. And as you hate losing - you always have to be the winner - when the Lancers lose it leaves you gutted.'

14

'I already know I'm not a good loser. But you're right, I feel let down personally when they miss a goal. Is that why twits like Jenkins make me so angry?'

'Jenkins hasn't made you angry. You were angry already, Zak. You're like your father there - there's a lot of anger inside you. Jenkins only triggered it.'

'Hmmm... you think I'm like my dad?'

'Yes. He came back from the war carrying a huge load of anger, and knew no better than to let it out on his wife and kids. He was feeling bad, you see - anger does that to you - and he had to get rid of it. So, when you yell yourself hoarse at a soccer match, you're throwing out anger too. But, when your team lose, you go home carrying an even bigger load of it with you.'

'And I don't have a wife and kids to take it out on, so what am I supposed to do - go ballistic? I tell you, mate, if I really exploded, there'd be not much left of you, or me, or of anything!'

'Rubbish Zak! You're not that cosmic! Put on your running shoes, and run twenty times round the block. If you really pushed yourself, and you came back exhausted, that would do it. There are non-destructive ways, you see, of releasing anger - ways that don't harm other people or yourself.'

'Yeah, you're right. I should go running more often. Keep me fit for the birds!'

'But don't misunderstand me, Zak. There's nothing wrong with anger. It's a basic human emotion with high survival value. But a lot of awareness is needed to harness it, and use it creatively.'

'I'd say it's why I'm such a success - because I'm an angry young man!'

'Yes it can work like a dynamo and give you great energy.'

'That's me. They call me the Earl's Court energy phenomenon!'

'You've certainly been blessed with a special gift from existence there.'

'Special gift - bollocks! Everyone who's alive has energy. And I've no patience with the people who say they haven't any. When a woman starts making excuses that she's too tired, that's always a total turn-off for me.'

'Have mercy on them Zak! It's exhausting keeping up with you. You live at such a fast pace, and you always try to pack in so much.'

'Ha ha! I live like I drive my car - fast and furiously!'

'Because then the adrenalin keeps pumping, and you stay on a high.'

'That's the only way to live.'

'But what are you learning from it all?'

'Well one thing I've learned is how to stand up to people. Taking on my old man toughened me up, and then there were all those fights I got into as a kid. They made me resilient, and trained my reactions. I've been in some very tricky situations, where I've had to make split-second decisions, which always turned out to be right. So now I know I'd be able to handle any emergency.'

'Then use these strengths, Zak, to create something you can be proud of. Instead of wasting so much of your wonderful energy, learn to employ it wisely. And don't forget to take a rest sometimes, or you'll be burnt out before you're fifty.'

'Fifty will do me fine. I don't want to get any older than that. I'm going to live my life to the full, with all the stops pulled out, and go out with a bang - that's my philosophy.'

THIRTIES

No one who knew me when I was a young hoodlum would have expected me to do so well. I've risen very swiftly up the career ladder. They recently made me a senior manager - at the age of thirty! Take a load of that! So to what do I owe my success? Not to any great talent for brokering as far as I can see, but to sheer will power. When I want something I go for it with no holds barred, and I'll let nothing stand in my way.

I see me in my office hunched up over my desk. It's 2am and I'm scheduled to give a paper at an international business conference tomorrow. I've only just found the time to start on it, so I'm under great pressure. The ants in my pants are biting again, making it hard for me to sit still, and I'm coming out in a hot sweat.

Sod it! A page of statistics is missing from last year's report, and it's the very one I need! I leap up, knocking over my chair, and pace up and down the room hitting my forehead with my fist, expletives exploding from my mouth. Where are my fags? I have to find them. Here they are in the drawer, and I light up inhaling sharply and deeply. That's better! Next I make another cup of black coffee. Then I start going through the files in search of the lost page. This set-back means it's going to be a fight to get finished in time, but I'm determined to succeed, even if it kills me!

I write the last line as the light of early dawn is filtering through the office windows. Then, instead of going to bed, I snatch an hour or two of kip on the office couch, and drive straight to the conference.

Later that morning, I'm up on the platform strutting my stuff in front of an audience of delegates. Though I say it myself, I'm giving a good performance, presenting my points in a punchy sort of way, and loading them all with strong conviction. I finish to a round of applause, and afterwards one of the directors comes up to congratulate me.

'That was a brilliant paper, Ramsdale,' he says, 'and a most spirited delivery. You're a shining example to us all of totality and dedication.'

Later, when I'm standing outside during the break, having a quiet fag, I hear IG's voice again.

'So all's well that ends well! But why do you always leave things to the last minute, Zak?'

'Perhaps it's because I like putting myself under pressure. Being in an emergency situation opens up my deeper energy reserves.'

'You mean rising to a challenge empowers you?'

'Yeah, it makes me feel larger than life - as if I could conquer the world.'

'You get the satisfaction of proving to yourself and others that you can win against the odds, but at a price! The constant state of stress you create is very wearing, so why not approach things in a more relaxed way for a change?'

'If I relaxed I wouldn't be productive.'

'Ah ha! But relaxed doesn't mean passive, Zak. It means loose and easy. Also more relaxed equals more aware, and some extra awareness would increase rather than decrease your effectiveness.'

'Nah! I'd never get anything done. The tasks I set myself are hard, see? I have to brace myself, steel my every fibre, and not let up until I'm finished.'

'And you don't even allow yourself a rest then. When you've reached your goal, you start looking round for some new project to throw yourself into.'

'That's the best time, when I'm at the start of something and it's all ahead of me.'

'In other words, after making all that effort, you don't wait around long enough to enjoy the fruits of your labours!'

'No, I let others do that.'

It's Valentine's day and I've a date with Gloria, the fabulous redhead I've been chasing. I'm putting on my best shirt and my hip-hugging jeans. I grab my brown leather jacket, and on the way out I glance at myself in the mirror. Handsome bastard! No wonder I'm seen as highly eligible - what with my sex appeal and my big salary! But gorgeous Gloria is proving to be quite a challenge. So far she's continued to dance just out of my reach. But my gut feeling says this is about to change, and my gut feeling is rarely wrong. Tonight's the night!

We're seated at an intimate table for two in a posh restaurant in Earl's Court, that's all decked out for the occasion with pink paper hearts. We've finished our main course, and the waiter is serving the desert, and I'm gazing across the table into Gloria's teasing green eyes. I've been playing the 'enfant terrible' all the evening, shocking and seducing her with anecdotes from my delinquent past. But now I've turned into a big, cosy teddy bear with eyes that plead, 'Take me to bed with you, do!' Ha! Gorgeous Gloria's not falling for it. She's still in her power trip of playing hard to get - the little vixen!

'Tell me, Pete, how many women have you slept with in your whole life?'

You see what I mean? That's the very question guaranteed to flummox a man like me!

'Oh I've lost count,' I reply airily. 'I've been sowing my wild oats far and wide like any healthy male animal. But, now I've turned thirty, I'm thinking of settling down. So I'm on the lookout for a woman who's strong enough to tame me. Do you know one?'

There's an important piece of information I'm withholding from Gloria. It's the fact that, once I've conquered a woman, she loses all her mystery. And I lose all my interest in her. It's the chase I relish rather than the kill, but there's always a chance that Gloria will be the exception.

Whether it was the challenge I threw out, or the champagne, or the paper hearts - who knows, because women are enigmas - but after the meal Gloria agrees to take me home with her. There we sit drinking wine and talking, until she's so tired it's no big deal to get her into bed. Around four in the morning we finally make love and, once again, it doesn't live up to my expectations.

Breakfast is a silent affair without any of the witty bantering of the night before, and soon I'm looking at my watch.

'I have an appointment at nine, so I've got to run,' I say gulping down the rest of my coffee.

Gloria gives me a passionate goodbye kiss at the door.

'See you soon, babe,' I call as I vault down the stairs three steps at a time. But, by the time I've arrived at the office, and I've got stuck into my work, there's nothing further from my mind than fixing up another date with Gloria.

As the days pass, I'm increasingly disturbed by the persistent voice of IG, who seems to be trying to get my attention. He's taken it upon himself to play the role of my conscience!

18

'You still haven't got in touch with Gloria! How do you think the poor girl's feeling? Seduced and abandoned, I shouldn't wonder.'

'Hey! Don't you come poking your nose in here, or I'll send you back to Hades where you belong!'

'You gave her the impression that you really cared, and now you don't even bother to phone her!'

'Well, if she's sitting there, gormlessly waiting for the phone to ring, it just goes to prove she's not my type. If women want to be treated as equals, they have to take equal responsibility for what happens in a relationship, and not try to manipulate by playing the damsel in distress.'

'Hmmm... you've distressed quite a few damsels in your time, Zak.'

'Well Gloria's a big girl, and perfectly able to look after herself! So mind you own business!'

'Zak! What you lack is empathy, and it's leading you down the path to loneliness. Have you ever asked yourself why you're not close to anyone?'

'No, because I know the answer - I value my freedom too highly. I want to be able to do what I like when I like, without having to consider other people, and without having to make compromises.'

'Well it's certainly easier to gratify your own needs, when you're oblivious of the needs of others.'

'If I didn't look after number one, I'd soon sink to the bottom of the pile in the corporate world. Everyone there is motivated by self-interest.'

'Yes, you get ahead faster when you don't count the casualties. But there's a price to pay for that kind of success. Your heart becomes deadened. You become incapable of feeling.'

'That's just the sort of thing women say when they're giving me a piece of their mind. A woman can be pretty cutting when she's been rejected. One of them even called me a sexual predator once!'

'Now we know why you haven't called Gloria - you don't want to hear her say things like that!'

'No, it's because I've been rushed off my feet at work, but I'll get round to fixing up another date with her. Gorgeous Gloria may still have some potential after all.'

A full day ahead! I'm on my way to a board meeting, and I'm anticipating a showdown with one of the directors. The bastard is bent on opposing one of my pet schemes. But he's got a shock coming. He's going to find that creating opposition only arouses my fighting spirit. This time, however, the board is bent on presenting a united front against me, and they stand firm, even when I bring out my heavy guns.

In the end the meeting is adjourned before I've been able to secure my victory, and I return to my office in the vilest of tempers.

A junior rep is waiting for me with a favour to ask, and I listen to him with mounting impatience. He feels it and begins to stutter and, before he can reach the end of his sentence, I've exploded in exasperation. The little twit is so alarmed that he nearly falls backwards out the door. Ha ha! He won't return in a hurry!

My staff are used to me. They know I have a short fuse, and keep out of the way once the blue touch-paper has been lit. My secretary, for example - a docile girl who can't say boo to a goose - has become an expert at recognizing the signs. She'll hurry ahead, removing obstacles from my path in a desperate attempt to avert an explosion. But sometimes all her efforts fail, and I'm seeing such a scene now.

I'm dancing round the office in the throes of a massive temper tantrum. The energy I'm throwing out is like the blast of a bomb with enough force to shake the whole floor of the building. My secretary is cowering in the corner like a frightened rabbit, looking guilty. And so she should because it's her fault for fucking up.

'You're wrong, Zak. It's not her fault. It's the load of anger you're carrying that's the problem. It's true she made a mistake, but how you reacted to it is your responsibility.'

'Well, don't go and make a big thing of it. I'm just letting off steam. It won't last long and, when it's over, I'll forget all about it.'

'You might forget, but what about your poor secretary? She's going to be traumatised for days.'

'Well, if that's the case, the girl must be abnormally hyper-sensitive. She needs to toughen up a bit.'

'And what about you? You're abnormal - a grown man behaving like a two-year-old!'

'I was provoked. I couldn't help it.'

'Then do some self-inquiry like you've been taught! Look at the situations that trigger your wrath and try to understand your pattern. When, for example, does your anger arise?'

'Usually when I'm thwarted, or when something goes wrong, and I get held up - especially when there's a deadline to meet.'

'And what else do you feel on those occasions besides anger?'

'Helplessness.'

'Yes, and helplessness is something you can't deal with, Zak, because it arouses your deepest fears. If you were willing to work on yourself, and bring in more awareness, your pattern of violence could be changed.'

'Why should I change? I like it like that.'

'Then you must be getting some benefits from losing your temper.'

'Of course I do. It helps me get what I want. It's like using a blowlamp to clear the path ahead of me. Others soon jump out of the way when they get a blast from it.'

'As long as you have an investment in a behaviour pattern, and think you're profiting from it, you're won't be able to grow beyond it. So we'll just have to wait for the crunch to come.'

I suppose I should be grateful to my inner wise guy for pointing all this out. I mean if I took his advice, I'd be a changed person. I'd be somebody else. But, hang on, is that possible? I've taken the Aries medallion, and I've become Peter Ramsdale, who's by definition an angry young man. So it would mess everything up if I changed. And, anyway, do we know for sure that an editing option has been built into our life-scripts?

MIDDLE AGE

So how's life treating me now I'm middle-aged? Excellently! I left the firm two years ago to set up a brokering company of my own which, judging from the huge profits we've been making, was the right career decision. So at the age of forty-two I can say I've achieved everything I set out to achieve in life - top job, big salary, big car, penthouse apartment. I've reached the top of the ladder and it's like where do I go from there?

You see, I'm an ideas man, and my strength lies in developing new projects. But I'm increasingly prevented from doing this by the administrative duties that now lie heavy on my shoulders. Also, though I'm strong at motivating people, and can give my members of staff a good kick up the pants when they need it, what I lack are people-skills. I've no patience for the daily dealings with my staff, whose petty and time-consuming problems just annoy me, and there's always the office politics to contend with. I'm a straightforward guy, who expects others to be as upfront with me as I am with them, so I get taken for a ride by the cunning and the devious.

There's a knock on my door. Sod it! Another disturbance! When the hell am I going to be able to get on with my work? Sally enters.

'Excuse me, sir, I just wanted to tell you, sir, that I'm not able to work late this week because my child-minder is sick.'

'That's not my problem!' I retort angrily. 'What does it say in your contract?'

'That I'm expected to work flexible hours, but...'

'No buts allowed! When we have a rush on like now, and I say you're needed, then you have to stay late. So kindly rearrange your life accordingly.'

Sally bursts into tears at this, which makes me even angrier.

'Either find a solution, Miss Riddlesdown, or you're fired!' I shout.

'Alright,' she sobs. 'Then I'll have to get my sister down to look after the kids. But I had hoped, sir, that you'd have more sympathy for a single mum like me!'

'I'm in this business to make a profit, not to be kind to people,' I say gruffly.

Something about Sally reminds me of my ex-wife. I know what it is - it's the manipulative way she tries to appeal to my feelings. I got married in my thirties, in the belief that I'd found what I was looking for - an Amazon of a woman who'd go through thick and thin with me. But, once she'd got her husband and her house, Suzie turned into a domestic cabbage like all the rest. Okay, our marriage lasted seven years, but I got bored with it long before that and went back to having affairs - openly because that's how I do things. She even reproached me later for not keeping them a secret from her!

When it came to the showdown, Suzie accused me of a whole list of crimes including not respecting her. She said I'd violated her emotional and physical boundaries - 'invaded her space' were the words she used. I've never been able to understand what women mean by that, though it's slowly getting through to me that I'm not aware enough of the other person. My perception of myself has always been round and clear, whereas my perception of others is hazy. So, if I barge into you, it probably wasn't intentional. I just didn't see you coming!

Well, in the end, Suzie went to a solicitor to get an injunction, and had me thrown out of the house. So I lost my home as well as my kid. Yes, I have a boy of six, name of Ned, a little menace - just like me at that age! Of course, Suzie was granted custody. Now she's wreaking her revenge by resisting my visiting rights. I have to fight my way through all kinds of hurdles before I can get to see my son.

So I don't have a family any more, but it's something that I'm used to. My relations with my dad are still strained, and my brothers have gone their separate ways. We don't keep up - women are better at that. So I'm footloose and fancy-free, which has its advantages. I can come home as late as I like, as no one is waiting up for me. And, when I need company, I fix up a date with one of the many attractive divorced women I know, who see me as a great catch.

My hair may have started to recede, and the little pointed beard I sport is turning grey, but otherwise I'm in my prime. Playing squash has kept me in good shape, and I have the money to enjoy myself in any way I like. So why do I keep getting the feeling that life is slipping away, and I'm missing out? And why are the pleasures I used to enjoy no longer satisfying?

'Do I hear you embarking on some self-inquiry, Zak?'

'Oh, it's you again, IG! Well this is your territory, isn't it? So perhaps you can tell me why my life is losing its taste.'

'I'd say it's because you've got no one to share it with. You've got no friends.'

'Well, I suppose you're right. Although I know plenty of people who I'd call my friends, none of them are friends in the real sense of the word - why's that?'

'It's because you're used to seeing other people as rivals, and a rival can never be a friend by definition.'

'Well, I inhabit the corporate world where it's about the survival of the fittest. We're like a crowd of sperm all racing to be the first at the ovum.'

'And you were trying to be the winner, until you realised that there are no winners - only losers.'

'Shut up, will you?'

'Why?'

'Because I see losers as duds.'

'And, if you showed yourself to be dud, would other people think the worse of you?'

'I'd think the worse of myself!'

'Then it looks as if you've got an ego problem, Zak. You've been putting yourself under pressure to win, because you need to boost your ego so badly.'

'Then why are women always telling me that my ego's too big. One of them called me a monster of egotism once!'

'She's right - you have a big ego, but it's hollow. Prick it like you prick a balloon, and when it pops what's left? A flabby little bit of rubber symbolising a low self-esteem!'

'That's not how I see myself!'

'Zak, if you feel threatened every time you're asked to give way over some small matter, and you have to fight over it, that proves you have low self-esteem.'

'Okay! So I'm not as self-confident as I appear, but I make up for that with my willpower. When I want something, my will is so strong that I always get it.'

'The wise man knows when to exert his will, and also when to surrender.'

'Surrender! That word doesn't belong to my vocabulary!'

'Because you see surrender as weakness. But, until you've learned the art of surrendering, Zak, you'll never achieve anything really great in life!'

I'm at the cash desk in the petrol station. It's late - well after midnight - but they're open all night. I'm the only customer, and the old geezer behind the till is just about to hand me my change when a thug in a balaclava appears from nowhere shouting,
'This is a hold-up! Up with your hands!'
I see immediately that the thing he's pointing at us isn't a real revolver. So I take a swipe at it, and knock it out of his hand. Then I tackle him and, in the tussle that follows, I'm just getting the better of him when I'm hit over the head from behind. All the lights go out and, when I come to again, I'm lying on the floor with the old geezer bending over me.
'You okay, mate?' he keeps saying in a quavery voice. 'You didn't see his accomplice come up from behind, did you? I saw him too late to warn you. But that was a brave act - tackling that hoodlum like you did. I only hope he hasn't done you an injury.'
I've received a head wound, and have to go to A&E to have it dressed. It's left me with a splitting headache, and I had to wait at the police station for them to take my statement, but I got my picture in the paper. 'Company Director tackles Bandit' was the headline. And I'm just thinking that I'll cut it out and send it to mum, when the telephone rings and she's on the line.
'Pete, I've got some bad news,' she says. 'Your dad is dead.'
Apparently he'd been ailing for some time, but he wouldn't go to the doctor. Then, when she woke up this morning, she found him dead in the bed beside her. Will I come? Of course I will. I drop everything, get into my car, and drive the three hundred miles to where she lives without a break. When I arrive, I find mum looking very old and frail. How long is it since I've been to see her? Too long!
The next morning she asks me to drive her to the funeral parlour to say her last farewells. In spite of my great reluctance, I agree to do it for her. As we enter the room where he's laid out, I notice that my hands are shaking. But when I see the corpse my fear turns to amazement. The towering ogre of my childhood has shrunk to a tiny, wizened creature - so frail it seems I could pick him up with one hand. Mum and me stand there in silence, and suddenly I feel hot tears running down my face. I'm too late! Too late! I wanted to see him once more to have a closure, but now he's gone and died on me!

Mum looks so exhausted she can hardly stand. I have to give her my arm as we walk out of the room. And, it's not until we're back in the car that she breaks the silence.

'He was talking about you only the other day - saying how you was the pick of the bunch after all.'

'I thought he hated my guts,' I reply.

'Not any more he didn't. He'd boast about you to his friends - tell them how much you'd achieved - which shows he was proud of you really.'

'Well he never let on about it to me,' and saying this I realise it was the one thing I'd always wanted to hear - that my dad was proud of me.

My brothers arrive for the funeral, and we have an emotional reunion. I never would have thought it but my eyes fill with tears when I embrace my youngest brother. I start to remember the good times we had together when we were kids. They've brought their wives and children and, when I see them with their families, I'm angry with Suzie for not being there with Ned. I'd love to show off Ned to them.

It's a novelty at first, but soon all the sitting around, and drinking cups of tea, and chatting about old times begins to pall. I've a load of work waiting for me back in London, and I'm impatient for the funeral party to be over so I can get away.

I drive back at night down a clear motorway, keeping my foot hard down on the accelerator. But then, when I'm back home, instead of going to bed, I sit in the kitchen smoking and draining the best part of a bottle of whisky. Perhaps it's because I lack sleep - I haven't had a good night's sleep since dad died - or perhaps it's the after-effects of the head wound, but I'm in a very strange mental state. I end up lying on the kitchen floor as it's getting light, bawling my head off. Even when I was a nipper I don't remember crying like that. It's as if something deep inside me has become unblocked, and opened the floodgates.

'There's nothing wrong with crying, Zak. It's good for you, and funerals tend to bring up your tears.'

'Well, if you think I'm crying for my old man, IG, you're wrong. He was seventy-five, and at that age you have no quality of life. No, I'm crying for Ned who's growing up without a dad. I used to blame Suzie for that, but I know it's my fault really. The reason she won't let me see him is because I lost it once and gave him a thrashing. He was getting on my nerves, as kids do, not doing anything really bad. Poor little lad!'

'It's how your dad treated you. You didn't know any better.'

'Yes, but hitting children does more harm than good.'

'Then you won't do it again.'

'It's why Suzie got custody, but our relationship was doomed before that. She was weak and let me get away with too much. It would have been different if she'd stood up to me. She should have had the gumption to fight me.'

'Perhaps she saw no point. You'd have never given in.'

'True, but all the same a relationship should be more equal if it's going to work.'

'Yes, and your relationship wasn't equal. You did the all the taking and Suzie did all the giving. Perhaps the reason why she let you have your way was because she pitied you.'

'She what!'

'She saw that underneath all your bluster you felt insecure. And she knew about your potency problem, so she deferred to you to boost your manhood.'

'You make me sound like a right wimp!'

'If you were man enough to admit your vulnerability, Zak, you'd be able to relate to women on more equal terms. Your weakness is that you deny your weakness.'

'Hmmm... well you're my inner guide so you should know. What do you think - if I found a woman and got married again, would I have a chance of making a success of it?'

'That would depend on how much you've learned from the first time round. If you've understood your patterns, and you're willing to make a conscious effort to change them, your future need not be a repetition of your past.'

I've lost all my zest for my work. It feels more like a treadmill now than a passion. I could easily take early retirement - I can afford to - but I'd go bananas if I had nothing to do. Okay, so I'm a workaholic! I have to keep my nose to the grindstone to stay sane, but I'm the one in the end who gets ground down by it all. In the brokering business you live on a knife-edge, because you're dependent on cash flow, and you get chased by clamouring creditors all the time. Well so far I've managed to keep ahead of them, but my wheeling and dealing can go pear-shaped, as I've discovered to my cost.

A couple of years ago, one of my investments failed so badly I thought I'd bankrupted the business. The shock of it knocked me out of kilter and I started drinking heavily. Then my liver began to play up, which scared the daylights out of me. I've always relied on my robust health, which I took for granted, so it was a shock when I had to go to hospital for treatment. During the time I was off work I got badly depressed.

You see I'm used to living in the fast lane, with phones ringing and meetings to attend non-stop, and suddenly there was nothing - just emptiness. I was alone with myself, and discovered I didn't like myself very much. Luckily this phase didn't last long. And, after my recovery, I managed to pull the company together again, so we bounced back.

I'm sitting in my office and Hilary Spooner has just been shown in. She's a customer who's been defaulting on payment and has run up a considerable debt. She's explaining that a creditor of hers has forced her into a position where she's unable to pay. And, as she speaks a smile starts curling my lip, because I've never liked the woman, and now she's giving me a chance to put in the boot.

'If your business isn't healthy enough to withstand a crisis,' I say, 'you'll never survive in this line. So you might as well pack it in. Declare bankruptcy, sell your assets and get out!'

'Oh I can't do that! I'm divorced with three children to support. I'd not be allowed a bank account, and I'd not be credit worthy. And because I'd be obliged by law to declare my bankruptcy to a prospective employer, my chances of finding another job would be zero.'

That's right, I think, they kick you when you're down! Once you're in the gutter, it's hard to get out again! She goes on to explain that her company is not the only one under threat, as there could be a knock-on effect. If she's forced into bankruptcy there would be a cascade, and the number of small businesses who rely on her payments could also go bust. So she's come to beg me to be magnanimous and forgive her debt, so the collapse of a chain of businesses can be avoided.

Well it seems that I'm being given the choice of biting off the rat's head, or throwing it to freedom again, and once again I choose the latter. Instead of sticking to my guns, I agree to cancel her debt, and the woman is so grateful she nearly falls at my feet and kisses them. And, after the door has closed behind her, I notice that I'm feeling good for a change. I've got a nice, warm feeling inside.

OLD AGE

I'm sixty-five, and still incredibly fit and productive for an old geezer. And I wanted to die at fifty! Ha ha! Well, if I'd continued the way I was going, I'd be dead now. I'd be in my grave. I only survived because I made the right life choices back in my forties. It was all triggered by my girlfriend of the time getting pregnant. When Louise broke the news to me, my first reaction was to get her an abortion. But then, when I thought about it, I realised that, having missed out on Ned's childhood, what I really wanted was a second chance to be a dad. So I bought a big house with a big garden and I married Lou.

After Adam was born, I changed my lifestyle so as to make more time for my family. My first step was to sell the business that was enslaving me. I wanted a job that would allow me to leave the office at five every evening, and be home in time to read Adam a bedtime story. So I accepted a post in a rival brokering company, on the condition that they'd never ask me to do overtime or work weekends. They agreed, and I've been with them ever since.

A second baby followed - a sister for Adam - who we called Emma. Every Saturday morning I'd take the kids to the park for a game of football. I used to stand in the goal, yelling encouragement, while they shot one ball after another at me. I was trying my best to be the sort of father to them that I would have liked to have myself.

'Come on Adam - into the left-hand corner! Oh bad luck old chap! You hit the post, but it was close! Right Emma - your turn. Yeah - nice and strong and straight! That's my girl!'

It was Emma not Adam who grew up to be a football ace. She plays in the women's county team now. I always said it was a pity she wasn't the boy, because Adam is arty and not into sport at all. It was quite a challenge for me to accept this, and stop harassing him. Lou and I get on all right in our way. Living with me has turned her into a real old battle-axe, and we fight a lot - but fighting is healthy, isn't it?

I've just been retired - forcibly of course, because I wouldn't go without a putting up a fight. But the management had lined up some bright-eyed, bushy-tailed thirty-year old to step into my shoes. Well that's the way it goes! So here I am, put out to pasture with time on my hands. Watching sports programmes on TV, and going for jogs round the park, is not enough to keep me out of mischief, so I've become a coach at the kids' football club, and get a lot of satisfaction out of bringing on the young talent. But even all this is not enough to tire me out it seems, because I have insomnia. I'll toss and turn all night and not get a wink of sleep, so I thought I'd consult my inner agony aunt about this problem.

'Why can't I get to sleep, IG?'

'Because you can't relax,' he replies.

'Ha! I don't do relaxation, you know that.'

'Then it's time you learned. Make it your goal to become the master of your energy.'

'How do I do that?'

'Try martial arts - something like aikido would do it.'

'What - me prancing round like a sissy in white pyjamas!'

'Aikido will teach you to tense up your muscles when an effort is needed, and afterwards, when no effort is required, to let go and fall into a natural relaxation.'

'No thank you! It doesn't sound like my thing!'

'Well you're probably too old now anyway to win a black belt!'

'Too old! Too bloody old! Just you watch! I'll have that black belt before you can say Jack Robinson!'

Well, it wasn't quite as quick as that, but I'd got it by the time I was seventy. Now I'm seventy-seven and running out of steam. I used to take my superior strength and energy for granted, but I've lived long enough to see it all fritter away. Only when it was gone did I appreciate what a wonderful gift it had been. But I'm not complaining, because I've had a good run for my money. The important thing now is to keep going, and not to lean on poor old Lou. I can't stand the idea of being helpless and dependent.

Perhaps you wonder what I'm doing up this ladder - well today's a big day. After all these years my team, the Lancers, have finally won the cup, and we're celebrating. I've erected a flagstaff over the front door, and I'm going to hoist my green and white flag on it.

'Pete, you old fool, what are you doing up there?'

My wife is shouting and gesticulating at me through the kitchen window.

'You know you're not steady enough to climb ladders. Wait! Let me come and do it for you!'

Stupid woman! Always worrying about me - just because I once had a dizzy spell. I'm taking no notice of her. But, by the time I've climbed up a few rungs of the ladder, I'm short of breath, and, when I get to the top, everything starts to swim before my eyes. Ruddy hell! I'm losing my balance! And, clutching at the air, I fall heavily to the ground.

Lou comes running out the house all flustered.

'Oh no! Pete, Pete! You silly old fool! I told you not to climb that ladder! Why do you never listen to me?'

From a bird's eye view I see myself lying motionless on the garden path, with Lou bending over me. But I seem to have double vision, because I can also see inside my skull, where blood is oozing from the wound to my head, and seeping into my brain. My wife is in a panic now. She's running indoors to dial 999. Poor old Lou!

The next thing is I'm being carried on a stretcher into an ambulance, and a medic gives me an infusion as we forge our way, siren blaring, at break-neck speed through the rush-hour traffic. I'm lying there happily and feeling no pain. For the first time in my life I'm totally relaxed. I also notice that IG is at my side. I can see him now very clearly, and we have one of our little chats.

'I'm not going to make it to the hospital, am I? This is the end of the road.'

'I'm afraid so, Zak.'

'Well don't be - I'm not sorry to go. It's no fun being in an old, impotent body. In fact I can't wait to be free of it.'

'Don't be so impatient! You've still got five minutes to go before your heart stops beating. Just cool it!'

But of course I can't cool it. Instead I lie there impatiently counting the minutes, and then suddenly - pop - I'm out of my body, and out of the ambulance, and floating in a void. And the next thing I hear is IG's voice bringing me back with some post-hypnotic suggestions.

'Five, four, three, two, one. Now you can remove your blindfold and open your eyes. Welcome home Zak!'

'Thanks! Well now, I suppose you've been keeping the score? So tell me how I did.'

'You got full marks for growing a big ego!'

'Don't be funny! That would surely lose me marks!'

'You're right that spiritual development is ultimately about dropping the ego, but you have to have one to drop in the first place, and that has been your achievement. You started that life with shaky self-esteem and an insecure sense of identity. But, as you passed your tests and grew in confidence, your integrity increased, and you became more secure in yourself. You get full marks for fighting your battles bravely, and sticking to your convictions, even though they were sometimes misguided.'

'Yes, and I learned from my mistakes, didn't I? Otherwise I wouldn't have been able to marry Lou and be a good dad to Adam and Emma.'

'That's right. You turned it around in your middle years, and the reason you could do so was because your heart had opened.'

'I could have easily stayed single and hooked on success, and gone on working like a maniac. But instead I made something of my life that I can feel good about now.'

'That's the most important thing - to feel good about your life once you reach the end of it. So well done Zak for absolving the incarnation group with honours! And now you can take a well-earned rest.'

'A what?'

Life 2
NEL the TAURUS

With IG's soporific music in my ears, I lean back comfortably in my chair, happy there's nothing more to do for the next seventy years or so but watch the story of my life unfold. Now Nel, I tell myself, you're not going to let anything upset you this time! You're not going to suffer! You just have to remember that it's all only a film, even when the amnesia begins to kick in.

Oh - it's started! I can see a womb and I'm looking straight into it, as if through the x-ray eye of one those cameras they use to make scans. Curled up inside is a baby girl, and I know instinctively it's me. I have sort of double vision. I'm seeing the baby as if through the camera lens, and at the same time I am the baby and can feel what she's feeling. She's cuddled up to her own body, sucking her thumb, doing nothing but dozing her time away, soothed by the thud-thud of her mother's heartbeat.

It's cosy and warm, and I've felt very safe in here so far, but now the scary bit is beginning. The first odd thing I become aware of is a shuddering like a series of earth tremors, and then the walls of my cave start pulsating. It gets much worse when they begin to squeeze me from every side. Be sensible, Nel, I tell myself. This only means that your mother has gone into labour These are contractions, stupid, and nothing worse than that. But babies don't listen to reason.

Now I'm being propelled headfirst downwards towards the mouth of a very sinister looking tunnel. I'd rather die than go in there. So I struggle against the force that's pushing me, and manage to twist my body round into a horizontal position and to dig in my heels. Me as observer is saying,

'Silly baby - that's just the wrong thing to do! Now the birth will be hard labour and long drawn-out!'

But baby, bless her heart, doesn't understand.

I hold my obtuse position till I've not enough strength left to resist the call of nature. Then I'm swirled upside-down, and pumped straight into the tunnel headfirst. Mercifully it's all over quickly, and I emerge on the other side into a place full of violent light. I can feel my new lungs inflating with air, and I'm screaming full force, and no wonder because I'm being held upside down by my feet, while someone is spanking my bottom. A most undignified entrance into the world!

When I've been washed and dressed, and given to my mother to hold, I stop crying. Enfolded in her arms, I relax again into the familiar feel of her. I'm joined to her body once more, and can hear her heartbeat, which is telling me it's safe to fall asleep. The date is May 6th 1944, and I like my new name. It's Lucy Angelica Bullock.

THE KID

Two long years have passed in earth time, and baby Lucy has grown into a chubby toddler. She's a picture of health with shiny pink cheeks and bright blue eyes. It's teatime, and I move inside her again, because I don't want to miss eating my favourite cereal which is groats! Clutching my little spoon tightly in my fist, I eat greedily, shovelling the next spoonful in before I've swallowed the last. Cereal is soon overflowing from the corners of my mouth, and running down my chin. My pink bib is sodden with it, and the pool of cereal on the floor is getting bigger.

'Lucy Angelica you mucky pup! Just look at the mess you're in!'

And mummy strips me of my sticky clothes, and pops me into the tub. A rub-dub-dub a scrub and a rub, and I come out clean again and pristine pink. Now I'm sitting on mummy's lap in front of the fire, cuddled in a big, soft bath towel. She's singing that song to me about old Macdonald and his farm.

'With a moo moo here, and a moo moo there. Here a moo there a moo, everywhere a moo cow!'

I'm wearing my prettiest frock It's primrose yellow and has pink rosebuds all over it. We've put on our best clothes today, because we've got visitors coming to tea - mummy's sister Muriel and my cousins Julia and Janet. That's why I'm allowed to wear my hair loose! Mummy is brushing it with her silver hairbrush to make it shine.

When we've had our tea, we're sent upstairs to play, so mummy and auntie can talk in peace. But I'm not enjoying my cousins' company at all. I'm standing glowering in the doorway, while Janet and Julia pull all my toys out of the cupboard, and scatter them over the floor. The puppet strings have got tangled, and the pony has lost her tail, and I'm getting more and more upset.

Now Julia has discovered my best baby doll, and started to undress her.

'Leave my doll alone!' I shout, but Julia takes no notice.

Meanwhile Janet has pulled the dolls' house out of the corner and opened up the front. Now she's changing all the furniture around, which makes me very cross indeed.

'Stop it,' I scream at her. 'Stop it! Stop it!'

'But auntie said we could play with your toys.'

'Well you can't because they're mine!'

I give Janet a hefty push and she stumbles, grabbing my hair as she falls. Ouch! I know she did that on purpose, and it makes me see red. The next moment I'm screaming, and pummelling her with my fists, until mummy and auntie come running upstairs and pull us apart.

'Lucy Angelica! What's the matter with you? That's not a nice way to treat your cousin!'

I try to explain how she'd provoked me, but I'm so red in the face and speechless that I can't get a word out.

'Come with me,' says mummy firmly, leading me downstairs to the kitchen. 'I've got something for you. Now, if you promise to be nice to your cousins, and let them play with your toys, I'll give you this.'

My eyes light up when I see the chocolate bar.

'So are you going to be a good girl and share your things?'

'Yes mummy,' I say meekly, and the chocolate bar is mine.

Ha! No one's going to make me share this! I'm going to eat it all by myself - down to the very last bit!

TEENS

I'm sweet fourteen and mummy has bought me my first bra, which I'm in the process of trying on. There are three mirrors on my dressing table, so I can see myself from the front, the side and the back. Its surface is cluttered with my collection of favourite things - china animals, a pink powder puff, strings of beads, a picture of a horse in a silver frame and sea-shells.

When I see how neatly the lacy cups encase the mounds of my budding breasts, a thrill of excitement runs through me. Next I pull a low-cut sling top tightly over them, and slip into my stiff petticoat and flared skirt. I can't do up the waist buttons because of the bulging roll of puppy fat around my midriff. Never mind!

Make-up next! I select a strawberry pink lipstick and midnight-blue eye shadow for my lids, and I blacken my lashes with thick mascara. With half-closed eyes, I throw a sultry look at an imaginary admirer standing behind me in the mirror, and flutter my eyelids at him. That's it - Marilyn Munroe! Then a squirt of Femme Fatal before slipping my feet into my high-heeled sandals, and out the door I go. Head held proudly high and heels clacking, I set off down the street in the direction of the park.

Although I'm feigning disinterest in everything and everyone, I'm keeping a lookout all the time for a certain boy with blonde hair.

Yesterday I found him in the park, and he followed me all the way home. Every time I turned round he dodged into the bushes, while I pretended not to see him. If he does it again today I have a plan. I'll let him come after me, and all of a sudden I'll spin round and walk towards him. When we pass I'll look him straight in the eye. We'll see what he does then!

TWENTIES

I'm waiting for the stylist to arrive to get me ready for the fashion shoot. I got rid of my puppy fat through stringent dieting, and I've shot up to nearly six foot in height.

'With that figure you should be a mannequin,' said my friend Carole, who has connections in the fashion world.

It was Carole who introduced me to Brad the famous photographer, and now I'm working for him as one of his models. My big break came a year ago when I made the front cover of Vogue, and after that my career took off in a spectacular way. Now I'm in high demand, and earning lots of lovely money! In fact at twenty-three I'm earning more than my father, who had to slave for thirty years to reach his high-income bracket!

I take a peep at myself in the mirror. I've been dressed in a stretch satin corset with a short diaphanous chiffon skirt, and I'm wearing a fabulous pair of white leather boots that make my long legs look even longer. The stylist is putting the final touches to my hair, which has to hang down straight from its centre parting, and Brad is fiddling with his camera. Now we're ready.

During the shoot, Brad barks out instructions like a sergeant major on parade ground, and I have to obey very promptly. I take up one pose after another. Flash! Flash! He'd like my hair hanging over my left eye please, and the stylist rushes up to comb it into place. Flash! By the end of the morning all my muscles are aching because the poses are tiring to hold. I'm also thoroughly fed up, although I don't show it, because I have to look as fresh as a daisy in each shot. That's part of the job.

When I'm not working, I like going out and having a good time. I've got money to burn, so I eat in expensive restaurants, and treat myself to shopping trips to Paris and Rome, and stay in luxurious hotels. And I'm always buying clothes and shoes. I can't afford the outfits I model, of course, but they've made me thoroughly spoilt, and it has to be designer gear for me now or nothing.

I've just discovered this stunning little boutique in South Kensington, and it's where I'm heading this morning. Soon I'm moving my fingers swiftly along the rows of hangers on the rails. I run an expert eye over the items that catch my attention. I must say I like their range but I'm choosy. It will have to be something special before I get my chequebook out.

Now I'm in one of the plush changing rooms, trying on a selection of their little creations. And half an hour later I'm smiling wryly as I write a cheque for over two hundred pounds. I emerge into the street laden with carrier bags, and wave down a taxi. 'Fortnum and Masons,' I say. They have the best chocolate éclairs in town, and I'm going to treat myself today. I deserve it - I work hard enough!

Lucy Angelica may be making a frivolous impression, but I assure you that she also has a sensible streak. I'm very aware that I should be investing my money in something solid while the going's good, which is why I've bought a flat in an up-and-coming area of town. We moved in last May - we being me, my boyfriend Hugo who works in an auction house, and Bruce the cat. We've had fun furnishing it with some gorgeous pieces that Hugo was able to pick up cheaply. We both agree that antique furniture is not only elegant and stylish, it's also a good investment.

However, there's a problem with having valuable stuff in your home, and that is you're more likely to get burgled. That would be my worst nightmare come true. It makes me so upset when I lose something. Last month my car was stolen from outside our flat, which nearly broke my heart because she was my dearest possession - a sweet little white VW cabriolet with red leather seats. I was devastated when I discovered they'd discontinued that model, so she couldn't be replaced.

'That sounds like an over-reaction, Nel.'

'Who's Nel? I'm Lucy.'

'Your real name is Nel, and I'm IG your inner guide. Have you forgotten the incarnation group? We used to do self-inquiry exercises together.'

'I sort of remember.'

'Don't worry - it's the amnesia.'

'Though your voice sounds familiar, as if it's always been there in the background. Are you like my conscience?'

'More like your higher self - an older and wiser part of you that has an overview of your life.'

'Then you can see into the future. So tell me, am I going to get my car back?'

'No, it's a gonner, Nel. I know you find this hard to accept, but life gives only to take away again.'

'So I'm going to lose other things too? Oh no!'

'Gain must always be balanced with loss, just as receiving must be balanced with giving.'

'Then I'll have to write off my little cabriolet. That's so tough!'

'It's how things are. Life is teaching you the lesson that all attachment leads to misery. But, tell me, why are you falling in love with things? Have you no people in your life to love?'

'Well, there's Hugo - I love him very much - and mummy who's always there for me. Since I've become a famous model I'm the bee's knees in her eyes. I love my dad too, of course, and then there's Bruce, the most beautiful cat in the world. I adore him. In fact I can truly say I love all animals great and small - even spiders.'

'And do you love yourself?'

'Myself? That's a funny idea! No, not really, though I can be awfully self-indulgent.'

'Self-indulgence is not a sign that you love yourself - just the opposite. And do the things you treat yourself to make you happy?'

'Only for a short while, and then I start wanting something else. I've realised that I'm happier when I'm looking forward to buying something than when I've actually got it.'

'That's an important insight. Do you remember when you were little, and your parents were hard up after the war? You had to save up your pocket money for weeks, before you could afford to buy something you'd set your heart on.'

'That's right, and today I've so much money I can buy all I desire straight away, which makes the things I purchase seem less valuable, and buying them less of a thrill.'

'That's a good thing to realise, because you're engaged in defining your values at present. So are the things you buy worth the time and money you put into them?'

'The answer's no, because sometimes I go wild when I'm out shopping. Then I come home with things I don't really want, and I know I'll never use.'

'And what were you feeling inside on these days? Were you a bit depressed, for example? And did you treat yourself to those things to try and cheer yourself up?'

'Very likely, because I'm often depressed about what happens at work. People always think that being a fashion model is terribly glamorous, but it's hard work both physically and emotionally. And you have to put up with a lot of bitchiness from the other girls. There's blood on the catwalk as they say.'

'So you go shopping to get a lift when you're feeling down and, when you're feeling empty, you go to Fortnum and Masons, and stuff yourself with a chocolate eclair. That can happen when you don't love yourself.'

'But how can I love myself when I don't know who I am?'

'Quite right, Nel! You can't define your values until you know who you are, which brings us to the central question: who is this self we are inquiring into.'

'You should be able to tell me. You're my inner guide.'

'I can't, because we all have to find that out for ourselves.'

When I look at myself in the mirror I don't see myself. I only see what's wrong with me - that there's a spot on my chin, or that my nose is looking big, or that I've got a bad hair day. Although they're very clever at covering up the blemishes when I'm being prepared for a photo shoot, I still worry about my appearance all the time.

And it's a drag to have to watch my weight, especially with my weakness for chocolate. Hugo can laugh, but I know he wouldn't fancy me if I was fat, and my figure is my fortune in my profession. So I indulge in the calorie-rich foods I love until my tape measure says 'stop', and then I go on a diet to shed the extra inches I've put on. But this stop-and-go way of eating isn't good for my body.

Whenever I see my picture in a magazine or up on a billboard, I can't identify with it. I just don't believe that girl is me, because, when I'm modelling, I have to act a part that usually has no relation to what I'm feeling inside. I'm not myself, and outside working hours I can't be myself either, because I have to keep up appearances. When I go out I must be seen wearing designer clothes, and my hair must be styled just right, because I can't afford to look a fright in public. A roving photographer might take a picture of me, and the next morning it would be spread all over the gossip pages.

'So you're a bird in a golden cage, Nel.'

'Yes, that's what it feels like, IG.'

'You're under pressure all the time to represent some ideal of beauty that's determined by the fashion industry.'

'Yes, so I can't be authentic.'

'Well, first you need to define beauty in your own terms.'

'That's difficult, because different people have different ideas about what's beautiful.'

'It's not about other people, Nel. It's about you. What do you find beautiful?'

'Um! Well, fat and clumsy is ugly, and slim and elegant is beautiful. Young and glowing is beautiful, and old and faded is ugly. But it seems to be more complicated than that, because beauty comes and goes. On some days, when I look in the mirror, it's there very strongly, and then it's gone and nothing I can do will make it come back.'

'That's because beauty is like a blessing. The goddess Venus blesses us with it when she decides to favour us, and some are favoured more than others. Seeing your good looks I'd say you're one of her firm favourites, Nel.'

'At the moment perhaps, but I'm aging by the day and, if I think about what I could look like in twenty years time, it makes me shiver.'

'You dread growing old?'

'Of course, because where will I be when I lose my looks? Out of a job for one thing, and Hugo will stop fancying me, and go off with someone else. And, if I'm old and ugly, I won't be able get another boyfriend, so I'll be lonely and poor and wretched.'

'But the good news is you'll be free at last. You'll be able to be yourself, because you'll no longer have to please other people.'

'That's not much consolation! I think I'll just curl up and die right here and now!'

'Poor Nel! It's harder for a beauty to lose her looks than for a girl who's always been plain. That's one disadvantage to being beautiful, and there's another - you're never sure whether you're being loved for yourself. Beautiful women are seen as trophies by men, and, if you're rich as well as beautiful, that's double trouble. Then you'll worry that you're only being loved for your money. And may be you are, because both beauty and wealth create greed in others and the desire to possess.'

'I'm seen as both rich and beautiful at present, so that means I could be exploited.'

'Yes, but you can also exploit. Beauty has its market value, as you've discovered, because you use it to earn your living, and it can also be used to gain power over people.'

'It gives me power over men, I've noticed that!'

'That's right, and you must wield that power with great awareness, because when beauty is used it's abused, and when beauty is abused it's bruised, and then it dies like a flower.'

'I like that. I think I'll write it down... So are you saying that it's not okay for me to make myself attractive? I mean I love glamorous clothes, and wearing expensive jewellery, and I spend a fortune on body care. You should see my bathroom - it's bursting full of jars and bottles!'

'Delight in the body, Nel, and enjoy all the pleasures of the flesh. But always remember that, when it's the real thing, beauty is always natural. It's enough unto itself and needs no outer ornament, because it's a light that illuminates you from within.'

The next part of the film of my life is just starting and it's May, my birthday month. In a few days time I'll be thirty and - guess what - I'm still together with Hugo! I see us sitting at the kitchen table together eating Sunday brunch. We're both wearing silk kimonos and nothing else, as we've just crawled out of bed. There's a vase of tulips on the table and a bowl of strawberries. The croissants are still warm from the oven, and a delicious smell of freshly brewed coffee hangs in the air. I can't resist coffee, so I slip back inside Lucy's body.

I'm immediately wracked with pangs of love for Hugo. He's so good looking in his tousled, hunky way. As I watch him dunk his croissant in his mug, tears spring to my eyes, which I hide by gazing out of the window. The old pear tree in the garden is covered with pink blossoms. We're going to get a bumper crop, and the birds, busy among the branches, are all singing full throttle. Everything in the garden is lovely, as they say, but beneath the sunny surface of our life something isn't right.

Just now in the bedroom after making love - which as usual went much too fast for me - I made the mistake of bringing up our taboo subject. It seemed a good time as we lay cuddling in bed, with Hugo in his Sunday mood. But the way he reacted left me feeling tearful. The gist of the matter is this: I want to get married and have babies, but Hugo, for some reason that I fail to understand, won't commit. And this has been going on for some time, with me broaching the subject, and him putting off giving me an answer. I pretend I don't mind, but deep down I'm hurt that Hugo isn't keen on marrying me. It makes me wonder whether he loves me so much after all.

It's not as if we couldn't afford a baby, as we're well set up financially, although I'm no longer earning. I gave up modelling last year for health reasons. I was becoming increasingly anorexic, so my doctor advised me to find another job. Well I haven't been trying very hard, because I planned to get married and have babies in my thirties. That will happen soon, and in the meantime there's plenty of work to do on the house.

I kept an eye on the housing market, and three years ago, when prices had risen, I sold my flat in town for a huge profit, and Hugo and I bought our cottage together. It was built in the 1820's, and is situated on the edge of the Green Belt with a mature garden. There are old-fashioned climbing roses straddling the porch, and hollyhocks grow along the wall in summer, and it has enough land at the back to graze a pony. At present we're living on Hugo's earnings, which is all right by me, after all I kept him when I was earning and he was growing his business. But Hugo seems to resent it.

'Let's go to Mexico for our next holiday,' I say. 'It's supposed to have wonderful beaches.'

'That's another of your extravagant ideas! You'll have to pay for yourself, love, you know that.'

'I thought you might invite me as my thirtieth birthday present!'

'Can't afford to at present, love. Take some dosh from your savings account if you really must go.'

Hugo can be so mean sometimes. And, if I didn't keep reminding him, he'd very likely forget my birthday altogether. Why doesn't he understand how happy it makes me to receive a nice birthday present?

'If you think I'm going to touch my savings,' I say, 'you've another think coming. I need them for my security!'

'Then Mexico will have to wait until you start earning again.'

I'm becoming more and more agitated, but I don't let it show for fear of spoiling our lovely Sunday brunch.

'So what shall we do for my birthday then? It's the day after tomorrow.'

'I'll take you out for a meal.'

His offhand tone of voice is the final straw, and I can't prevent myself exploding in an angry tirade. The grudges against him that I've been hiding away come pouring out now - but not my deepest grudge, which remains hidden.

Maybe I didn't handle that very well I think, after Hugo has upped sticks and left. Bruce comes in from the garden and rubs himself against my legs. He always feels my distress, and that's his way of comforting me. I pick him up and fondle him.

'Bruce my sweet pussikins! You're my heart-throb, you're the one I love!' And I kiss his little pink nose, and bury my face in his fur.

I know where Hugo's gone and what he's doing. He's round at his best mate Tony's. They'll be sitting in Tony's living room with the curtains drawn, smoking pot and listening to modern jazz records. I hate that kind of music, and what a waste of a sunny afternoon! We should be out in the country going for a walk together. And in my imagination I see us walking hand in hand through fields of sprouting green corn, and my eyes fill with tears.

Oh Lord! Why am I so emotional this morning? I suppose it's because the day got off to a bad start with bad sex. And I've noticed I always get very worked up about injustices around money. They bring out the warrior in me, and then I'm ready to fight for my rights down to the last penny.

'I'm glad to see you doing some self-inquiry, Nel. When you know your patterns better, you'll be able to break out of them.'

'Hallo, IG! Can I ask you for some advice?'

'About your relationship?'

'That too, but first about my investments. I want to make sure I'll be able to keep up my present lifestyle in the future, so I need to invest my savings wisely now.'

'I can't give you assurances about the future, Nel. Lives are always composed of lean years as well as fat, and we must learn to survive both wealth and dearth.'

'And is there no way of cheating the system, and getting the wealth without the dearth?'

'No, because everything has to balance out. But it's good you're thinking about these matters, because you're learning in this life to become materially self-sufficient, and provide the security you need.'

'But what if Hugo's business collapses? I worry about that, I really do.'

'You should never worry, Nel, because when you worry you're focussed on the future, and the future doesn't exist yet. Try to live in the present instead, because you can only be happy in the present moment - never in the future or in the past.'

'I'm unhappy at present - very unhappy actually - because Hugo isn't being nice to me. Since he met Tony and started smoking grass he's a changed person. I've heard that marijuana saps your energy, and it seems to be true in Hugo's case, because he used to have much more verve. He's become so passive lately, and his sex-drive is at an all time low!'

'Perhaps you're to blame too.'

'Me? I've tried everything, and still he won't come on - which is a big problem for someone like me. Tauruses need a lot of sex in order to feel good in their bodies. And Hugo knows that - the bastard - but he still won't give up smoking pot!'

'Perhaps it's his protest against the way you're trying to plan his life.'

'Well, he knows I want to spend my thirties bringing up children, and he's accepted that he's part of the plan.'

'But you can't go ahead without his agreement.'

'Hmmm.... The awful thing in our generation is that we have a choice about when to have babies, whereas, in the old days before the pill, women just got pregnant, and the men had to marry them, and that was that!'

'Nel! If you're planning to force his hand think twice, because it's not going to work out.'

'Then should I tell him that I've stopped taking the pill?'

'Of course! It's the ethical thing to do. But, Nel, are you sure Hugo is the right man for you? If you value sex so highly, at least that side of your marriage should be hunky-dory, and that's not the case, is it?'

'Only because he smokes so much pot. We used to have a great scene at the start of our relationship. We used to say we were ideally suited in bed. But, when the baby comes, I know he'll stop smoking, and everything will come right. So I'm not going to allow you to put me off marrying Hugo, IG. I've made up my mind, and nothing you can say is going to change it!'

It's six months later, and I'm down at the health club receiving a luxurious massage. I felt I needed pampering today. So here I am, lying on the massage couch in a treatment room, naked except for a thong, while the masseuse runs her hands over my big, pregnant belly. We chat in a cosy, woman-to-woman way about pregnancy and breast-feeding and, when the treatment is over, my body feels supple all over. And not only that - my skin smells scrumptious and my soul feels deeply nurtured. I dress slowly, putting on my jewellery last, a pearl necklace, a bracelet of coloured stones and two rings - one engagement ring and one wedding ring. Yes, Hugo and I got married last September.

The good thing about being pregnant is that it gives you an excuse to concentrate on yourself. So I'm busy satisfying the needs of my body. I make sure I get plenty of healthy food, and I get my fresh air by going on long country walks. I never realised that trudging along muddy footpaths can be a sensual experience. But it's as if being pregnant has put me in touch with mother earth, so I can see, hear, smell and taste more of Nature than before.

It's also kept me busy at home, as there's so much to do before baby arrives. My friend Carole, who's an experienced mum now, having had her first baby last year, has helped me go through the catalogues. Together we've chosen the bath, the cot and the pram, and she's also passed on to me some sweet little baby clothes in different sizes! Even Hugo has started looking forward to it, now he's got over his initial shock. He's going to make a wonderful father. As for my mother, all she can talk about is the baby, and dad's just as bad. They can't wait to be grandparents.

'So you see, IG, me getting pregnant has brought the family closer. Then it wasn't such a bad thing to do, was it? And I'm feeling much more fulfilled. I don't nag Hugo like I used to, so we're getting on better - except for one small problem.'

'What's that?'

'He's stopped having sex with me. He says we should wait until after the baby's born in case we harm it, though that's not the medical opinion. So I'm worried it's because I've become fat, and that's turned him off.'

'But it's natural to put on weight when you're pregnant.'

'In the front maybe but not all round so you look like a beer barrel! My problem is I'm addicted to chocolate.'

'If you listened to your body, Nel, you'd find it's not so keen on chocolate bars. It's your mind that's addicted to them. When you were anorexic, you listened to your mind instead of your body, and as a result your body lost it's balance. But the body is wiser that the mind, so why not start listening to it again, and find out what it wants?'

'I know what it wants - to be fat! As soon as I relax my control it starts growing a spare tyre. But when I'm fat I don't feel desirable, and when I don't feel desirable I lose my self-confidence!'

'Girls of your generation have been brainwashed into believing that fat is bad, and skinny is good, and that has made you negative towards your natural body shape. But it's time to free your mind from its conditioning, and to love your body the way it is.'

'I hear what you're saying, IG, but I have a strongly developed aesthetic sense that sees flabby as ugly, and fat as plain disgusting!'

'That's due to your conditioning. All variations on the female form are beautiful when they are natural. Change your mind-set, Nel, because, if you feel negative about your body, you'll feel negative about yourself. Listen to your body, allow it to regulate itself, and it will be graceful, and find it's own style of beauty.'

MIDDLE AGE

We've moved forward twelve years to 1986. I'm standing in the bedroom of a house I'm refurbishing, discussing colour schemes with my client. I suggest to her that we paint each wall a different pastel colour, and crown the effect with a brilliant yellow ceiling.

'That way the atmosphere in the room will be subtly differentiated,' I say, 'and the walls will be encouraged to relate and start up a dialogue with each other.'

The lady looks dubious. 'I think I'd sleep better in the bedroom if it was painted magnolia, because that's what I'm used to.'

I sigh. Why are people with money such stick-in-the-muds? As we pass the mirror, I take a quick glance at myself, and note with satisfaction that my tailored suit gives me a slim waistline, and my bottom doesn't look as enormous as I feared. I dress very smartly now, in keeping with my role as an interior decorating consultant. And, though I say it myself, I'm in good nick. People are amazed when they hear I've turned forty, because I still take a size thirty-eight.

'What's your secret, Lucy?' they ask.

'I've learned to listen to my body,' I say.

Yes, no more chocolate bars and cream cakes for Lucy. Her body has said very clearly that it prefers fruit, so fruit is what it gets. And taking up yoga has also helped me keep my shape. Nevertheless it's a miracle I still look so young considering what I've been going through. My hair should have turned grey, and my face should be lined with deep furrows of sorrow, because Hugo and I are getting divorced.

After our daughter Melanie was born, Hugo abandoned his failing antique business, and got a job as a buyer for a big antique trading company. And when Melanie started nursery school, I decided to have a career again, and trained as an interior designer. Then, once I was qualified, I set up my own consultancy business. Hugo and I went on happily for a while, though we lived separate lives, until I discovered he was having an affair. A woman Carole knows wised her up to it, and when she told me I nearly fainted with shock.

'But, darling, surely you must have guessed something was afoot! We women always sense these things!' Carole exclaimed.

No, I trusted Hugo and never thought he'd do anything like that. I was amazed when further investigation revealed that the affair had been going on for years and years, I was also very indignant. There was me staying faithful, although starved of sex, while all the time another woman was getting what should have been rightfully mine!

I took the bull by the horns and confronted Hugo about it. He denied it at first, but, when I persisted, he broke down and confessed. He tried to appeal to my pity, going on about how hard it was for him to lead a double life, and how he couldn't face separating from her, but neither could he face losing his home and family.

'It's tearing me apart,' he said, and he begged me to put up with it, and go on as we were.

'What - share my husband!' I exclaimed, outraged. 'Not on your Nelly!'

'But Lucy, you've been sharing me all this time!'

'That was different. As long as I didn't know about her, there was no skin off my nose. But, now it's out in the open, I won't tolerate it. I'm going to have you thrown out of the house, unless you promise to stop seeing her!'

Hugo, who knows very well how stubborn I can be once I've dug my heels in, left with his tail between his legs. And the next thing I hear is that they're living together. He hasn't come back to collect his stuff. There's a cupboard in the bedroom still full of his shirts. In fact, everywhere I turn, I'm confronted with his things. It's awful! But the worst pang I get is when I think of them together in bed. That's like a great big thorn in my flesh.

I realised I had to do something, so I went to my solicitor and started divorce proceedings. As I'm very much the injured party, and I've spent a great deal of money on Hugo over the years, I thought the least the law could do for me was get some of it back. But I had another think coming! I got a letter from Hugo's solicitor telling me he's claiming half my house - yes, you heard right! Hugo the highwayman, who only contributed a measly two thousand when we bought it together, now wants a hundred thousand back! If he wins the case my future is grim. Either I'll be crippled by serious debt, or forced to sell my beloved home.

'Poor Nel! It's hard I know, but you've only yourself to blame.'

'You mean because I got pregnant without Hugo's consent? It's true, IG. If I hadn't acted as I did, Hugo wouldn't have married me, and I wouldn't be going through this horrendous divorce. Well, I'm certainly being punished for my sins!'

'Your fault was your obstinate blindness to the truth. Hugo was not behaving in a loving way, his heart was not with you, but you closed your eyes to this. You'd set your mind on marrying him and nothing could deter you.'

'So instead of seeing things as they were, I saw them how I wanted them to be.'

'That's right. It's an old pattern of yours to gloss over problems, and try to repress anything that threatens to disturb the smooth surface of your life.'

'But I was always a good wife to Hugo. I was always loyal, and look how he repays me - by torturing me!'

'You're torturing yourself, Nel.'

'That's ridiculous! Who's behind those solicitor's letters that cause me so much pain?'

'They may derive from Hugo, but how you react to them depends on you. At the moment you feel like a victim, and you're allowing disempowering thoughts and feelings to sap your energy. That's why you feel bad, but you have a choice.'

'What choice do I have then?'

'Accept the situation instead of fighting it, and you'll suffer less. Your mind is full of negative thoughts and destructive feelings at present, but this can be changed. If you could replace them with positive feelings towards Hugo, you'd feel better immediately.'

'I daren't think positively about him, because then I'd get sentimental. I'd start remembering how I used to hold his arm when we walked down the street, or how he'd make me a cup of tea in bed in the morning. Oh dear! Now I've started crying again. The truth of the matter, IG, is that I still love Hugo.'

'It's good to recognise that love is still there beneath all the hurt and anger, because love is generous and wishes the other well, and love is healing. And, if you love Hugo, you'll be able to let go of him in gratefulness for what he's given you, and move on.'

'But not when the creep is trying to get half my house! He doesn't deserve any generosity. And I feel more like cursing him than wishing him well. May all the plagues of Egypt fall on his head and on the head of his floozy!'

Six months later I'm divorced. The verdict went against me, and Hugo won the case, and it's nearly bankrupted me. I've had to remortgage the house, but at least I'm still able to live in it. The chattels have to be divided equally. So Hugo is coming round tonight to claim what's legally his, and I've arranged for Melanie to sleep over at a friend's house. I'm anticipating a battle, and thought it wise to get her out of the way.

So here we are - Hugo and me snarling at each other over our stuff, like two dogs fighting over a heap of bones.

'The rosewood sideboard is mine because I paid for it!' I say.

'Yes, but who found it and brought it home? Me - so that makes it mine!' retorts Hugo.

We each refuse to give way, and it's the same with the silver coffee pot, the studio ceramics and the best teaset. I've always loved that teaset. It's Royal Worcester and a particularly fine design in red and green, with a delicate gold rim. But now I hear myself threatening to smash it to smithereens rather than let Hugo have it. He's so appalled by this, that he hands it over to me without further argument.

It's past midnight before we're finished. Hugo has loaded his stuff into a van now and driven it away, leaving awful gaping spaces in all the rooms. I'm sitting by myself in the kitchen, emptying a bottle of wine, and nursing my grievances. Well, IG, I'd be a saint if I could feel generous and forgiving towards Hugo at a moment like this!

But I've got the message. I understand that harbouring negativity is bad for me, and that's why I'm making a decision to stop dwelling on the past. I've decided to make a new start. I'm going to pick up the pieces of my life, and stick them together again, and I'm going to replace the big centre piece that was Hugo. And as for my precarious financial situation - I know there are lean years ahead but, if I'm economical, and I work hard, I know I'll be able to recuperate my losses.

It must be several years later now, as I'm sitting in front of my first PC. I work long hours, but my business as a free-lance consultant is building. Now that I've found the right consumer group to target - single men who need a representative pad but fear they have no taste, and divorced men hoping to impress the ladies - the assignments are pouring in. I'm motherly towards the young bachelors, and flirt discretely with the middle-aged divorcees. Charm and an attractive appearance are great assets in this line of business. And I predict that, if things continue the way they're going, I'll be back on my feet in less than five years. Then the mortgage will be paid off, and I'll have no more worries about money.

'If I know you, Nel, you'll still feel insecure even then, unless you change your pattern. You've always been afraid your savings are not enough, and believed you needed more.'

'It's true, IG. I'm a bit neurotic in that way.'

'Then let's do some self-inquiry.'

'I'm not sure that self-inquiry is helpful, because even if I've understood some point about myself, I'm not going to change.'

'But just recognising a pattern can make a lot of difference. Then you're free to decide whether you want more of the same or not.'

'But I don't like changes.'

'Not even changes for the better?'

'Perhaps, but basically, IG, I'm an old stick-in-the-mud.'

'Most people are driven by two things - fear and greed. Greed makes them want more than they've got, and fear makes them cling to what they have for fear of a future lack. But then they never get to enjoy anything.'

'I'm a bit like that.'

'So, if you wanted to step out of the clutches of greed and fear, your first step would be to define your needs. When you're able to distinguish your needs from your desires, then you'll know what to keep and what to dispense with. And you'll be able to set your savings a reasonable limit.'

'That's all very sensible advice, IG, but you can see what a spoilt brat I am. I count as needs what others see as luxuries - for example my self-indulgent bathroom, or my super-modern kitchen or my conservatory full of exotic plants. I must have all that around me because, if I had to dispense with quality and beauty in my life, I'd wither away.'

'All right Nel, then try at least to live in the here-and-now, so you enjoy the things you have. Because, when we live in the present, greed and fear don't affect us. They only have power over our minds when we're in the past or in the future.'

Guess what! I've got a new lover! Neil is a plasterer - one of the tradesmen I do business with - and he's very sweet when he's not plastered! He's fifteen years younger than me and, with his body builder's physique, and his muscular arms covered in tattoos, he's a very different kettle of fish from the decorous middle-class men I usually go out with. He drinks beer instead of wine, he's a soccer fan instead of being into cricket, and I can't talk to him about anything that interests me. But these problems fade into the background when we're in bed together, because the sex is so good.

So I'm having that whale of a time that I missed during my marriage. However there's one fly in the ointment - my daughter. Melanie doesn't like him. She's grown into the sort of stroppy teenager who protests loudly and vociferously at everything that displeases her. So, if she comes home from school and finds Neil in the shower, or she catches him helping himself to something from the fridge, she's likely to be extremely rude. But Neil takes it all in good part. He says he's used to being sworn at!

Six months have passed in this vein, and I've just arrived home after a busy day at work. Melanie is staying with her dad, so I have a bite to eat and then collapse on the sofa. I've got into the habit of bumming out in front of the TV set every evening. I watch whatever's on, even if it's a load of rubbish, and I wonder why I do it. It must be to relax, because I'm always wound up after a day at work. But a bit of self-inquiry produces another reason - I keep my mind occupied with moronic programmes to avoid thinking and feeling.

I'm tired tonight and decide to turn in early. So I switch off the TV and the lights, and go upstairs. But, when I'm in bed, those worrying thoughts I've been trying to ignore start going round and round in my head, and keep me awake. I've been watching Neil and Melanie, and I don't like what I see. Neil is definitely trying to butter her up. The way he pays her compliments, and brings her little presents, makes this obvious. He may declare that she's like a daughter to him, but I know something is going on.

Melanie takes the presents, but refuses to say thankyou with a kiss, and there's something definitely coquettish in her way of snubbing him. So I'm feeling very uncomfortable about it all. And just when I thought I'd got everything nicely sewn up - with the house, and a job I like, and a beautiful daughter and a lover to gratify me!

'I need your advice IG. Am I being irresponsible in allowing Neil the run of the house, when he has his eye on Melanie?'

'It depends whether Neil is the type of man you want your fourteen-year-old daughter to consort with?'

'Definitely not.'

'And is he the type of man you want to consort with yourself?'

'Well, to be honest I would prefer a nice respectable husband, if I could find one. Neil is wearing a bit thin.'

'Yes, because a relationship based on lust rather than love can never be fulfilling in the long term.'

'And why's that?'

'Because lust means using the body of another for your pleasure, and, when you treat another human being like a thing, you degrade him or her. Love, in contrast, bestows dignity and value on the other. It respects the body, and also values the spiritual being within.'

'That sounds a bit moralistic, IG. I don't take it so seriously. After all Neil and I are just having a bit of fun, and I give as good as I get. Neil doesn't go home hungry! Okay, our sex is very animal but we're all animals basically, aren't we? And sex with Neil is so liberating.'

'Yes, you were carrying a load of frustration, Nel, that you needed to release, and sex is a natural catharsis.'

'It was high time to free myself up sexually, after my inhibited upbringing, and my frigid marriage. I've been able to break all my inner taboos in bed with Neil, and get rid of my hang-ups.'

'That was the gain, but there's also been a loss, because love was missing. You've never loved Neil.'

'No - at least not in the way I loved Hugo.'

'Then perhaps it's time to say goodbye to him, in gratefulness for what he's given you. Sexual pleasure is the root of our capacity to enjoy, but it should be a beginning and not an end in itself. Because it can open the door to the greater joys of the heart and spirit that you'll share with a future partner.'

OLD AGE

Two senior citizens are dozing in deckchairs under the apple tree on a hot summer's afternoon. It's me and my second husband, Len, and on my lap there's a ginger cat curled up asleep. The present Bruce, who shares his name with a long line of predecessors, is a ginger tom like the first, and I love him to bits. I also love Len. When we met eight years ago he was freshly widowed, and so disorientated that he proposed to me on our first date!

'At our time of life we have no time to lose!' he said.

Well, I'm not one to leap before I look, especially when it's into the state of matrimony, where I'm once bitten and twice shy, so I replied,

'Give me six months to get to know you, and then I'll give you my answer.'

And, by the time the six months were up, I was sure that Len was Mr Right, so I allowed him to lead me to the altar.

The first big decision we had to make was whether to live in his house or mine. Well, as I had no intention of leaving the house where I'd lived for thirty-five years, and put down such deep roots, I dug my heels in. So Len agreed to move in with me. He rented out his four-bedroomed house and, as rents have risen steeply in recent years, he's getting a very nice income from it, which goes to augment his pension.

When I married Len, I decided to give up my interior decorating business, and embark on a life of ease. And it was high time, because the profession had been overrun meanwhile by hordes of youth with college degrees, and there was fierce competition for clients. Besides, when my mother died, (my dad had passed away ten years earlier) and her house was sold, I came into a small fortune, as property prices had gone through the roof. So at last I could accept that I have enough money. As I always say to Melanie,

'The advantage of being an only child is that you don't have to share your inheritance with any siblings!'

Len is also retired. He's had a career as a bank manager, but he says the banking business has also changed for the worse, and he's happy he's no longer part of it. He spends the day on his computer, surfing the net, and keeps fit by playing golf and mowing the lawn. Len is a very agreeable man to live with - placid and even-tempered - and we both value a regular lifestyle. We get up at eight o'clock in the morning, after a cup of tea in bed, and eat lunch punctually at one. Dinner is at seven, and we always go to bed after the ten o'clock news.

Len enjoys his food, and I keep myself busy cooking the sort of old-fashioned meals that make his eyes light up - steak and kidney pie, lamb stew with dumplings, always followed by some kind of pudding with custard. Of course I eat all these meals with him - I can't resist food!

I'm standing on the bathroom scales and - oh Lord! - I've put on half a stone! That's not good news, as I've just gone out and bought myself a smart new summer suit and, unless I lose weight, it's not going to fit. I could always pass it on to Melanie, of course, and perhaps the style's too young for me anyway. The short skirt doesn't do anything for my knees, and I don't want to look like mutton dressed up as lamb.

Melanie, who's in her thirties now, is the spitting image of me at that age, and she turns heads. It felt strange the first time I noticed the men giving her the eye instead of me, when we walked down the street together. I was both proud and envious of her at the same time! Yes, I've been blessed with the gift of beauty, which is vanishing now. But the inner beauty remains, and in some cases it only becomes visible when the outer has faded. I also know that Len loves me much more than all those men who used to chase me when I was young and gorgeous.

Melanie is very different from me in other ways. I always know exactly what I want, but she's all over the place. I always have my finances sorted, and manage my money sensibly, whereas Melanie, who's a single mother and on benefit, is continually hard up. She'll ring me and say, 'Jamie needs a new pair of winter shoes, mum, and I'm broke. Can you help us out?' or 'The rent's due on Thursday, mum, and I'm in the red. Can you lend me a couple of hundred?'

I always say 'yes', which leaves me feeling like a soft touch. I wish she'd be more financially self-sufficient.

My grandson, Jamie, is four and I love him to bits, but he's a handful. She's always asking me to take him while she goes up to town, and muggins always says 'yes'. But, after a short dose of Jamie, the house always looks as if a tornado has struck. And it takes hours afterwards to put everything back in its place. Perhaps I need to do some self-inquiry about this.

'Why can't I say 'no' to my daughter, IG?'

'That's right, Nel. Instead of blaming Melanie, ask yourself what you contribute to the situation.'

'Well I think somewhere inside me I feel guilty, and it's to do with the divorce. Because I wanted Melanie all to myself when Hugo had gone, so I tried to stop him seeing her. And I badmouthed him to her to drive a wedge between them, which wasn't right, I know.'

'And have you talked to Melanie about it?'

'I can't because she gets angry every time I broach the subject. Hugo and his floozy live in Spain. They bought a villa on the Costa Blanca, and Melanie flies out with Jamie to holiday with them. Jamie gets thoroughly spoilt every time they go there, and he's always out of control by the time they get back!'

'It sounds as if you still haven't let go of Hugo, although it's over twenty-five years since the divorce.'

'Which still seems like yesterday.'

'If you could finally let him go, and close that chapter of your life, your relationship with Melanie would improve, and you'd all get on better.'

'Huh! I'll get on with Melanie better when she's found a job. I was so upset when she threw in the last one - she'd only been there a month! The truth of the matter is that she doesn't want to work. She'd rather stay at home and be a mum, and let me foot the bill!'

'If you stopped trying to plan everything for her, and to organise her life, she'd have to learn to stand on her own feet.'

'I doubt it, because she's such a scatter-brain. She never thinks ahead. She keeps running up debts on her credit cards, without having the faintest idea about how she's going to pay them off!'

'So what is the worst that could happen?'

'Well, if she goes on like that, she could end up in the gutter!'

'Perhaps she needs to experience insecurity for her growth. You've chosen the safe option, Nel - a fully insured life with every comfort and convenience. But Melanie obviously prefers living on the edge. That's a different life choice and, if you're willing to learn from her, she could teach you how to keep the spark of adventure alive.'

'You mean I should be irresponsible?'

'No, there's a middle way. Between your organised set ways, and her chaotic spontaneity, is a middle point where you're securely grounded, but you still remain flexible and part of life's flow.'

Thirty years fly past as time gallops faster and faster. My ninetieth birthday comes and goes. I'm doing a little dusting today. I move round the room dusting all the familiar objects I know so well, and love so dearly. Nothing has been changed. There's Len's chair. It's empty now he's gone, but otherwise everything is still in its accustomed place - the ornaments, the books, the pictures. They will all outlive me.

The house is overflowing with half a century's worth of clutter. And it will be a nightmare for Melanie to clear it out after I'm gone. But she won't mind once she discovers how much she stands to inherit - over a million when death duties have been paid. I hope she won't spend it all at once!

When I've finished my dusting, I let myself down slowly and painfully into my chair. It's curved as if, over the years, it's taken the shape of my body. I've had to give up yoga, but I still practise the meditation I learned in the yoga class. I close my eyes and watch the rise and fall of my breath, and soon I feel that familiar feeling of relaxation flooding over me. My body, cradled by the chair, is warm and comfortable, and I can smell the freshly mown grass, and the fragrance of roses wafting in through the open window. My ears pick up the sounds of the summer garden - all that bird and insect life buzzing and chirping busily - and I enter that blissful state in which I lose all sense of time.

'Nothing is lacking,' I say to myself. 'When the body is relaxed and happy, the being inside is relaxed and happy too.'

When I've finished meditating, I go to the cupboard and take out my nail file, a bottle of scarlet nail varnish and some acetone, and start doing my nails. It's not because I'm vain, it's more a question of self-respect. As I'm housebound now, I have a hairdresser who comes to wash and set my hair every week, and I always put on my lipstick when I'm expecting a visitor. Today I am expecting death.

Melanie dropped by earlier this afternoon. She was a good daughter to me at the last. After Len's passing, she took care of me as well as she could in her scatterbrained way. And, when it was time for her to go and we embraced, we both knew this was the last time. I had to struggle with my tears, and, although I couldn't say it out loud, I said to her in my heart,

'Goodbye my dearest Melanie! Our relationship was not an easy one, because we're both so different, but deep down we both know we love each other very much.'

All of a sudden I'm shaken by a spasm that comes like a bolt from the blue. I clutch the arms of my chair so hard my knuckles turn white. But the other part of myself - the part called Nel who is the observer - stays calm. She knows that I'm suffering a stroke, and that it will soon be over. It's also a comfort that IG is at my side.

'You must let go of everything now, Nel,' he says. 'Say goodbye to your house, and all your things, because you're going to have to leave them behind.'

'Can't I even take my handbag? There's some things inside I can't do without.'

'You won't need them where you're going. And, last of all, say goodbye to your body.'

'Good gracious! That's weird! There's my body over there, slumped in the chair, and here I am, perfectly alive and well, and more clear-headed than before. '

'You're out of your body, that's why.'

'I'm having an out-of-the-body experience, and I don't even believe in them!'

'You are your real self again - you're Nel.'

'And I feel about sixty years younger. This is so much better than the treatments they offer on those health farms. My skin is smooth again, and I've got my figure back!'

'Astral bodies are very plastic. They take the shape of our thoughts and dreams.'

I thought it would be hard to part from my body, because I'd got very attached to it after all these years. But now I find I don't mind, because it's worn out, and threadbare and no use any more. And I've got a gorgeous new one in exchange - although it's a bit intangible, a bit like a fine mist.

'I'm going to bring you back now, Nel,' says IG. 'I'll count slowly from ten backwards, and when I reach one you'll wake up.'

And I do, and I find myself back in the group room. Lucy has vanished for ever, my virtual life is over, and I'm left to mull over all that's happened to me.

Life 3
BOB the GEMINI

'Here we go. Hold tight!'

I'm flying through space, and there are pieces of cosmic debris whizzing past. We keep just missing head-on collisions. No time to observe or examine these objects in detail, but my guess is they're fragments of some giant planet that exploded billions of years ago, whose pieces are still orbiting the sun, because there's no one around out here to clean them up!

In no time I feel solid ground under my feet, and things begin to fall into place. I can perceive three-dimensional space now and physical form. What I can make out, because it has dimensions of length, breadth and height, is a shape that might be a house. It takes some moments for my vision to adjust to the earthly way of seeing, and then I'm able to distinguish the details.

It is a house, and one of a row of similar semi-detached dwellings. The paint on the window frames is cracked and peeling, and the front garden is overgrown. That's its physical condition, but I can also read from the information field around the house that there's a woman in labour inside. Standing by the front gate, I watch the doctor arriving and, judging by the look of his car, I'd say we're in the 1940's,

Cut! And the next moment I'm whizzing down a tunnel at high speed to emerge at the other end into blinding daylight. And that's all I'm aware of concerning my birth, which is so quick I question whether it happened at all. But there's the proof before my eyes - a newborn baby lying in a carrycot. With his round face, round eyes and big ears, he looks just like a monkey. Must be me! Yes, that supposition is being confirmed by the conversation going on around me in the room. I learn that it's June 10th 1944, and that my name is Laurence George Twinsett. Well I'm blowed! This time I'm a Larry!

The door swings open and in come my brothers. There's a lot of scuffling and giggling, and then I see their two round faces peering down at me. Up to now I've been enjoying a non-local perspective with a wide encompassing vision, but suddenly my viewpoint has narrowed down to that of the baby. I'm inside the cot. And as I look up at them in wonder and awe, one brother sticks out his tongue. 'Boo!' cries the other.

Oops! They've picked up the carrycot and are carting me off in it. Now I've been shoved under a bed! Above me I can see bedsprings and bits of old felt, and my brothers have run off with shrieks of laughter, leaving me alone in the dark.

'What've you gone and done with the baby?' screams ma.

'Hidden 'im!' they cry gleefully.

THE KID

I'm at an age where I'm into everything, and nothing is safe from my prying hands. I've already decimated the clock, and unscrewed the knobs from the radio. As my dad's a salesman and travels, and ma works at the post office, we're home alone a lot. Then my brothers, Stuart and Gary, look after me. I follow them around the house, copying whatever they do, and time flies. But on days when they've gone to school, and old Mrs Botton comes in to sit with me, it crawls. I'm a bright little button of a lad who's forever asking questions, but you don't get much out of Mrs Botton, who always gives you the same old answer - 'I dunno I'm sure! Ask yer mum when she gets back!'

My favourite place is on the wall by the front gate, because from there I have a view all down the street. And that's where I'm sitting now, drumming my feet, while I watch the postman on his round. I make a mental note of the houses that get letters from his big sack, and wonder if we'll be one of the lucky ones. Hurrah! He's stopped and is holding out a big, brown envelope.

'Give it to yer ma!'

So I put it beside me on the wall.

The next passer-by is a big, gangly dog. He comes loping up, and stops to sniff at my shoes before lifting his leg. Oops! The envelope has gone and got sprayed, which makes me laugh so much I nearly do a Humpty Dumpty and fall off the wall!

There's a bus pulling in at the bus stop in the distance, and I spot Stuart alighting. In my excitement I forget that I'm not allowed to leave the front garden, and dash off down the street to meet him. But Stuart takes no notice of me, as I trot along at his side chattering nineteen to the dozen. He's lost in thought as big boys often are.

While Stuart is eating his tea, I pinch his satchel, and crawl under the table with it. I'm curious about the things he keeps inside, especially the pencil case, which is the main object of my interest. I empty its contents of pens, rubbers and pencil shavings out onto the carpet. When Stuart sees what I've done, he clouts me round the ear.

'Larry you friggin' pest! You know you're not allowed to touch my school things!'

And this time it's me who takes no notice.

Cut again, and now it's as if the film of my life has fast-forwarded to when I'm seven years old. My brother Gary is small for his age, and me and him are like two peas in a pod, so people mistake us for twins, although he's a year older. We have to share a bed, and right now he's trying to read his comic, while I'm pretending to be a sea-monster, thrashing about under the bedclothes, and creating a commotion that I know will wind him up. Sure enough, soon he's started yelling and is raining down blows on my head.

Ma bursts into the room.

'If you two don't pack it in and go to sleep, you'll both get clouts round the ear-'ole!'

That shuts us up because ma's clouts don't half hurt! Then she turns out the light and goes downstairs, but Gary is sly. He has a torch, and goes on reading his comic under the bedclothes. Crikey, I think, that story must be exciting if he can't put it down! Perhaps I'm missing out on something. I'd better try harder to learn to read!

TEENS

At fourteen I'm small for my age and my friends call me tich. I still pretend to be under twelve to get a child's fare on the bus. I'm on my paper round, pedalling along with a basket of newspapers on the front of my bike. I skid to a halt, grab a paper, drop the bike, in at the front gate, stuff it through the letterbox, out again - that's the routine. Sometimes, through undrawn curtains, I catch glimpses of things not meant for my eyes. So I've learned a thing or two about the intimate lives of people in our neighbourhood, which gives me a certain prestige, as I always have a new piece of gossip to relay to me mates.

While I'm cycling to school in the morning, skimming along and dodging the parked cars and pedestrians, I like to pretend I'm Batman. Then I have huge wings growing out of my shoulders, and I imagine myself taking off, and flying along in the air high above the street. And, through pedalling my bike faster and faster, I get that cool, free-flying feeling I love.

But then arriving at school is like falling out of the clouds, because the secondary modern I attend is a drab, dark, miserable pile of Victorian boredom. And as it's well nigh impossible for me to hold my tongue for more than two minutes on end, I'm always getting sent out for talking in class. Sometimes I think I spend more time outside the classroom than in! But I usually have some dog-eared paperback in my pocket to read, or I'll chat with the caretaker and the dinner ladies. So time passes pleasantly out there in the corridor, until the bell marks the end of the lesson.

The best thing about school is me mates. There's a gang of six of us who meet behind the bicycle shed in the dinner break to share a packet of fags. I'm the chatterbox amongst them. And, as I'm good at making witty rejoinders, and generally taking the mickey, we always have plenty of laughs.

On some days I'll play truant. I'll slip away and scale the wall behind the gym, and drop down on the other side into the back alley that runs behind Woolworth's. It's my favourite escape route, because that alleyway is hardly used and you're unlikely to be seen. Then I'll wander round the shops until quarter to four, or slip into the Majestic by the back entrance without paying, and watch the matinee.

TWENTIES

Twenty-one now, and I've got the key of the door, but not to ma's house because I've moved out. I'm sharing a flat with my brother Gary and a couple of mates. Not that they see much of me, because I'm up to my ears at the moment, trying to hold down two jobs at once. The first is delivery work, and the second is behind the counter in a coffee bar, where I operate the coffee machine. On top of that I'm studying for my A-Levels at night school, which goes to explain why you find me with my nose in a book every spare minute.

Some mates who rolled up at the caff the other night were pulling my leg about it.

'Belt up,' I said. 'I've got a syllabus to get through.'

'A silly what? What kind of bus when it's at home?' was their response.

I mean a lot of people don't get it - why I'm into books when there are birds, and why I bother to pinch so many from the bookshop in the High Street - books, I mean, not birds. They think I must have a screw loose or something! Anyway, talking of buses reminded me of a joke, which I proceeded to tell them.

'Paddy and Seamus are in Dublin for a night on the town, and it's late and they've missed the last bus home to Cavan. They happen to be passing the bus station, and Paddy has a good idea - they could borrow a bus and drive home in it. So he breaks into the bus station while

Seamus keeps a look out. Soon he hears a terrible commotion - a crashing and a bumping coming from inside - and at last Paddy appears driving a big double-decker. 'Sorry it took so long,' he says, 'but the bus for Cavan was right at the back!'

They killed themselves laughing.

It's the early hours and I'm at my desk studying. I've got the radio on for company, and I'm drinking black coffee to keep awake. Well it's the only time there's any peace in this place. During daylight hours it's like Piccadilly Circus, with pop songs blaring, and streams of visitors coming and going. The trouble with me is I get easily distracted. If a mate drops by, and I just pop out for a minute to have a word with him, sure as Bob's your uncle we'll go on nattering the whole evening, and then I won't get my revision done.

Having missed out on an education at school, I'm getting one now - though I did leave with five O-Levels, which proves I've a good memory but not necessarily that I'm intelligent. It was all about learning stuff by rote there, and spewing out the facts they'd stuffed into you in the exam. So you had to do your revision, but my problem has always been my low boredom threshold. Revision is old hat, and old hats could never hold my interest. That's caught by the new hats that appear.

As I'm lighting up another fag, I get a fit of coughing, and then I notice that the air in the room is thick with smoke.

'You're smoking way too much, Bob my lad,' says a familiar voice in my head.

'Hey! Who are you to talk?'

'I'm your old friend IG, standing for inner guide, an older and wiser part of yourself.'

'And I'm Larry. Bob's my uncle!'

'You may think you're Larry, Bob, though really you're Bob, Bob. But don't worry - it's normal for people to forget their names once they've incarnated. It's a side effect of the amnesia.'

'Amnesia - that's a new word! I'll note it down. Well, IG, if you think you can persuade me to give up smoking, you've another think coming. Because I've been smoking since the age of ten, so it's a deeply ingrained habit.'

'Aha! Then it must be a behaviour pattern carried over from your last life.'

'My last what? Now you're not making sense!'

'Poor Bob! You can't think outside the box any more, now that your mind has become conditioned by the materialist paradigm.'

'Paradigm? That's another new word! So what does it mean?'

'Weltanschauung.'

'Give me a break! I don't spreche Deutsch.'

'World picture! But don't confuse being knowledgeable with being wise, Bob, because they're not the same thing.'

'And don't split hairs, IG, because I haven't many left to split - Larry is going bald. But I must say I'm enjoying chatting to you - saves me from talking to myself!'

'I am yourself.'

'Then I'm not going to let myself get a word in edgeways, because I talk the hind legs off donkeys, though what good a donkey's hind leg is when it's off I don't know!'

'About as good as a cigarette butt! So here's a riddle for you, Bob - what do chatting and smoking have in common?'

'Search me.'

'Both stem from a compulsive need to keep the tongue and the lips occupied.'

'Ha ha! But I know a better way of doing that - give a girl a French kiss!'

'Then you'd better get yourself a girlfriend quick!'

'Meaning I smoke because I'm not getting enough sex?'

'Well done, Bob! You've just cracked the first bit of your code.'

'Cracking codes sounds like a job for MI5. All I can crack are jokes. Hey man, if I can wisecrack does that make me wise?'

'You won't be wise, Bob, until you know yourself. And you won't know yourself until you self-inquire. Don't you remember those self-inquiry exercises we used to do together?'

'I remember I had a life coach.'

'Who is now your inner guide.'

'Hey! So, if you're my inner guide, can you help me make up my mind?'

'What about?'

'Well, I'm planning to go to university, but I can't decide what to take. The trouble with me is I'm interested in everything.'

'I thought French was your favourite subject?'

'Because I'm into French kissing? That's a good reason to do a degree in modern languages! And a year abroad, as part of the course, would suit me fine, because I'm into continental women - especially French and Italian girls - not the Scandinavians because they're too tall. I went out with a Swedish girl once, and I had to carry a stool around with me all the time.'

'Whatever for?'

'To stand on when I wanted to kiss her. Ha ha!'

'Look at you, Bob - you're lighting up another cigarette without noticing what you're doing. And that's how you go on, allowing your unconscious to run your life, though you think you're in control and you are making decisions.'

'And as a cure for that you recommend doing self-inquiry? Well, it's a subject I haven't looked into. But, tell you what IG, when I've finished my exams, I'll pop down to the bookshop in town and pinch a few books on it!'

I passed my A-Levels, and I've just received the news that I've been accepted by Cardiff university to do a degree in modern languages, so I'm throwing a party to celebrate. A whole crowd of friends have turned up and squeezed themselves into our tiny flat. I've been spinning round like a top all evening, talking non-stop. I always get over-excited at parties, as if I'm running on some special high-octane energy. The record player has been belting out rock and roll, but now it's past midnight and people have started pairing up, so smoochier numbers are required. I put on a blues record, and invite Barbara with the long blonde hair to dance with me.

It was my brother Stuart who brought her along. He's been going out with her, but I take it for granted that he'll share her with me. Then, while we're dancing entwined, I notice Elaine, the girl I've been dating, sitting in the corner looking glum. So, as soon as the track is finished, I pull Barbara over and we both collapse onto the sofa beside her.

Now I'm pig in the middle, sitting pretty between two pretty girls with an arm round each, and flirting with both at once, turning the tap of my teasing, boyish charm full on. But, instead of a frolicking threesome, a rivalry develops. Now they both want me, and they both want the other woman out of the way. Well, I've been there before. Double trouble is the name of this game, and I'm going to need all my juggling skills to keep both balls up in the air at once.

Elaine, who's had a couple of drinks too many, has started insulting Barbara, who is being abusive back. And, although the sight of two pretty girls doing battle over me flatters my ego, a cat-fight would spoil the party. So I try to lighten the mood by cracking some jokes, which go down with the girls like lead balloons. In the end Stuart intervenes and takes Barbara off my hands.

When Elaine comes to kiss me goodbye, she says,

'Larry, I want you to promise me that you'll give me a ring tomorrow.'

'What kind of ring, darling?' I say. 'An engagement ring - a wedding ring?'

'A ring on the phone,' she replies. 'That's all I'd accept from the likes of you.'

And I promise to call her the next day, although I know I won't, because I'm not in love with her any more. I'm in love with Barbara with the long blonde hair.

'That's very fickle of you, Bob.'

'Hallo, IG! Come to morally reprimand me?'

'No, I've come to get you to inquire into why you change your mind so often.'

'Why do I change my mind? Well, when I promise a bird I'll phone her tomorrow I mean it, but then tomorrow never comes, does it?'

'That's no excuse for being inconsistent.'

'Well everyone knows what I'm like, and they don't mind. The other day I promised a mate I'd go jogging with him before breakfast but, when the alarm went off, I didn't feel like it, and went back to sleep. So he went off and jogged alone - it's what he'd expected anyway.'

'Then why make promises in the first place, if you know you're not going to keep them?'

'Well part of me intends to keep them, but then a different part takes over - a part that didn't do the promising, and so doesn't feel responsible.'

'It sounds as if you have a split personality, Bob, as you're always in two minds. But then, instead of you changing your mind, your two minds change you!'

'Ha Ha! But who's this we're talking about? Is it Larry or Bob or you, my higher self? I seem to be all three.'

'That's right, so you should be careful about using the word 'I' unless you're certain what it stands for.'

'So who is I?'

'You have to find out.'

'Well, what I've noticed is other people believe in my 'I' more than I do myself. For example when I told Elaine I loved her, that seemed to make sense to her.'

'And how often have you told a woman you loved her, and afterwards changed your mind?'

'Never and often. Because I always mean it in the moment - that's to say, part of me means it. But later on another part - the one that likes having fun, and never falls in love - takes over.'

'Very confusing for the ladies!'

'They soon learn not to take me seriously.'

I'm never happier than when I'm on wheels. I started out with a bike, and graduated as a teenager to a motorcycle, which I'd ride through the fields. Then, as soon as I was old enough to get a license, Stuart taught me to drive a car. Now I own a van, which is my lifeline because, whenever I feel suffocated by this town, I can get away.

I'm planning another trip before the term starts. Gary's coming with me this time, and we're driving down to Italy through France and Switzerland, and then back up the German autobahn. Gary is worried that's too much mileage to put under the bonnet of an old banger like my van, because last year she broke down, and left me stranded in the sticks. But that was the start of one of my interesting adventures.

I hitched a lift and was picked up by this grand monsieur in a Citroen Déesse.

'See these vineyards,' he said, 'à droite et à gauche? I possess them all. Ils sont tout à moi!'

He was a wine grower you see. We had this fascinating conversation about the Common Market while we drove along and, when we reached his village, he said he liked the cut of my jib - 'le coup de mon giblet' or something like that, and invited me home to sample some of his choice vintages.

It turned out that he was a bachelor, living alone in a huge château. The old boy seemed glad to have someone to talk to and, while we sampled some genuine vin superieur, he told me the story of his life - about his mother, who died five years ago - quel malheur! - and his sister in Nanterre who has five children and sixteen grandchildren. His hospitality extended to a bed for the night, and I didn't say no. It made a change from sleeping in the van. He was so concerned about my comfort he kept appearing in my room to ask if there was anything more that I needed, and the next morning he arranged for the van to be towed away and repaired.

When I tell this story to Gary, it makes him even more worried. We may look alike, Gary and me, but characterwise we're very different. I'm a nomad - never happier than when I'm on my way somewhere and not yet arrived whereas Gary is the solid settler type.

'So you keep on the move, eh Bob? That way life never gets boring.'

'Hallo, IG! Time for more self-inquiry?'

'How did you guess! But turn the radio off first.'

'I can't. When I was two I took off the knobs and lost them, so now it's always on - even when I'm in the bath.'

'It's like your mind. That's always left on too!'

'Well, it's company when I'm alone in the flat. If I didn't have the radio, there'd be a deafening silence in here.'

'And silence freaks you out. But, only when you can listen to silence, will you hear the things that are truly significant.'

'Everything's significant if it's interesting, IG, and I have to stay informed. I must know what's going on in the world.'

'But all that information on so many different subjects just clutters up your mind.'

'There's no need for you to worry about my mind. I never miss a trick. The only flies on Larry are on his pants!'

'So what relevance does dairy farming in Dorset have to your life? It's what they're going on about at present.'

'Who knows? But what I learn now could come in useful later. Each bit of information I collect is like a small piece of a jigsaw puzzle that's slowly getting put together.'

'I understand - you're trying to make sense of things, and you believe that one day you'll be able to see the complete picture?'

'Yes, because there's a system behind everything and, once you know all the parts, then you'll know the whole.'

'Not necessarily because the whole is always more than the sum of its parts. And the problem is that, when you see the facts you gather as all equally valuable, you lose the power to distinguish between important things and trivia.'

'But we have to start with simple facts if we want to understand the world.'

'And what is a simple fact?'

'Something that's been scientifically proved, and fits into the logical system of human thought.'

'You'll find no certainty there, Bob. It's better to start with self-knowledge because, once you know yourself, you'll know everything worth knowing.'

THIRTIES

I see a young man in a pair of tight jeans with holes in them and a faded T-shirt. His hair is long and unkempt, and his skin looks as if he hasn't washed for a fortnight. Larry at thirty plus still lives in a shared flat. You can hardly open the door to his room because of the piles of books gathering dust on the floor on the other side. If you manage to squeeze in, you'll find it sparsely furnished apart from a bulging bookcase. There's an unmade bed, a desk piled precariously with papers, and a table littered with torn envelopes, dirty crockery and an overflowing ashtray.

It's not exactly home-sweet-home, I think, but I only use it to sleep in, being out most of the time. I eat in cafes and read in the library, and life is so full-on I've no time to look for something better. You see, I'm not only earning my living, I'm also doing a PhD. Even if I told you the subject of my post-graduate work you wouldn't be much wiser, as it involves research into an obscure semantic problem that's still little more than a bee in my professor's bonnet.

At this rate I'm reckoning on my thesis taking years to finish, as my present job is so high-powered. I work for Harry, who publishes a free local rag that advertises businesses and forthcoming events in the city. I took on the job because I hoped I'd be allowed to write articles. I fancy myself as a journalist, but now I find I'm glued to the telephone all the time. Harry has discovered my talent for sales talk, and has given me the job of persuading potential advertisers to buy our advertising space.

It's early morning. The latest edition is hot off the press, and I'm driving round in the van delivering bundles of papers to the shops and cafés we use as outlets. They all know my face.

'Hi there, Larry,' they call. 'How yer doing, mate?'

If I've got time, I'll sit down for a chat while I smoke a reefer, and drink a cup of tea with them.

But this morning I have to be back at the office promptly, because Harry has called a meeting. I find the team sitting round the table, discussing the paper's format. I have a lot to say on that subject. I favour a change, and present my views in a long speech in which I leave no pauses between my words, and never come the end of my sentence. It's a tactic I learned in student discussion groups that successfully stops other people from butting in.

I'm so involved in my ideas I don't notice that Harry is getting impatient. In the end he interrupts me. He says he disagrees. We don't need a change, and he goes on to say why. I'm soon so convinced by his arguments that, when I next come to speak, I contradict all the views I previously expressed, and argue in favour of Harry's proposals instead. And my rhetorical skill sways the balance, so Harry's proposals get adopted. Afterwards he compliments me on getting the message across so well.

'You've certainly got the gift of the gab, Larry,' he says.

We're down at the pub, my mates and me, sitting at our usual table. With a few drinks under my belt, I'm getting into my stride, wisecracking and raising laughs, and we've just got onto the subject of footwear when I look up, and see a cute bird with long blonde hair coming in at the door.

'Hey kid!' I call out. 'I like your sneakers. Where did you get them?'

Her reply is lost in the drone of voices and jukebox music that fills the room. I watch her as she looks around, as if perplexed, before making for an empty chair.

The mates are talking about cricket so I put in my two-penny worth, though I've not been following the test match. But I can always find something to say about cricket as about most subjects. And all the time I'm keeping my eye on the girl with the long hair. She's up at the bar now, buying herself a drink. Every now and then she'll glance in the direction of the door, as if she's expecting someone to walk in. If this is my lucky night, he won't turn up!

A short while later, while I'm sitting enthroned in the gents, I hear IG's voice coming through loud and clear.

'This is a good opportunity to do some self-inquiry,' he says.

I groan. 'Don't you have any other games up your sleeve?'

'Bob,' he says, 'I'm only doing my job! You can enjoy yourself with your mates and self-inquire at the same time. You just have to keep watching yourself, and note what motivates what you say and do. For example, what have you noticed about yourself this evening?'

'That I like the sound of my own voice!'

'Good! And what are the benefits you get from talking a lot?'

'Hmmm....well popularity, I suppose. People find me entertaining, and they enjoy my company.'

'Right, and you also need to talk to feel connected. Because, as long as you're talking, and holding other people's attention, you don't feel so alone.'

'Is that why I always strike up conversations with strangers on buses?'

'Maybe, because feeling alone in the big, bad world can be scary. But then, if you don't watch out, you become dependent on other people's company.'

'Ha ha! That's right! I can't even go to the loo now without taking my inner shrink with me! There should be a notice on the door of this cubicle saying "Free Psycho-anal-asis"! Ha ha!'

'And what motivates all this facetiousness?'

'You mean why do I keep cracking jokes? Well, I suppose it's to lighten the mood. When you're out with your mates for the evening, you don't want things to get heavy, do you? Bernie, for instance, can get very maudlin about his ex-wife and, once he gets going on that theme, the evening's a write-off. So then I'll step in and crack a joke to get everyone laughing.'

'So, by keeping the conversation flippant, you prevent people from talking about things that really matter.'

'What really matters to me right now is to pull the plug, and get back to the bar. I have to see what that chick with the long blonde hair is up to.'

She's sitting there on her own, smoking a fag and looking fed up. So, as I pass her I say, 'Hi kid! Have you been stood up?'

'Looks like it.'

'What! A pretty girl like you! I don't believe it! Well then, if you're tired of sitting all on your lonesome, why not come over and join us?'

'I don't mind if I do,' and she gets up and follows me.

'So what's your name, darling?'

'Sally.'

I introduce Sally to the mates by recounting an amusing anecdote about each, and soon she's in fits of laughter. Then I start asking her a few personal questions, and in no time I've collected all the necessary information. No, she doesn't have a steady boyfriend. The bloke who stood her up this evening was a first-time date. Yes, she's left school, and works at the newsagents up by the station. Right, I think, I know where I'll be buying my fags from now on! And, when it's closing time, I offer to drive her home, and Sally accepts.

Each time I go into that newsagent's shop it gets harder to leave. I'm beginning to feel quite at home there. I'll sit on the stool in the corner nattering to Sally while she serves the customers, or restocks the shelves, and time flies by. Sally is interested in everything I have to talk about - even in my research subject! Whereas, usually, when I start on that theme, people's eyes glaze over.

'Listening to you is an education in itself!' she remarked the other day. I found that very gratifying.

On our first date we go to the flicks. I pick her up from the shop at closing time, and we go to see *Kramer v Kramer* with Dustin Hoffman and Meryl Streep. It's a tearjerker of a film, and Sally cries buckets, though my eyes stay dry as usual. It's a long time since I cried, and I could never understand why people cry at the flicks.

When it's over, we go for a coffee, and then I take her home in the van. She lives six miles out of town, deep in the countryside. And, before we get to her village, I drive off the road onto a cart track. It leads into a field where I stop the van, and turn off the engine. The

67

cows scatter. I'm not expecting much but, as it turns out, Sally knows the ropes better than me when it comes to sex, although she's only seventeen. I'm the shy one not her, and she lets me go all the way!

And that's how things go on - I take her to the flicks a couple of nights a week, and on the way home we always stop in the same field. The cows have got to know us, and greet us with loud moos when we drive in. Then one Monday morning, when I arrive at the newsagent's to buy my fags, I find Sally looking pale and decidedly weird.

'I was hoping you'd come in today, Larry,' she whispers, 'because I've something to tell you.'

There's a customer in the shop, flipping through the magazines in the rack, so she beckons to me, and I follow her to the storeroom at the back, where she drops her bombshell.

'I'm pregnant,' she announces.

I'm speechless. Yes, for the first time in his life, old Larry is lost for words.

'So are you going to marry me, or what?'

'Er....this needs to be thought through, love,' I mutter, panic rising in my throat.

'Well, you'll have to think it through quick,' she whispers, 'because I'm already eight weeks gone!'

'IG, I can't handle this alone. I can't think straight any more.'

'You don't have to think, Bob. It's your heart you should ask, not your head.'

'My heart says escape - jump in the van, drive down to Dover and cross the Channel double quick. But then I'd feel like a right sod.'

'It's about taking responsibility, Bob.'

'You want me to take responsibility for a wife and kid! I'm not even able to take responsibility for myself?'

'You're thirty-four, Bob. You're no spring chicken.'

'But I've always been like Peter Pan, the boy who never grows up. I don't think I'm mature enough to be a dad.'

'Well, if you're clear about that -'

'I'm not, because I'm in two minds as usual. One mind is a coward and can think up plenty of reasons to do a bunk. The other says it would be a good thing to have the baby, and marry Sal - sober me up and all that - because I've been living too flippantly. I took my affair with her too lightly. I should have asked her if she was taking the pill. I just presumed she was, and it was a mistake to leave something like that up to a teenager.'

'If you go deeper than your split mind, Bob, you'll discover a more essential part of you, a part with moral courage and sticking power. So find this place of strength, and then you'll have the courage to face the consequences of your actions.'

The next day I tell Sally that I'm not ready to be a father, and that it's too early to think about marriage.

'You'll have to have an abortion, love,' I say. 'Of course I'll pay for it.'

But, at the mention of the word, Sally gets upset. It turns out that her family are Catholic, and some of the values of the Catholic church have rubbed off on her, though not the one about chastity.

'We can't kill the baby. We can't kill the baby!' she keeps saying.

Her parents want a word with me. Jesus Christ - she hasn't gone and told them! I have to come round to talk to them. The prospect scares the living daylights out of me. I imagine her mum and dad descending in a fury, and dragging me bound and manacled to the altar. And once again I'm tempted to do a bunk, but I don't.

The front door is opened by a small girl. And, inside, the house seems full of screaming, romping children - Sally's younger brothers and sisters. And there I see a gleam of hope. They are a family of seven, Sally being the oldest, so I conclude that her mum must like babies. In which case the more the merrier, and another one wouldn't make much difference!

And, indeed, Sally's mum turns out to be more laid back about the whole thing than I expected. Apparently she got pregnant with Sally when she was only seventeen, so that could explain it. They say they're against abortion on principle, so there's no question about it - Sally must have the baby. But they don't want her to rush into marriage at her age. They want her to go on living at home, and the child can grow up with Sally's younger brothers and sisters, but of course I'll have to foot the bill. And, when her dad tells me how much a month I'll be paying, I go weak at the knees.

'It's your legal obligation,' he says sternly.

So now poor Larry, who was always footloose and fancy free, is trapped! I can't throw over my job when I feel like it any more and go abroad, because I have to have a regular income coming in to pay for the kid. On the other hand, I'm proud of myself for doing the decent thing, though I feel like a butterfly that's been caught, and pinned down in an insect collection, but is still alive and wriggling. And seven months later I become the absent father of a big, bouncing boy called Jake.

By the time I'm in my forties my head is a bald dome, surrounded by a fringe of hair like a monk's tonsure. It's as if too much thinking has worn my pate thin on top! And I've put on weight, I'm no longer the will-o'-the-wisp I used to be, but sport a cosy little potbelly. I see myself sitting in front of my first computer, typing something with two fingers. It's romantics now instead of semantics! I'm writing a reply to the replies I've received from my lonely-hearts ad.

It's out-of-character I know, because I've always said I want to stay single, because singles have more fun. But that's only half the picture. The other half is that I hate being on my own. And, as you get older, and your friends marry or move away, it becomes harder to make new friends, so you're forced to spend more and more time in your own company.

I stopped seeing Sally after Jake was born. She was a sweet girl, but her mental horizons were simply too narrow for my needs. I decided that I require a woman with an intellect. But I've done my duty by Jake, and religiously kept up the monthly payments. I used to go round to see him but, after Sally found another man and got married, Jake said he didn't want me to come any more.

'I've got a new dad now,' he said, and so the visits stopped.

I've had a number of other relationships, but for one reason or other none of them lasted. I used to believe that chopping and changing did no harm, that what I needed was variety. And I also thought I was playing clever by avoiding ties, but this is how I've ended up   a balding middle-aged man, living alone in a bed-sitter, with no one to date on a Saturday night. And I'm beginning to think there's something wrong with me.

'IG, why have none of my relationships lasted?'

'A good question, Bob. Let's crack that bit of your code.'

'Perhaps it's because I've been going for married women.'

'Maybe. What benefits do you get from having married girl-friends?'

'Well, it feels safe with them I suppose. I can be sure they aren't plotting to marry me, and they won't allow me to make them pregnant. So married women are a safe bet.'

'That must have something to do with Sally.'

'Yes, I certainly don't want a repetition of what happened there. But now I feel I'm ready for a long-term, committed relationship. I just have to find the right woman. So what I've done is put an ad in the lonely-heart's column of a big national paper, and you see that huge pile of letters over there? That's all my replies. I've got my work cut out now to go through them.'

'So what kind of woman are you looking for?'

'I've advertised for a blonde, long-haired, intellectual, twenty-something nymph.'

'I see. And what about your PhD?'

'Oh that's been put on a back-burner. I'll be ninety at least before I'm Dr Larry Twinsett!'

I'm writing a letter to duplicate and send round to my replies. Dear blank, I begin, and then my mind goes blank. I decide to start with the facts, so I write:

"I am a graduate in modern languages. After failing to get an academic post, I did a Dip. Ed. and worked as a journalist on a paper until it folded. I am presently teaching French at a sixth-form college. I am also engaged in research for a PhD thesis. I am into European literature, travel, films, Miles Davis and trying to catch my own tail."

Then comes the witty bit. "As a single I was living a double life, but my dream is to be a double living a single life. How to describe myself - I am in good nick for my age, playful, urbane, emotionally illiterate (but willing to learn), a good communicator, interested in everything, with bags of GSH."

But, if I look critically at what I've written, all I can see are clichés. Parlez vous cliché? It's going to be embarrassing when I actually meet these women, and have to come over in a way consistent with my letter. But what I dread most is having to choose between them. How will I manage to select the pick of such a very large bunch of ladies?

'IG! You'll have to help me.'

'You'll help yourself if you do some self-inquiry.'

'What if none of them turn out to be long-haired, twenty-something nymphs? Then what criteria should I use to make my decision?'

'How did you decide which computer to buy?'

'I looked through the catalogues, and picked the one that had all the features I wanted.'

'Which is exactly how you shouldn't choose a girlfriend!'

'Why ever not?'

'Bob, how on earth are you going to assess another person? You haven't even assessed yourself, as your ad goes to show. You want to fall in love, but who is there to do the falling? And you don't know anything about love in the first place.'

'On the contrary - I'm an expert on the subject. I wrote a research paper on the concept of love in 19th century French literature when I was at uni.'

'But the more you know about love, the more it prevents you from loving. Love must be experienced in the heart, the blood and the marrow. If you want to find love, you have to turn down the volume of your head, and turn up the volume of your heart.'

'Spare me the metaphors, IG. Just tell me plainly how to love - preferably in ten easy steps.'

'Well, the first step is to recognise what's been preventing you from loving up to now. And in your case it's your habit of abstracting yourself from your feelings. You talk about feelings a lot, and analyse them, but you avoid actually feeling them.'

'So, if I understand you rightly, you're saying the egg must come before the chicken. I must develop feelings for someone, and then I'll know in my marrow whether it's love, and if I've found the right chick. Or is it the other way round? Do I find the right chick, and the feelings develop afterwards, in which case the chicken comes before the egg?'

'Bob! You're a hopeless case!'

A year has gone by, and I'm sitting at my computer with the telephone receiver cocked under one ear, and a cigarette hanging from the corner of my mouth. I'm smoking, drinking a mug of coffee, typing a document, and talking to a student on the phone all at the same time. That's multi-tasking for you! On the desk in front of me there's a photo of a pretty girl with long, blonde hair. It's Helen, the sole survivor of the lonely hearts who replied to my ad. Helen lives in far-away Liverpool, but we talk to each other every day on the phone.

I've finished my thesis at last! About time, you'll say, because you've been at it for fifteen years! And, if PCs hadn't come in, I'd be still at it now. It was word-processing that came to my rescue by allowing me to collate my copious notes, because I'd gone on reading, and accumulated more and more material, until I was snowed under. The trouble with me is, whenever I discover something interesting, I have to jot it down. So my folders are bulging with scraps of scribbled paper, and, even with the aid of a PC, it was a Herculean task to type up all those notes, and organise them into a digital filing system. But I got there in the end and finished my thesis, which has proved to myself, and everyone else, that I have sticking power after all.

But it's also led to me catching the computer bug in a bad way, and I've become a real nerd. I stay up late at night, and miss my sleep, exploring new software and learning to programme. I seem to have a natural talent for this sort of thing.

'Something else to inquire into, Bob. How did the computer get such a hold over you?'

'Well, IG, when I'm on the computer, I forget everything else, and I think that's why I've got addicted. My attention gets riveted onto the screen, and I lose all sense of time. That means I never get bored, which is a big plus for someone like me.'

'But there's a downside too. It's isolating you, Bob. For instance, you no longer go down to the pub in the evenings to meet your mates.'

'Ha ha! They've all caught the computer bug too! But the fact is, IG, I don't need other people so much as I did in the past. My computer is company enough.'

'And what about your search for true love?'

'That ended when I found Helen - that's her in the photo. Helen lives in Liverpool. I've been up there to visit, and she's been down here to see me a couple of times.'

'So, whenever you want to see each other, long train journeys are involved?'

'I've no problem with that. I enjoy travelling by rail, and between you and me, IG, it's a good thing there's some distance between us. That way we each keep our space and, on the occasions when we do meet, it's always special.'

'It sounds to me as if you've found yet another way of avoiding closeness, Bob. But you won't get away with it much longer. Love will soon be arriving on your doorstep, and put you on the spot!'

It's late in the evening, I've switched on the lamp as it gets dark early at this time of year, and drawn the curtains, and I'm looking forward to getting engrossed in a new video game I've bought, when I hear the doorbell ring. So I go downstairs and open up to find Helen standing on the doorstep together with four bulging suitcases. I draw a blank.

'Hallo, Larry,' she says. 'I've come to stay with you. I got fed up with Liverpool, and thought I'd have a change - come down to London and find a job. Hope you don't mind?'

'Er, no, of course not,' I stutter, 'but why didn't you give me notice of this, Helen?'

She carries her cases purposefully one by one into the hallway, and when they're all safely stowed, she explains.

'Okay, I know I'm not being very fair, but, if I'd asked you beforehand, it would have put you in a dilemma. And this way at least I spare you the prolonged agony of indecision.'

She's hit the nail on the head, so there's nothing more I can say. Helen is the kind of blunt, no-nonsense northerner who will have no patience with my dithering, and it looks as if I've met my match in her.

To begin with Helen seems happy enough. She finds a job, and keeps herself busy in her spare time cleaning the flat from top to bottom, putting up new curtains and throwing out all the stuff she decides I don't need any more. However, as she soon discovers, there's someone else in my life - and it's someone I have no intention of giving up. So while she sits on the sofa of an evening watching telly, and hoping, no doubt, that I'll come and cuddle up beside her, I'm sequestered with my computer in the bedroom, getting stuck into a new piece of software, instead of a new piece of her underwear.

In the end she does what all modern women do when they run the gauntlet, she asks for a 'sharing', and that, I've learned, means I'm going to be confronted with some uncomfortable home truths.

'Larry, I love you, I really do, but it's not working out. You're either on your computer, lost to the world, or you're here, but you're not here because you're talking. I've never known a man talk as much as you. You even go on talking while we're having sex. Orgasm comes and goes without you taking time to pause for a comma!'

'But Helen, if I'm talking to you, it stands to reason that I'm with you. Anyway, I thought we'd agreed that being able to talk is of prime importance in a relationship.'

'Yes, but not when the conversation is always one-sided. You talk and I have to listen, and, once you get going, I can't get a word in edgeways, so I end up feeling not seen and not heard. And another thing - listening to you drains my energy. You get energy from others when they're paying attention to you, which is why most people prefer talking to listening, but some have forgotten how to listen altogether.'

'Meaning me?'

'Yes you, Larry, or if you do listen it's only with one ear.'

'Must be my right ear. It's bigger than my left. The left one got too many clips round the ear 'ole from my mum.'

'You might have a PhD Larry but, most of the time, what you say is not very edifying. You're either taking the Mickey, or you think out loud and give a running commentary on every trivial thing that passes through your head.'

'But I have to put my thoughts into words, Helen. Otherwise I'd never know what I think about them. You should be pleased that I allow you to be party to my thought processes.'

'Very kind I'm sure, but I see through it! It's nothing more than a male domination strategy. And, when I say something, and you respond with a facetious remark to shut me up, that's a typical male trick to disempower women!'

'Jeepers creepers! I'm shacked up with a rampant feminist!'

'And having the last word doesn't necessarily prove that you're right.'

It's getting too much for me to cope with, so I seek help from my brother Gary. He's been married three times, and divorced twice, so he's more experienced than me when it comes to women. Gary says he knows why Helen has become so bitchy.

'She's getting broody,' he says. 'She's thirty-eight now, and her biological clock is ticking, and she knows it. What she wants from you, bro, is a baby!'

I'm immediately on the alert, because this is the very thing I've been dreading. So I decide to test the waters by mentioning to Helen that I'm thinking of having a vasectomy, and the emotional way she reacts proves that Gary is right. My next step is to go ahead and have the operation, and soon afterwards, sure enough, Helen packs her bags and departs to Liverpool. And that's the end of that.

'Not quite, Bob, because there's a lesson for you to learn here. Did you get the point Helen was trying to get over to you?'

'That I talk too much? I knew that already, IG.'

'No, what she was saying was that no real communication happens when you talk. As long as you talk at people and not to them, you're not really relating. You have to remain aware of the other person, and how they're taking what you say. Are they really interested, do they want to say something themselves, or do they simply wish you'd shut up?'

'You mean I'm not good at communication? That's funny because every reference I've ever been given has always called me a good communicator.'

'But that doesn't mean you know how to talk to women. Women listen to your tone of voice as much as to the content of what you're saying.'

'What I've noticed is that you can't have a rational discussion with a woman.'

'Because they come from the right, intuitive side of the brain, not the logical left side, and you're a very left-brained person. Poor Bob! Now you're totally at sea. I know this is a hard part of your code to crack.'

'Never mind, IG. Keep on sending me nuts, hard ones too. I'll crack them all with my nutcracker in the end, unless they drive me crackers first!'

OLD AGE

I see an old geezer who's close to his sell-by date. He's losing his teeth, and his skin is so wrinkled it could do with an iron. I see him in his accustomed place, sitting at his computer, a state-of-the-art version of that first PC bought way back in the eighties. It's yours truly - Bob alias Larry - though I hardly recognise myself. Larry might age but Bob never gets a day older, and I'm Bob on the inside.

A lot has happened in the meantime, so I'd better bring you up to speed. I'd packed in my teaching job by my late forties, having become thoroughly bored with it. By that time I no longer needed to pay child support, and was free to go travelling, so I went abroad. Altogether I spent seven years out of the country, and during that time I earned my living writing tourist guidebooks. This went well to begin with, and, for the first time in my life, I actually managed to save some money. But, as more and more authors climbed onto the bandwagon, the travel literature market became flooded.

So I moved back to London and took up computing, which led to a new career as a free-lance IT consultant. Soon I was in high demand, with small businesses and private customers as my clients. I started dividing my time between working in London, and staying at my country cottage in the Dordogne. Yes, I've bought a little hideaway in rural France, and the advent of cheap flights has meant I can afford to commute there regularly.

My next-door neighbour in the very French village where it's situated is a merry widow called Margot, and I fell in love with her chou farci chasseur before falling in love with her. Margot's a wonderful cook and great fun to be with. There's nothing I like more than sitting by her log fire on a winter's evening, my stomach full of a delicious three-course dinner, sipping cognac and listening to all the amusing anecdotes she tells. Yes, you heard right, in my old age I've actually mastered the art of listening!

This lifestyle suits me, straddling the Channel with one foot in England and one in France. At present I'm back in London, because I'm in need of medical treatment. And, although I'm very fond of her, I never miss Margot when I'm over here. I enjoy being free to spend my evenings surfing the net, and we stay in touch by sending each other text messages on our mobile phones.

Today's technology is mind-boggling. The stuff on offer on the world wide web when you go online is enough to feed my information hunger for lives on end. For example, I've just googled Jaques Brel, who is Margot's favourite singer, and get a load of that - or in his case an overload! There are hundreds of references to explore! Another benefit of the internet is it gives you an opportunity to make new friends. I'm in touch with many interesting people now, scattered all over the globe. You should see my buddy list - it's pages long!

First I'll get my emails done, and then I'll visit some of my favourite chat rooms. But then I'm shaken by a violent fit of coughing, and I feel so dizzy afterwards that I have to go and lie down. The truth is I'm a very sick man. The doctors have diagnosed lung cancer. I know, I know - you all warned me. And I've tried to give up smoking. In fact nobody has given up smoking as often as I have! I should go down in the Guinness Book of Records!

The silence in the room is suddenly broken by my mobile phone playing a cheery 'Pop Goes the Weasel'. I pick it up.

'Hallo?' I say.

'Dad? Dad!' says a strange voice on the other end. 'It's Jake. I'm in London. In fact I'm in the phone box by the bus stop. I'm on my way round to see you.'

'Jake... is it you? I haven't heard from you since, well, since you were a little kid.'

'I know, and it was my fault. I shut you out of my life, but now I want to see you again.'

'Well, I'm busy tomorrow, and the day after that I have to go to the hospital...'

'Please dad! It's got to be tonight. It's very urgent. I'll be there in ten minutes.'

He rings off and I rise unsteadily to my feet, whereby I have to hold onto a chair, because I've come over all of a tremble. Where shall I start? Make something to eat? Is there any beer left in the fridge? And the next thing I know the doorbell's ringing, and I'm going down to let him in.

He's a big man, broad in the beam and a good foot taller than me. I clear the newspapers off an armchair, so he has room to sit down. Then I sit opposite him, and we stare at each other uneasily for a while. It's Jake who starts talking and his voice is thick with emotion.

'The reason I didn't want you in my life,' he says, 'is because I hated you for abandoning me and mum. I was angry with you dad - very angry. But last year I got divorced, and then I had a nervous breakdown, which led to me joining a men's group, and that's where I got in touch with my anger. I've been working on myself, dad, and now I can honestly say that I don't hate you any more. I've forgiven you for everything, and I've come here tonight to have a closure.'

'I see,' I say, 'then what about a cup of tea?'

When I get up to put on the kettle, Jake gets up too. Then, before I can avoid it, he steps forward and puts his arms round me, and gives me a great bear hug. It's the first time in my life I've been hugged by a man, and I find it weird at first. Well, we stand there for what seems an eternity, me small and frail clutched up against his big, strong breast. And, when he finally lets go, it leaves me feeling high and strangely elated.

'I have a son!' I say to myself, 'I have a son!'

'I need you, dad, so I've come to ask you to be part of my life again.'

'Of course I will be,' I reply, ' though sadly it's a bit late in the day.'

And I break the news about the cancer, and how the doctors have given me only three more months to live. This is a shock for Jake. He bursts into loud sobs, and that makes me cry too. Tears course down my cheeks and drip onto my collar, but in my chest there's a feeling of fullness, as if the volume of my heart has been turned up.

Jake puts me in touch with Sally, who's divorced and lives in London - in fact only a short bus-ride away. Little Sally has made something of herself, in fact she's grown into the sort of woman I admire - strong and determined, with both feet firmly on the ground. Now a taxi comes and takes me to her house every week for Sunday lunch, and Jake is usually there too. I look forward to it as the highlight of the week. Sally can always be relied on to do a good old-fashioned English roast.

But now I have a problem, and I've been there before. Sally and Jake have asked me to spend Christmas with them, but Margot is expecting me to spend it with her in the Dordogne. And I can't split myself and be in two places at once - or can I?

It's Christmas Eve and I'm lying in bed feeling very weak. They've arranged for a night nurse to come and be with me. I'm not in any pain, but breathing is difficult and, if I try to speak, I cough. No problem - I've said everything worth saying long ago, and plenty that wasn't into the bargain. But Margot was disappointed when I told her I couldn't come for Christmas. I didn't tell her how bad I am, as it wouldn't help matters. So I wasn't surprised when I got a text from her this morning.

'come please get next plane.'

'cant,' I text back, 'not well enough'.

'tant pis bon noel!'

I shall share her sumptuous Christmas meal in my imagination. And Sally and Jake will be preparing the turkey and boiling the Christmas pud, but there's going to be an empty chair at their table too - or is there?

'Hallo, Bob, my lad!'

'Hallo, IG, old man! You always were my better half. If I'd listened to you, I wouldn't be where I am now!'

'It's never too late.'

'It's too late to stop me smoking, IG. Even the doctor's given that up, and allows me to do it when he's visiting. Well, we've all got to die of something, haven't we? And I'm doing it my way. So have I got through my syllabus, IG? Have I completed what I set out to do in my life?'

'Yes, all the boxes are ticked.'

'Good because I'm starting to get restless. You know me - always on the move. So I don't want to stay in this dying body any longer. I want out. But where's the exit? Can you show me?'

The next moment I'm whizzing down a tunnel at high speed to emerge into a brightly lit space at the other end, and it's over. And that's all I'm consciously aware of concerning my death, which was so quick I question whether it happened at all.

It's Christmas day and I've successfully split myself into two - impossible when I was Larry, but it's feasible now I'm Bob again. One part of me is spending Christmas in the Dordogne with my friend Margot. Little does she know it, but the empty chair at her table isn't empty at all. And the other part sits at Sally and Jake's table, where it looks as if Christmas dinner will be a sad affair, as they're grieving for me. So, to lighten the atmosphere, I play a little joke on them. I replace the pound coin, cooked in the plum pudding, with one euro. And, when she finds it, Sally immediately denies putting it there.

Jake's eyes light up.

'It must be dad who did it,' he says. 'And that means he's with us now. He was always in favour of abolishing the pound and adopting the euro!'

Life 4

MAB the CANCER

I've always been drawn to Cancers, so it's nice to know I'll be born a Cancer this time. If I've understood IG rightly, I'm going to lead a Cancer sort of life in what is called virtuous reality. I'm not sure what that means, but I dare say I'll soon find out.

The music he's playing is beautifully soothing and relaxing, and it carries me away to dreamland. A brass knocker appears, decorated with a goblin's face, and I can make out the porch and front door. I'm about to knock, but the door opens by itself so I step inside. The light, falling through a high stained glass window, creates a pattern of coloured shapes on the parquet floor. There's a polished wooden table with a vase of flowers on it - they're carnations I think. And I can hear a familiar sound - the tick, tick, tock of the grandfather clock in the corner. I greet him like an old friend.

Then I notice that there are people in the room. A young woman is lying on the bed, and an older woman dressed in a uniform, who could be a nurse or a midwife, is seeing to her. And who's that sitting in the rocking chair in the corner? It's my daughter Mabel, who's old and grey now. She has just become a grandmother.

And who's making all that noise? It's a teeny-weeny baby girl. Ah the darling! She must be newly born because she's all red and wrinkly, and crying her eyes out, and no wonder after what the poor mite's been through! One minute she was lovely and warm and safe inside her mummy's tummy, and the next she's cast out into the big, cold world!

After she's been washed in a bowl of warm water, and dried her with a towel, she's given to grandma Mabel to hold. Mabel wraps her in a soft, woollen shawl that she knitted herself. And now my mummy is sitting up in bed, laughing with joy and relief. And, if that's my mummy, then the little baby girl must be me!

It's strange this virtuous reality. It's like watching a film, and being in it at the same time, because I both see the baby and I am the baby. I also see the room in every detail - the faded pink rosebuds on the wallpaper, and the chintz curtains. I thought virtuous reality would be like dreaming, but it feels more real than that. I'm so happy that I've been born into my own family, and I'm back in my own home. It's July 15th 1944, and my new name is going to be Marjorie Charlotte Crabbe - Charlotte after my great-grandmother.

THE INFANT

Look at me! I've grown into such a bonny child! I'm three years old, and I've got auburn hair, chubby legs and freckles on my nose. We're on our way to the village shop to buy some groceries, and I hold very tight to mummy's skirt as we go up the step and through the door. Tinkle, tinkle goes the bell.

'A pound of sugar, half a pound of butter and some baking powder, please.'

We're going to bake a cake, and, if I'm a good girl, I'll be allowed to lick out the bowl. The lady behind the counter is new, and, when she asks me my name, I'm shy and dive into mummy's skirts to hide.

'Her name's Marjorie - Marjorie Charlotte.'

'Ah that's nice!' says the lady.

When she spies me peeping out, she offers me a lollipop, which I take from her hand quickly.

'What do you say?'

'Thankyou,' I lisp.

'Ah the little poppet!'

We've made the cake and put it on the tea table. It's a surprise for daddy but, when he comes home, he's in a bad mood, and he doesn't even notice it. While we're eating our tea, he starts arguing with mummy, and, because his angry voice makes me frightened, I slip down from the chair, and disappear under the table. It's like being in a cave under here, with the long table cloth reaching down to the floor all round me.

It's late, and I know I should be asleep, but I'm lying awake in my bed listening to mummy and daddy's raised voices. They're having another row. When I hear mummy crying, I want to go to her, but if I get up I know daddy will smack me. So I lie as still as a mouse, waiting till they are quiet and I know it's safe to fall asleep.

THE KID

I'm growing up fast. Mummy plaits my hair every morning, and ties two bows on the ends. But here in the hospital no one has time to do it, so I wear my hair loose. I've just had my tonsils out, and I'm sitting up in a high hospital bed, that smells of rubber sheeting, clutching my teddy bear and crying my eyes out.

A nurse comes in with a plate of jelly.

'Look what I've brought you, you lucky girl. This jelly will slip down without hurting your poor throat.'

82

'I don't want it,' I sob. 'I want my mummy!'

'Come on, Marjorie, be a big girl. You're seven now, so you should stop crying.'

'I want to go home!'

'Look Marjorie! The other children are laughing at you, because you're such a cry baby. Come on - eat up your jelly like a good girl.'

I open my mouth just wide enough for the jelly to be spooned in. Then, as soon as the plate is empty, I dive down under the bedclothes, and pull them over my head. There I lie for the rest of the day, sucking my thumb. It's my place of refuge in this ward full of strange children who stare at me.

'She's been very homesick.'

Nurse is talking to mummy who has arrived to fetch me home.

'Yes, Marjorie is a bit clingy. Normally she won't let me out of her sight. Perhaps it's because she's an only child. She'd like a little brother or sister to play with - wouldn't you Marge? But sadly that's not to be. Hurry up, poppet, and put on your shoes!'

I'm so relieved to be home again, sleeping in my own little bed, with all my toys around me. Daddy was especially kind today, and he hasn't shouted at mummy at all. I tell my doll Brenda about where I've been, and what the nasty doctors did to my throat, and I play hospitals with her again and again. Brenda has to be very brave every time she says goodbye to her mummy, and goes into hospital to have her tonsils out!

TEENS

I'm fourteen, and what the lady doctor who does the school medical calls 'well developed for my age'. In other words I've got big breasts, but I don't like them, though the other girls in my class are envious. I flatten them by wearing tight vests. I'm going round to visit grandma Mabel this morning. She lives on the other side of the village in a sweet little cottage.

Grandma was bombed out of her house at the end of the war, which was a horrible thing to happen, because she'd lived there all her life. And it had been in her family for generations. It's where I was born in 1944, and six months later it was reduced to rubble. But it's nice that grandma still lives close, because we can pop round and give her a hand if need be - like this morning when she's feeling poorly.

As I walk up the garden path, I suddenly have a feeling of foreboding. Grandma is getting old, and I know she's going to die soon. Perhaps this is the last time I'll see her alive! Suppose she's already dead. What will I do if, when I go in, I find her dead in the bedroom?

I lift the latch on the back door very slowly, and enter with a beating heart. What a relief when I see her sitting in her usual chair - a sweet, elfin creature with a halo of white hair. I run across the room, and throw my arms round her.

'Dear grandma,' I say in my heart, 'you must never, never die because I love you so much!'

First I mop the floors, and then I scrub out the bathroom. When I've done that, I peel the vegetables for lunch. I know just how grandma likes them - boiled until they're tender. The poor soul hasn't a tooth in her mouth, and she won't wear her false teeth because they're uncomfortable, so she has to chew everything with her gums.

After we've finished eating, I fetch down the photo albums. I love looking at the sepia-brown pictures of great-uncles with pipes, and aunts in wide-brimmed hats, and cousins several times removed.

'That's my poor mother,' says grandma, pointing to a woman in a high-necked frilly blouse with a cameo brooch pinned beneath her chin. 'She died very young. You've always reminded me of her, Marge - you've got her eyes.'

I've heard her say that before, and it makes me feel I've got a special bond with my great-grandmother Charlotte!

TWENTIES

It's my twenty-first birthday and my wedding day all in one. We're just coming out of the church - me in a long, white, satin dress with a train. I had to have a white wedding, because it's always been my dream, although mummy thought it inappropriate as I'm clearly no longer a virgin. There she is, close behind me, sobbing into her handkerchief. Dave my handsome young bridegroom is at my side, and kicking and struggling in his arms is Mark our two-year-old.

Now we're lining up for the photographer - mummy and daddy on my left and Dave's mum and dad, who are not his real parents because he's adopted, on the right. In the row behind are my uncle Arthur and auntie Eva, and my cousins Jerry, Roger and Jude together with some members of Dave's family I don't know yet.

Uncle Barry is also there. I've never met him before, because my father quarrelled with him before I was born. But now their estrangement must be over, because he's come up from Wales for the wedding, and brought my Welsh granny with him. So at least I've got one grandmother here, because, sadly, grandma Mabel didn't make it.

She died a couple of years ago, and I still miss her sorely, though I find comfort in knowing that she's a beautiful angel in heaven now, watching over us.

Dave is literally the boy from next door. We met when we shared a pram. Mummy was looking after him while his mum went shopping. He first asked me to marry him when we were aged six. Of course I said yes, so we've been engaged for a record length of time - fifteen years in all.

Although we always knew we were destined for each other, when I got pregnant, mummy said we must wait because I was only eighteen. She said I was too young to know my mind. I expect she was hoping I'd meet someone better - a budding bank manager perhaps - and marry him instead. Because Dave is only a cook, and that doesn't carry much status. But I only had eyes for Dave.

So, after Mark was born, I went on living at home, and Dave went on living next door, and mummy helped look after the baby. Then I got pregnant for the second time and, when it turned out that I was expecting twins, mummy became very anxious for us to tie the knot. So I was allowed to wed my childhood sweetheart at last.

After the wedding, we'll be moving into our own home. We've found a sweet little terraced house not far away that we think we can afford. There's some decorating work to be done before we move in, and some carpets to be laid, but we hope to be finished by the time the twins arrive. Dave is a handyman, and good at DIY, and he has plenty of time during the day, as he always does the evening shift at his restaurant.

It'll be a relief to be in our own four walls, because living at home has become quite a strain. Daddy has always been difficult, and his moods have put a blight on our family life. And mummy, though I love her to bits, can get on my nerves. She still treats me like a baby, although I'm twenty-one! But she's been good about looking after Mark while I'm out at work, I'll say that. I don't know what I'd have done without her!

'It'll be so hard for me to lose you, Marge,' she keeps saying. 'I dread you going, I really do!'

'But mum,' I reply, 'it's only round the corner. It's not like I was going to John o' Groats or something! You'll be able to pop round and see us whenever you like.'

'Yes, but that's not the same, is it?'

We've painted each room in a different colour, and laid wall-to-wall carpeting, which we bought with grandma Mabel's money, bless her!

We've also got some pieces of furniture from her cottage that have been in storage since she died.

'We can't let the rubbish clearance people take it all, dad,' I said. 'These are family heirlooms!'

Among the bits and pieces we've inherited is the double bed she rescued from her bomb-damaged house. It had belonged to her mother, my great-grandmother Charlotte, who was given it back in the eighteen-seventies on the occasion of her wedding. Dave and I will be snuggling up in it now.

So our little nest is feathered, and we've moved in, and we're very cosy in it - so cosy in fact that I hate leaving it to go to work. At the moment I still go to the office every day, but soon I'll be leaving. Dave has agreed to me becoming a full-time mum when the twins are born, though this will mean less money coming in. But, with three children under the age of four, I don't have much choice, do I?

It's Sunday today so I can have a lie in. I'm propped up in bed, busy knitting some baby clothes. The knitting needles rest very comfortably on my big tummmy, and I'm just getting to the end of the second little jacket when the doorbell rings. That will be my friend, Sheila, come round for a cup of coffee. I hope she won't mind sitting here in the bedroom amongst all the clutter!

In Sheila's opinion I've made a big mistake in saddling myself with three kids at my young age.

'You're missing out on life,' she says. 'You're sacrificing your youth! And don't give up work whatever you do. Get yourself a childminder, or give them to your mum, but keep your foot in the door.'

'But what if I want to stay at home, Sheila?'

'Then you can say goodbye to a career, because when you try to come back later, all they'll have to offer you will be some lowly, badly-paid job.'

'I've got a lowly, badly-paid job at the moment. I've never enjoyed clerical work, but at least I've continued working until now. My mother stopped working the moment she got married.'

'That's what women did in those days, but we're more emancipated in the nineteen sixties. Haven't you got any ambitions, Marge?'

'Not really. I'm old-fashioned in that way. I believe a woman's place is in the home. Families are happier when the mothers stay home to look after their husbands and children.'

'But you'll have no money of your own - you realise that? You'll have to ask Dave every time you want to buy yourself a new pair of shoes!'

'That's okay by me, and it's okay by Dave too,' I say cheerfully.

But afterwards, when I think about what Sheila said, I'm not so sure. Maybe having babies is the soft option. Maybe I'm afraid of asserting myself out in the world, and I married Dave because I want to be taken care of. While I'm pondering these ideas, I hear a voice in my head that I think I recognise.

'Hallo, Mab dear! How are you getting on?'

'You're IG my inner guide!'

'That's right! So the amnesia hasn't completely deleted your pre-birth memories. I wanted to remind you that I'm available, in my role of life coach, to answer your questions.'

'Then I'd like to ask you whether I've done the right thing in choosing to have children so young, or have I gone and messed up my life like Sheila thinks?'

'You didn't choose anything, Mab. You tumbled into it, or rather it was the other way round, and your children chose you. But motherhood is a good path for you to be on.'

'I'm relieved to hear that! Then you think being a mother is as worth while as having a career?'

'It can be more worth while, because in giving your children a happy childhood with plenty of love, you're giving them the best start in life. And you're also giving something valuable to the world of the future. Because the love that your children receive from you will be passed on to their children, and from there on to future generations.'

'That's a lovely way of seeing it! Oh IG, I do so want to be a good mother and to get everything right!'

'You're going to make mistakes, Mab, because perfect mothers don't exist. However, you can learn from them. Because bringing up three children is not an easy task - in fact it's highly challenging but it will make you mature.'

'IG, can I ask you about a problem we have with Mark? At the moment he's disturbing us at night, and I'm getting quite sleep-deprived. He'll wake up and start crying, and he won't stop until I've fetched him into our bed. Dave doesn't like it. He says I'm too soft with him.'

'Then inquire into why you do it. You remember the self-inquiry exercises we used to do together?'

'Vaguely. Hmmm...perhaps I'm trying to make it up to him, because I have to take him round to my mother's every morning. She looks after him while I go to work, but he doesn't want to go. He'll start screaming and clinging to me, which always makes me feel guilty.'

'Yes, that may be why you're finding it hard to say 'no' to him. You let him have his way instead of using tough love.'

'What's that?'

'It's saying 'no' when it's for the good of the other. And it would do you good, and Dave, to get a good night's sleep for a change.'

'But I can't leave Mark alone in his room when he's crying and upset. It wouldn't feel right!'

'And were you upset and crying, and left alone in your room when you were small?'

'Sometimes.'

'Then Mark could be triggering some old, painful feelings in you. If you identify with him in that way, it would also explain why you always give way to him. You see, Mab, the main thing is to be aware of what you're doing, and why you do it. Then you'll be able to make decisions that feel right.'

The next time Sheila comes round for a cup of tea I tell her about tough love, and she likes the idea.

'If you always run to comfort Mark every time he cries,' she says, 'he's going to stay dependent on someone to soothe him even when he's grown up. I know men who have stayed babies like that, and who expect their wives to mother them then.'

'But Mark's still so tiny Sheila.'

'Okay,' she replies, 'when a child is small he needs nurturing, but also some independence. It's like a lot of nurturing and a little independence to begin with. But then, as he grows older, the balance changes, so when he's a teenager, he'll need a lot of independence and hardly any nurturing.'

Sheila knows a lot about it because she's studied psychology, so I listen to what she says. And I decide to use more tough love in my treatment of Mark, though this will be hard as it goes against my nature!

I'm now the proud mother of two sweet little girls. It was an easy birth considering I was having twins, and the whole thing was over in under four hours. The midwife was very pleased with me. She said my build helped.

'With your broad hips you could easily give birth to a whole brood of children!' she said.

I'm breast-feeding them of course - no formula in my house any more! I'd have breast-fed Mark for much longer, but I had to go back to work. So he got put on a bottle, poor mite! It's six o'clock in the morning, and I'm stretched out in bed with a baby at each breast. Dave is still snoring, and Mark is lying between us, cuddling up. I love the feel of their little bodies pressed against mine, and to smell their sweet baby fragrance!

While the twins suck at me, I luxuriate in the erotic throbbing that starts in my nipples and floods all over my body. I imagine I'm a fountain of milk and honey - milk to nourish their bodies, and the honey of love for their souls! It's in moments like these that I feel complete. Nothing is lacking, and I think to myself that this is happiness!

Polly and Amanda seldom cry, and at night they sleep the sleep of the blessed. I think it's because they were wanted, and were welcomed into the world. Not like their father who was illegitimate. His mother couldn't keep him, so they took Dave away from her the moment he was born. I find that heart-rending, and when I imagine how he must have felt - such a wee, helpless mite, abandoned and given into the hands of strangers - it brings tears to my eyes.

'You're very tender hearted, Mab, but there's no point in upsetting yourself about things that are past and gone. That's a waste of emotional energy.'

''You're right, IG, and I need all the energy I've got now. Can I ask you something about Dave? Sometimes it's difficult to know what's going on with him, because he never says much at the best of times. And, when he's in one of his moods, he closes up like a clam. Then, if I try to put my arms round him, I get pushed away and that hurts.'

'Perhaps he's feeling neglected.'

'Well, the children do take up a lot of my time, but that's natural at their age. I've often thought Dave could be jealous of Mark, because he doesn't like it when Mark sleeps between us.'

'Then try to consider Dave's needs as well as Mark's. You must always remember that you may be your children's mother, but you're also Dave's wife and lover.'

I'm taking my babies out in the pram, with Mark riding behind on his tricycle. Polly and Amanda look a picture in their little pink dresses and white frilly hats. I always dress them alike, and I'm so proud when people stop and admire them. We drop by at mummy's house, and of course she wants me to stay and have a cup of tea. I see at once that she's feeling upset, so I agree to come in for a minute.

We sit in the garden. The twins are asleep in their pram, and Mark is playing in the sand pit, and I sit there listening to all the gory details of her latest row with daddy. It seems such a shame. Why must my father be like that? He's been blessed with a good wife, and three beautiful grandchildren, not to speak of me, his daughter, so why can't he enjoy us?

Then I remember what I've heard about his childhood. Those were hard times. My grandfather died in the trenches in the First World War, leaving my grandmother to run the farm in Wales and bring up the children alone. Poor daddy was bullied by his older brother, uncle Barry, and that must have left some scars. Oh dear! I can feel my eyes filling with tears. I mustn't let the children see me crying, so I make an excuse to leave. Then, on the way home, I have a little comforting chat with my inner guide.

'The past needs to be revisited from time to time,' IG says, 'because you need to understand it in order to understand the present. You suffered during your childhood from the tensions between your parents. But, if you want to make sense of things, you'll have to go further back, to the time before you were born. However, this will require some courage, Mab, because then you'll uncover things you'd rather not know about.'

'But mummy never talks about her life before she got married, so I won't get anything out of her. And, when I ask her about dad's long-standing quarrel with uncle Barry, she always says, 'We don't want to dig that up again. It all happened such a long time ago!' Oh I wish things were different in our family! If my father was a proper husband to her, she wouldn't come round to our place so often, because she's beginning to get on Dave's nerves. He calls her an interfering busybody. The trouble is she's always convinced that she knows best, but I don't say anything. I don't want to hurt her feelings.'

'Perhaps you should try using tough love towards your mother as well, because it sounds as if you're having trouble with boundaries, Mab.'

'But it's so hard for me to say "no" to her, because she's had such a rough time all these years with my dad, and I feel so sorry for her.'

'You're not your mother's mother, Mab.'

'And there's something more - an even deeper reason why I can't turn her away from our door.'

'That's right, my dear, inquire into it.'

'I think I'm afraid of rejecting her for fear I should lose her love. Yes, that's what I'm afraid of deep down.'

'So perhaps you think you weren't loved enough as a baby?'

'Possibly, because I was brought up by the old-fashioned method of feeds every four hours on the dot. And in between I was never picked up and nursed, even when I cried and cried. And I was a child who needed a lot of cuddling, so I must have felt love-deprived.'

90

'So perhaps, deep down in you, there's still a fear that your mother doesn't love you. But even our deepest patterns can be changed, if we become aware of them. And the more you understand yourself, Mab, the better you'll understand other people.'

THIRTIES

I'm pacing up and down with my arms wrapped round me, as if I'd fall apart if I didn't hold myself together. What's happened is my father's walked out on my mother, and I'm worried sick. I can't imagine how she'll cope! He left a goodbye note, but it didn't give an address, and she hasn't heard a dicky bird from him since. She's been coming round to us every day since it happened. She says it gives her the creeps to stay alone in that big, empty house.

Of course I want to be there for her in her hour of need, but we need our privacy too, which she refuses to understand. And she's not good company, Dave says, because all she does is whinge.

'It's so cruel,' she keeps saying, 'after I sacrificed my whole life for him - not that he ever appreciated it. And now that I'm old, and I need someone to lean on, he just casts me off like an old sock!'

And she goes on and on in that vein.

I don't know how she's going to make ends meet, because there's no sign that my father made any provision for her, and she's only got a tiny pension. Perhaps she'll have to go out to work although, knowing mum, she wouldn't be much use to anyone. She hasn't a clue! She's started coming round here with her electricity bills and her bank statements, because she doesn't know what to do with them. She'd never even signed a cheque before - my father took care of all that!

But the more we help her, the more she expects us to do, and however much we do for her it's never enough. Dave says it's driving him nuts, and even my patience is wearing thin. But I can't turn her away from our door, especially now she's all alone in the world! She is my mother after all!

This horrible cold I've caught is dragging on and on, and making me feel so run-down! And the housework isn't getting done either. I have no energy for it when I feel so low. Oh dearie me! Now I'm starting to cry. Where are you, IG? I need some of your kind words of advice.

'What's the matter, Mab?'

'I don't know. Perhaps I'm just feeling sorry for myself.'

'It looks to me as if you're grieving.'

'But no one has died.'

'No, but we still need to grieve sometimes. Perhaps you're grieving for the loss of your father, because he's not only left your mother - he's also left you.'

'You're right, and actually I'm very hurt that he went off like that without saying goodbye. But he never loved me much, I know that now. Do you know, I can't ever remember him taking me on his knee, although I was a sweet little girl and very affectionate. He was always so wrapped up in himself.'

'You're angry with him, Mab.'

'Am I?'

'Yes, if you do some self-inquiry, and dig a little deeper than your pain, you'll find a layer of anger.'

'You're right as usual. Deep down I am angry and I've a right to be, because I had to do without the love and support that daughters are owed by their fathers. My dad's a selfish bastard! Yes, that's what he is - a bloody, selfish bastard and I hate him! Oh my - hark at me! I'm sorry, IG, for letting myself go like that.'

'No need to apologise, Mab. You are expressing your authentic feelings, which is your right. And it's never wrong to be angry, but it's wrong to cover up your angry feelings, and pretend that they're not there.'

'Oh dear! Now I've started crying again. It's all too much for me at the moment, IG. I don't think I can cope.'

'Those negative feelings you're holding inside are sapping your energy. But, now you've started to acknowledge them, you'll feel better.'

'That doesn't solve my problem with mummy.'

'So what exactly are you afraid of there?'

'I'm afraid she's going to cling to us more and more until in the end she strangles us.'

'That can only happen if you allow it. If she has a hold on you, Mab, it's you who are giving her the power. So start inquiring into how she always gets you to do what she wants.'

'Um - I think it's her way of implying that, if I refuse, then she's going to suffer even more. And, as she's suffering so much already, because she's old, and her health isn't good, and she's had such a hard life, I can't refuse to do her that little favour.'

'Well done, Mab. Your mother is being emotionally manipulative, and you've seen through it. This will help you change the pattern.'

'And I've noticed something else. She gets me to do things for her by appealing to my maternal instinct. Because she always appears to be so helpless, I react to her as if she's an ailing child. Then I have to do everything in my power to make her feel better.'

'So your roles are reversed - she is the child and you are the parent - whereas it should be the other way round.'

'Yes, you're right! I see that very clearly now. Thank you IG!'

My mother is sitting in an armchair with her hat and coat on because the room is cold. We haven't lit the fire yet, as we've only just arrived back from a weekend away. The phone went as soon as we came in the front door, and she was round here within half an hour, full of reproaches.

'You didn't phone me once, Marge, to see how I was doing!'

I'm on the brink of reacting in the old way. I nearly start apologising and trying to reassure her, but then I stop myself. 'Mummy, I have to tell you something,' I say, 'so sit down,' and then I begin.

'It's my wish,' I say, 'that we phone each other less, and that we see less of each other too. Now that you're through the first difficult phase after daddy's departure, we feel it's best, me and Dave, that you try to stand on your own feet, and become more independent. Because you've got to make a new life for yourself, you know.'

She immediately gets upset, as I knew she would.

'Those are hard words coming from you, Marjorie! I thought at least you'd understand. If I can't rely on my own daughter to be there for me in my hour of need, then who else can I turn to?'

Oh dear! I can feel myself getting upset that she's upset. But this time I manage to control myself and say,

'Mummy, I know it's not your fault that you've never had a life of your own. You belong to a generation of women who were brought up to sacrifice their needs to the needs of their families. They weren't supposed to be independent. So it's natural that you're at a loss, now you have no family at home to look after. But this is your time, mum. You're free to live in the way you want to at last. So you should get out more - find new interests and make new friends. Then you'll be able to enjoy the rest of your life, instead of sitting there all sorry for yourself, and feeling like a martyr.'

I feel very good about the way I put that over, and it seems to have had an effect, because mummy doesn't reply. She just sits there looking thoughtful.

MIDDLE AGE

As I pass the hall mirror, I catch my reflection in it. I'm wearing my pink dressing gown and my old, fluffy slippers, and I've got curlers in my hair. My figure, always on the full side, has started to bulge, and my pretty auburn curls are turning grey. Marge, I say to myself, you're beginning to look middle-aged!

I've made a hot water bottle to take up to bed with me, and, before I turn off the light, I glance round the room once more. It's cluttered with the sort of paraphenalia that make a home - embroidered cushions, framed photographs of the children, knick-knacks and holiday souvenirs. There's a sickening feeling in the pit of my stomach, because change is in the air.

Dave is on night shift as usual. His restaurant closes at eleven but, as he has to supervise the clean up, I'm not expecting him until after midnight. So I'm going up to bed alone as usual. I lie clenched up between the cold sheets, waiting for my body heat, and the warmth from the bottle, to spread and envelop me. And even then I can't drop off.

It feels as if an era is coming to an end, what with the twins gone away to college and my poor dear mother no longer with us. I shiver. She passed away last Christmas, and I still can't believe that she's gone. When I turn the key in her front door, I always expect her to be waiting for me in the hallway, like she used to.

It wasn't a very happy Christmas, as you can imagine. I normally throw a big family party, as it's the time of year when families should get together. So I'd stocked up on special Christmas fare, and we'd bought the tree and put up the lights. The twins were home from college, and they'd brought their boyfriends with them.

But then we got a shock on Christmas Eve, when mummy collapsed and was rushed to hospital. She died on the operating table. They found a tumour the size of a melon in her gut, and it had been there for some time, they said. Well, she'd been complaining of indigestion, but we hadn't taken any notice, because she was always going on about her aches and pains. I reproach myself for that now. Anyway, instead of a Christmas party, we had a funeral.

Yes, an era has come to an end, as my father's gone too. He passed away five years ago, and we knew nothing about it until the funeral was over and uncle Barry phoned us. My father had moved back to Wales after he left mummy, and all these years he'd been fighting a lawsuit against Barry over the farm. So the two brothers had been at loggerheads again. I don't know what's wrong with our family!

In a way it's a relief my mother and father are not around to worry about any more. They've gone to a better place, and left me free to get on with my life. And I've got a lot to do, as I'm clearing out mummy's house, and it will be a long job, because there's piles of stuff to go through. Poor mummy never could throw anything away. She kept all the clothes I wore when I was a child, so Polly and Amanda inherited them. They used to run around in the same little cardigans and dresses I'd worn a generation earlier!

Mark helped me empty the drawers and cupboards, and we've piled their contents in heaps. Now I'm going through them, deciding what to keep and what to throw away. Memories come flooding back as I pick up one familiar object after another. There's cards I made for Mother's Day, and my school reports, and seaside postcards I sent her when I was on holiday - so much of sentimental value I can't bear to throw away. The things I want to keep I put into a suitcase.

While I'm going through the cardboard boxes in the attic, I come upon some bundles of old letters. And, when I start reading them, I realise that they contain family secrets. They were written by my Welsh granny to my mother soon after I was born, and, as I read, I piece the story together.

It seems my mother worked on their farm as a land-girl at the beginning of the war, and daddy and his brother Barry became rivals for her love. At first she preferred Barry and got engaged to him. But, when he was called up and joined the army, my father seized his chance. He stepped in, and got her to marry him, and soon after the wedding mummy discovered she was pregnant with me.

Barry had been home on leave two months earlier, and my father got it into his head that I was his brother's child. When I was born with red hair, this seemed to confirm it, because Barry is a red head, whereas my father's hair is black. Mummy swore I wasn't Barry's child, and my Welsh grannie didn't believe it, but nothing could persuade my father.

When I grasp the meaning all this has for me, I come over faint. Perhaps my father is not my father! Or was it his jealousy causing him to imagine those things? But it explains a lot about his treatment of me and mummy. And I wish I had found these letters before mummy died. Then I could have asked her about it, and I'm sure she would have told me the truth, but now it's too late. And my father and my welsh grannie are dead too, so there's only uncle Barry who would know, and I'm too scared to ask him! If he was really my father, it would be awful, because he's not a very nice person.

Now that mummy's house belongs to us, we have to make a big decision. Shall we move into it? It was mummy's dying wish. The last time I spoke to her, before the ambulance took her away, she said she wanted me and Dave to live in it. She said she couldn't bear the thought of strangers in her home. But I don't know if I want that, so I'm in a dilemma. Perhaps IG will tell me what to do.

'Never ask anyone to tell you what to do, Mab. Always try to decide for yourself. Just close your eyes, and go inside. Then if you can go a little deeper than your mind, you'll discover what you really want.'

I try it for a minute, and then I say,

'I feel split inside, IG, because on one hand I'm at home here - it's where I grew up. But I can also feel a lot of sad psychic stuff from the past hanging about these rooms. So, if I lived here, I imagine I could get depressed. But it was my mother's dying wish, so I ought to comply with it.'

'You believe you should go on obeying your mother even after she's dead?'

'Well, she brought me up to always do what she said. But in the mean time I've become my own person, haven't I?'

'That's right. You don't have to go on living the way your mother wanted you to live.'

'Because then I'd become more and more like her, which is the last thing I want!'

'Yes, you don't have to repeat your mother's life. You can break out of the pattern, once you've become aware of it.'

'And I will! I see now that it's not a good idea for us to move into mummy's house. So what I'll do is I'll put it up for sale, and we'll stay where we are!'

I'm dusting the sitting room. When I get to the wedding photo on the mantlepiece, I run the duster carefully over its gilt frame. There I am, I think, a slim young bride, clinging shyly to Dave's arm, and him smiling down at me so proudly. We were so much in love then. And an even earlier memory comes up of us in our school uniforms, walking home from school with our arms wrapped round each other. My eyes fill with tears.

We always used to hold hands when we were out, but we've stopped doing that now for some reason. And our days of cuddling up together on the sofa in front of the telly are over too. When Dave comes home after the night shift, I'm always in bed. Then he'll sit downstairs drinking beer, and watching late night telly, until he falls asleep in his chair. Even on his days off he'll drink, and then there's no feeling of closeness any more. But I'm not complaining because, compared to some I know, Dave and I are happily married.

It's a blessing we still have Mark at home. He's a dashing young man of twenty-four now, and the apple of my eye. Mark and I have a deep rapport. We know instinctively what the other is feeling, and sometimes he'll put into words something that was just going through my head. I was never as close as that to the twins, though I love them both dearly, but they have each other anyway.

One thing, however, disturbs me. It's like a thorn in my flesh. Mark has got this girlfriend who I don't like. Ellen's her name, and he's been going out with her for more than a year now. I try to be welcoming when she comes, but she isn't the easiest person to get on with. I've told Mark very clearly that he can bring her home to a meal whenever he likes, but I draw a line at her staying over night in my house. I may be old-fashioned, but I don't like it.

'It sounds as if you're jealous of her, Mab.'

'No I'm not! It's just that I don't trust her, because I know she's plotting to take Mark away from me. She keeps talking about them moving to London, and she's started applying for jobs there. But Mark is in no hurry to leave home, and why should he be? He's got everything here that he needs.'

'Young men are pulled from their mothers by their biology, Mab, and you must accept that Mark needs independence now - not nurturing. So don't make the mistake of clinging too tightly or, when the break comes, it will be painful for both of you.'

'As long as Mark needs me, I'll be there for him.'

'It's time you were there for yourself, Mab. I watch you doing so much for him. You cook him nice meals, mend his clothes, clean his shoes. Every time he goes out the door, you call after him to make sure he hasn't forgotten anything. That way you manage to stay preoccupied with him all day long.'

'Well I like looking after people, and I can't look after Dave. He's too self-sufficient.'

'You're someone who needs to be needed, Mab.'

'May be, but Mark is such a big child. He's always so forgetful, and a bit helpless. He needs a woman to look after him.'

'Perhaps he's like that because you've been too over-protective. When he marries Ellen, he'll be as dependent on her as he has been on you.'

'Then he's in for a shock! If I know Ellen, she won't have time to look after him properly. There'll be no supper on the table when he gets home from work, and his bed won't be made either. But then at least he might appreciate how good he had it at home with me!'

'You're comparing Ellen unfavourably with yourself again, Mab. And have you noticed that, whenever Mark says something positive about her, you respond by drawing his attention to one of her faults?'

'Well, it annoys me to hear him putting her on a pedestal. And Dave's another one who's soft on her. He always said he found her attractive, and sometimes I catch him staring at her legs.'

'All the more reason for you to see her as a threat.'

'She is a threat, but for Mark's sake I'm doing my best to be nice to her.'

'That's no solution. Instead of concentrating on Mark and Ellen, you need to turn your attention back to yourself. Start thinking about what you're going to do with your life when you no longer have Mark to look after.'

I'm lying in bed feeling very angry. Mark and Ellen have moved to London, and, no sooner were they settled in, than we heard they'd got married - in a registry office with only a couple of friends of Ellen's as witnesses! It felt like a slap in the face! My son getting married, and without a proper church wedding and a reception, and missing the chance to invite all the family! It was a terrible disappointment to me, and I blame Ellen for it.

I doze a little, but then I'm awoken by noises downstairs. I put on my dressing gown and slippers and go down to investigate. As I thought! Dave is asleep on the sofa and he's left the TV running. There's a half-full glass of beer in front of him, and four more empty bottles on the table. I give him a shake.

'What! What's the matter?'

'You've fallen asleep in front of the TV again! Come to bed, love, or you'll catch your death of cold.'

'All right. I'm just coming. You go ahead.'

But I don't. I sit down beside him instead, because we've got some talking to do.

'Dave, when I see all those empty bottles I worry about you, love, I really do.'

'Well you don't have to. You know I need a drink when I get home from work, and I never touch a drop during the day.'

'Cut it out, love, for my sake.'

'I know how much I can take!' he says irritably.

'But it's changing you, love. You don't notice it but it's making you withdraw more and more into a world of your own. We don't talk to each other any longer, and we don't make love, and that's not good for our marriage.'

'What's not good for our marriage is your nagging! It's like you have to have everything under control - even how much I drink! I can't move a finger in this house without asking your permission.'

That wounds me.

'But Dave,' I protest, 'I'm only thinking of your own good!'

He gets up without another word and goes upstairs.

'You see what alcohol does to people, IG? Dave, who was always so kind and considerate - that he should turn on me like that! He'd never have said such hurtful things if he'd been sober.'

'I think you should listen to what he's telling you, Mab. He says you're too controlling, so are you?'

'Well, of course I care about what he's doing to himself. I love him after all.'

'It's more than that. If you could be Mab for a moment instead of Marjorie, and stand aside and watch yourself, you'd see how insistent Marjorie is that her will be done. Within the four walls of the house, Marjorie is queen. All Dave can do is fit in.'

'You make me sound like my mother!'

'And the last thing you wanted was to become like her!'

'I don't understand how I can be Marjorie and Mab at the same time, but you know best. I wish you'd give me some advice about how I can help Dave.'

'Try the Alcoholics Anonymous people.'

'Oh Dave would never go there! He doesn't believe he's an alcoholic, you see. He thinks the amount he drinks is normal.'

'Then you'll just have to wait until he admits to himself that he needs help. And, in the meantime, Mab, instead of preccupying yourself with other people, face up to your own problems. What are you going to do with the rest of your life? Have you thought about going back to work?

'Dearie me no! I've been out of things for far too long! I can't imagine anyone giving me a job!'

'A negative belief like that can be a self-fulfilling prophesy. But perhaps you're creating an obstacle to shelter behind, because you're afraid of the big, wide world outside your home.'

'That could be it.'

'Then always remember that your fulfilment lies in your own hands. You believe you're dependent on others for your happiness - on Dave, or Mark or the twins. But only you can make yourself happy, and only you can create a future for yourself in which your potential can be fulfilled.'

I took this to heart, and plucked up courage, and went round to the job centre to see if they had any work for me. There I got a shock because things had totally changed in the mean time. They said I can forget my shorthand, and I'd have to retrain before I'd be employable. Today that means becoming computer literate, and learning to do word processing.

Well, nobody can say I didn't give it a try! I got hold of a second-hand computer, and went to classes twice a week, but I drew a blank. I couldn't get my head around all those soft windows. My mind doesn't seem to work that way. So, by the end of the course, I'd hardly managed to learn the basics, and the teacher said I'd have to do the module all over again.

Then I began getting these stomach pains. I went to see my doctor, who's a very nice man - always so kind and fatherly. And he discovered a stomach ulcer. I was prescribed some medicine for it, and he told me to stay at home until it had cleared up. That's why I had to give up the computer course, and I won't say I wasn't glad.

OLD AGE

It's a bitterly cold afternoon. The wind is howling down the chimney, and I'm sitting by the fire trying to keep warm and knitting a pair of socks for Mark's Christmas present. I'm a widow now. Poor Dave was taken four years ago come February. It's a comfort to think that we grew closer again in our old age.

However there was a crisis to weather first. His drinking problem got so bad that, in the end, it cost him his job. But that turned out to be the best thing that could have happened, because the shock brought him to his senses, and he finally agreed to go to the AA. There he met some wonderful people who helped him get his life back on track. He stopped drinking from one day to the next and he never relapsed. I went along with him to some of the meetings, and there I learned that I was what they called 'co-dependent'. When at last I'd understood what that meant, I was keen to solve our problem together.

We found this wonderful counsellor through the AA, who gave us couple therapy once a week. He helped us come to terms with our childhood traumas. And, as a result, Dave learned to stop closing down and sulking when he was cross with me, and I learned to accept him, warts and all, and not nag. So we spent some happy retirement years together, before the day came when Dave passed away. He died in my arms.

There have been some additions to the family as well as losses. When Dave was gone the house felt very empty, so I got myself a little dog. Now I have Candy to keep me company. There she is - curled up in her basket, the sweetie. She's just lapped up a whole saucer of tea, and eaten two chocolate biscuits!

I've also become a doting grandmother. Polly followed my example and became a teenage mother. By the age of twenty-one she had three girls, and Amanda has a lovely little boy. Four adorable grandchildren to still my baby-hunger! As Polly lives close by, only down the road, I see a lot of them. I'm always being called upon to baby-sit, and Amanda is only a bus ride away. Ellen and Mark are still in London. They are childless. Mark, I know, would love to be a dad, but Ellen never wanted to have children. She's a hard-bitten career woman.

I miss Mark very much. London always seems so far way away, although it's only fifty miles. I look forward to the times when he comes down alone to visit me and stays the night. His bedroom is left exactly as it was when he was a little boy, with his toys still on the shelves, and his posters on the wall. Oh dear, thinking about him makes me want to give him a buzz, but, if I get Ellen on the line, she'll snap at me. She thinks I phone Mark too often.

Oh, is that my telephone ringing? I answer it and it's Mark of course. The telepathy between us is still working. But I immediately sense that something's up.

'Mum,' he says, 'Ellen's been taken to hospital. I think she's having a miscarriage!'

'Good heavens Mark! I didn't even know she was pregnant!'

'She didn't want to tell anyone yet, but she's in her seventh month. Do you think the baby will survive? Oh mum, I'm in such a state! Could you come up and be with me - just until all this is over?'

'Of course, my dearest, I'll be up tomorrow on the first train after the rush hour. Don't you fret!'

He sounded relieved. Poor lad! He's such a sensitive soul, and he gets so easily worked up. I'll have to take Candy round to Polly's. As I pack my case and make my arrangements, I'm feeling quite light-hearted inspite of the circumstances. It's because I'm getting to spend some time alone with Mark. But why did Ellen want to hide it from me that she's pregnant? That's what I'd like to know!

As soon as I've taken off my hat and coat, Mark pours out the whole story. Ellen had a pain two days ago, but ignored it because there was a rush on at her office. Then late last night her temperature shot up, and they called the doctor. He sent for an ambulance, and she was rushed to hospital. The baby was delivered early this morning by ceasarian. It's a boy, and he's just about alive but small and very feeble. He's in an incubator, and Mark was able look at him through the glass when he went to the hospital this morning. Apparently some membranes in Ellen's womb had ruptured, and she'd developed septicaemia. And, because the infection was already in her blood stream, they had to do a ceasarian to save the baby's life.

The next day Mark takes me to see my new grandson, and he's a heart-rending sight - such a poor, crumpled up little mite, with the face of a ninety-year-old! They call him Boris, and the doctor has put his chance of survival at fifty-fifty. Ellen is in intensive care because of the peritonitis. She has to have blood transfusions. I must say Mark is dealing with the anxiety of it all much better than I'd have expected, and he's so grateful that I'm there to support him.

Ellen has been allowed to come home, but Boris, who seems to have a strong will to live, must stay in his incubator for several months longer.

'Your wife needs care,' the doctor tells Mark. 'She must remian in bed until she's finished her course of antibiotics, and it will be several weeks until she's back on her feet. So could your mother stay and nurse her?'

Well, I was planning to leave as soon as Ellen returned, but now I agree to stay of course.

When I brought Ellen her lunch today, I found her sitting up in bed looking much brighter. She's a woman of few words and, although she always thanks me politely when I do something for her, if I try to make conversation, she'll answer in monosyllables. Nevertheless, when I collect her tray, I say brightly, 'You're looking quite perky today, Ellen - as if you're on the road to recovery.'

'Thanks,' she says. 'I do feel better. Sit down a minute, Marge.'

Notice that she never calls me mother! So I sit myself down beside the bed, and wait to see what's coming. She's silent for a moment, and then she blurts out,

'It's awfully good of you to do this for me. I'd like to say how grateful I am, but I find it difficult, because you're not an easy person to talk to.'

'Well you don't try very often!'

'It feels as if there's no point, that I'll never get through your hard shell.'

Well blow me down! It's her who's hard not me!

'I think you've got me wrong, Ellen,' I say. 'You're the one who's unapproachable!'

'Not with other people,' she says, 'only with you. I think it's because I can sense you're critical of me, and I know you've never approved of me marrying Mark.'

'That's funny,' I say, 'You feel that I don't like you, and I feel that you don't like me.'

'I've got nothing against you as a person. But I don't like the way you boss Mark about. It's so controlling.'

Oh dear - have I become like my mother then without noticing it?

'But you have a kind heart under your hard shell,' she goes on, 'and I know you mean well.'

'I could say the same about you,' I reply. 'Perhaps the time has come to stop being suspicious of each other, and try to get to know each other instead.'

And, quite spontaneously, I bend over and give her a kiss on the cheek. At last I feel I can accept her as a daughter.

I'm really ancient now - eighty-seven last birthday! I can't remember things very well any more, so I depend a lot on my children. Polly cooks my meals and does the housework, and Amanda does my shopping and sees to the laundry. My grandchildren are all living their busy lives, but they come to see me whenever they find time. Boris is my favourite. I know I shouldn't have favourites, but I can't help it. He's so much like Mark at that age.

The house is very much the same as it was when Dave and I moved in, sixty-five years ago. But the village around has changed beyond recognition. I doubt if I could find my way down to the shops any more! Mark wants to take me to London. He says he's found a nice care home there for me. To be sure I'd like to be nearer to Mark and Ellen, but I can't face leaving my home after all these years.

I often have double vision. For example I'm sitting in my chair, and I see myself sitting in my chair as if from above, both at the same time. Now I understand what IG meant when he said I was two people - Marjorie and Mab. Mab is watching Marjorie wandering about from room to room. She's looking for something, but she can't remember what it was. Oh dearie me! She's getting more and more absent-minded by the day. Poor old biddy, doddery and wandering in her mind! The children are right - she's a hazard to herself, living here alone. But she's determined to stay in her house until the day they carry her out in a box!

'Hallo, Mab!'

'Hallo, IG! Can you tell me what's going to happen next?'

'You've nothing to fear. Whatever happens will be for the best. You know that, don't you?'

'I do, IG. It's what my life has taught me, but all the same I would hate to live in a strange place amongst strangers.'

'Your life has taught you that it's best to dwell on positive thoughts and feelings because, when you worry about things, there's a dark shadow over you. It could be a lovely sunny day, but you won't be able to enjoy the sunshine because of the black clouds inside your mind.'

'Yes, and I've also learned that, when you have negative feelings about other people, it can poison your relationship with them, because you don't see them how they really are. That happened between me and Ellen.'

'True, Mab, whereas, when you think the best of people, you bring out the best in them.'

'That's right! Oh IG, I've come to understand so much with your help, but there are still days when I feel lonely and sorry for myself.'

'But you're not alone, Mab, when you're surrounded by so much love from your family. It's the love you gave them when they were small that's coming back to you.'

'Yes, I can feel it. But please tell me I won't have to leave my home. It would break my heart!'

'That's what the caterpillar was worried about, when it was time to leave her cocoon. But, once she was out, and she'd spread her wings, she discovered that the whole sky was her home.'

I'm lying in bed and I'm having difficulty breathing. This little white cell with its smell of disinfectant, its checked chinz curtains, and its vase of plastic flowers on the sill is my whole world now. Nurses in white glide in and out of the door, my children and grandchildren appear and disappear, and the days and nights slip past in a haze. I've absented myself from the world, and I'm living in my inner world instead.

It's luminous and miraculous there. I meet fairy-tale figures from ages long past, together with real people that I have known. Sometimes I see my poor dear mother, standing by my bed wringing her hands, and sometimes grandma Mabel flies in through the window to see how I'm doing. And once I saw Dave waiting for me at the end of a long tunnel. He was dressed like a bridegroom.

My heart is weaker now. I can feel it fluttering like a small bird learning to fly. And through the half-drawn curtains I can see the moon - full and bright. In the moonlight all the threads of gossamer, that connect everything to everything and make it into one whole, are illuminated like a spider's web covered with dewdrops. I watch in wonder while the radiant web weaves its colours into patterns around me. It's creating something that's very like a cocoon. How thin the membrane is, and how easy it will be for the butterfly to break through!

Then I hear IG's voice. It's coming from outside me now, and he's giving us the familiar post-hypnotic suggestions.

'Four - three - two - one - welcome back Mab!' he says, and I open my eyes to find myself in my reclining chair in the group room. The eclipse is over.

'You see, Mab, there was nothing to be afraid of. It was easy, wasn't it?'

'Yes,' I say, 'but I feel a bit shaky. Dying certainly takes it out of you!'

'Then take your time. Come to your senses gently.'

Goodness me! That was a weird experience. I really believed I was a lady called Marjorie. Virtuous reality is certainly very real. And it will take me a while to get used to real reality again!

Life 5
ROY the LEO

When IG asked me what I wanted most, I said fame. I've been an 'also ran' too often in the past, so this time I want to be a winner. I could drop a few names - Raphael for example. I was one of the young, aspiring painters who assisted him in his workshop. But, whereas every one has heard of Raphael, my name's been forgotten. In the eighteenth century I was a portrait painter, and a member of the Royal Academy, where I hobnobbed with the likes of Sir Joshua Reynolds. But, whereas his pictures are on public display in leading art galleries, mine lie gathering dust in the basement storerooms, which I naturally find galling.

So my aim this time is to go down in history. And, having worked hard at developing my talents in my past lives, I know they are all ready to flower. So I've composed my life-script accordingly, although, as IG explained to me, life-scripts do not determine our future. They incline our fate without compelling it. All the same I'm confident that this time round I'm going to achieve something great. And which of the twelve signs has fallen to my lot? Lo and behold it's Leo the lion - the most brilliant sign in the whole zodiac!

So I'm lying back in my reclining chair with my eyes closed, feeling relaxed and confident. And soon a spectacular light show starts unfolding before my inner eye. A multitude of swirling colours meet and merge to create what can only be described as a painting in motion, a mobile artwork! I savour the spectacle, which, alas, is not long lasting.

And now hardly any light at all penetrates the cave in which I lie curled. I'm in a womb I presume, with nine long months ahead, during which I have nothing to do but grow myself a body, and enjoy being lazy. I can allow things to proceed at their own momentum. And I can rest assured that I'm wanted, as I am destined to be my mother's beloved first-born child, and the kind of son my father has always dreamed of having.

The less said about my birth the better, as it was nasty, brutish but fortunately short, and I soon see the light of day, where I find a welcome committee waiting. Besides my mother, who of course is present, there's my father, the doctor, the midwife, the housemaid and the chauffeur - five faces all peering down at me, as I lie there in my cradle, freshly washed and swaddled. And everyone is delighted with what they see.

'What a beautiful baby!'

'What a noble forehead!'

'He looks like some exotic Eastern prince with that golden skin and those fine, dark eyes!'

I get my colouring from my mother, a dusky society beauty, who is also an artist of some repute. The year before I was born, she held an exhibition in Chelsea that caused quite a stir in art circles. But I'm her greatest work of art, of course, and she's quite prepared to dote on me, as are all the rest of the household.

This virtual reality, as it's called, is most peculiar. It's as if I'm experiencing everything in duplicate, being simultaneously the infant in the cradle, and the objective observer of the scene. The latter notes the date as August 1st 1944, and hears I'm to be christened Lionel George Stanton-Gleaves - a name that I approve of. Lionel has a noble ring about it, and the Stanton-Gleaves are an ancient lineage with their own coat of arms.

THE KID

Some months later I'm sitting upright, split naked on a leopard skin rug. My father, who's a keen photographer, is preparing yet another photo session. He's set up his box camera on a tripod, and is shining a bright lamp on me. It feels pleasantly warm on my bare skin. And there's my mother standing behind him, smiling and waving. But all her efforts to coax a smile to my lips fail, and I stare back in grandiloquent disdain.

I've been a martyr to photography since the day I was born. In fact I doubt whether there's a child in London whose first year of life has been recorded in more photographic detail. When this new set of prints have been developed, they'll be added to the collection in the thick, vellum album with my name embossed on the cover, that is full of photographs of yours truly.

I've grown apace, and in the next scene I'm coming up to three.

'Lionel, my precious, come and dance for us. Show us how you dance the jig!'

My mother is seated at the piano ready to play and, with a condescending smile, I start dancing to the music of a jolly sailor's hornpipe. Spurred on by my audience, who are clapping to the beat, I dance more and more wildly until I fall over and bump my head.

Though normally I'd make a fuss, I'm aware that all eyes are upon me. So I manfully suppress my tears and, struggling to my feet, I dance until the last chord has been struck. Then I conclude my performance with an elegant bow, which is rewarded by a burst of applause.

I'm used to being the centre of attention, because in our home everything revolves around me. My mother showers me with love and kisses, my father is proud of each new thing I learn, Nora, my nanny, spoils me horribly, and the housemaid is my humble servant. Mummy finds the imperious way I treat her amusing.

'Look at the little precious! Don't you think, Percy, that he has a regal manner - as if he's born to command?'

So I'm growing up in the belief that I'm someone very special. It's therefore all the more of a shock, when a baby brother appears out of the blue to oust me from my throne. I see my mother gazing at the puking little usurper with adoration in her eyes. And I see my father laughing at his antics, as he dandles him on his knee, and I become petulant and horrid.

Time flies by in this virtual life of mine, and soon I'm seven and starting prep school. I see myself sitting at a new desk in a new classroom looking nonplussed, the reason being that I've lost the status I enjoyed in my previous school. No one here knows me or knows of my talents, but this can and should be rectified. Therefore, when a suitable occasion arises in the playground, I announce to my classmates that I intend producing a play.

'Who wants to be in it?' I ask.

'Me! Me! Me!' they clamour, and soon I'm surrounded by a bevy of would-be thespians all wanting parts.

This is where I come into my own, as I allocate the roles and direct the action. Not a line of the script needs to be written down, as seven-year-olds are able to ad-lib without inhibition. So my play, that centres round Robin Hood and his merry men, takes shape. I am not only the producer, but of course I also play the main part of Robin himself.

When our little drama is ready, teacher allows us to perform it in front of the class. Desks are moved aside to create the space for a stage, and the head teacher comes in to watch, which inspires us all to give our best performance. When we reach the end, we are clapped profusely, and I take a bow and receive a special round of applause, which is like music in my ears.

Afterwards, I am able to bask in the popularity that this achievement brings me, but not all my classmates have become my fans. Some reject me, and set themselves up as my rivals, and some have become open enemies. And I begin to wonder if a desire to have special status, and a desire to be popular, cancel each other out.

TEENS

My ability to split my vision, and both be myself and watch myself being myself, slowly fades in the course of my childhood. And, by the age of sixteen, my consciousness is firmly entrenched in the slender form of Lionel Stanton-Gleaves. I'm just emerging from puberty, and fluctuate between the two extremes of self-confidence and self-consciousness. Where clothes are concerned I tend towards flamboyancy, and my tastes are always on the expensive side. Luckily I have a compliant mater who's willing to foot the bill. My hair is so long now that it reaches to below my shoulders.

'Go and get your hair cut,' the pater growls. 'You look effeminate!'

And it's true, because I'm often mistaken for a girl. But the mater approves.

'I like it long,' she says. 'It makes him look like the young Byron. Don't you agree, Percy, that he has that Byronic blend of aristocratic suavity and dishevelled genius?'

When it comes to class, I admit that I'm an awful snob. I cringe at the charlady's vulgar tones, and have taken to accentuating my upper class drawl when I speak to her. I've also noticed how she hangs her head when she's addressed, and she never looks us in the eye. So, in order to distinguish myself from those of her caste, and to appear taller than I am, I've taken to holding myself stiffly erect. And I look people directly in the eye when I speak to them.

They've sent me to an expensive private school in Hampstead, one that's favoured by the bohemian set because of its liberal attitudes. Short back and sides are not written into the rulebook there, but instead individuality and idiosyncrasy are cherished.

I'm the heartthrob of a bevy of girls from the lower forms, who always wait for me outside the gates after school. Sometimes I'll engage them in a bantering exchange, but I usually hurry past taking no notice, because our chauffeur is waiting round the corner with the Bentley. But, although I may seem off-hand, this female adulation is very welcome, as it serves to boost my self-esteem, which is suffering sorely at present under the pater's preference for my brother Nathaniel. My father is a rugby fan, and Nat has turned out to be an ace on the rugger pitch. It's the pater's dream to see him play in the national team one day.

'Are you coming to the match this afternoon to cheer your brother on?' he'll ask.

That's the last thing I want! Watching Nat's exploits on the rugby pitch, and seeing the pride in my father's eyes, would make me feel diminished. I'm not good at sport, and I've never tried to be, lacking as I do all ambition in that direction. In fact I look down on sporty types like Nat as lesser mortals, grosser and coarser than myself, and far less intelligent. Instead of wallowing in the mud, and getting hot and sweaty, I prefer to spend my free time painting in watercolours, or doing some etching. It's more civilised.

My mother, who hopes I'll become an artist like herself, allows me to use her studio. However, I confess that I'm lazy, and, instead of labouring to improve my painting and drawing skills, I prefer to lounge in those dives so fashionable amongst my generation, where frothy coffee is served from hissing, bubbling machines. I'll find a seat in some prominent place, and sit there cultivating my image.

The fact that we own a chauffeur-driven Bentley serves to arouse romantic fervour in the teenage beauties who congregate there. This evening I've invited two of them to visit my mother's studio. They've just arrived, and are standing by the door, watching me in admiration while I throw great globules of paint at a very large canvas.

'It's action painting,' I explain, 'in the style of Jackson Pollock.'

They nod, though I doubt whether they know who Jackson Pollock is, and I have only a vague knowledge of him myself. I ask them if they'd like to model for me, and explain that it will entail posing naked in front of the canvas, while I throw pots of paint at them. By this method we will create an original artwork in the form of a multi-coloured silhouette. Hoots of laughter!

After some hesitation the prettier one, who's name is Muriel, agrees, and takes off her dress and bra so that all she's wearing are her knickers. We're just discussing whether she should be allowed to keep them on or not, when the door opens and in walk my parents, accompanied by some very illustrious guests. Good grief!

The mater, who instantly sums up the situation, comes to my rescue.

'And this is our son Lionel. As you see, we are encouraging his interest in the arts by allowing him to be creative in his own original ways.'

'And this young lady has kindly agreed to pose for me,' I add.

Muriel's face is as red as a beetroot. She dresses hurriedly and makes her escape, and the incident goes down in the family annals as an early example of my impending bohemian decadence.

TWENTIES

I'm studying architecture, and in my third year at university. In spite of an inner knowledge that I'm destined to become a great painter, I realised that I needed an income to support my luxurious lifestyle. I therefore decided against studying fine art and starving in a garret, and chose to learn a lucrative profession instead.

What interests me in architecture first and foremost is its aesthetic dimension. I see its social relevance as secondary, and find the technical side of the subject tedious.

'What is a building?' I am wont to say. 'Nothing but a piece of sculpture, materialised out of form and space and light!'

It's my ambition to save our towns and cities from the uglification of the industrial era. I intend to beautify them with buildings that are not only functional, but are also works of art. My inspiration will be taken from the great architects of the past - Bramante, Brunellesco, Bernini - names with an eternal ring to them - whose work is still admired today after nearly five hundred years.

We've been given the task of designing a new municipal library for this term's study project, and I feel I've come up with some original solutions, and created a building that is both functional and elegant. So, unsolicited, I pass my drawings on to the head of the department, and ask him whether he'd care to comment. This man has had an illustrious career as a leading London architect, so I'm highly gratified when he praises my design profusely. I'm also aware that, if he chose to do so, he could help me up a few rungs on my career ladder.

Although I'm dedicated to my subject, I never allow it to distract me from leading a vibrant social life. I belong to the bright and beautiful set - the crème de la crème of the students of our year - and this evening we're invited to a party. The host is one of our professors, and I'm informed that a number of important people will be present.

As I arrive at the house, which lies in a salubrious area of town, the brightly lit Georgian windows welcome me from afar. And, on entering the portico, I'm greeted by the dazzle of the impressive cascading chandelier hanging in the hallway. I'm wearing my latest statement piece - an item of gear picked up on the King's Road. It's a mixture of medieval cloak and Mexican poncho in black velvet edged with gold. My set are into way-out clothing, and I know people will splash out this evening on their party gear, so I'm planning a dramatic entrance. And indeed, when I sweep through the door in this eye-catching attire, all the heads turn in my direction.

My favourite mannerism these days is to be effusively polite. So, while I sashay round the room champagne glass in hand, I'll say things like, 'Please, please don't mention it!' or 'The pleasure is all on my side!' or 'How extraordinarily kind of you,' which may sound affected, but has the right calculated effect. In passing, I overhear a lady ask,

'Who is that interesting young man?'

And I'm gratified to hear one of our senior lecturers reply,

'That's Lionel Stanton-Gleaves, third year architecture. A student of some promise so I hear, and most proficient at painting in oils.'

On hearing myself described in such terms I glow inwardly. Though I'm always careful not to show my gratification when I receive praise. My response is always a humble one when I'm paid a compliment.

'And why is that, Roy?'

'Hallo, IG! Is it you, the voice from the cellarage?'

'Your humble servant! If you'd like to do some self-inquiry, we could start by analysing your false modesty.'

'Modesty is good taste.'

'But it's insincere when it hides an avid hunger for praise.'

'Everyone likes being praised, IG, though I personally find it slightly embarrassing.'

'That's because you don't know how to receive praise and appear modest at the same time. And what do you do when criticism comes your way?'

'Deny all charges, argue defensively. You see if you want to be successful, you have to nurture your image. Self-presentation is everything. And things are going well for me. My life so far has been a pure success story!'

'Success is not about impressing people by playing to the gallery. Success is about having the courage to be your authentic self.'

'But I'm a thespian by nature, IG, so I delight in role-playing. Besides, like in eighteenth century Venice, masks are dress code in our society.'

'So, when you go around blowing your own trumpet, you don't believe in the image of yourself you're promoting - you're just acting a part, are you?'

'No, on the contrary I have an unshakeable belief in myself and in my talent. And a lot of other people believe in me too - not just my mother but also my tutor and my professor at the university.'

'Yes, I know they think you're a promising student but, in the end, it's not about how others see you.'

'It's about how I see myself, I know that, and I see myself positively. Besides being multi-talented, I'm entertaining and fun to be with. I have charm and charisma, and a great sense of humour, and I also have leadership qualities.'

'Then why waste your energy through trying to make the right impression on the right people? Have you forgotten that public opinion is fickle?'

'But, whenever a man achieves something of lasting artistic value, it will always be acknowledged, even though recognition comes posthumously.'

'So what is motivating you, Roy? What lies behind your determination to make your mark on the world?'

'I don't know, but the knowledge that I was born to achieve something great has been there ever since I was born.'

'Perhaps there's some deficit in you.'

'What do you mean?'

'Perhaps you secretly suffer from an inferiority complex, and you need success and recognition to compensate for it.'

'I more likely suffer from a superiority complex. My ego is enormous.'

'But a big ego is an indication of deep insecurity. Like a building with shaky foundations needs wooden piles to prevent it from collapsing, so the ego is needed to prop up a shaky sense of self.'

'Just why are you deconstructing me like this? Surely, as my life coach and my inner guide, you should be supporting me instead!'

'I'm only doing my job, Roy! Self-inquiry is your way forward. It will give you the distance to your self that you need to identify your patterns. And, when you come to know yourself, and you've discovered your intrinsic value, then neither approval nor disapproval will shake you, because you'll be standing on a firm foundation.'

THIRTIES

We're ten years further down the line, and I'm pleased to report that I'm doing splendidly. I left university with a first class honours degree and, through making use of my connections, landed myself a job with Musgrove and Musgrove as junior architect. There I immediately made an impact. I was never given the menial tasks to perform but, recognising my gifts, they involved me in their more significant projects from the start.

In social circles I'm seen as a party lion of the first magnitude. I'm a member of a rather exclusive club, where the young and the beautiful are perennially on display. It's the place you go to catch tomorrow's high-flyers, frequented as it is by all the young meteors, as well as by established celebrities. I've been known to spend a whole week's wages there in a single night, which set my overdraft spiralling.

The waiter is showing me to my accustomed table, and before long my friends join me. I'm wearing a pale grey suit with a golden tie, and I carry an elegant cane - a style flaunted by the young Aubrey Beardsley in the 1890's. As I reach for the menu, I take off my shades to reveal my large dark eyes, veiled by a-tick-too-long lashes. Men are inclined to fall for me as well as women, drawn perhaps by that hint of the hermaphrodite in my appearance. And I enjoy playing up to this ambiguity, which serves to make me all the more intriguing.

I am thus a different species from my brother Nat, who inhabits the world of rugby clubs with their pubs and pints, their society blondes and sports cars. And I go out of my way to go out of his way, because, every time our paths cross, Nat is a pain in the arse.

'So what does your brother do that gets up your nose?'

'I'll tell you, IG. Last time we met he called me a stuck-up prig and a pompous little squirt!'

'Well, if that galled you, it proves there's some truth in it. Admit it, Roy, you can be arrogant and over-bearing!'

'It's Nat who's the arrogant one. That's why I have to cut him down to size!'

'You're just sore because he doesn't look up to you as you think a younger brother should. But Nat is the last person in the world who's going to join your fan club.'

'Then I'm very sorry for him, because he must be eaten up with envy.'

'Or is it the other way round, and you're the one who's envious? Because Nat has some things going for him that you lack.'

'Only his beefy physique and a measure of sporting success.'

'Come on! Nat is a fine figure of a man - broad-shouldered and virile, muscles like a body-builder and...'

'A big prick! Say it! But I find comfort in the fact that my impact on women has always been greater than his. They buzz around me like bees round a honey-pot.'

'Then perhaps you're irked by the fact that your father takes so much pride in him. He goes to all his matches, and Nat, it seems, is turning out to be the kind of son he always dreamed of having.'

'That's a bit close to the knuckle IG! No, as I see it, my brother has very little going for him. He's less intelligent, less cultured and far less gifted than me. In fact he's nothing more than a clumsy oaf, and I told him so to his face the last time he insulted me.'

'Roy, have you noticed that, whenever someone says something negative about you, your hackles come up and you immediately retaliate? You leave no time for the criticism to sink in, which is a pity because it might have been helpful. Always pay more attention to your detractors than to what your admirers say.'

'Alright, if I'm honest, I'll admit I feel both superior and inferior to Nat.'

'Yes, and there we have it. The root of the trouble lies in your habit of comparing, because, when you're in your ego, you always need someone you can feel superior to. Life for the ego is a race in which there are people behind, and people in front. When you look at the people behind, you feel good because you're beating them. But you feel discouraged when see the people ahead of you. So why don't you withdraw your attention from other people altogether, and focus on yourself? Try beating your own best time instead.'

I left Musgrove and Musgrove two years ago, because I felt I wasn't being appreciated there as I deserve. My next step was to move to Brighton where I set up my own practice, for which the pater kindly coughed up the necessary funds. So far we're doing splendidly. My connections from school and university are bringing in the commissions. And I already have a number of larger projects to my name that I can be proud of.

As I am wont to say, an architect's reputation is carved in stone. What we build becomes our monument, and will be so judged not only by our own generation, but also by the generations to come. The great Wren churches, or Pugin's gothic pinnacles, go on bearing witness to the artistic genius of their creators. So I'm always aware that what I'm building now will become my epitaph!'

I've surrounded myself with a loyal and deferential team of bright young things. They are like planets held in the gravitational field of my central sun. Last week, when the news came through that we'd successfully landed a big contract, I ordered in a crate of sparkling wine, and we celebrated our victory with a wild party. Very little work got done that day, but work hard, play hard is my motto. Everyone got riotously tipsy, and the great guffaws of laughter following my jokes echoed so loudly through the walls that the people from the office next door came to complain. Of course they were persuaded to join the party!

As long as things are done according to my specifications, I'm an easy-going and tolerant boss. I never dictate what my staff should wear, or the hours they should be at their desks; but nothing happens in the office that I don't know about, and I'm something of a control freak concerning standards. Everything we turn out has to have my stamp of approval. The downside is I'm inclined to take on too much. I know I should delegate more to my staff, but I simply don't trust anyone here to do the job as well as I can.

A client has arrived for an appointment, and Cressida - a highly decorative art student, whose role it is to hover - has fielded him. She engulfs him in a deep-cushioned sofa, and serves him Turkish coffee in a gold-rimmed cup. I then stage-manage the interview so the desired outcome is reached. As clients are wont to do, this customer has envisioned something that's wildly impractical. So, in a tone of quiet authority, that plainly says there can be no doubt I'm right, I persuade him that he doesn't want what he wants, but he wants what I want instead!

Despite a full diary, I always find time to paint, and I'm planning on having enough canvases filled by the end of the year to hold my first exhibition. I have hung some examples of my recent work on the office walls. They are always praised profusely when people want something from me. But I feel that little Janice, my secretary, is sincere in her appreciation of them. She also asks intelligent questions about my painting techniques, and listens absorbed when I air my views on contemporary art.

'The girl has brains as well as beauty!' I tell the mater.

'But does she have the right qualities to make you a good wife?' is her reply.

My parents are keen on me getting married. Now I'm approaching the watershed of thirty-five, they think my life should be put on a more regular and even keel. So my eye has alighted on Janice. Is she the right woman? Well, I pride myself on being something of a connoisseur when it comes to the fair sex, having enjoyed a number of glamorous love affairs in my time. Yes, I've been somewhat notorious in that respect, and sown my wild oats all over the town, but now the time has come to marry and procreate.

When Janice confesses to me that she dabbles in oils, I invite her to come round and paint in my studio. She's thrilled. She duly turns up with her paints and brushes, and I notice that she's also brought a basket of goodies for lunch. Now I like a girl who shows that kind of foresight! Come midday she tosses up a delicious salad from the simplest of ingredients, which we consume with a baguette and a glass of dry white wine.

Although Janice spends more time fetching and carrying my things than on her own creative efforts, she is obviously enjoying herself.

And, when it's time to pack up at the end of the day, she's happy to wash out my brushes as well as her own. Then she whisks round the studio, and in the twinkling of an eye it's all tidied up. I say a warm thank you for relieving me of this drudgery by taking her in my arms, and giving her a hug and a kiss.

Soon Janice has become as invaluable in my private life as she is in the office, and I've reached the conclusion that she'd make the perfect wife. Compared to the models and aspiring actresses I've been out with, Janice doesn't turn heads. She's not what is normally considered beautiful - at the most you could say she's attractive. But I'm not one of those men who need a trophy wife to boost their self-esteem. And I even see her low-key looks as an advantage, as they mean she will never upstage me. Neither will she attract admirers all the time, so I won't have to keep my eye on her.

The wedding is held in May, when the rhododendrons are out on the lawn in front of the five-star hotel that has been booked for the reception. It's a big society wedding, and the bishop himself has come down to marry us. I see a row of Rolls-Royces and Bentleys parked outside the church, and Janice is wearing a spectacular wedding dress. Its long, lacy train reaches half way down the aisle, and her six bridesmaids have their work cut out carrying it!

When we leave the church to the strains of Mendelsohn's wedding march, a press photographer is waiting outside. And the next day our photo appears in the local paper as part of a whole-page spread, under the heading *Leading Brighton Architect Marries In Style*. All excellent publicity!

We've acquired a spacious apartment in an elegant Regency crescent, where we live our busy, creative lives. Janice is an excellent housekeeper and provider, and is always very supportive of my work. She's encouraged me to enter the latest architectural competition announced by the corporation, although it means she'll see very little of me in the months ahead. It involves a high-profile public building for the town centre. And, if I win and we land the commission, it will catapult my career to new dizzy heights.

I submit my drawings on time, and hear via the grapevine that I'm on the short list. Soon afterwards I'm invited to meet the mayor and council representatives on site to expand on my ideas. It's a day with strong, blustery winds from the Channel, and gusts of rain that blow horizontally. The illustrious party are huddled together, macs flapping, on the brown-field site. And, although the wind is so loud I have to shout to be heard, I'm ebullient with confidence and very full of myself. I draw myself up to my full five foot six and a half inches of height, and wave my arms about in the air to give my words more emphasis.

'What concerns me is the visual impact. We need to place an accent on this rather bland skyline,' I say. 'So what I've envisioned is a piece of architecture that turns its back on all the historical precedents with which this town is overloaded, and makes a statement that is blatantly and uncompromisingly modern. The weak-hearted may find the design I've come up with too confrontational, but it is going to make people sit up and take notice of us, and that's what we want.'

Politicians, as I've discovered, know very little about architecture. What concerns them is how the general public will react, and whether the project will stand their party in a good light. And, by the end of the meeting, I've managed to persuade them that what I'm offering will put Brighton on the map, not only nationally but also internationally.

I'm honoured and highly gratified when, some weeks later, I hear that I've have been awarded first prize. Congratulations come flooding in from every quarter. The mater is over the moon, and the pater doesn't spare his praise, but of course there's one detractor.

'Oh my God!' exclaims Nat on hearing the news. 'He's too big for his boots already. Now the bastard will be even cockier!'

However, once the jubilation has died down, I discover that this commission carries with it heavy responsibilities. And, in the months ahead, my workload increases to such an extent that I no longer have the time to paint, which puts me in a quandary. The venue has been booked for my exhibition, the advertising has gone out, and I'm under pressure to finish four or five more canvasses by the end of the month. But for some reason my creative juices have run dry, and just when I need her most my muse has deserted me. In desperation I turn to my inner guide.

'IG, I've been managing very well without you, but in my present dire situation I'd be most grateful for some advice.'

'What's the problem, Roy?'

'I must be suffering from artist's block, because my creativity has ceased to flow!'

'Then perhaps you're trying to force it. Don't push the river. You're never the doer when you do your best work. It happens when you open up, and become a channel for the creativity of existence to flow through you.'

'But I can't afford to wait for that to happen! This is an emergency, IG. It would be most embarrassing if I had to cancel my exhibition, as I gave the committee the impression that I've paintings galore to choose from.'

'Then you're trying to save your face? But is your face worth saving? And why are you holding an exhibition in the first place?'

'That should be clear! It's because I'm not only an architect, I'm also a painter of some talent, and it's high time this was generally recognised.'

'You mean you're an exhibitionist, Roy. That's why you're holding an exhibition!'

'This is no joking matter!'

'It's my job, old man, to press your buttons and get you to self-inquire. Yes, it appears to me that this whole exhibition idea is nothing but ego embellishment.'

'You can be so irritating! It's about expressing the talents I've been born with, and what else are talents for? Should they be buried in the earth like in that Bible story?'

'Yes, because talents are like seeds. They contain within them the impulse to grow into some plant or tree, and in the right conditions they'll grow of their own accord and produce fruit. But, if you try to force them to grow before their time, you could kill them.'

'But, as I see it, unless I make an effort, nothing is going to happen. I'll stay mediocre, and my life will be wasted while I sit around on my backside.'

'So you're doing all this to avoid being mediocre?'

'Ha ha! There's no danger of that, IG. I've already enjoyed considerable success as an architect. My present project is receiving a lot of attention in the national press and, if all goes well, they could offer me an OBE in a few years time, like they did to old Musgrove.'

'Only an OBE! Why not a knighthood?'

'Yes, why not?'

'Roy, do you really need the queen to acknowledge your worthiness before you can believe in it yourself? No achievement however high can increase the value of your being, which cannot be improved on. And you won't receive more love through becoming famous either.'

'Yes, I've heard the theory that celebrities seek love from their public because they don't love themselves. But in my case I'd say I love myself too much. I'm the narcissist per excellence.'

'You're self-obsessed, Roy, and that's a different matter. It happens when inside you feel inadequate.'

'I certainly feel inadequate with this exhibition looming over my head. Oh my God! What am I going to do?'

'Inquire into the primal wound to your self-esteem, Roy, because, if you can turn that round, then whether you succeed or fail in the eyes of the world will no longer matter. Once you value yourself, you'll no longer need validation from other people.'

This talk with IG leaves me thoughtful and, after further deliberation, I cancel the exhibition.

MIDDLE AGE

I've acquired a plot of land in a salubrious location, and built us a house on it to suit our needs. As it also serves as a show house, it boasts of some state-of-the-art architectural features. It has five bedrooms, a sumptuous fireplace for log fires in winter, a Spanish-style patio with a swimming pool for lazy summer days, and solar panelling on the roof. The basement has been turned into a spacious play area for the children, and the attic has become my studio, my sanctuary as I call it. We have four offspring - three lovely girls followed by Thomas, the heir to the throne.

As I'm never tired of saying, Janice is the best thing that could have happened to me. She's made a wonderful wife. Her very presence is reassuring, and she's always ready to listen to my problems. It's a boon that she sees rearing children as more worthwhile than pursuing her ambition to paint, as I rely on her to hold the domestic fort.

I'm up to my neck in work now, but I still find time to play with my children. When I arrive home from the office, little Thomas will say,

'Daddy, put your womping trousers on.'

And I change out of my suit into my leisure wear, so I'm ready for a romp before supper. They love it when I give them piggy-backs up and down the garden, or chase them round the rhododendron bush. However, as I'm now rather tubby, I soon get out of breath, and I fear that I cut rather a ludicrous figure puffing along behind them. I'll have to cut down on the business lunches, or my wardrobe of elegantly tailored suits will no longer fit me!

I've recently landed the contract for yet another prestigious development. It involves a tower block containing flats, offices and shops that is to be erected on a brown-field site in the city centre. However, the residents' association are up in arms, and there's been a deluge of protest. They've lodged an objection claiming that the infrastructure in the city centre is inadequate to cope with a high-density development of this nature, and a study has been commissioned by the urban planning office. If it finds the location unsuitable, the whole project could be placed in jeopardy.

Another annoyance is that my work has become the subject of some scathing articles in the local press. The wretch who is writing them labels my proposed building 'a monstrous eyesore', and has the audacity to accuse me of, I quote, 'failing to have a long-term vision for the area.' Balderdash! The real reason for the furore is that my style of architecture is too visually challenging for morons like him to appreciate.

So I've come to the conclusion that the public must be educated to appreciate a visual impact of this magnitude, which is why I'm replying to his accusations with an article of my own. In it I defend my vision in the simplest terms that even the grossest idiot could not fail to understand. And when it's finished I send it to the editor of our local rag.

I am mortified when he refuses to publish it.

The report commissioned by the planning office confirms the choice of location, but demands that a number of revisions be made, before the project can pass from the drawing board to its execution in bricks and mortar. I have no other option but to comply with their demands. But even then the enterprise remains jinxed, because the most unlikely problems keep cropping up, which I'm called in to solve. It's also uncanny how many key people fall sick, and are off work when they're needed. And not only that - we are let down left and right by contractors, and suppliers fail to deliver on time, all of which makes chaos of the work schedules.

As if this was not enough, I start having staff problems. My original, amenable team have now left, and the new lot who have replaced them, like many of today's youth, are querulous and insurgent. They have banded together to resist doing overtime, and are making other outrageous demands. My response has been to assert my power more conspicuously, and to tighten my control.

Then, when two out of the three paintings I submitted for inclusion in the Arts Council's annual exhibition are refused, and the painting that is hung is torn to pieces by the critics, I start comparing myself to Job. As you may remember, Job was the undeserving victim of a number of horrid plagues from heaven.

It's a further blow when friends - or so-called friends - seeing me thus weakened and under duress, desert my flag. I recently bumped into G. M. Petherington, the president of the Arts Association, with whom I've always been on friendly terms, and I was appalled to hear him referring to my exhibited painting in very derogatory terms.

'Why is this happening to me, IG? Surely it's not in my life-script!'

'Our life-scripts must sometimes bow to karmic necessity. You know those medieval depictions of the wheel of fortune, Roy? Well, you've risen up on one side and reached the top. But, however hard you try to stay there, the wheel must go on turning and carry you down on the other side. The only thing you can do now is to take comfort in the knowledge that, when you've hit the bottom, you'll start ascending again.'

'Hmmm... old Petherington had a jeer in his voice the other day. I seem to have become an object of ridicule.'

'The people who criticise you have their own reasons for doing so.'

'That's true. Petherington's paintings, for example, always received less acclaim than mine. He's under the illusion that he's a great talent, when in fact his work is merely mediocre.'

'Through denigrating a rival's work, you can indirectly raise the value of your own. You know that Roy.'

'All the same I'm mortified by betrayals such as these from people who I always saw as my friends.'

'In your eyes a friend is someone who says positive things about you and your work. So, when they start saying negative things instead, does that make them an enemy? In that case your enemies do you a greater service than your friends.'

'Hmmm... If I'm honest I'll admit that, although I know a lot of people, there's none among them that I can truly call a friend. The sad truth is I stand alone and friendless.'

'That's because you've become a leader. The captain of the ship is always set apart from the crew. Leaders may have fans and hangers-on, but these can never be their friends, because they are not their equals.'

'That's the situation in the office. I had a vision of us all being part of one team that was total in work and total in play. I wanted to be treated like one of the lads, but my present crew won't even show me respect! There's one young man in particular who does his best to undermine my authority. I'd fire him if I could, but he'd take me to a tribunal for it.'

'So how do you keep him under control?'

'When he makes a mistake, I make an example of him in front of the others. I've found that, if I can make him lose face, it takes the wind out of his sails.'

'That's a strategy rulers have always used to hold onto their power - shaming and wounding their opponent's ego. But it's not helpful to demoralise your staff, Roy, because, by disempowering them, you diminish their enthusiasm for their tasks. And, when that happens, it's you who suffers, because their performance is impaired, and then your practice goes down the drain.'

'Good grief! We don't want that to happen! So what's the alternative, IG?'

'Listen to your crew like a good captain does, and take their views into consideration. Don't try to dominate through exerting your power, but become a mentor to them. Trust them enough to delegate responsibility, and then you'll further their talents and bring them on.'

'Yes, I've never been very trusting. That's why I used to have to exert so much control.'

'When your love is stronger than your fear, instead of loving power, you'll wield your power with love.'

That's good advice old IG has come up with. But, before I can start putting it into effect, I will have to arrive at the bottom of the wheel.

The bedroom curtains are drawn. Although it's noon, I'm lying semi-conscious in semi-darkness. I hear the doorbell ring, and footsteps sound on the stairs, and Janice knocks at my door.

'It's Andy and Penny from the office with an enormous bunch of flowers.'

'Send them away. I told you I want to be left alone for Christ's sake!'

That's not like me, but I'm not my usual self at present. I've lost all my joie de vivre, and I've sunk into a slough of despond.

The tower block that was surrounded by so much controversy was finally completed, and ceremoniously handed over in the presence of the mayor and councillors, and with wide media coverage. But it wasn't long before a structural fault was discovered for which the contractors held me responsible. Now they are threatening to sue me for a vast sum of money, and my broker informs me that my insurance policy provides inadequate cover. If they win, not only will my practice go down the drain, but - even worse - I'll be branded for ever with the stigma of professional incompetence.

As soon as the news went round, customers started backing out. Client confidence had clearly been shaken, and we lost a number of important contracts. Rumour has it that we're not expected to last until the end of this financial year.

I'd reached the point where I felt I couldn't take any more hits, when the news reached me of my father's sudden demise. I hurried home to be with my mother and help her arrange the funeral. And at the funeral I came face to face again with my estranged brother, Nat, who I hadn't seen for ten years. I decided to be friendly, as I knew it was dear to my mother's heart that we should be reconciled.

'How's it going, Nat?' I ask.

'Oh fine, fine!' he replies, though he doesn't look fine. In fact he's looking decidedly the worse for wear. He's let himself go, and he's lost his superior physique.

'How's the wife?

'Fine, fine!'

'And the girls?'

'Doing brilliantly - academically gifted both of them - not like me, eh? Harriet is at St Andrews reading history, and Jessica, who takes her A-levels next year, is set on getting even better grades than her sister. She wants to go to Oxford! And what about yours?'

'I can't trump that,' I say. 'My girls all left school at sixteen. Two became nurses and the other's a nursery school teacher. So it's all down to poor old Thomas, who's finding it a struggle to get a few O-Levels.'

After the service, Nat and I are left alone at the graveside. Nat says, 'I've got something to tell you, Lionel, and this is as good an opportunity as any.'

'What then?'

'He wasn't your real father,' he says, pointing at the little mound of freshly heaped earth. 'While he was away in the war, the mater had a love affair with an Indian, who got her pregnant. The pater was very decent about it. He offered to adopt you, and bring you up as his own son.'

It's like being hit over the head with a sledgehammer.

'When did you find that out?' I gasp.

'Last year when the pater was talking to me about his will. He made me promise not to tell you as long as he was alive, because he didn't want to spoil his relationship with you.'

'An Indian?' I mutter. 'I hope at least he was a Maharaja.'

'No, he was a carpet salesman.'

I look at Nat in sheer disbelief.

'If you don't believe me,' he adds, 'go and ask the mater - though it's not a good time now, while she's grieving.'

When I get home, I go upstairs to my sanctuary without speaking to anyone, and I lock the door behind me. I don't re-appear. Janice has to bring my meals up on a tray. She passes my message on to the office that I've contracted hepatitis, which is a fiction. The truth is that all the stuffing has been knocked out of me. I'm flat on the floor and out for the count.

'You're having a hard time, Roy!'

'Hard! You see before you a broken man, IG, a ruin of his former self. How are the mighty fallen!'

'I see it as a great opportunity. When the outer props of the ego have been taken away, we have the space to discover our true being.'

'Is there justice in the universe, I ask myself. I've dedicated my life to producing architecture of the highest standard to grace our city. I have laboured to create works of art in which others can delight, only for it all to end in utter ignominy!'

'Nothing ever ends, Roy. We just go on and on. And, if I know you, you'll have the courage to pick yourself up and start again.'

'No no! This great blow has felled the mighty oak. It lies shattered on the ground.'

'It's your pride that has been shattered, Roy.'

'Ha ha! Pride comes before a fall!'

'False pride came before your fall; true pride can come after it. And in the mean time you are learning some important lessons.'

'What for example?'

'Patience and fortitude in adversity, a deeper understanding of life's patterns, and perhaps more compassion for others.'

'Ah yes! I haven't been very compassionate, have I? I used to look down on most people, but now it's turned out that I'm not a cut above them as I thought. I'm a cut below them. I don't even have a pedigree any more, now I'm no longer a Stanton-Gleaves. I'm just an ordinary, common or garden bastard!'

'But you're more human, Roy. You're softer and more in your heart.'

'Perhaps. I see my former self now as selfish and attention seeking. I wanted to be appreciated, though I never thought of appreciating others. And I took up all the space, so nobody else had a chance to shine.'

'If you see that clearly now, your pattern will change. You'll be more generous in the future, and more supportive of other people.'

'And I no longer crave fame and recognition, IG. My only wish is that the contribution I have tried to make through my creativity will one day be appreciated.'

'It is appreciated, Roy. You have always used your talents to add value to the world.'

'Really? Well that's good to know! Hmmm... Andy and Penny from the office turned up this afternoon with a bunch of flowers. I'm sorry now that I turned them away so rudely. It was a kind gesture, and I thought they couldn't stand me!'

'Now that you're in your heart, you're going to meet with more love and sympathy. And people will be compassionate towards you, when they feel you have compassion for them.'

OLD AGE

It's my sixty-fifth birthday party, and I'm sitting at the head of the table, a rotund, jovial figure with a mane of thick white hair. Beside me sits my dear wife Janice, and round the table I see the smiling faces of my four children and my eight grandchildren. Thomas has brought his digital camera to record the occasion, and we all say 'cheese'. This latest photo will be added to the pictorial record of my life that I have preserved in the shelves full of photo albums.

After suffering a minor heart attack last year, I decided to squeeze the juice out of every remaining moment. So I'm celebrating this birthday in style. A marquee has been erected in the garden, and I've ordered ten crates of the best champagne. The caterers have been called in, and this afternoon more than eighty guests will be arriving for a garden party. Among their number will be my brother Nat, with whom I am now reconciled, and his wife Cynthia and all their sundry offspring.

These are happier times. The wheel of fortune continued turning, as IG said it would, and soon I was rising up on the other side. The inquiry into that structural fault in the tower block, for which they tried to make me responsible, ended fortuitously. It could be proved that the cause lay in a material fault rather than in a design error, so I was acquitted. And this gave me the impetus to bounce back with renewed vigour, and I was soon my old, cocky self again - but only outwardly. Inwardly I was a chastened and reformed character.

However, by the time I'd reached my mid fifties, my career had passed its zenith. Fashions in architecture were changing and, stubborn as I am, I found it hard to move with the times. Society was now dominated by a barbaric youth culture, and age and experience were no longer at a premium. The plum assignments were all going to the young bucks who were in vogue, and I had to make do with scraps from their table so to speak. But I took this philosophically - I'd learned a thing or two in my slough of despond!

So I'm now semi-retired, and have plenty of time to devote to my life-long passion - painting. My attitude to it has changed, however. I now paint because it's what I love doing, and not because I need acclaim. I'm also more relaxed about whether my pictures are exhibited or not, because I take neither my talent nor myself as seriously as I used to.

During the course of supper I give the little speech I've been preparing.

'I'm going to find it hard not to brag', I say, 'because I've been blessed with a wonderful life and a wonderful wife! I am proud of producing not only fruit from my loins,' and with a sweep of my arm I indicate my assembled children and grand-children, 'but also a body of work that I can be truly proud of, both as an architect and an artist.'

'Hear! Hear!' chorus a number of voices.

'Looking back with my architect's hat on, and recalling what I've created in my time, I feel not only pride but gratitude. I see myself as privileged to have had the opportunity to express my talents, in comparison with many from the lower social classes, whose whole energy is taken up with earning their bread. I've been allowed the satisfaction of seeing my visions materialise and become reality.'

My speech was extracted from my memoirs. Last year I decided to put pen to paper, and record some of the highlights of my life, so that the things I've experienced will not be lost to posterity. However, while I was writing down my reminiscences, a curious feeling came over me. It felt as if I was writing fiction rather than biography, that the character emerging from the pages was not the real me. And I found that I no longer believed in Lionel. That brought me back to a basic question, that has dogged me throughout all my inner dialogues with IG - who am I?

'Ah ha!' IG replies mysteriously, when I ask him. 'That's what we're trying to find out.'

'I mean, I know my name's Lionel, and I know my biography, and can list my achievements. I know what I think about myself, and to some extent I know the opinions others have of me. So am I then the sum of all these factors?'

'Lionel is a virtual character, leading a virtual life. Roy is more real and permanent.'

'I don't know anything about him at all!'

'Roy is the face you had before you were born, and the face you will have after you die.'

'I see.'

'You've been many different characters in your time, because you've often been on earth before, and you'll be here many more times.'

'I've always said, if reincarnation exists, I must have been an artist in the past, because painting and drawing came so naturally to me. I had a talent for it from an early age. Was that because I'd studied it in my last life?'

'Very likely! But there are many of your ilk alive at this very moment, whose achievements are on a par with yours. I'll show you if you like.'

And before my eyes arises a vision of a great throng of people - men and women, white, black and brown, of different races and nationalities, each standing proudly in front of the pictures and sculptures and books and edifices that they've created.

'That's sobering,' I say when the vision fades. 'It certainly puts me and my achievements into perspective. Thank you, IG!'

A short time later, while I'm trying to hang one of my larger canvasses, I'm surprised by a sudden pain in my thorax. I let the painting fall, and it crashes to the floor, while I lean against the wall panting for breath. My chest has become a bellows, and it's being deflated with great force from either side so I can't breathe. I'm unable to call for help, and a moment later I fall heavily to the ground.

I am now being squeezed by the bellows upwards from my chest into my throat, and, although the passage is a narrow one, I discover that I can pass through it with ease. I pop out through a small hole in the top of my head, and immediately everything becomes more spacious. That's better, I think! Now I have room to breathe.

'Hallo, Roy!'

'Hallo, IG! I'm so glad you're here. I seem to have had another heart attack.'

'You've left your body.'

'Good grief, you're right! There it is over there, lying in a heap on the floor. How amazing!'

'Don't miss this moment, Roy, because, if you can stay alert and aware, it's a time when you may catch a glimpse of your essential self.'

I am looking down on events from a height. First I watch Janice discovering my body, and her shock and grief are hard to bear because, it appears, I have no means of comforting her. Although I keep shouting, 'Here I am - up here in the corner of the ceiling!' she can neither hear nor see me. But nothing fazes Janice. She always does the right thing in an emergency. And, in the days that follow, I watch her bearing her bereavement with fortitude, supported by the family who rally round her. The funeral is arranged according to the instructions I wrote down after I suffered my first heart attack, which Janice follows meticulously.

I never miss my own funeral, as it's fascinating to see who comes, and who doesn't bother to attend, and I enjoy eavesdropping on what people say about me. The vicar's address is not very inspired. I could have done better myself! He goes on about my outstanding achievements, and my amusing quirks of character. But the obituary that appeared in *The Times* was good for a laugh!

I finally say goodbye to Lionel in the churchyard. Hovering round the open grave, together with my family and other mourners, I watch my coffin being lowered into the ground and covered with earth. I say goodbye to Lionel without regret, but bidding my nearest and dearest farewell is harder. However, I know we are all going to meet again. Then, before I finally take my leave, I check the tombstone to make sure they've got the inscription right. Yes, there it is:

Lionel George Stanton-Gleaves,
artist and architect.
Born 1st August 1944, died November 10th 2012
'Let my creations be my epitaph.'

Life 6
MEG the VIRGO

What have I let myself in for! I must confess I feel slightly worried, because I've got everything so well sorted at present. My life up here is running like clockwork. So, although I have a sincere wish to improve myself, it could be seen as somewhat foolhardy to let myself in for an experience that's sure to be unsettling.

It was my life coach, IG, who urged me to incarnate. And I see his point, because in a sense I am treading water. I'm not doing as much as I should do to fulfil my potential and, as everyone knows, a new incarnation is the best way to accelerate your personal growth. So here I am, on the brink of my big adventure, and feeling a tick apprehensive, as I lie back in my reclining chair and do my best to relax.

Oh bother! It's not working! IG's hypnotic suggestions, and that soothing music he's playing, are having no effect at all. I'm too wound-up I suppose. But then, if the hypnosis doesn't work, I won't experience anything, and then what shall I do with myself for the next threescore years and ten? Sit here twiddling my thumbs, or what?

I'm just beginning to think it would be wise to call the whole thing off, when some coloured lights appear. As my eyes are still closed, I conclude they must be inside rather than outside me - in other words an optical illusion. However, the way they bob and twinkle has a calming effect on my nerves and is very pleasant. I wonder how it's done? Through stimulating the pineal cone perhaps? No, that's the wrong word! What's that little gland in the middle of your forehead called? I should know, but it's slipped my mind.

I see a room in a hospital. There's a woman lying unconscious on the operating table, and I recognise her as my new mother. I've just been delivered by caesarean four weeks prematurely. The gynaecologist decided to operate as the lives of mother and child were at risk. My mother, you see, is an elderly forty-two, and she'd come to the end of her strength, having been in labour for more than thirty-six hours!

I'm relieved to unite with my new body at this advanced stage in the proceedings, and be spared the ordeal of going through a difficult and protracted labour. Amnesia, it seems, has its positive side. I watch myself being washed and weighed, after which I'm shown to my mother, who is just coming round from the anaesthetic. She manages a weak smile. My impulse is to cling to her and cleave to her breast, which seems the only safe place in this new, alarming world. But, no, I'm not allowed to! Instead I'm whisked away and put in an incubator.

Of course I understand the necessity for this measure, because I'm premature and under-weight. But, as I can also feel what the baby is feeling - namely her acute distress - I'd say that, psychologically speaking, it's not right because the baby is bewildered and confused. She doesn't know where she is, or who these people are, or what they are doing to her body. So it's logical that she wants to remain with her mother. But I soon get used to the incubator. I have to, as I'm to spend four long weeks in it!

When my mother comes to fetch me home, she's understandably nervous about me catching an infection. So she does her best to reproduce the same sterile conditions I had in the incubator. My cradle, my bath and my pram are disinfected as regularly and thoroughly as my feeding bottle and teat, and my baby clothes and nappies are boiled to kill all the germs.

I've made a mental note of my new name. It's Marion Jane Goodchild, and my date of birth is August 25th 1944.

THE KID

At the age of two I'm a tiny, fairy-like creature with wispy blonde hair. I'm following my mummy round the house helping her do the housework. In my hand I carry a miniature feather duster that's like a fairy wand. We dust the furniture and sweep the floor in that order. Otherwise, if you swept the floor before you dusted, the dust that falls down wouldn't get swept up, would it?

'Mummy, where does dust come from?'

'From the air.'

I'm puzzled by her answer because I can't see anything in the air at all. Then one day a shaft of sunlight falls obliquely through the curtains, and they appear - billions of particles of dust moving in a grand, slow dance. They are all shimmering with lovely colours, and they don't look at all like the enemy they are made out to be.

When we reach my bedroom, and mummy sees the mess it's in, she gets very cross.

'Marion! Go and pick up those toys, and put them back where they belong. What do we always say? A place for everything and everything in its place!'

I'm sitting in my high chair, swaddled in a bib, staring at the pile of uneaten food on my plate.

'Eat up your carrots, dear, they're good for you,' and mummy tries to push another spoonful of the nasty, cold pulp into my mouth.

'Ugh!' I spit it out.

'Now look what you've done, you naughty girl!'

I look down and see a large orange stain spreading over my snow-white bib, and I'm so alarmed that I start coughing and choking. Mummy is worried that I'll bring up my whole meal, so I'm allowed to get down.

Mummy works very hard. She's like a busy bee buzzing about from morn to eve, because daddy needs looking after as well as me. He's been disabled in the war, and has got a gammy leg, which is why he's always at home sitting in his chair by the window. I've got two grown-up sisters, Anne and Mary, who go out to work. Mummy says Mary's the difficult one. She calls her 'Mary, Mary quite contrary'.

I've grown somewhat. I go to school now, and I'm in Mrs Wilson's class. This morning we're doing a handwriting test, and I'm taking great pains to form every letter in the way we've been taught. When I get to the end, I take a peep at Howard's exercise book. Howard, who sits at my table, is one of the naughty boys, and, when I see his writing that's all smudged and messy, it makes me feel quite smug.

'You're not holding your pen properly, Howard,' I say. 'You'd be able to write much better, if you held it like this!' - and I show him.

I only meant to be helpful, but Howard doesn't take it that way. In reply he flicks his pen in my direction, landing a big blob of ink right in the middle of my neat page. I burst into tears. Mrs Wilson, however, saw what happened, and comes over to scold Howard, who says it was an accident. Oh my! Now he's gone and told a fib! His nose is going to grow until it's as long as Pinocchio's!

'Never mind, dear,' Mrs Wilson says. 'I'm still going to give you ten out of ten for neatness.'

TEENS

At fourteen I'm underdeveloped for my age, with a chest that's as flat as a pancake. Also my mother, who cuts my hair by putting a pudding-basin over my head, has given me an unflattering bob. So I'm not feeling very glamorous when we depart on our shopping expedition to buy a new winter coat for me, and a pair of shoes. Father's pension from the war office doesn't stretch far, and it's hard to make ends meet, so big items like coats and shoes have to be budgeted for.

I don't like any of the coats I have to try on, and the sensible shoes that mummy chooses for me are not what I had in mind.

'And who are you to be so picky and choosy, miss?' she snaps.

I make allowances for her, as she's always on edge when we shop for expensive things. But then she goes and embarrasses me by saying to the shop assistant,

'My daughter is at the difficult age. Turns up her nose at everything! It's enough to try the patience of a saint!'

The girl, kneeling at my feet with a shoe in her hand, is not much older than me, and I blush with shame. I'm feeling a right twit anyway - sitting here with both shoes off, and exposing my darned socks for all the world to see!

We arrive home with the sort of coat my mother would wear, and a pair of ugly, lace-up clodhoppers. The girls in my class are going to laugh their heads off when they see them. They've all become so fashion-conscious of late, and they doll themselves up so glamorously when they go out. It's nylons and high heels for them! And there's some in our class I could name who've already got steady boyfriends!

'Never mind!' I say to myself. 'When I'm dressed in this coat and these shoes, the last thing I'll have to worry about is boys. They'll run a mile when they see me coming - even our Andrew will.'

Andrew is the head choirboy, and of late he's taken to staring at me when the choir progresses down the aisle. The other day I was both flattered and alarmed, when a friend revealed that he'd said to her he liked me.

Sunday comes round, and I accompany my mother to church dressed in the frumpy coat and the clumpy shoes. I'm so ashamed I keep looking down at my prayer book so as to avoid meeting Andrew's eyes. But then, after the service, while I hang about while mummy has a word with the churchwarden, I spot him coming out of the vestry. And suddenly I come over all awkward, as if I don't know what to do with my arms and legs, and I stand there as stiff as a poker. Luckily it starts to rain at that moment, which puts me out of my misery, because we've forgotten our umbrellas, and so we have to make haste and hurry home.

I enjoyed a measure of success at school, though I worked hard for it. And in the end I left with three A-Levels in maths, physics and chemistry. My marks would have been good enough to get me a place at university, but mother was against me going, as it was unprecedented in our family.

'We've made a lot of sacrifices, Marion, to keep you on at school,' she said. 'So it's your duty to go out to work now, and earn your keep.' As I was good at science, the school careers officer suggested I apply to the local branch of a big drug company. And you can imagine how pleased I was when I was offered a place as a trainee lab assistant! At first all they gave me to do was to wash out the test tubes, but then I came to the notice of Dr Carson, the head of our department. He was standing behind me one day, watching me work, when I heard him remark on the careful and meticulous way I performed my task. I was very chuffed to be praised by Dr Carson himself! And I was even more chuffed when, a few months later, his assistant left to have a baby, and I was asked to replace her!

I see myself hard at work, checking samples and ticking them off one by one on a long list covering four pages of close typing. I'm wearing a long, white overall that I've washed and ironed myself, and my hair is combed back tidily under a hair band. I note with approval that my appearance is neat and unassuming.

This sort of work demands my full concentration as mistakes are easily made, and I'm very aware that one small error could jeopardise the success of the whole trial! That's a lot of responsibility for a trainee lab assistant, but I'm determined to prove to Dr Carson that he can rely on my accuracy. When I've finished that job, the next thing on my list is to set up rows of sterilised test-tubes. I'm very quick at this kind of work as I have agile fingers. Sometimes I think they know what to do without having to receive instructions from my brain!

'You're getting on like a house on fire,' says Dr Carson, who has just come in the door. 'You did that in half the time it used to take Pauline!'- Pauline was my predecessor.

I flush with pleasure at this compliment, and Dr Carson stays for a while, talking about this and that, while I go on with my work. I studiously avoid looking up and meeting his eyes, because Dr Carson has started giving me long, intense looks of late, that make me feel vaguely uncomfortable.

When I get home at six, my working day isn't finished by a long chalk. Daddy's leg has got so bad now he can hardly walk, and my mother's health is not the best, so it's fallen to my lot to be their carer. I cook their lunch before I leave for work, and shop on the way home, and get the washing and ironing done in the evenings after supper. On Saturdays, following my mother's example, I give the house a thorough clean from top to bottom, so my only free time is on Sundays when we go to church.

I must confess that there are days when it all gets on top of me, and I become an old misery guts. Then I give myself a little scolding.

'What are you moping for, a great girl like you?' I say. 'You should be ashamed of yourself. You have so much to be thankful for!'

'Excuse me, Meg, but I have to butt in. I'm IG your inner guide. You remember me, don't you, from the incarnation group?'

'I've never been to an incantation group in my life!'

'Incarnation, dear, but don't worry if you've forgotten. It's an effect of the amnesia!'

'Amnesia? That sounds serious. If I had amnesia, I'd be very worried indeed!'

'It's normal to have amnesia when you incarnate, so no cause for concern. I just popped by to see how you were doing.'

'And found me having a moan. I'm sorry.'

'Don't apologise, Meg. It's good to express your feelings.'

'Well most of the time I'm patient, and try to bear my burdens cheerfully, but, when I compare my life to the lives of other girls my age, it does seem a bit unfair.'

'Then perhaps you need to be reminded that you chose these circumstances. I can remember us writing them into your life script. It was your belief then that a good life is a life of sacrifice and service.'

'That's what I still believe.'

'Then are you open to doing some self-inquiry?'

'As long as it's not too upsetting.'

'If a thing upsets you, Meg, that's a sure sign there's something behind it that you need to understand better.'

'Alright, I'll do it.'

'Then tell me why you don't allow yourself any me time?'

'That should be obvious! I've got a full-time job, and two decrepit parents on my hands. But, if I have to work my fingers to the bone, it's my sisters' fault, because they left me to carry the can. Mary has emigrated to New Zealand, and you can't get further away than that, and Annie very conveniently lives up in Scotland!'

'Meg, do I detect some bitterness in your voice?'

'Hmmm.... well maybe deep down I am resentful, because I feel they're getting off too lightly.'

'But, if your life is all work and no play, you're also to blame. You make extra work for yourself by having such high standards.'

'Yes, I know I'm a perfectionist. I've always believed a job worth doing is a job worth doing well.'

'But beneath a belief like that could lie an irrational fear of making mistakes.'

'Mistakes shouldn't happen and, if they do, it only proves your mind's not on your job!'

'You're very hard on yourself in that respect, Meg, and I've noticed you coming down hard on others too. That's the trouble with being a perfectionist - you expect everyone else to be perfect too!'

'I know I can be critical but, when I draw someone's attention to a mistake they've made, I'm only trying to be helpful.'

'Other people don't see it that way. And to err is human, Meg.'

'Tell that to Dr Carson! We can't afford to make mistakes where I work. It could cost people their lives.'

'Yes, you need to maintain a high standard there, but, when you try to keep up such high standards at home too, you don't get any free time, and that makes you resentful.'

'But I'm not often in a bad mood, IG. I usually go about my work cheerfully enough.'

'If you deny your negative feelings, Meg, you'll never be able rise above them.'

'I have positive feelings too. I haven't become a carer merely out of a sense of duty. It's out of love.'

'I know that, Meg, because I can see into your heart. And all the love you're giving out, through looking after your parents so well, will return to you one day. But, in the meantime, make space to do things that you enjoy doing, and that are only for you.'

TWENTIES

Dr Carson has entrusted me with running his present series of trials. He calls me his good fairy, because he says I have the magical gift of creating order out of chaos. However there's one little fly in the ointment. The other day, when we were alone together in the lab, Dr Carson started to get personal. And in an intimate tone of voice, that was rather inappropriate in the circumstances, he started telling me about his marriage - how he and his wife didn't get on, and how they had these awful rows.

And then he added, 'I should have married someone amenable like you, Marion, instead of my virago of a wife.'

Well! I wanted to sink through the floor, and I must have been blushing all over like a beetroot, but somehow I managed to go on with my work as if nothing was amiss.

But now I'm on my guard, and I feel myself tensing up every time Dr Carson comes into the room. The trouble is I can't stop thinking about him. It's as if he's got a hold on my mind, and this makes me feel very guilty, because Dr Carson is a married man. And it puts me in another dilemma, because now I don't know whether I love Andrew still or not. We'll have to see when he comes back from university for the Christmas break.

I'm going to church alone tonight because mother's not feeling up to it. I'm wearing my best kid gloves, and carrying my prayer book bound in white leather that was a confirmation present. As the choir start to enter through the transept, I feel a thrill of anticipation, and sure enough there's Andrew bringing up the rear, and looking as handsome as ever. He throws me a sultry look as of old. And, as they launch into the first hymn, I hear his warm baritone again blending in with the chirping of the choirboys.

When the service is over, and we emerge into the frosty night air, I join the group of chattering parishioners at the gate. Everyone is talking at once. They all have a lot to say to each other, having kept quiet for a whole hour during the service. I'm keeping my eye on the vestry door, and at last I see Andrew emerging. To my surprise he comes straight over.

'Can I walk you home?' he asks, very friendly.

'If you like,' I reply, nonchalently.

Our progress up the hill is slow, as we're engaged in an animated discussion on the nature of the trinity. I must say I'm shocked to hear him expressing some views that are highly unorthodox. And, when he starts criticising the vicar's sermon, I start to wonder whether it was a good idea for him to go up to university.

We arrive at my front gate, and stand there for a moment looking at each other. There's an awkward silence. Then in one foul swoop he encloses me in a steamy embrace. As Andrew is long and lanky, and I'm a good head shorter than him, my face is now pressed up tightly against his collar. And all I can see is a large spot on his neck that has grown a white head, and is at that stage when it's just about to burst.

We stand there for what seems an eternity before he bends down and plants a kiss right on my mouth. I know this is my cue to respond, but I dither because I don't know how. In the end I give him a peck on the cheek, which unfortunately is immediately misunderstood.

'You virgins are all the same!' he exclaims in a bitter voice disentangling himself. 'You should have gone up to university, Marion. That would have loosened your morals!'

Then, with a mocking little bow, and 'Farewell till we meet again', he vanishes into the night, leaving me feeling like a worm that's just been squashed.

'And how was the service, dear?' mummy asks, as I let myself in the front door. 'Were there many people in church?'

Of course she's curious, so I have to sit down and tell her about it. She wants to know whether Mrs Norris was there, and whether the vicar remembered to announce the Women's Institute whist drive. But I can feel a headache coming on, which I use as an excuse to seek the solitude of my room. Once the door is closed behind me, I have a little cry, although I know that this won't do, and that I've got to pull myself together.

'What's the matter, Meg?'

'You don't know, IG? Then just look at me! I'm about as sexy as a barge pole!'

'On the contrary! Men find your brand of demure shyness very appealing, and they can sense the sensual woman inside you that's wanting to get out.'

'If that is the case, then why am I so uptight?'

'Perhaps it's due to your conditioning. If you feel shy and gawky and you're afraid of sex, it probably has to do with your upbringing.'

'Hmmm.... Perhaps it's because I believe that sex before marriage is a sin.'

'And where did that belief came from?'

'It's what we were taught in the confirmation class, and my mother also has strong opinions on the subject. She never talks about sex openly of course, but she's made it very clear that the worst thing I could ever do would be to get pregnant before I'm married.'

'So you're afraid of sex because your mother's afraid of sex!'

'Yes, but she can't help it. It was the way she was brought up. Poor mother! Her marriage to dad couldn't have been much either, seeing how disabled he is.'

'Then don't take her as your role model.'

'No.... The trouble with me, IG, is I don't know how to respond when a man starts making love to me - like Andrew did this evening. What do you advise?'

'Making love is like dancing, Meg. If you think about which foot to put forward next when you're doing the polka, you'll trip up. But, if you let go and trust your feet, you find they can manage very well by themselves. So leave lovemaking to your body, Meg, because it knows what to do. Just make sure that your mind doesn't interfere.'

'Oh dear! I'm not sure I trust my body. What about my animal urges? Surely I should keep them under control?'

'When the body has to obey the mind, it loses its natural sensitivity and spontaneity. Then you become like a severed head, and you're not able to sense your body any more, or to enjoy physical pleasure.'

'That's just what it feels like.'

'Then always remember that mind and body are not separate. You only see them like that because of your belief system. The truth is they are one. The body is the outer layer of the mind, and the mind is the inner layer of the body.'

I've changed my job. In a way I was sorry to go, because it was such a privilege to be able to work with a gifted research scientist like Dr Carson. But my job satisfaction was being marred by the liberties he continued to take with me.

The day came when he received an invitation to speak at a big scientific conference in Sweden, and invited me to go with him. My first reaction was to feel chuffed, as it was an opportunity to meet scientists of international repute, whose publications I had read and admired. So I agreed, and Dr Carson went ahead and made the arrangements.

I enjoyed the flight because it felt as if we were going away on holiday, and Dr Carson was in such a jolly mood. But, when we landed in Stockholm, and arrived at the hotel, I was alarmed to discover that he'd booked us both into the same double room. As I stood there beside him at the reception desk, watching him sign me in as his wife, I thought about saying something, but in the end I held my tongue, because I didn't want to make him look foolish in front of the receptionist.

There was a sinking feeling in the pit of my stomach as we were going up in the lift and, sure enough, when the porter showed us into our room, and put down our cases, my worst fears were confirmed. I found myself staring in dismay at a king-sized double bed. Dr Carson must have noticed that I looked worried, because he came up behind me and slipped his arm round my waist.

'We're going to be very comfortable here tonight, aren't we my darling?' he whispered.

Well, I had to do some quick thinking. If I refused to be his bedfellow, Dr Carson might very well hold that against me, which could spoil our good working relationship. On the other hand, I knew I couldn't handle the thought of sleeping with him in that enormous bed. It might all go horribly wrong, and then there would be even worse repercussions. I'd never be able to look him in the face again. And what about my long-preserved virginity? Hadn't I vowed to keep it intact for my husband-to-be?

This thought helped to concentrate my mind. And I turned round so that I was looking him in the face, and in a trembling but determined voice I blurted out,

'I'd like you to be so kind as to book a separate room for me, Dr Carson!'

And that's what he had to do in the end.

I was right about repercussions, because something changed radically after Stockholm. Instead of joking and jollying me along as he used to do, Dr Carson's manner became formal and aloof. Then a new lab assistant was taken on - one who was pretty, and bubbly, and fresh from school. And I soon noticed that he was paying her the same kind of attentions he used to pay to me. But she responded differently. She was blatantly flirtatious, and her low-cut tops, and the way she wiggled her hips soon got on my nerves. So I let her know in no uncertain terms that her dress and manner were inappropriate for the workplace.

'You're just jealous, you stupid bitch,' was her reply.

I was very shocked, and took a big step back after that.

Then the day came when I entered Dr Carson's room on some innocent pretext, and surprised them in the act of cuddling and kissing. He was seated in his big leather chair, and she was sitting on his lap in what I can only describe as an indecent embrace. I retired in confusion. And afterwards Dr Carson even had the nerve to tell me off for forgetting to knock!

All of this upset me more than I ever could have imagined, and I decided that I had no other choice but to hand in my notice. So that's the story of how I came to leave, and good riddance to Dr Carson and his philandering I say. But my feelings thought differently, because there was a pain left behind in my heart, which made me wonder if I'd really loved Dr Carson instead of Andrew after all.

THIRTIES

I've always liked the idea of working in a government laboratory, so I decided my next step would be to take the Civil Service entrance exam. I managed to pass it with distinction, and was offered a post in one of the larger government laboratories on the outskirts of London. This meant a longer commute, but in return I'd enjoy the benefits and security of Civil Service status. Well, I've been an executive scientific officer for ten years now, and I must say that, on the whole, I'm contented with my lot - at least it could be a deal worse.

I still live at home. It's seven years since my father passed away, and my mother, now in her seventies, has poor health. After living the life of a semi-invalid for years, she's been finally diagnosed with chronic fatigue syndrome.

Her condition, however, has had the benefit of making us more health conscious and, as a result, we've both become vegetarians. My poor father wouldn't have liked that at all. He loved his sausages and his Sunday joints! But, as he's no longer with us, mother and I feel free to follow a meat-free diet, and we always eat plenty of fresh fruit and vegetables.

That's one of the reasons why I've taken up gardening. The others are that it's a useful way to spend my free time, and it gives me fresh air and exercise. This summer I managed to grow most of our vegetables myself, and it's such a relief to know that what goes into our stomachs is pesticide-free.

It's a warm Sunday morning in September and, when I get home from church, I immediately set to work in the garden. I've carried mother's chair out onto the lawn, so she can sit and do her sewing in the sunshine. Every little counts, I think to myself, watching her busily ply her needle. We have forty more kneelers to finish before Christmas!

Yes, I'm still an active member of the church, and they've put me in charge of the campaign to raise money for Ethiopia. So I wasn't keen on taking on the kneelers as well, as it's a huge task because they all have to be hand-embroidered. But I was promised plenty of help, so I could hardly say 'no'. And initially there was no shortage of volunteers, but, one by one, they all dropped out, leaving mother and me to soldier on alone. However, I don't complain because it's for a good cause.

'But you are complaining, Meg. I can hear it in your tone of voice. Why do you always take on so much?'

'Well, I always think I ought to be able to do all these things, so I say 'yes'.'

'And why do you think you ought to?'

'Because otherwise I'd blame myself, especially when it's for a good cause. But then it gets too much for me, and I end up feeling put upon.'

'You're not being selfish when you say 'no' to people, Meg. You're just looking after yourself as you should. It would help if you always started by setting your priorities.'

'I try. I write little lists of my jobs, and cross them off when they're done. But, as it's my principle not to put off till tomorrow what can be done today, I often end up trying to do everything at once.'

'And what about that other saying - 'Man comes home at set of sun, but woman's work is never done' - does that apply to you too?'

'I'm afraid so. Because, unless the house is spick and span, I can't relax in it and neither can mother.'

142

'So you're always on the go.'

'Well, I've never been afraid of hard work, but things you rely on have a nasty habit of breaking down and holding you up. Last month it was the washing machine, and we had to wait three weeks for a technician, and by that time there wasn't a clean tablecloth left in the house!'

'Poor Meg!'

'I'll often have a go at fixing things myself. Once I've understood how something works, I can usually discover how to fix it. But in the case of washing machines you need technical know-how.'

'Yes, you've a lot of practical skills and a good eye for detail.'

'That's vital in my present job. Do you think I'm cut out for the work I do, IG?'

'Certainly, though it does involve a lot of routine, which many people would find monotonous.'

'But that's what I like. Routine gives structure to your working day, and makes your life generally more predictable!'

MIDDLE AGE

Glancing at myself in the hall mirror, I get a shock to see how stooped my shoulders are getting. I immediately make a mental note to think of my posture and sit up straight. I'm also looking decidedly frumpish! Perhaps that's because I'm wearing my mother's clothes. They were too good to throw away, so I thought I should get some more wear out of them. 'Waste not want not,' mother would say.

She was taken from us last November, though everyone said it was a happy release, because the poor soul had been bedridden during her last years of life. This, of course, made extra work for me, but Mary was moved to come home from New Zealand to give me a hand. And this at least enabled me to take my annual leave and get away for a fortnight.

But, otherwise, having sister Mary in the house was pure stress, because she's such an untidy person and very clumsy. She'll break the handles off the cups when she does the washing-up, or knock over her wine glass and stain the tablecloth. And she was forever forgetting to change her shoes when she came in from the garden. So we would find nasty, muddy footprints all over the lounge carpet.

I couldn't help nagging her about this, which understandably got on her nerves. So, while she was staying here, our relationship became rather fraught. But the hardest thing to put up with was her pop music. Mary, who is into disco sound, insisted on playing her ghastly records at all times of the day and night. I would go round with my fingers in my ears, though mother, bless her heart, seemed to like that sort of music.

'At least it's nice and cheerful!' she'd say.

When the time came for mother's will to be read out, and Mary learned that she'd left the house all to me, she returned to New Zealand in a huff. She'd only received a small legacy, and so had Annie, but at least Annie had the goodness to say it was fair like that. She also thanked me profusely for all I'd done for both mum and dad, and this acknowledgement, coming from my big sister, brought tears to my eyes. But I was feeling a bit weepy anyway, as it was soon after the funeral.

The day before Mary left to catch her plane back to New Zealand something slipped out. Mother had always called me 'an afterthought', because I'd been born many years later than my two sisters. But Mary now corrected this by telling me, not without some relish, that I was not planned and not wanted. Dad had come home on leave for Christmas 1943, and that's when it had happened. In other words I was a mistake. So there's me, who's always been so afraid of making mistakes, and now I discover that I owe my very existence to an error!

Yes, last year was a particularly hard one, but it's over now, thank goodness! Mother has departed to a happier place, and I am liberated from my role as a carer after all these years. But I miss her very much! Not having my mother to look after any more has left a gaping hole in my life.

'What exactly do you miss, Meg?'

'Hallo, IG! Well, I think I miss the structure that looking after mother gave to my day. Now it feels as if my life has lost its purpose, and I'm wandering about like a lost sheep.'

'I can understand that, but what about the church? Your involvement there used to give your life a meaning.'

'I've stepped back a bit recently. In fact I'm having a little crisis of faith.'

'Tell me about it.'

'Well, when I look at my mother's life, that was so blighted by ill-health you could hardly call it a life at all, I can't believe it was the will of a loving God that she should suffer like that. And mother was always so devout - she never forgot to say her prayers before she went to sleep!'

'Her faith must have been a great comfort to her.'

'But it's not a comfort to me any more, that's the trouble! There's always been this contradiction in me, IG. On one side I'd only accept something as a fact if it's been scientifically proved, and on the other

I believed in the Biblical miracles! But, when recent research cast doubt on the authenticity of the gospel texts, I started wondering whether the Bible was the word of God after all.'

'It must be hard to reconcile the scientist in you with the believer.'

'Yes, and the conclusion I've reached is that the virgin birth and the resurrection from the dead must be myth, because God wouldn't create the universe to run according to natural laws and then make exceptions, would he? That wouldn't be acceptable, because, by definition, laws should not have exceptions or else they are not laws.'

'That's what your reason says, but faith is a matter of intuition. Perhaps worrying your mind about these issues is a way of avoiding your feelings, Meg?'

'What do you mean?'

'Well, you're going through a very unsettling time emotionally. Not only are you grieving for your mother, but Mary's revelation has also upset you.'

'Yes, it was a shock to hear I was a mistake, but, when I think about it, it could explain why my poor mother was so terrified of me getting pregnant.'

'Yes, and it also explains why you were so fixated on serving her. Deep down you knew you were an unwanted child, and perhaps you were unconsciously hoping that, through becoming indispensable, you would earn her love.'

'And did I earn it?'

'Love doesn't need to be earned. But your mother was taught a lesson, because the child she had rejected at the outset became the faithful daughter who stayed by her, and nursed her through her long years of ill health.'

'Yes, and she grew to love me - I know she did. So that proves that everything turns out for the best, doesn't it!'

After mother's funeral Annie and I grew closer. And now I've accepted an invitation to go up to Scotland and stay on her farm. We're going to go hiking in the lovely hill country around where she lives, and I've gone and splashed out on a new pair of walking boots for the occasion. But first there's three more months of slog to get through at the office.

The fact that I'm crossing off the weeks until my holiday proves I'm no longer happy in my job, because the Civil Service is not what it used to be. Long-standing procedures have been changed of late to create even more bureaucratic red tape for us to wade through. But the main reason why I don't enjoy going to work is that I don't get on with my boss.

Henry Heath is a domineering little man, who addresses us in the sort of tone that white plantation owners used to their slaves! He's always giving me work to do that is outside my job description, and which he should be doing himself, and I allow myself to be loaded with it like a patient donkey. Blessed are the meek because they never protest! I've tried to escape his clutches by getting myself transferred to another department, but my application was turned down - probably because he refused to back it. And now I don't know what else to do.

'Well, Meg, you could try some self-inquiry.'

'Alright, IG, because I've got to find a solution.'

'So tell me what your options are.'

'Well, either put up with Henry Heath or leave.'

'And there's a third one - you could stand up for your rights and resist being exploited.'

'Oh dear, but I'm not very heroic. I usually keep my head down. Although I think I'd be able to stand up for myself better if I had a woman boss. It's because Mr Heath is a man and moreover a misogynist. Everyone knows he doesn't like women.'

'Or is it the other way round, Meg, and you don't like men? I've noticed there's been no man in your life for quite a while.'

'And that's how I like it. Men only create trouble.'

'It's what they are there for! Women need stirring up every now and then.'

'No thank you! I can manage very well without them!'

'But deep down you're disappointed that the man of your dreams has failed to turn up so far.'

'I no longer believe in his existence. The various specimens I've been out with soon cured me of that illusion. They were either married, like that womaniser Dr Carson, or they were hopeless cases from the start. For example there was Simon - talking to him was like trying to hammer nails into a brick wall. And then there was Bill who was so careless about his personal hygiene that you wanted to hold your nose when he kissed you!'

'And then there was Andrew...'

'He married another. And, according to church gossip, he's now joined the ranks of the married womanisers, so I'm left with the old maid card!'

'You're very hard to please, Meg. The fact is no man has ever been good enough for you. But focusing on their faults can blind you to their virtues. So you need to change this pattern, or it will condemn you to stay single and sexually frustrated all your life.'

'Huh! If there's one thing I don't miss it's sex! Though that's not a socially acceptable thing to say today. Morals have been turned upside down since I was a lass. And, yes IG, I do know what I'm talking about, because I'm no longer a virgin.'

'Oops! And I thought that, as your higher self, I knew everything about you!'

'I've kept that well hidden. Do you remember that fling I had with a Spanish waiter on the Costa del Sol in 1980 - a rather sordid interlude? Well, that's when it happened. Are you shocked?'

'No, I'm pretty unshockable. I'm more concerned about your repressed feelings. They don't just go away, you know - they go on accumulating below the surface. And, unless you find ways to express them, they can be detrimental to your health.'

'But what can a single girl like me do?'

'Change the way you relate to men. Focus on their good points rather than on their faults, for example.'

'And what if they have no good points?'

'Everyone has something going for them - even you, Meg! But I know why you're keeping such a tight lid on your feelings. It's because you've been once bitten, and now you're twice shy. The wound that Dr Carson inflicted on your young heart went deeper than you realised. But a new love interest in your life will help that wound to heal.'

'A new love interest indeed! My immediate problem, in case you've forgotten, is how to deal with Henry Heath.'

'You'll just have to be brave, Meg, and stand up to him.'

Things have come to a head. I've finally challenged my boss, and this is how it happened. As you know, I've always been a bit neurotic about making mistakes, and it's my habit to check and double-check everything. Well, last week I found a mistake when I was going through a report, and it was one that Henry Heath had made. It had caused a whole section of our current trials to go totally haywire. The poor lab assistant got the blame for it, and was in disgrace. But here was the proof, before my very eyes, that Henry Heath was the culprit. And what do I do? Instead of keeping my head down, as I would have done in the past, I march into his office, bold as brass, to have it out with him.

And guess what - the great man didn't even have the guts to own up. He tried to lie his way out of it instead, and was abusive towards me into the bargain. Well, I've lost every ounce of respect for him now, if I ever had any in the first place, and I'm thinking of handing in my notice, and quoting this incident as my grounds. What do you say, IG, shall I go ahead and quit?

'Taking decisive action is always empowering, Meg. It's better than grumbling and putting up with things. That makes you feel like a victim.'

'But wouldn't it be rather reckless of me to quit the Civil Service at my age?'

'What have you got to lose?'

'My security in the first place! Civil servants have a job for life, and the house is getting so expensive to run. There's some costly maintenance work that will soon need doing, so I need to have a regular salary coming in.'

'But, if I know you Meg, you'll be able to manage very nicely on a reduced income. You're someone who enjoys having to be economical.'

'True. I take after my poor mother there. She always scrimped and saved, even when she didn't have to any more. 'Look after the pennies and the pounds will look after themselves,' was her motto. So, if I leave the Civil Service, I'll have to get another job, which might not be so easy at my age.'

'Don't start out with a negative expectation. Recognise your talents instead, and acknowledge your achievements. That will boost your self-esteem, and help you find a job, because as we value ourselves so we are valued by others.'

'If that's the case, I've been a self-saboteur most of my life, because I'm always putting myself down. I'm so worried about sounding boastful and arrogant that I'd rather hide my light under a bushel.'

'But this can be changed. In the end it's about self-respect, and you're feeling much more confident now that you've had the courage to take on your boss. So go ahead, Meg, give in your notice and good luck!'

I did it. I handed in my notice but, instead of mentioning Henry Heath, I cited health reasons as my grounds, which wasn't very confrontational of me, but it avoided bad blood. Now I'm unemployed for the first time in my life, and feeling guilty about being a burden on the tax payer. But it's good to have a break to recuperate before I apply for a new post.

I've been catching up on all the necessary jobs around the house and garden, and looking forward to my walking holiday with Annie. Now it's the night before I'm due to leave. This time tomorrow I'll be in Scotland, and as usual I've planned my journey right down to the last detail. But, instead of getting my beauty sleep, I'm lying here awake, worrying about all the things that could go wrong on the journey tomorrow. I don't know why but, since I left work, I seem to worry much more. And it's about all sorts of silly little things, like whether I've forgotten to turn off the gas or lock the back door.

'You're in the habit of worrying, Meg. So, now the responsibilities that came with your job are gone, your mind has replaced them with a lot of trivial cares instead. You'll have to do some self-inquiry there.'

'Hmmm... Perhaps my habit of worrying has to do with my need to have things under control. I always try to plan ahead to prevent something unexpected happening, but then I still worry that I've overlooked something.'

'And what's so scary about the unexpected?'

'I might find myself in a situation where I don't know what to do.'

'You don't trust yourself to be able to cope?'

'No, and that's why I become prey to negative thoughts. And it's such a bother at night when I want to sleep. They keep going round and round in my head.'

'Perhaps they are serving a purpose. For example, they keep your mind busy, and that prevents you from feeling certain feelings.'

'What for example?'

'Sadness, loneliness.'

'I don't like to admit to being sad and lonely.'

'Everyone feels sad and lonely sometimes. So what does worrying do to you, Meg?'

'It makes me feel bad.'

'Then you could be feeling bad unnecessarily, because most of your negative expectations will never materialize. And, while you're worrying, you're missing the chance to feel good in the present moment.'

'Yes, I see that now. So is there any cure?'

'Mind training is the only solution. If you can train your mind to stay in the present, you'll be able to enjoy the gifts of the present moment. And, as far as the future is concerned, what you need is trust - trust in God or in existence, but most important of all trust in yourself.'

I've just arrived home from the hospital. I received my diagnosis today, and I've got breast cancer. The consultant assured me that the majority of breast cancers are curable nowadays, and I've been given an appointment for an operation to remove part of my left breast. This is to be followed by a course of chemotherapy. Oh dear! I really don't know how I'm going to get through the coming weeks!

I'm in the library. I thought to myself the first thing you must do is find a book on it. And there's plenty of cancer literature on the shelves. Most of the books describe the orthodox treatments, but there are some on complementary therapies. Although I'm usually sceptical about practises that are unscientific, because they are not evidence based, I feel attracted to these books, and I take a couple out to read at home. Then, as I'm leaving, the librarian hands me a brochure about a cancer self-help group that meets locally.

The operation is successful and, when I come out of hospital, Annie is waiting there to look after me. Once again she becomes my big sister, and I'm her baby who needs to be loved and cared for. Annie understands how vulnerable I'm feeling, and she's very patient and considerate.

Lying here in bed brings up memories of our poor mother. And the alternative health book I'm reading helps me to see her debilitating illness in a new light. If it's true, as they maintain, that all health problems have psychological causes, then perhaps my mother's belief system helped create her condition. She always saw herself as a victim of her complaint, and would never have taken any responsibility for it. But now I start wondering whether she had some investment in being ill. Perhaps it was her way of getting the love and attention that my poor father was unable to give to her.

When Annie has left, and I'm back on my feet again, I get round to ringing the contact number on the self-help group brochure. I'm invited to attend one of their meetings and, as soon as I walk in the door, I feel I'm among friends. Isadora, a plump, jovial lady, gives a talk in which she has nothing positive to say about orthodox medicine.

'All it can do for cancer is cut, burn or poison it,' she asserts.

She then goes on to describe some of the miraculous cures that have been experienced by patients who opted out of conventional treatment. And her conclusion is that cancer is a 'wake-up call'.

On the table by the door I find a lot of books and pamphlets. I flip through one about chemotherapy, and discover some facts that the doctors don't tell you. For example that chemotherapy involves being dosed with pure poison, which your body then has to detoxify. I find this idea quite horrific, and start wondering whether I should cancel my chemotherapy.

When I ask Isadora what I should do, she answers, 'Just listen to your body!' So, sitting in the bus on my way home, I have a go at it. At first all I can hear is some muffled digestive gurgling, but I slowly get the knack. And, when I'm able to tune in to what my cells are saying, I hear a clear 'no' to chemotherapy. Oh dear! How am I going to tell that to my doctor? He's gone and made all those arrangements for me now, and I do hate being a bother.

But then I think, 'It's my body after all!' So, gathering courage, I phone him and say, 'I know it's going against your advice, doctor, but I've decided to call off the chemotherapy. I'm going to go for a programme of alternative treatments instead.'

'Then you're making a very grave mistake,' he replies. 'It's been statistically proved that chemotherapy considerably increases the survival rate of breast cancer patients. So think it over again very carefully, Miss Goodchild, and then perhaps you'll see reason.'

But I've been seeing reason all my life, and look where it has got me!

I book a consultation with a nutritionist, who gives me some dietary advice, and tells me how to boost my immune system with herbs and minerals. And I join a spiritual-healing group who meet weekly to practise positive thinking and meditation. There I learn to use affirmations and visualisation to re-programme my body on a cellular level. At first it all seemed a bit too hippy-dippy, new-age for me, but then I notice that I feel a great deal better - not only physically but mentally too. And, most important, I'm learning to relax and to think positively.

Also the talks and workshops organised by the self-help group deepen my understanding of the psychosomatic links between my cancer and my belief patterns. I see now how all my life I've tried to be a good girl, and do what was expected of me, which often went against my grain. And, through trying to please others, I lost touch with my own centre. This resulted in the deep inner insecurity lying at the root of my irrational anxieties. I understand now how stressful thoughts and emotions can weaken the immune system, and come to the conclusion that my tendency to bottle up my feelings, as well as my habit of worrying, have led to my cancer.

During our group sharings people often break down and cry. At first I found that embarrassing, but now I'm able to see shows of emotion as positive. One day, while I'm telling the group about my long years as a carer, I'm overcome by an uncontrollable fit of weeping. In the past it would have been unheard of for me to let myself go like that in front of strangers, but now it feels very releasing. Afterwards, one of the men, who is new to the circle, comes over to me and gives me a hug.

'I was very touched by your story, Marion,' he says. 'It struck a deep chord in me.'

And that's how Michael came into my life.

Michael is very much the English gentleman. He's in his early sixties, tall and white-haired. He tells me he lost his wife through cancer three years ago, which led to him becoming a Buddhist. When the meeting is over, we sit together and talk, and we soon find that we have a lot in common. For example, we both love the countryside, so we decide to join forces to explore some of the local beauty spots. In the course of these walks, I discover to my great surprise that I trust Michael sufficiently to share my deepest thoughts and feelings with him.

And when, a few months later, Michael asks if he can move in with me, I say a reckless 'yes'. It feels as if I'm taking an enormous risk, but - surprise, surprise - I discover that I actually like living with a man, at least with a man like Michael. So, at the ripe old age of fifty-two, I have a boyfriend again, and I'm experiencing a nourishing relationship for the first time in my life.

'I'm not a virgin,' I confess shamefaced in an intimate moment.

'Your spiritual self is virgin,' he replies. 'It's eternally pure and luminous. But I'm happy if your physical self is a fallen woman!'

OLD AGE

With Michael's support, I was able to give my life a new direction. I'd become very knowledgeable about alternative health through my brush with cancer, and decided to train as a therapist. I chose reflexology and, when I was qualified, Michael converted the front room of the house into a treatment room for me. Mother must have turned in her grave to see what was happening in her lounge!

It took a few years, but gradually I was able to build up a thriving practice working from home. I felt as if I'd discovered my true calling, and over the years this work has given me a great deal of fulfilment. I've found a way of being of service to people, whereby I am also of service to myself.

With so much positive going on in my life, I could hardly believe it was true when I learned the results of the scan. Secondary tumours had appeared in my liver. They were discovered during a routine check-up, and Michael was even more devastated than me. We'd both believed that my battle against cancer was won. After all, I'd been free of it for nearly fifteen years!

'I'm puzzled, IG! Why is this happening to me now? I mean, I've learned to listen to my body, and I'm no longer as emotionally repressed as I was, and I don't worry like I used to, so it doesn't add up.'

'Life never adds up, Meg, because it's not a sum. It's a tremendous mystery.'

'But it seems so unfair. I've tried so hard to do everything right - health-wise I mean - and now it seems I've failed.'

152

'Don't see it as a failure, my dear. And it's not a punishment either for not looking after your body well enough. Nature in its wisdom requires every body to die, each in its own good time. And when our time has come, we have to accept and let go.'

'So, is that my present lesson then - to learn acceptance?'

'Acceptance and trust. You have done everything you can, and now there's nothing left to do but to relax. So just enjoy yourself, Meg. Savour each moment that life gives you. Take pleasure in little things - for example your daily shower, the blackbird singing in the cherry tree, or a cup of tea. Welcome each new moment as it arrives, and be grateful for all your blessings.'

I know I'm going to leave my body soon. And I've come to accept that my body in its weak and wasted state is no longer a good housing for my soul, so I'm ready to let it go. Michael is beside me holding my hand, and Annie and Mary have come to say goodbye to me. I feel very loved by them all. IG is there too. I can see him now, hovering between the floor and the ceiling, and I indicate that I want to speak to him.

'It's a funny thing, IG,' I say, 'but in the past when I thought about dying, I always imagined I'd die alone. But, as you see, things have turned out quite differently.'

'Life is full of surprises, Meg. As I see it, all that loving care you gave to others is returning to you now. But it's time to take leave of your body. Slip out of it very gently, as if you are casting off a garment and, as you let it go, thank your body for its long and faithful service to you.'

I thank my body, and we part company.

After a short space flight at a speed which, if I was still in a body, I would have found alarming, I arrive back in the group room, and it's as if I've never been away. Time seems to have hardly moved up here. I notice that the last bit of shadow is just receding from the earth, which means the eclipse is over. So how long did that take? Less than an hour I calculate, and yet it feels as if I've been gone a whole lifetime. Well, that proves the universe isn't logical. It's a tremendous mystery way beyond our comprehension, isn't it?

Life 7
LES the LIBRA

I've been in love with Isolda for aeons, though on earth our paths have so far failed to cross. So, when the opportunity arose to plan my incarnation and create my life-script, I wrote her into it. You see I've always felt incomplete - like half a soul wandering in search of my soul mate who will make me whole. But the universe is vast, and peopled with as many other-halves as there are pebbles on the beach. Thus it's been a hopeless task so far.

However, now that she's there in my script, I'm confident that I'll soon meet her in the flesh, although as IG explained, the future remains essentially undefined. It is, however, in our power to establish tendencies, which will be as strong as our desires. So, because my desire for Isolda is overwhelming, I'd say I have a fair chance of finding her again.

But, as I settle back into my reclining chair, all ready to begin my new life, a disconcerting thought crosses my mind - has Isolda planned me into her life-script? There's no way of knowing that. But if I am not in her script, and the wish is a one-sided one, will it take effect? And then there's the problem of the amnesia. It would be tragic if I bumped into her down there and I failed to recognise her!

My new life is beginning! A film is playing in my head in black and white, showing scenes of war-torn Britain. At first the frames move in slow motion before my inner eye, but then they speed up and sound is added. I can hear dance music, and a hall comes into focus, crowded with men in uniform. It's the sort of place where sailors on shore leave go to boogie-woogie with their girlfriends.

My inner camera lens zooms in on a couple dancing the quickstep. The man is very good-looking in a Nordic way, with gentian blue eyes and a blonde moustache. But his girl, who could be as young as eighteen, is a beauty - dark, shoulder-length hair, big doe-like eyes and lips as red as a rosebud! She moves so gracefully that I can't take my eyes off her!

They have danced the last waltz now, and the hall is emptying. I wait until they leave, and follow them as they stroll down the street, arms entwined, towards a small hotel. Once alone in the privacy of their room, they behave as if there's no tomorrow, and there may not be. There's a war on, and the man is due back on his ship at eight tomorrow morning, and the waters of the submarine-infested Atlantic await.

So the moment is fast approaching when I'll be required to spring into action. I realise that, to stake my claim, I must be first at the ovum, which will not happen if I'm my usual polite self and say 'After you!' But, when circumstances demand it, I can also be relentless, and, after some distastefully uncouth pushing and shoving, I am indeed first past the goal post. And the consequence is that, four weeks later, the girl with the rosebud lips discovers to her horror that she's pregnant.

Oblique rays of sunlight, falling through the high Victorian windows, illuminate the tiny blood-covered infant lying on the table. I can hear mewing cries and the sound of water splashing in a basin. The newly born is being washed and dressed.

'There now! Don't he look smart! Such a handsome little gentleman!'

The exhausted mother, lying on the bed, stretches out her arms. 'Give him to me nurse! Let me hold him!'

'Wait till I wrap him in his little blanket.'

As soon as I'm in my mother's arms I cease crying, and stare with wide eyes up into her face.

'Look! Oh look, nurse! He's smiling!'

'New-borns don't smile, dear. That's what's called a reflex action.'

'But he looked into my eyes, and smiled as if he recognised me! Oh the darling, the little sweetheart!' and she covers my head with kisses. It feels more like heaven than heaven.

'So what you going to call him?'

'William!'

'That's a nice name!'

So I'm entered in the registry as William Tristan Lovelock, born September 30th 1944. Lovelock is my mother's name. My father is entered as unknown.

THE KID

At two I'm a little Christopher Robin of a boy. My dog-eared teddy bear, Tod, goes with me everywhere. Mummy is sitting in the chair. Why won't she look up?

'Look mummy, I can hop!'

And I hop all round the room, but she can't see me because her eyes are closed. Then I notice tears on her cheeks. My mummy is crying, and I come to a halt dismayed.

'Mummy, mummy!' I wail, but she takes no notice.

'Mummy!' I wail more loudly, and run to her and tug at her skirt until she lifts me onto her lap.

'You're the only one I've got left, William,' she sobs, holding me very tightly. 'You're my little man now!'

I discover later that, after he'd been demobbed, my father returned to his wife and children. And I honestly have no recollection of writing that into my life script. On what grounds would I have chosen an absent father? I am perplexed, but then I remember IG explaining that the life script inclines, but does not determine our fate. There are deeper laws at work over which we have no control, such as the law of karma.

I see myself at seven walking home from school together with Chris, my best friend. I'm a pretty child with regular, clean-cut features, eyes with long lashes, and hair that curls softly down the nape of my neck. Although I'm friends with everyone in the class, and I'm invited to all the birthday parties, I'm happiest when I'm alone with Chris. So, as we approach the corner where our ways must part, I try to persuade him to come back home with me.

'But what could we play?' he asks.

I know what he likes most - it's kicking a football around. But as we haven't got a garden, I'll have to think of something else to tempt him.

'My mum's bed makes a whacking good trampoline,' I say. 'If you come back with me, you can have a go on it!'

Then, throwing my arm affectionately around his shoulders, I lead him talking and laughing to our door. I find the key in its usual hidey-hole. Mummy doesn't get home from work until six o'clock, and I hate being at home by myself.

I'm out shopping with mummy and uncle Trevor. We're in the shoe section of a big department store, because I need a new pair of plimsolls for gym tomorrow.

'They are over there, sweetie,' mummy says. 'Go and choose a pair that you like.'

And she sits down to continue her conversation with uncle Trevor. I walk disconsolately up and down the row of gym shoes, bewildered by the many different styles. I don't know which to take. Mummy calls over, 'Will, darling, hurry up and try some on. The shop will be closing soon!' which makes me even more nervous.

Why isn't she helping me? She's talking and laughing with uncle Trevor instead! Then a loud bell starts to ring, and a man in uniform comes to shoo us out.

'Sorry folks but it's closing time. Come back tomorrow!'

But tomorrow will be too late! I need my plimsolls first thing in the morning! I can feel the tears pricking my eyes, but mummy and uncle Trevor just think it's funny. They see it as a great joke that we have to leave without buying my shoes.

'That's Will for you all over. He can never make up his mind!'

Mummy and Trevor remain deep in conversation all the way to the bus stop, while I lag behind dragging my feet. It's not fair! She said she'd help me choose, and then she left me alone! Disgruntled, I watch Trevor kiss her goodbye. At least he's going, and when we're on the bus I'll have her to myself.

'Are you cross with me, Will?'

'No.'

'You are!'

'No.'

She's more interested in her carrier bags than in me. And, when we've found a seat, starts taking out all the pretty things she's bought.

'The question is will this go with my silk blouse? What do you think, Will?' and she holds up a frilly skirt that's printed all over with purple and white roses.

'It will look lovely!' I say.

I'm back in my role of her little man again.

TEENS

From where I sit I can see her profile outlined against the window. It looks familiar in a way that's strangely touching. I'm drawing it on the back of an envelope. Her hair is combed up into a ponytail, leaving little curls nestling round the lobes of her ears! I draw them very carefully. The coffee bar is crowded with grammar school girls all chattering excitedly.

'Sonia!' someone calls over to her.

So now I know her name! It's Sonia like the girl in *War and Peace*. My eyes follow her as she goes up to the counter, weaving her way between the tables with all the grace of a ballet dancer. I must get to know her, I think, but that's not so easy when you're fourteen, and the sexes are divided by an invisible boundary line that cannot be crossed without inviting ridicule.

I've found out where she lives, and now I do regular detours past her house on my bicycle. The day comes when I catch sight of her in the garden and I wave, but she just looks blank. I've found out other things about her too - like what she orders when she meets her best friend in the coffee bar on Saturday mornings. It's a strawberry milkshake. So now I always contrive to be passing when she's likely to be there.

One day I see her sitting alone at a table so, taking the bull by the horns, I march in and order a strawberry milkshake. My heart is beating so loudly that I'm afraid she'll hear it.

'Hello Sonia! Fancy meeting you!' I say.

She gives a sigh.

'Alright, if you're a good boy, you can come and sit here with me, and watch me slurp my milkshake.'

I know that, beneath her cool exterior, she's as shy as I am, so I try to find things to say to put her at her ease. And we sit there, deep in conversation, all the morning, during which time I discover hundreds more things about her. And everything she does and says confirms my inner feeling that we were made for each other.

After that encounter, it's not long before all our friends and classmates have accepted that we're an item - 'Sonia and Will' said in one breath and seen as one unit. When I'd used the word 'we' in the past, it had always referred to me and my mother. Now it stands for me and Sonia.

'You two make a handsome pair!' mummy exclaims with pride in her voice, as if finding a pretty girlfriend is an achievement equal to getting good marks at school. And she keeps saying, 'I'm so glad you've got Sonia. Now I needn't feel so guilty about leaving you alone when I go out!'

Because my mother is in the throes of a new relationship! Clive is the latest in a series of uncles who have come and gone over the years. None of them hung around long enough to be called 'dad'. But, with Sonia in my life, I no longer suffer from feeling excluded. A threesome is awkward, because there's always an odd one out, but a foursome, like the equilateral twosome, moves naturally into a state of balance.

Mummy and Clive have got tickets for a concert this evening, and I've invited Sonia round, knowing they'll be out. I've beautified my room for the occasion with some Indian shawls, and a pair of silver candlesticks borrowed from my mother's bedroom. The bottle of wine I bought with my pocket money looks very sophisticated, standing there on the table beside the two cut-glass goblets, and my guitar is lying casually on the bed. Before Sonia arrives, I light the candles.

Sonia is wearing make-up, and I'm glad to see she hasn't gone to town on the lipstick. Her choice of a white cotton blouse, together with a fashionable pencil skirt, also shows her good taste. She's sitting opposite me sipping her wine, when she notices the guitar.

'Oh Will! Is it yours? Can you play it?'

That's the cue I've been waiting for, so I strum a few chords before launching into my party piece. And all the time I'm thinking ahead. When I've finished playing, I'll offer to give her a guitar lesson, and then she'll come and sit beside me on the bed, and then it'll be as easy as pie to put my arms round her and kiss her. I shiver. The moment of our first kiss, which I've been imagining as something wonderful, is approaching!

And it all works according to plan, proving that I'm a smooth operator. Soon Sonia is sitting beside me, and I'm gently leading her fingers up and down the strings. Our first kiss is about to happen, and it seems nothing can prevent it, but suddenly there's the sound of the front door opening, and we jump apart with a common reflex action.

A moment later Mummy and Clive poke their heads round the door. And, when Clive sees us sitting side by side on the bed, he comes out with one of his crude jokes that makes Sonia blush. I could wring his neck.

'It's getting late,' says mummy. 'Sonia's mother will be worried, so you'd better take her home now, Will.'

It's a half an hour's walk, and on the way I apologise profusely for Clive's vile behaviour.

'He's the grossest yet,' I say, 'but he won't last long. None of her boyfriends have lasted so far.'

And I tell Sonia about the succession of men who have passed through, starting with my father.

'That was during the war,' I explain. 'My mother loved him very much, but he was married and he didn't tell her.'

'He double-crossed her then? Does it run in the family?'

'No, I'm not like him,' I say. 'I'm the faithful type!'

I'm imagining what will happen when we reach her gate. I'll put my arms round her and hold her close, and we'll kiss and time will stand still, and we'll be in heaven. But we arrive at her house to find her father waiting on the doorstep, rattling the milk bottles. So she says a quick goodbye before scampering off indoors.

I had to wait another three weeks for our first kiss to happen, but then it totally blew my mind.

I'm taking my A-Levels next summer, and then I want to go to university, but - typical me - I can't make up my mind what to study. Luckily the school careers officer knows what I'm cut out for.

'Your teacher's report says you have a logical mind and good communication skills. William. So we could make a solicitor of you. Have you ever thought of studying law?'

I hesitate because I'm wondering whether Sonia will approve. Her interests are arty, and solicitors have a dry and stuffy reputation compared to actors and musicians. Perhaps she'd prefer her future husband to have a more glamorous profession.

'Can you see me as a solicitor, Sonia?' I ask.

'Yes, it fits,' is her reply, 'because you're good at talking, and you'll charm the socks off your lady clients. Or you could be a barrister, because you never answer a straight question!'

I'm perplexed by this reply, as I can't decide whether it's meant as praise or blame. Sonia has become critical of late. She's definitely less starry-eyed about me than she used to be, but I brush this thought aside. The fact remains that we're getting engaged at Christmas, and we plan to get married when we've got our degrees.

My mother likes the idea of me studying law, so I go ahead and apply to Nottingham. And I'm overjoyed when I get a place, because Sonia has applied to go there to do a degree in English. But then my dream of us both going to the same university is dashed when she fails to get her first choice, and has to fall back on Dundee.

So our ways part at the start of the autumn term. We say a tearful goodbye on the station platform, promising to write to each other every second day. And we actually keep this up for a fortnight, after which our correspondence becomes lop-sided. I continue to send her detailed descriptions of everything I do, think and feel to which Sonia replies cryptically. Also her letters become increasingly infrequent until the black letter day arrives.

'Dear Will,' her last epistle reads. 'I've discovered that I don't love you any more, so I want to split. I hope this doesn't hurt too much, but honesty is the best policy - as you always say - although how honesty can be a policy I fail to see! Wishing you a happy rest of your life. Yours Sonia.'

I am stunned by her simplicity and directness. If I'd written that letter, I'd have gone round and round beating about the bush in an effort to make the bitter truth palatable. But why does she sign herself 'yours' if she isn't any more?

I'm in the telephone box at the Student's Union, and my small change is dropping through at an alarming rate. They are looking for her. At last I hear the echo of approaching footsteps, and Sonia's familiar voice says, 'Hello!'

'Sonia, I'm coming up to see you. I'm catching the night train.

We've got to talk!'

'No, don't come, Will. It wouldn't help because... because I've met someone else. That's why.'

This new fact immediately explodes my dream and creates a cataclysm of cosmic proportions! For five years Sonia has been the pivot around which my life revolved, and now I'm thrown out of orbit. I'm like a dislocated planet, doomed to wander for all eternity through the lonely reaches of outer space.

'Hallo, Les.'

'I beg your pardon - I'm Will.'

'Only for this incarnation! Otherwise you're Les, and I'm IG, your inner guide. Surely you remember me, or is your amnesia total?'

'It's total. I've a total blackout. I'm hardly eating, hardly sleeping, missing lectures, so it's not surprising.'

'This is your first big life crisis, Les. But never fear - your inner guide is near, ready to lend an ear.'

'That's comforting, because I urgently need someone to talk to. Sonia has cut off all communication, so I have no way of knowing what went wrong. I don't understand it, IG. We were going to get married!'

'And live happily ever after? Poor Les!'

'Her feelings must have changed, because she promised to love me forever. Those were her very words!'

'Human relationships are temporary arrangements full of trial and error. Their main purpose is to function as learning experiences.'

'Then, with respect, where does love come in? What about that great Shakespearean sonnet - 'Love's not time's fool, though rosy lips and cheeks within his bending sickle's compass come. Love alters not with his brief hours and weeks, but bears it out even to the edge of doom'?'

'Sonia will go on loving you in eternity, but down here it's all change. Do you remember how you were fixated on your mother? You never wanted to let her out of your sight. But then you moved on. You fell in love with Sonia, and now you hardly give your mother a thought.'

'She's gone and married Clive, that's why. She's compromised her ideals.'

'A romantically inclined young man like you, Les, may find this hard to accept but, when two people fall in love, they enter a dream world. Each projects the image of his or her ideal partner onto the other. Then, as reality slowly kicks in, the dream fades and they see each other as they really are - warts and all.'

162

'Sonia hasn't got any warts! What does that new boyfriend of hers have that I don't have? That's what I want to know!'

'A good question, Les, because it can lead you deeper into yourself, and self-inquiry is what you need most at present.'

'How do you do it?'

'Start with the warts, and tell me about your faults.'

'Hmmm... Well, perhaps I'm too much of a mister nice guy. And, as you see, I try to steer clear of difficult subjects. I also hate quarrelling, so I'll go out of my way to avoid a conflict.'

'Yes, peace at any price is your motto. But, when the problems in a relationship are glossed over, it soon begins to feel phoney.'

'Sonia may have thought that.'

'It's always a mistake to sacrifice authenticity for harmony.'

'So, if I change, will she come back to me?'

'Who knows? But my advice to you is, instead of fantasising about the future, or living sentimentally in the past, stay in the present. You're in your first year at university, Les, and there's a whole new world out there waiting to be explored.'

TWENTIES

But, instead of taking IG's advice, I spend my first year at university in mourning for Sonia. I convince myself that her new relationship is a temporary blip and that, come the next vacation, she'll be back with me again. Thus I remain hooked on her memory. And I shun the women students who make approaches to me, preferring instead to hang out with a gang of male friends.

I'm with them tonight. We're seated round a table in the Student's Union bar, and I'm immaculately turned out as usual. It's my habit to choose my clothes with the same good taste I use to decorate my room. When dressing, I always consider how the different items of clothing will work together, and it shows. I also go to an excellent hairdresser. Well, looking attractive is important, isn't it? It brings you advantages socially.

It seems my role in the group is to bring people together, and be a connecting link. I also ensure that the machinery of social intercourse is well lubricated. So, if I notice that someone is being left out and is feeling neglected, I'll do my best to draw him in and include him in the conversation.

'Yes, you have a talent for that, Les,' says IG, who is also present though invisible. 'But why are you so sweet and friendly to everyone all the time? Are you so desperate to be liked?'

'It's my nature,' I reply. 'I have a genuine interest in people. I'm always inviting friends up to my room for coffee to catch up on their lives.'

'You overdo that. Perhaps your time would be better spent at your books.'

'But creating a network of connections is also important when you're at university. It can stand you in good stead later on.'

'You need your friends more than they need you.'

'I need them when there's decisions to be made. Then I'll go around asking everyone what I should do, and they'll all tell me something different, so I get more confused. But I notice how flattered people are to be asked for their advice.'

'Then getting on well with everybody is more important to you than your sincerity. You say what you think the other person wants to hear.'

'Is that bad? I'm only trying to keep the peace most of the time. And if a quarrel does flare up - which can happen between the best of friends - I'll step in and try to mediate between them.'

'That's a role you learned to play early in your life when your father still visited you. He would come round to see you and your mother, though his visits always ended in tears. You couldn't bear to see her get upset, so you'd try to divert their attention to prevent that happening.'

'So I was a peacemaker from the cradle - that's interesting!'

Time has passed, and in the next scene I'm already in my second year. I'm on my way to a tutorial with Laura, my favourite lecturer. A quick glance in the cloakroom mirror reveals that I'm looking nicely tanned after yesterday's swim. I undo my top shirt button, and make my way down the corridor to her room where I knock on the door.

'Come in!'

She looks up from her desk and gives me a smile.

'Ah, there you are, William! Have you got your essay? Then take a seat and read it to me.'

I read as if I'm reciting a speech by Shakespeare, making the dry-as-a-bone subject matter sound dramatic which, judging from her chuckles, Laura finds amusing. When I get to the end, I sit back and enjoy watching her while she talks. She must be thirty-five if she's a day, and yet this woman is still gorgeous! I'm impressed by her poise and sophistication, as well as her excellent dress sense.

When we've finished discussing my essay, the conversation moves on to other topics. She's aware that I'm admiring her, because she keeps giving me little sideways looks out of the corner of her eye. Yes, there's no mistaking it - my tutor is flirting with me! Then out of the blue she asks me whether I have a girlfriend.

'Unfortunately not,' I reply.

'Excellent because I'm in need of an escort on Saturday evening. I've been invited to this dinner dance - a rather grand affair. Are you game, William, or would you find it a frightful bore to partner me?'

'I'm game,' I say.

'No, on second thoughts I'd rather you were the game-keeper, then I can be Lady Chatterley!'

We both laugh. It looks as if I've made a conquest!

After the dinner dance, things move forward at a gallop, and soon Laura and I are sleeping together. It is her wish, however, that our love affair should remain secret. So, when our paths cross in the faculty, we give the impression of having a normal student-teacher relationship. But sometimes Laura can't wait until we're alone and, when I pass her door, she'll leap out and grab me, and pull me into her room where we exchange passionate kisses. Or I'll find erotically suggestive comments, written in her hand in the margins of work that I've handed in. Yes, it's Laura who is making the running, while I play coy and hard to get. Well, it's all part of the mating game!

'So what is this relationship giving you, Les?'

'Hallo, IG! I'm not sure I want to discuss it with you. You'll open me up and lay bare all my secrets.'

'That's my job!'

'Well, alright, I admit that I'm flattered to receive these attentions from a woman of Laura's age and standing.'

'Then is it a status thing?'

'Not with me, but it is with her! She's thirty-something - she won't reveal her exact age - and a successful academic, who's achieved everything in life except a husband. So she's in need of someone like me to be her gallant swain.'

'We're not talking about Laura, Les. We're talking about you. What do you get out of it?'

'Well, an education in the erotic arts for one thing, and an introduction to an elite social circle, where I meet a lot of interesting people. Laura says she's making a man of me, and I'm certainly more self-confident now.'

'Your ego, that took a battering from Sonia, has been put back on its pedestal. Though, if people knew what you two were up to, they would call you her toy boy.'

'That's not very nice!'

'So do you love Laura or not?'

'I don't know. In a way I love her, and in a way I don't. I certainly don't feel the same as I felt for Sonia, and I'm clear that I don't want to marry her. So the answer is 'no' I suppose.'

'You don't know where this affair is going?'

'No, and sometimes it feels unreal - as if I'm not being myself, but I'm playing a part.'

'So, if you're not yourself, then who are you?'

'Whoever she wants me to be. I take my cue from her. It's as if Laura has got this image of what her partner should be like, and I do my best to fit the bill.'

'It sounds like a very unequal relationship to me.'

'I suppose it is. Laura's a strong-minded woman. She wears the trousers and I do as I'm told.'

'In other words you give in for the sake of a quiet life!'

'Well, it makes things simple if I let Laura decide. For example, when we're in a restaurant, and she asks me what I want to eat, I'll say, 'I don't mind - what are you having?' And if she says she's having the steak, I'll say, 'Then order one for me too,' because I never know what I want anyway!'

'You can't know what you want if you're always focused on Laura. You lose touch with your own needs that way, and end up surrendering your power.'

'Well, it may look like that from the outside, but there's plenty of power to be had from behind the throne!'

Laura is stressing me out. Those who know her from the faculty, where she's the personification of intellectual detachment, would never believe she could be such a drama queen. Yesterday, for example, I was having an innocent tete a tete in the common room with a girl from our year, when Laura sailed in and immediately jumped to conclusions. As soon as she'd got me alone, she accused me of chatting the girl up, and made a huge scene.

'But Laura, darling,' I replied, 'we were only discussing our course work.'

'Oh no you weren't! I saw you laying on the charm, and that little flirt was lapping it up!'

In the end I had to go to bed with her to make things okay again.

My end-of-term exams are approaching fast, and I urgently need to get down to work, but Laura still expects me to do things for her. For example, she's asked me to hold the fort tomorrow at her apartment, because she's expecting the delivery of a piano. I'm not at all keen to do this for her. I'd prefer to work in the library where the books I need are available, but as usual I say 'yes'.

'I can rely on you, can't I, Will? You'll be round at my place by eight?'

'I'll be there on the dot.'

'Good boy!'

I take up my post feeling grouchy. And, when her telephone rings, I answer it thinking it's the piano man, but it's one of her friends who wants to leave a message. While I'm noting it down, my eye falls on Laura's diary lying open on the desk. Last Friday's entry reads '7pm: Hamish dinner'. Hamish? That's her ex-husband!

Thinking back to last Friday evening, I remember her telling me she was going to see her mother. That's weird, I think! And, flipping back through the pages of her diary, I discover Hamish's name appearing at regular intervals. So is she still seeing him and not telling me? I'm so upset by this idea that I can't get on with my work. There's no alternative, I think, I'll have to have it out with Laura!

But this is easier said than done, because finding the right moment to broach such a sensitive issue is no easy task for me. So the weeks pass by and I keep putting it off, although I'm wracked with suspicion every time she says she can't meet me, and doesn't give an explanation.

'It can't go on like this, Les. You must take the bull by the horns and talk to Laura.'

'But I'm so loathe to open a can of worms, IG. It would spoil the nice time we have together. Isn't it better to let sleeping dogs lie?'

'When you repress uncomfortable feelings, they don't just go away. They remain in your gut and gnaw at your insides.'

'But IG, Laura will be furious when she discovers that I've read her diary, and I'm not strong enough at present to stand another scene. What I need is harmony!'

'It's an uneasy harmony that's achieved at the cost of truth, Les. So, when cracks appear in your relationship, don't just ignore them and pretend everything is okay when it isn't. Because, when your outer behaviour no longer corresponds with what you're feeling inside, you become phoney, and then your relationship becomes phoney too.'

'But I feel a great reluctance to broach such an unpleasant subject.'

'And why? Inquire into it.'

'Perhaps it's my fastidiousness. It wounds my aesthetic sensibility when we quarrel. And it hurts me to see Laura lose all her beauty and become ugly and coarse when she makes a scene.'

'Beauty cannot be without ugliness to complement it. If you accept one contrary and reject the other, your view of the universe will always be partial, and your consciousness will never be whole.'

IG has convinced me that I have to have it out with Laura. So on our next date I pluck up courage, and confront her about her ex-husband. She admits that she's still seeing him, and she doesn't see anything wrong with that.

'Sometimes I need to be with a man of my own age,' she explains.

I'm shocked because I've always taken it for granted that sexual fidelity is part of the package when you're in a relationship, and her 'Don't worry it's only platonic!' doesn't ring true in my ears.

'But, Laura, you go berserk if I drink a cup of coffee with one of my classmates. That's not very fair, is it?'

'Life's not fair,' she replies airily. 'We're all made differently, and what's sauce for the goose isn't necessarily sauce for the gander.'

I can't believe my ears! How can someone like Laura, a lecturer on British constitutional law, not be in favour of equal democratic rights? After her confession I lose all my trust in her. And not long after that we decide to call our relationship off. This time I get the post-mortem that Sonia denied me.

'You're very sweet, William, but why are you always so bloody tactful? I can never have a proper discussion with you, because you won't say what you really think. Where do you stand on current political issues? What are your religious views? I've never been able to find out!'

'They're the same as yours.'

'How boring! I've decided I need someone who's more my match - a macho sort of guy - somebody who takes control.'

'I thought you needed a sensitive, modern man, who was considerate and attuned to your needs?'

'No, that's all too wishy-washy!'

So my ego was knocked off its pedestal again, but retrospectively I can see my affair with Laura as a learning experience. She held a mirror up to me in which I saw myself more clearly, and she taught me what love is not. For example, it's not a trade agreement for the mutual profit of the parties concerned. And it can't be imposed from without, because, unless it takes root in the heart, and grows from the inside like a bulb in the dark, it isn't love.

168

THIRTIES

When I'd finished my degree, I spent a year at law-college before being articled to one of the medium-sized law firms in London's West End. After my two-year traineeship, I specialised on family law, knowing that a position would soon become vacant in that department. I also knew they were keen to keep me on. So now I'm a fully-fledged solicitor, living in an elegant apartment in one of the London squares.

We are holding a dinner party - 'we' now standing for me and my girlfriend Virginia. The dining room with its high ceiling and Regency plasterwork is coming into its own tonight. The long table is a-gleam with silver cutlery, and the colours in the central floral decoration perfectly match those of the tablecloth and napkins. I go round distributing the place cards. I put Virginia on my left and Joan, the head of our department, on my right. The other seats will be filled by various people of note, because wining and dining them is the way we attract clients of substance - and fill our coffers!

I'm on good terms with all the partners in the firm. I join the men's coalition in the pub at lunchtime, and I never forget to order flowers when a lady partner has a birthday. I've even found favour with our founder - a venerable old patriarch. We exchange pleasantries in the hallway, me standing with a polite smile on my face and my hands folded deferentially behind my back. As he moves towards the door, I follow respectfully several paces behind.

To put a solicitor's work in a nutshell, it's about resolving conflicts of interest, which is right up my street. I have what is called a legal mind, which means I can argue both for and against a case, and spot the loopholes in an argument. People skills are important in our trade, and I pride myself on being able to handle even the most difficult of customers. When they become agitated, I'll sit there calmly, nodding as if to give credence to everything they say. And, if they start shouting, I'll continue to speak slowly and insistently in an even tone of voice, which always calms them down.

I never cease to be fascinated by those representatives of the human race who beat a passage to my door. A large percentage of them are women seeking divorce, and it's my practice to offer some marriage guidance counselling during the first interview.

'Why not sit down and talk to your husband instead of plunging into litigation?' I'll say. 'If you could only see your husband's point of view, and meet him half way, agreement could be reached amicably.'

Whereupon one woman threw the inkstand at me. And my kind concern can be misinterpreted in another wrong way, as there are women clients who fall in love with me. So I've taken to wearing a large, gold wedding ring on my left hand as a deterrent.

One day, when I'm sitting there twiddling my ring, I hear IG say, 'It's funny, Les, but here's you pretending you're married when you're not, when your father did it the other way round - he pretended he wasn't married when he was.'

I'd never thought of it like that, but in both cases there was pretence and deception. And this triggers the continuing debate inside me about whether Virginia and I should marry.

'So what are the pro's and cons?' IG asks, trying to be helpful.

'Well,' I reply. 'There's a lot I could cite in favour of tying the knot. For example, I've reached the age of thirty, which is a respectable age to marry, and my present partner is of the breed that makes good wives and mothers. She also comes from a long line of solicitors, and her father is head of a London law firm.'

'Good heavens Les! Then what can be cited against?'

'Well, I suppose I hear too much about the seamy side of marriage from my unfortunate clients, and I'm aware of how emotionally scarring and financially crippling a divorce can be. And there's only one way to ensure you'll never be divorced, and that is never to get married!'

'Very true.'

'And Virginia and I are chugging along quite happily at present. Whereas, seeing the fate of some of our married friends, I've realised that legally sanctioning love is often the quickest way to kill it. In the past you would marry the first respectable person you met, and expect love to follow. What followed, however, was a brood of children, and these kept you so busy that the question of whether you loved each other or not never arose. But our generation has a choice, and that makes it difficult.'

'The crux of the matter is you're not sure whether you love Virginia or not.'

'Correct. And, in the case that I don't love her, would that be a ground for marriage? It would certainly be a ground for divorce!'

IG laughs. 'Your problem, Les, is you're carrying an image of your ideal soul mate, like a knight of old carried his lady's handkerchief. But romantic love is always more dream than reality, and it's not the best basis for marriage. There's another kind of love, however, that has more substance - one that deepens with the years. It is called loving kindness, and it's characterised by compassionate understanding, and concern for the other's well being. If that's what you feel for Virginia, then go ahead and marry her.'

'It's difficult to know what I feel, IG.'

I decide to let Virginia decide with the consequence that we're married within three months. And the following year her father makes me a partner in his law firm.

MIDDLE AGE

I've always nursed a fear of growing old, but at forty-two I'm relieved to find I still look presentable. The lines that have appeared in my face give it more contours, and my greying temples lend me a distinguished air. However, I've put on some weight round the waist, which I seek to redress by going jogging. Poor Virginia, on the other hand, is fighting a losing battle to keep her figure. I try to comfort her by telling her that I like buxom women, but she says she doesn't believe me.

This evening I arrive home with a bouquet of twelve red roses - one for each year of our married life.

'Happy anniversary, darling!' I say, greeting her with the usual kiss.

'And happy anniversary back.'

She's put some champagne on ice, and we drink to many more years of happy wedlock. Virginia and I have grown together like two trees planted side by side whose branches intertwine. We have two children: Amy who's eleven and Victor who's nine. Amy is like Virginia and Victor takes after me, so the family is like a neat multiplication sum - two times two making four.

Noticing that I'm feeling mellow after the champagne, Virginia decides it's a good time to henpeck me.

'It's such a drag when you promise to empty the rubbish bin, Will, and then you don't do it. You know I'm up to my neck now I'm back at work, and it's Molly's day off!'

I forgot - maybe intentionally as I've always had an aversion to the bin. Perhaps it's because I'm reluctant to soil my solicitor's hands, which must always lie clean and neatly manicured before me on my desk. However, as I don't want to get into an argument with Virginia on our wedding anniversary, I offer to take the bin out now.

'You can't because it's been done. Why do you always say you will, Will, when what you mean is you won't?'

'Don't forget that we're invited to dinner at the Wimpole's tomorrow.'

'That's typical! You always try to duck uncomfortable questions by changing the subject.'

'Remind me what the question was.'

'Why do you say 'yes' when you mean 'no'?'

'And why do you get so upset about trivial things like emptying the rubbish bin?'

'I'm not upset! It's you who's upset.'

'Not in the least - I'm fine.'

'No you're not! I can feel how tense you are. You go on talking in that irritatingly calm voice, when underneath you're seething.'

'Excuse me a moment - I have to make an urgent phone call,' and I get up and walk out the door. 'We'll talk about it later.'

Virginia emits a sound like an engine back-firing.

Well, I may be able to escape from Virginia, but I can't escape from IG, who immediately challenges me.

'Why are you running away?' he asks.

'Because I find it highly distasteful to engage in a slanging match with Virginia on our wedding anniversary.'

He sighs. 'You're still using the same old bag of tricks to avoid being confronted, Les. First you tried to change the subject. Then you answered her question with another question, and, when she still didn't give up, you ran away.'

'Well, it was the wrong time, and anyway, you're making a mountain out of a molehill.'

'I'm only trying to save your marriage.'

'With respect, our marriage is not on the rocks. Our friends are always citing it as an example of a marriage that actually works! No no, IG. This is a mere domestic tiff.'

'Then why get so upset?'

'Because, when I come home tired from the office, I'm in need of peace and quiet. But what do I find - the kids not in bed and the house in a shambles! Yes, I know children have their own agenda, but I happen to have a low tolerance threshold for noise and mess, which is why I get tense. And, if I'm required to discuss sensitive issues with my wife on top of that, it puts me under an unbearable strain.'

'So you acquiesce to Virginia's wishes in the nicest possible way, and then do as you please.'

'I give up!'

Virginia has gone back to work. She's a primary school teacher and her extra-curricular duties now require her to remain at school several evenings a week, and sometimes all day on Saturdays. So, left to my own devices, I've joined a tennis club, which serves the double purpose of keeping my figure trim, and offering me an interesting social life. Virginia isn't into tennis, but she's threatened to come to the dances and socials to keep an eye on me.

And very wise too, because men are a rare species at the club. Most of the members are well-heeled housewives with time on their hands. For an inveterate lover of beauty like myself, there's plenty on the courts to please the eye. And so I enjoy many lazy Saturday afternoons, sitting in a deckchair watching the young women play, their short skirts fluttering in the breeze as they serve and leap to lob.

Later on we gather at the bar. I'm standing beside one of these young ladies at present, and she's revealing to me how she keeps her body tanned and fit during the winter months. She goes to a fitness club for regular workouts, she says, where she has the free use of a sun-bed.

'And they have a marvellous indoor pool. So, if you want to come for a swim any time, I could take you in as my guest.'

'That's very kind of you,' I reply, although I think to myself, 'Before I show myself in my swimming trunks, I'll have to go on a diet. I don't want to look like lamb undressed as mutton!'

While I'm standing there, sipping my cider, a girl I've never seen at the club before catches my eye. She's seated at the table in the window, and I find myself staring at her profile. Her long brown hair is brushed up into a ponytail, and she's wearing silver earrings. Suddenly I find myself shivering as if I've caught a chill.

'Who's that girl over there?' I ask.

'That's Tina - home from university for the summer vac. She's got a very snazzy backhand I hear,' says my companion.

As if sensing my gaze, Tina looks up, and our glances meet. And in that moment I know her, and I know that I've always known her. We smile at each other, and it's like a smile of recognition. However, before I have a chance to talk to her, she gets up to leave. Thank goodness I'm wearing shades, because there are tears in my eyes. I've always known I was accompanied by an invisible love, and now miraculously it has taken form.

Thereafter I spend all my spare time at the club, hoping that she'll reappear, but in vain! And, when I make inquiries, I'm told to my chagrin that Tina has gone abroad for the summer.

A year later, however, I bump into her in the street. I've just left the office on my way to the little Italian restaurant where I eat lunch, when she emerges from a tube station as if materialising from the depths of my subconscious. A flash of recognition crosses her face and we stop. Yes, she remembers me from the tennis club. Yes, she's in London now, working for a company whose offices happen to be just round the corner. How incredible! It can't be a coincidence. I remember reading that, when synchronicities start occurring, something significant is about to happen, so what does it all add up to?

I ask her if she likes pizza and she says 'yes', so I invite her to lunch. And, as we sit there in the crowded cafe, our chairs crushed together, I'm once more stunned by her beauty. And every word we say to each other seems loaded with presentiment, or perhaps it's teleology at work, and the pull of the future has us in its thrall. Because you don't find love - love finds you!

Our meeting leads to more lunch dates, and more lunch dates lead to an outing in the country, and the country outing leads to the inevitable. I wasn't looking for an affair, but existence, it seems, has decided I should have one. And I arrive home that evening with grass in my hair, and a burr in my in my underpants, which I have to explain away.

The time Tina and I spend together has been neatly planned into my office hours, and the occasional evening when I'm supposed to be doing overtime. We meet in her flat, which is a short taxi ride from my office. Tina understands that we must never be seen together in its vicinity, as we could bump into my father-in-law, and so far so good. Virginia hasn't noticed anything amiss either, so I've been able to keep my life running on its normal track. But, as the feelings intensify, and I become more and more obsessed with Tina, my life comes dangerously close to a derailment.

'This is the nineteen eighties, IG, and men of my age are having affairs all over the place, so why do I feel so bad about it?'

'You vowed when you were small that you'd never to do to a woman what your father did to your mother.'

'I did? Then that could explain why I'm such an emotional wreck. One moment I'm as high as a kite, and the next I've plunged into the depths of despair.'

'But at least you're in your feelings! Your life as a solicitor was turning you into an emotional fossil, Les.'

'Yes, Tina is my salvation. She's so beautiful, IG, and it's such a gift to be in love with her!'

'So do you love her because she's beautiful, or is she beautiful because you love her?'

'I don't know - both at once.'

'As I see it, Tina has the power to evoke these feelings in you because she corresponds to the image in your subconscious that Jung called the anima. It's your anima, Isolda, who you're really in love with, Les.'

'Isolda? That's the name I used to give to my dream woman. But why must love lead to these moral dilemmas? I don't think I can stand going on deceiving Virginia for much longer.'

'Then go to her and make a clean breast of it.'

'I can't! It would hurt her terribly.'

'Knowing Virginia, I would say she'd prefer you to be honest with her. And telling her the truth would show more respect to her than continuing to live a lie.'

Honesty is the best policy. I know that, but it still takes me several months to summon up the courage to speak to Virginia. Then one evening, when the children are in bed, I take a deep breath and say, 'Sit down, Virginia, I've got something to tell you,' and I pour out the whole story.

When I've finished she's silent, while I look at her anxiously. Then she says, 'I knew from the start.'

'What!'

'It was pretty obvious, darling - all that strumming on your guitar and that pair of youthful jeans you bought, and the burr in your underwear!'

'And you didn't say anything?'

'Nope! Because I thought, if I close a blind eye, it will soon pass. You see I'd found out via the grapevine that she was only twenty! You miserable, middle-aged baby-snatcher!'

'So what do you intend to do?'

'I've done it already, darling. Two can play at that game, I thought, so I jumped into bed with Walter.'

I'm flabbergasted. 'What! Walter from your school - the one who drives the school minibus and chews gum?'

'That's him. So now the ball's in your court, as they say down at the tennis club. And, if you want your wife at your side again, you'll have to give up your bit on the other side!'

That's easier said than done, because I know that, if I abandoned Tina now, I'd wound her as deeply as Sonia wounded me. So I ignore the sword of Damocles hanging over my head, and do nothing. And for a while things go on as normal, except that Virginia moves into the spare room.

But now I'm haunted by the thought of that twit Walter hovering in the background. One night I dream that he elopes with Virginia in the school mini-bus, taking Amy, Victor, the dog and the hamster with him. It's sobering to think that he could have the power to rob me of my family, and that makes me realise how precious they all are to me.

I'm also worried that Virginia could tell her father about my extra-marital affair. I imagine a scenario in which he denounces me in front of the assembled staff as a scoundrel and a blackguard, and banishes me ignominiously from the firm. And this leads me to ask myself if I'm really prepared to sabotage my career for love of Tina.

It comes to a head when Virginia issues me with an ultimatum.

'Either you sever your connection with Tina,' she says, 'and promise never to see her again, or I'm going to leave you and move in with Walter!'

'And what about the children?'

'We'll share them out - one for you and one for me - that's only fair, isn't it?'

With my life now spiralling out of control, I turn in desperation to my inner guide.

'Virginia's got fed up with your prevaricating,' IG says, 'and is forcing the issue. Well, it's what you hoped would happen, isn't it? You knew that, if you sat on the fence long enough, one of the two women would decide for you, and that way you'd avoid the responsibility.'

'Look, IG, I've got a kidney complaint, and I'm suffering from nervous exhaustion, because I can't sleep without Virginia lying beside me. So, instead of lecturing me, just be a good fellow and tell me what to do.'

'If you're feeling under the weather, it's because you've been putting off making a decision. Prevarication always puts a strain on the system. So the sooner you can commit yourself one way or another, the better.'

'But IG, I'm in a lose-lose situation!'

'It seems like that because you're trying to use your mind to decide on an emotional issue. Your intellect serves you well in your work as a solicitor, but it's powerless in this situation, because it knows nothing of love.'

'Then what's the solution?'

'Listen to the voice of your heart. You'll recognise it because it always speaks very simply, and without complicated reasoning. It will tell you what to do. And then take action, Les, and never look back.'

I've realised that I need to find Sonia to exorcise her ghost. That's the first thing to do. It's twenty years since we last met, so she'll be forty-two - old enough to be Tina's mother. That's a sobering thought! Her parents still live at the same address, so I get in touch with them, and discover that she has a house in Worthing. They give me her telephone number and, as I'm dialling it, I notice that my hands are trembling.

'Hello!' she says.

'Hallo, Sonia! This is Will - a voice from the past.'

By the end of our short conversation, we've arranged for me to come down and visit her next Saturday. She says she's looking forward to it very much.

After explaining to Virginia where I'm going and why, I catch a train to Worthing. I take a taxi from the station to Sonia's house, and, while I'm paying the driver, I can feel my heart jumping around in my chest like a spring chicken. I ring the bell, the door opens and we stare at each other transfixed. She's aged of course. Her beautiful, long, chestnut brown hair is gone. It's been cut short and dyed blonde, and her mouth turns down at the corners. Life, it seems, hasn't treated Sonia very well.

Altogether I spend two hours with her, while we drink cups of tea and nibble biscuits. She tells me about her marriage and, as I listen to the long story of her acrimonious divorce, I feel as if I'm back in my office, and Sonia is one of my distraught women clients. All I want to do is get away.

'Don't go yet Will,' she begs when I stand up. 'I've prepared some lunch for us in the kitchen.'

But I decline. Sonia is so very needy, and I have nothing I can give her. When we part at the front door, she takes my hands in hers and, looking into my eyes, she says,

'As you see, Will, I've lived to regret my mistake. I should never have dumped you like I did. Do you remember how we used to say we were made for each other? Well, I still believe that to be true.'

But I don't any more.

'Say you'll come and visit me again, Will, and promise that next time you'll stay longer.'

'Sorry, Sonia,' I mutter, trying to free my hands. 'I can't promise that because... because I'm a married man, and... well... my wife wouldn't like it!'

When I'm halfway down the road, I turn and see her still standing there on the doorstep. She waves and I wave back. Goodbye Sonia!

OLD AGE

Time moves ever faster as you get older. And we must have fast-forwarded at least twenty years, because I'm watching my retirement celebration. I succeeded my father-in-law to become the senior partner in the firm, a position that I've held up to the present day. But now it's time to hand over the reins of power to the younger generation, and

I'm confident that my son, Victor, who is stepping into my shoes, will be a credit to the firm.

My family, together with my colleagues and the large number of friends who have responded to the invitation, are seated in the hotel restaurant. I'm wearing a smart new suit that my tailor made for the occasion, and flaunting a snazzy, puce-coloured tie to add a splash of colour.

The obligatory toasts have been drunk, and the meal has been polished off, and it's time for my speech. I'm feeling a tick nervous, but Virginia is at my side, ready to give me support. Virginia and I have been married for thirty-five years - time enough, you would think, to learn something about love. And, though what I feel for her is not the intoxicating love I felt for Sonia and Tina, it's deeper and more lasting. In fact it's what IG called loving kindness.

I've launched into my speech.

'Looking back on thirty-five years in the firm, I can truly say that I've enjoyed a rich and fulfilling career. The going was tough at times, but I feel I've completed the course honourably. Finally I'd like to express my thanks to the wonderful woman at my side, who's supported me through good times and bad with so much patience and love, by drinking her toast. To my beloved wife Virginia! Long may she live!'

Little did we know that Virginia would be dead within a year. The funeral was held in our local church, where she lies buried in the graveyard. They are keeping a space beside her for me. It's in a beautiful location, under a five-hundred-year-old yew tree.

'So here I am, IG, pottering round the house like a lost soul. I'm no good at being alone, you see. I get thoroughly miserable when there's no one to talk to. So I was thinking of visiting Amy this afternoon.'

'No, you went round there yesterday. Why don't you visit yourself for a change?'

'What do you mean?'

'You've been preoccupied with other people all your life, Les, which is one way of avoiding meeting yourself. But there's an opportunity now to change that pattern.'

'I'm too old to change!'

'Nonsense! As long as a plant is still alive, it's green and, as long as it's green, it can grow. It's important to learn to enjoy your own company, because, unless you can be happy alone, your relationships will all turn into dependencies.'

'I was very dependent on Virginia. That's why it's so hard now that I'm alone.'

'But Les, you were always alone, even when she was alive. You came into the world alone, and you'll be alone when you leave it again.'

'That sounds like a life sentence - or a death sentence rather!'

'And yet the paradox is that you're never alone when you're together with yourself. But, in order to discover this, solitude is needed. So use your time alone to go inside. Meditation can connect you to your inner being, and through your inner being you'll find you're connected to the whole of creation. And, once you've experienced this, Les, you'll never be lonely again.'

I take IG's advice, and join the drop-in meditation class that's held weekly in the local community centre. But, as it turns out, I don't have much time left to learn meditation or anything else, because, two months after Virginia's passing, I collapse in the street without warning. A passer-by calls an ambulance, and they rush me to hospital, but it's too late. The family say I died of a broken heart. And I'm relieved to have been polished off by a nice, clean coronary thrombosis, and so be spared a messy and undignified death!

Thus Virginia and I are reunited when my body is laid to eternal rest beside hers in the plot beneath the yew tree. And I know that, when my soul enters the other dimension, her soul will be there waiting for me.

Life 8
SUE the SCORPIO

In my first session in the incarnation group IG, my life coach, produced a twelve-sided dice. Instead of numbers it had signs of the zodiac on it, and my eye was immediately caught by the Scorpio glyph.

'It looks like a curled up snake,' I remarked.

'Roll it, Sue!' he said.

So I did and, when it came to rest with the Scorpio glyph uppermost, cold shivers ran down my spine.

'So you'll be our Scorpio this time round!' he said brightly.

'I knew it!' I replied.

I'd been very reluctant to reincarnate, but knew I had to do something. There was a huge shadow of remorse clinging to me and, as everyone knows, an incarnation is the best way to balance your karmic books. When the seeds we've sown in the past ripen and produce fruit, we must eat of it - even if it tastes as bitter as sulphur. And it was my belief that no compassion would be shown to one whose sin was to transgress the bounds of natural law. Surely I would incarnate in the most miserable circumstances, and live a life of pain and penury!

When I asked my life coach about my karmic repercussions, he replied, 'Your next incarnation will indeed be challenging. But joining an incarnation group is the best thing you could do, because now you'll prepare a life-script, and benefit from the services of an inner guide.'

'So is it good or bad that I'm a Scorpio?'

'It's good! In fact it's just what you need! You will have great moral strength at your command, and the warrior's skill of survival.'

'But they are such disgusting little animals. No one likes them - they sting!'

'Their poison is medicinal, Sue. And don't forget that the Scorpio archetype is also represented by the eagle, who takes wing and flies higher than all other creatures on earth. As a Scorpio you will have great power at your disposal, which you'll be able to use either for good or for evil.'

'I'll use it for good,' I say resolutely.

And this cheered and comforted me. So now, as I lie back in my reclining chair and close my eyes, I'm looking forward to my new life. It's going to be exciting.

I don't have to wait long before things start happening. What I see first is a dark red cloud shot through with blue and purple streaks of lightning. At its centre a naked man and woman are copulating, and the atmosphere around them is so charged that it attracts me like a moth to a candle. At the moment of groaning meltdown a vortex of light is created into which I am sucked, and I find myself spiralling downwards, deeper and deeper, until I reach the very point of combustion.

Then all light is extinguished, and I remain for what seems a long time in utter blackness out of which, in due course, a foetus appears. I see it floating in a luminous bubble. I can make out the contours of a face emerging at the bulbous end. Its eyes are black smudges, and its nose and ears mere rudimentary protuberances. In the place of arms and legs, the creature has newt-like flippers and, as I discover, my consciousness is able to move in and out of its one-and-a-half inch body.

When I'm inside it, I have a view of the interior of the bubble, which is full of water. It's as if I'm afloat in a salty ocean. But now I hear muffled and far away the sound of someone sobbing. An atmosphere of menace is spreading, and I no longer feel safe. Then I get a shock. A long, sharp object like a lance is approaching from the left, its point poking and probing. It is going to perforate the wall of my bubble and stab me to the heart. Then, as a scream rings out, I contort in a spasm of fear. I hear groaning and moaning, and the body encasing me winces with pain. Then the lance retreats as swiftly as it came, and the nightmare is over.

Six months later the foetus has become a fully formed baby girl, now so large that she fills the whole bubble. When my consciousness is located within her, I feel uncomfortably claustrophobic, as there's hardly room to turn. Where is the exit I wonder? Is it down there - that tiny opening like a plughole that looks much too small for me to pass through?

Help! Oh help me, IG! The walls of my bubble have started pumping like a pair of bellows so that I'm crushed between them. I'm going to be killed - but can I die before I've been born? Then I remember the power I have of changing my perspective, and gain some relief by switching to a higher vantage point. Hovering above the proceedings, I watch my mother, who has now arrived at the clinic, being prepared for her confinement.

'The waters have broken,' the midwife pronounces.

But it's tiring to maintain the perspective of the outside observer, and soon I'm drawn back into the womb again. My whole head is down the plughole now, with my face pressed out of shape like a screwed up rubber mask. But, most alarming, there's a cord like a hangman's noose wound so tightly around my neck that I'm close to strangling. And I must remain clamped in this position, as in a vice, for a whole day and night while my mother's contractions start, then stop, then start and stop again. Is it because I should have been hung in my last life that I'm on the gallows now?

I take a brief moment of respite outside, and notice the look of concern on the face of the midwife when she's checking my heartbeat through her stethoscope. For the umpteenth time she urges my mother to make a grand effort, but the poor woman has no strength left. She's failing fast, and at that point they make the decision to deliver me by caesarean.

Then it's all over very quickly. My casing is slit open, and a burst of light comes flooding in. A pair of green-gloved hands, that are larger than my face, descend from above to extract me. The cord is unwound from my neck, and I'm hung upside down like a skinned rabbit, and thumped several times on my back, while I protest with loud howls at this most unnatural entry into the world.

It's November 7th 1944 and my new name will be Kathleen Theresa Pitt.

THE KID

'You're very, very naughty!'

She drags me out from my hiding-place behind the sofa.

'Look what you've done - smeared dirty soot from the fireplace all over the wallpaper! You wicked girl!' and I get a hard slap round the face that makes me scream.

'Stop that racket, do you hear! It's driving me up the wall!'

But I can't stop, so I find myself being dragged into the hallway. I'm struggling to get free and kicking her shins. Now she's pushing me into the cupboard under the stairs.

'No, mummy, not in there!' I scream.

But, ignoring my cries, she slams the door shut and bolts it from the outside. I know this place well, and sniff the familiar smell of turpentine and boot polish. It's pitch black except for a slit of light along the top of the door. I find the old moth-eaten rug and curl up on it. I'm still crying - more in anger than in fear. I hate my mother!

Then I remember the spider, that big hairy one I once saw scuttling across the cupboard floor into a hole at the back. What if he comes out and starts crawling over me? I shudder. I'm sure I can feel something tickling my leg. Now I'm screaming again with all my might, and hammering on the door wildly.

'Let me out! Let me out!'

It's my daddy who opens it, come home from the office in time to save me from the spider.

'Daddy, daddy!' I sob, holding out my arms to him. He picks me up and holds me tight, while I wipe my wet face on his jacket collar that smells of cigarette smoke and trains.

'Now then, what's my little gypsy been up to?'

I like it when he calls me his little gypsy. Between my sobs I blurt out the whole story, and tell him how nasty mummy has been.

'And who played with dirty soot from the fireplace - was it you?'

I nod.

'Then you must say you're sorry to your mother,' and he leads me into the kitchen.

Mummy is making tea and feeding my baby sister at the same time. She gives me a black look.

'I'm very sorry,' I mumble, looking at my feet.

And she says, 'I've forgiven you.'

But I know that isn't true.

I was about three then, whereas in the next scene I'm at least eight. The class are walking in a crocodile to church - twenty-four little girls in dark grey uniforms. Heading the procession is a nun in a black habit with a long headdress. Another nun brings up the rear. Heavy crucifixes hang dangling from their necks.

Today is the feast of Saint Barnabas, our patron saint, and instead of doing lessons we're going to church. As I walk along in the crocodile my steps become lighter. I'm feeling light-hearted because church is better than school, and a million times better than home. Home is horrible now that daddy has left - or rather he was kicked out. My mother says he's a bad lot, and has forbidden us to talk to him.

'Keep away from that rat!' she told us.

But daddy is a clever one. He went to court and got visitation rights, and now he comes every Sunday afternoon to take us out in his car, and she hasn't the power to prevent it. After lunch on Sundays I go upstairs and make myself pretty for him. I put on my best dress, and undo my plaits so my hair hangs loose. Lucy, my sister, tries to make herself pretty too without success. She's got straight hair and sticking out teeth, and in any case daddy loves me best. That I know for sure.

When we arrive at the church, we file into the front rows of the pews. The priest, who's standing at the lectern, is reading from the book of Genesis, which is the first book of the Bible.

'And they heard the voice of the Lord God walking in the garden in the cool of the day. And Adam and Eve hid themselves because they were naked.'

My friend Veronica catches my eye, and we have to stifle our giggles. It's very shocking, but funny all the same, to hear a rude word like 'naked' spoken in church. But then there's the Lord Jesus, hanging life-size from his cross above the chancel, blood dripping from his hands and feet. He's stark naked except for that little cloth he wears around his loins to make himself decent!

The sermon is all about sin. And, when Father O'Leary asks us to remember the worst thing we ever did in our whole lives, my mind goes blank. There was something, but I don't want ever to think about it. And, after I'm confirmed and go to confession, I'll never confess it. I'd die of shame if Father O'Leary knew. But is it a sin, I wonder, to withhold confessing a sin?

'Be of good courage, dear children,' I hear Father O'Leary say. 'When the terrible day of your death and your judgement comes, then, if you are truly penitent, the Lord God will be merciful.'

But not if it's a mortal sin you've committed, I think. Then you'll go to hell, and nothing will save you - not even if you say twenty Hail Marys every day for the rest of your life!

TEENS

When I reach the age of fifteen my mother turns me out. My crime was I kept staying out later than ten o'clock - when the curfew she'd imposed began. One evening, when I arrive home after midnight, I find the bitch waiting for me.

'Where have you been, you little slut?'

'None of your fucking business!'

'Don't you swear at me, young lady! I'm sick to death of you, so get out! You can go and live with your father. And for all I care you can both go to hell!'

I'd switched off my feelings a long time ago where she was concerned, so I took her at her word. Ice-cold and aloof, I phoned my father, and arranged for him to collect me, and packed my things. My way of dealing with pain has always been to keep it under wraps. And, when the car arrived, I didn't even say goodbye to her, and all she gave me was a dark, livid look. Good riddance to bad rubbish, I said to myself.

'As long as I can remember she's always had it in for me,' I tell my dad, 'whereas Lucy's her golden girl who can do no wrong. But I don't envy her living with someone who's off her rocker. On some days she's like manic and on others she's depressed. She threatened to put her head in the gas oven last week.'

My father gives a wry laugh.

'I wouldn't take that seriously,' he says. 'The woman's deranged. No wonder you wanted out!'

It's a relief to be at my dad's place, because here I can do as I like. At first I resented Debbie's presence in the apartment - she's his new partner. But then I realised it was a good thing he was wrapped up in her, because it meant he didn't care what I got up to. So I'm free.

I've come home from school, done my homework and changed out of my school uniform. Now I'm getting ready to go out. I've smudged bright red lipstick on my lips, and attached a pair of false eyelashes. The pale foundation I've used on my face, and the circles of dark mascara round my eyes, make me look like some tainted creature of the night. I fasten my nylons to my suspender belt. They have seams up the back that make my legs look long and sexy in high-heeled shoes. No one will guess my age!

I've got a date tonight with a man I met in the pub last Saturday. I was out for the evening with Veronica (she's still my best friend - I have long and faithful friendships!) when I spotted him at the bar.

'Look over there - a fanciable bloke!' I said to Veronica. 'Just watch me pull him!'

I stared at him intensely until he felt my gaze, and looked in my direction. Then, once I'd got his attention, I started some steamy eye contact. Soon he was over at our table, asking if he could buy us a drink. He said his name was Rich, and, when he'd brought the vodkas we'd ordered, he stayed with us the whole evening. Veronica hardly got a look in. I had him totally transfixed.

I stride brazenly in through the swing-doors, not turning a hair about going into a pub alone, although many girls of my age would. The men sitting at the bar all turn to look at me. One wolf whistles, and another makes a joke that I don't catch, whereupon they all laugh. At that point Rich appears.

'She's my girlfriend,' he says roughly, 'so mind what you say about her!'

He takes me over to the corner, where we sit down at a table for two, and Rich orders a couple of vodkas. He's a man of few words, and, as soon as we've drunk up, he asks me if I'd like a ride in his new sports car.

186

'You mean the red MG that's parked outside?' I ask.

He nods.

'Very flash!' I say.

Some time later we're driving down a country road and it's just started raining. Then all of a sudden Rich drives into a hidden lay-by behind a hedge, and turns off the engine. It's getting dark now, and there's the loud sound of the rain hammering on the folding roof, but inside the car it's cosy and warm. Rich offers me a cigarette, and we smoke for a bit. I talk and he mutters a reply now and again. Then he shows me how the seats recline to make a double bed.

I knew from the first moment I set eyes on Rich that he'd be a good lay, and my feeling was spot on. In fact he turned out to be my best shag yet. By the time we're finished the windows are all steamed up, and I'm lying there thinking wow - what I experienced then was ecstasy! Yes, there's no other word for it. I've found the door leading out of the ordinary, grey world into a universe of energy, where we become so intensely and passionately alive that we shine.

A little later, we're lying side by side smoking, and it's still raining.

'How old are you?' asks Rich.

'Fifteen,' I reply proudly.

'Tut tut! What would mummy say?'

'If she could see me now, she'd do her nut.'

'I'd do her nut too!' says Rich.

'She's so screwed up about screwing, that woman. When I was living at home with her, she'd get my little sister to spy on me - tell her where I went and who I was with - as if it was her mission in life to guard my virginity!'

'Small chance of that with a sexy beast like you for a daughter!' laughs Rich.

Although he was a good lay, Rich didn't last long. He was too much on the surface for me, having nothing interesting to say and no deeper feelings to explore. Like most people I meet he lacked interiority.

TWENTIES

I'm dressed to kill. My new red shoes with their three-inch stiletto heels are crippling my feet, but they turn heads. They've bloody well turned Karl's head!

'Do you wear them in bed?' he enquired the other day, as we passed in the corridor.

And another time he asked, 'Are you getting enough sex?'

Cheeky bugger!

I'm in my second year of a degree in social science, and Karl is a psychology post-graduate, a so-called 'mature' student, and the energy is electric every time we're in radius of each other. I'm well aware of the power my sex appeal gives me over men, and I enjoy playing with it. However, once a man has surrendered, and is grovelling at my feet, the game is over because I've no patience with wimps. I need a he-man - someone brave enough to stand up to me, and who's ready to put the boot in when necessary.

One day I'm reading in the library when Karl comes up.

'What's your favourite position?' he whispers in my ear. 'Tell me what you like - it's for a research project.'

I fix him with a cold eye.

'You're asking the wrong person,' I say. 'I'm a committed virgin, and I'm saving myself up for Mr Right!'

'Cor blimey!'

The day inevitably comes when he takes the step of asking me out.

'There's a new horror film on at the Odeon that will scare your pants off. Will you risk watching it with me?'

Karl must be clairvoyant, because I have a weakness for horror films. Snake-tressed vampires, gothic castles and screech owls are right up my street, so I agree but on one condition.

'There'll be no hanky-panky in the back row,' I say.

And he must have taken me seriously, because he remains very respectful the whole evening, and even refrains from clutching my hand in the most blood-curdling scenes.

Afterwards, when we're walking home, he asks me about my commitment to chastity, and I reveal to him that I've been to a convent school.

'That explains everything,' he says. 'A catholic conditioning leaves a woman's mind in a very unhealthy state, because, when her sexual energy has been repressed, her nerves become distended, resulting in various forms of neurotic behaviour.'

His conclusion is that I have a backlog of sex energy to work through. He advises me to make a start on this right away, because compressed sexuality is like an unexploded bomb. It could go off at any moment, and cause a mental breakdown.

On our following dates, he continues to employ the full range of his Freudian know-how, and his considerable rhetorical skills, to persuade me to surrender what he terms my 'quaint and obsolete virginity'. All in vain!

However, I'm finding that, in the process of hooking Karl, I've become hooked on him. I am now passionately and viscerally in love with the bastard. So at this point I capitulate and agree to go to bed with him, but not before I've wrested a vow of commitment from him. I get him to swear by the one thing he holds holy - and that is his potency - that he'll always stay faithful.

'Which means that, if you ever dare cheat on me, you'll be struck impotent!' I explain.

'Christ! It sounds like a medieval curse, you old witch!'

And so we have sex together at last - a whole long night of it, as we discover that we're both insatiable - during which I successfully feign the breaking of my hymen.

There follows a summer of high passion in which Karl and I are besotted with each other. We pine for the other's body when apart, and devour each other when we fall together. But, by the start of the autumn term, some of the initial heat has been lost, and I realise that I'll have to box clever to keep Karl's eye on the ball.

We enter a stormy patch in our relationship in which we have horrific rows, and savagely tear each other to pieces. But each scene of devastation is followed by sex so incredible that it restores us to life again. Karl and I now live together and, shortly before my finals, I discover that I'm pregnant. When I break the news to him he says, 'Go and get an abortion!'

'Is that all you can say? I can't believe my ears! You want me to murder our child?'

He takes this as a cue to start on again about the Pope and my catholic conditioning. I can't take any more of that shit, so I start screaming and throwing books at him.

'I'll come back when you're rational,' he says, disappearing down the stairs.

I throw myself on the bed in frustration, and sob until all the emotion is out of me. Then, when I can think straight, I begin to see that he has a point. Having a baby at this stage would be inviting big trouble into my life. It would jeopardise the job with the social services that I've got my eye on, and drive my mother well and truly up the wall - not that I'd care about that! But I would care about losing Karl, who has always said that he doesn't want children.

I don't know what to do. And while I'm lying awake, in too much inner turmoil to sleep, I hear a gentle voice speaking to me.

'Are you ready to talk, Sue?'

'My name's Kathleen,' I reply, puzzled.

'Sue is your deeper self - the person you were before you were born. It's her I'm talking to.'

'Sue? It rings a bell.'

'I'm IG, your inner guide,' the voice continues, 'and, as your amnesia lifts, you may remember that I was your life coach in your life before this life.'

I remember a group of twelve, and a room like a space capsule with a view of the stars.

'IG!' I blurt out, 'you've got to help me! You've got to tell me what to do! Should I have an abortion or not?'

'It's not my place to make your decisions for you, my dear. I'm just here to help you with your self-inquiry. In a situation like this it's important we look inside, and discover what's making you so afraid.'

'Christ! I hope you're not some kind of psychologist. I've had so much psychology from Karl it's coming out my ears!'

'This isn't about theories, Sue. It's about your subjective experience. What does your deeper self want?'

'It wants the child, because it's Karl's child and I love Karl, so how could I kill something that comes from him? Besides abortion is unnatural and a sin - although I don't believe in hell any more, whatever Karl says.'

'And what does the other side of your mind say - the side that is tempted to have the abortion?'

'It says that having the child would be taking a great risk, because Karl's attitude is unlikely to change. Having a baby wouldn't serve to cement our relationship, just the opposite. I could lose him through it.'

'And what would happen if you lost Karl?'

'I'd go crazy, because I'm totally addicted to him. This was never an ordinary love affair, IG. It was a fatal attraction! And it's gone so deep that it feels like, if this root was pulled out, the whole foundation of my psyche would collapse.'

'I think not, Sue. You're underestimating your inner strength and moral purpose. It would be an ending and a kind of death, but you would resurrect.'

'But in what state? I'm like a junkie, IG. I get withdrawal symptoms every time Karl goes away for a few days.'

'You've become dependent on the high pitch of emotional and sexual intensity that this relationship gives you. But, though you call it love, it's more like an inflammation of the emotional body - an overheated state full of feverish lust, possessiveness and jealousy.'

'If I'm jealous, it's no wonder. The bastard is always flirting around with the undergraduates. But I see jealousy as something positive, IG. It proves that I love Karl and need him - that I'm not indifferent.'

'You say you love him, and yet you play games with him. You wax hot and then cold. You tease him by playing hard to get.'

'Well, I have to keep his interest up.'

'You're manipulative, Sue!'

'I know, but it's out of desperation. You see I'm always expecting him to do the dirty on me. I know what men are like!'

'Before you can truly love from the heart, you must rise above all that fear and suspicion.'

'And how can I do that?'

'Become the observer of yourself. Don't be so identified with Kathleen. Allow your point of consciousness to move to Sue, because she has a wider perspective. And don't forget to continue your self-inquiry. It would help if you paid a visit to your grandmother. She still remembers the time when your mother was pregnant with you, and she's ready to talk about it.'

So, following IG's suggestion, I go to see my granny, who I've neglected for years. She lives in Reigate in an old people's home, and, when she sees me coming in the door, her face lights up. I'm surprised that she's actually pleased to see me again, although I'm no longer a practising Catholic!

'Granny,' I tell her, 'I've got a problem - I'm pregnant!'

She looks at my left hand to see if I'm wearing a wedding ring. I'm not.

'Pregnant and not married!' she sighs. 'Well, I've seen that before.'

And then to my amazement granny opens the door of the family closet, and reveals a skeleton lying inside.

'Your father got your mother in the family way when she was just seventeen. He wasn't much older himself, and his people were against him marrying. So the priest made arrangements to send her to a home. It's what they did with unmarried mothers in Ireland in those days. They stayed there, working their fingers to the bone, and their babies were taken away and given for adoption.

But I didn't want to lose my only daughter in that way, so I sent her round to an old biddy in the village, one who helped women when they were in trouble. And she went quietly enough, but, when she was lying on the table with the needle already half inside her, she had a vision. She saw herself stretched on a rack in hell, and it was Satan himself who was torturing her. This gave her such a shock that she leaped up, and was out the door before the old biddy could ask for her money. Which is how you came to be born, Kathleen, so you can thank the devil for it! Well, in the end your father was persuaded to marry her, so she wasn't put in a home after all!'

After my visit to granny, I make the firm decision to have the baby. Babies should come into the world wanted and loved, and that's what I wish for our child. I intend to give it all the love and care I was denied, and nothing Karl can say or do will change my mind now. When I tell him this, and he senses my determination, he shrugs and says,

'Please yourself, Kathleen, but don't forget it's entirely your decision.'

It seems that the bigger my belly grows, the less I see of Karl. He's in the throes of finishing his Ph.D. and has to work late most evenings. I sit at home, watching moronic TV shows and biting my nails. One night, when I expected him at eight, he doesn't turn up until after eleven, and by that time I'm stewing in forebodings like a steak cooking in its own juices.

'Sorry, sweetie, I forgot about the time. I got so stuck into my work.'

'You can't pull the wool over my eyes,' I growl. 'I can smell the alcohol on your breath.'

'Well I had a quick drink with some students on the way home.'

'Any women in the party?'

'No, only blokes.'

'I don't believe you!' I say in a voice curdled with emotion.

'Give me a break, Kath. I feel as if I can't move without you breathing down my neck!'

The atmosphere in the room is so thick now you could cut it with a knife. Under the pretext of giving him a kiss, I go over and sniff at his jacket collar, and when I smell perfume the storm breaks, and Karl gets it full in the face.

'Let's sit down and talk about this like two rational people,' he suggests lamely, but I'm a long way beyond reason.

That night I refuse to have sex with him. Well, he has to know how bad he's made me feel! In fact I've resolved to starve him of sex for a week and, even if the bastard comes crawling to me on his bended knees, I won't relent. If he thinks he can run around with other women, and then come home and have it off with me, he's another think coming!

'I don't feel like it,' I say.

'I don't believe it! A nymphomaniac like you refusing a shag!'

'You're mistaken,' I say grimly, 'I'm not a nymphomaniac now - just the opposite! You wait and see!'

But when he's left for the faculty the next morning, and I remember the cute little student who does his typing, I'm in a frenzy of worry. I phone Veronica for comfort, but she's out. Then I remember my inner guide, with whom I have the following conversation.

'What's up, Sue?'

'I'm so mad at Karl I could kill him.'

'You can't help what Karl does, but you can help the state of mind you're in.'

'I think the bastard does it on purpose. He enjoys making me jealous! In some perverted way it makes him feel valued.'

'But he isn't making you jealous, Sue! He's triggering the jealousy you already have inside you. It's been accumulating for years - for lives even - because you always denied it was there. But, if you want your suffering to stop, you'll have to address it.'

'I'm desperate for it to stop. It feels as if I'm being eaten up inside by cankerous worms!'

'Yes, and those are the real hell fires - envy, jealousy, anger and hatred. They are the inner tortures. And the irony is that, although you believe Karl is the cause, and you see yourself as his victim, you're doing it to yourself. You're the cause of your own suffering.'

'If that's the case, then what can I do about it?'

'When jealous feelings are there, inquire into them. They will lead you into your past, and childhood memories will be triggered. Your relationship with your sister Lucy could be relevant.'

'Hmmm... I hated her! She was the goody-goody who could do no wrong in our mother's eyes, while I could do no right.'

'Jealousy is born of comparison, Sue. If you don't compare, you don't feel jealous.'

'It's my mother's fault. She always treated me as if I was inferior to Lucy.'

'And that's what you still believe deep down. I've watched how you judge yourself. You show yourself no mercy Sue.'

'Yes, I hate myself and that's the truth.'

'The wound to your self-esteem goes further back than this life, but there are keys to it in your childhood which you must uncover, because it's important to examine the self-rejection that lies behind your jealousy.'

'Hmmm... for example I keep comparing myself to that student who does Karl's typing. I see her as a threat because she's younger and prettier, and more bubbly than me.'

'Yes, the more you compare yourself negatively to others, the more threatening they will appear. So start by inquiring into the wound to your self-esteem, and search for therapies to heal it. And above all don't despair, my dear, because awareness is like an inner alchemy. It has the power to transform even the strongest and most deeply rooted jealousy into love.'

The baby arrives in February. It's a boy and we call him Dirk. After the birth, the disparity between Karl's life and mine becomes greater. I lose all my freedom, being tied to the home and a fractious child, while Karl's life is hardly affected. From the start he leaves Dirk entirely up to me. I'm the one who gets up in the night and cleans up the sick, and changes the full nappies. Moreover he seems to lack all paternal feeling, because he never cuddles Dirk or plays with him. And this annoys me.

'Dirk needs a father figure,' I keep saying. 'He needs to bond with you, Karl, but how can he when you don't spend any time with him?'

'You wanted that kid. I didn't!' is his reply.

I give a sardonic laugh.

'But you wanted the sex that made him, you lecher!'

'You mean you made me want the sex. Then, when I was in your power, you ratted on me. Admit it, Kath - you forgot your pill on purpose that night he was conceived!'

'I did no such thing!'

'It's the way you work, you devious bitch. But this time you're going to find that you've shot yourself in your own foot!'

I used to idolise Karl - put him on a pedestal - but now that the chips are down he's showing himself in his true colours. Scratch this card and, instead of the winning number, an ugly monster will appear!

My life would be emotionally less taxing if Karl and I separated. I know that I would be a good deal happier without him, but we've tried to split up so many times, and it's never worked. There's a strong magnetic force that always pulls us back together again. In my despair I turn to my inner guide.

'What shall I do, IG? My child needs a father, and I need a partner, and Karl is refusing to play ball!'

'You're still under the illusion that you can change him, Sue. But you can't make a person into something they are not. You'll have to accept Karl as he is, and start from there.'

'But you know me, IG. I'm a fighter. I never give up, and, when I see that something is wrong, I can't rest until I've put it right.'

'Which has led to you and Karl becoming embroiled in a power struggle from which you're determined to emerge the winner. But you're going to be the loser this time, Sue, because all the love there was between you is being destroyed in the process, leaving only anger and resentment.'

'But it's so unfair! Why should other women have husbands who are loving and supportive and not me?'

'We carry the psychological patterns that attract our circumstances. And, although you may have forgotten its origins, you are responsible for that particular pattern forming. It was created by the choices you made in your past lives.'

'Knowing that doesn't help when I can't remember my past lives.'

'You don't need to. Just remember that, because you created the pattern, it's in your power to change it. Patterns are habits of thinking and feeling, and, once you see them clearly and objectively, you can snap out of them.'

'Hmmm... I must have been a very bad person in my last life to have attracted all this negative karma!'

'But before this life began, Sue, you joined an incarnation group, where you worked with me to create a life-script. We ensured that you would have the chance to pay your karmic debts, and get the life experiences you needed to grow spiritually.'

'Yes, I can sort of remember that.'

'Then you should be able to see all that happens to you - even your most challenging circumstances - in a positive light, and that will help you be patient.'

Our relationship struggles on for another year by which time Dirk is walking, and needs to be watched every minute. I let him play in the garden, which is a safe space when the back gate is bolted. One Sunday morning, I have to go into town to the chemist's, and I ask Karl to do the child minding. Karl agrees for a change - he must be feeling guilty about something! So I go off to catch the bus, ignoring the feeling of foreboding in the pit of my stomach.

Two hours later I alight at the bus stop, and, when I turn the corner into our road, I see an ambulance parked outside our house. I sprint the last hundred yards, and arrive when they're just about to close the doors. Dirk is inside on a stretcher looking very pale and dead. Then I hear Karl's voice.

'Keep calm, Kathleen. He's not dead - only unconscious.'

'Christ! What happened? What have you done to him?'

'He ran out into the street and was hit by a car. The fucking driver didn't even stop!'

'You left the back gate open!' I scream. 'It's all your fault!'

Karl doesn't reply.

Dirk was in hospital in a coma for two days and nights, and then he woke up. I was at his bedside all those hours, and for the first time for years I prayed.

'Dear Lord God, be merciful. Let him live!'

The paediatrician tried to comfort me.

'He has concussion,' he said, 'but nothing's broken - no internal injuries. So I think he'll pull through.'

He never mentioned the fact that Dirk could have brain damage, and the police never caught the driver of the car.

THIRTIES

When I brought Dirk home from hospital, he was unable to walk, and he kept on getting fits. These scared the daylights out of me. My rage against Karl was immense. Dirk's life had been blighted, and I saw it as Karl's fault. His negligence in leaving the gate open on that fatal day proved his lack of love for us, and I had no option now but to throw him out.

'I want to erase you from our life,' I cried, 'and this time it's for final.'

Karl agreed it would be best, so he found a flat and within a week he'd moved out with all his things. This left me the sole carer of a disabled child. I'd planned to go out to work when Dirk started nursery school, but now all my career plans had to be ditched. I was also very poor, with only a carer's allowance to live on, supplemented by a meagre monthly cheque from Karl. And there was no one in my family I could turn to for help, as my father had gone abroad, I had quarrelled with my sister Lucy, and my mother in her twisted way insisted on seeing Dirk's accident as a punishment from God.

'He was conceived in sin, and he will be your scourge,' she pronounced ominously, 'like you were mine!'

I saw that I could expect no compassion from her as long as she remained stuck in her Old Testament view of life.

I had my work cut out getting Dirk assessed for the benefits he's legally entitled to. My first battle with the authorities was over his rehabilitation programme. I'd applied for the one I saw as optimal, but we were turned down. A long struggle ensued in which I went back and forth between the health authorities and the social services, with both of them trying to fob me off. But I stood my ground, and in the end my case was heard and we won.

There was a new battle to be fought when Dirk turned five. I wanted him to attend the local primary school instead of a school for handicapped children, as his intelligence was normal, although he was in a wheelchair. But my application was turned down. However, knowing that the law was on my side, I didn't give up. I started writing letters, and lobbied our MP, but it was only when I found a solicitor, and threatened to take the case to court, that the authorities backed down. So my tenacity paid off in the end. Dirk now goes to the primary school, and I'm seen by everyone locally as a right old battle-axe!

Although Karl has been banished from our life, I've found it impossible to banish him from my mind, and I often catch myself thinking about him. This old habit serves to keep my rage and hurt sizzling on a back burner. I know these feelings are bad for me, but I've never been good at forgiving and forgetting.

Karl only lives three miles away. I know his address, and sometimes I take Dirk for an outing to that area of town. Then I'll walk slowly up and down the street where he lives, pushing Dirk in the wheelchair.

'Just a minute, Sue. Why are you doing that? Are you hoping to meet Karl?'

'No IG, but I want him to look out the window, and see Dirk in his wheelchair, and be stricken with remorse. He must never be allowed to forget what he's done.'

'If you finger your wound, Sue, it will never heal.'

'There can't be any healing until there's justice.'

'You mean you want an eye for an eye, and a tooth for a tooth? If Karl had an accident now and was maimed, would that satisfy you?'

'Yes it would. Or I'd like to be the one who writes his life-script next time. Then I'd make sure he makes amends by paying a heavy karma!'

'You'd show him no mercy?'

'None at all! And why should I? He's blighted my life as well as Dirk's. Instead of being out having a career, I'm tied to the heavy responsibility of caring for a disabled child.'

'As I see it, Sue, your problem lies not in your situation itself, but in the fact that you can't accept it. You see yourself as a victim, and are blaming other people for your suffering. But the truth is you're creating most of it yourself.'

'I've never thought of it that way.'

'You need to start taking responsibility for your emotional states. Because there's no need to continue harbouring negative emotions that only make you feel bad, when you can let go of them and become lighter and brighter.'

'How does that work?'

'When you focus on negative thoughts and feelings, you're giving them energy and making them stronger. But, if you withdraw your attention from them, they weaken and lose their power over you. So, if you want to achieve happiness and peace of mind, learn to focus on the positive instead of the negative, both in other people and in yourself.'

197

What IG has just told me is very important, and I'll try to remember it, though that's easier said than done!

I've immersed myself in Dirk. My life revolves round him, and the last thing that I miss is a man in my bed. I'm as celibate as a nun, and yet I'm totally fulfilled and emotionally nourished through my relationship with my little son. He's such an affectionate child, and he has such a heavenly smile. It's like the smile of a holy angel!

Then one night I have a dream. I'm sitting on the slope of a volcano, and all around me I see brimstone and ashes. A ghostly figure appears, holding out a cup to me that contains a steaming, yellow potion.

'Drink!' it commands.

'But it's sulphur!' I protest, trying to push the cup away.

Again he lifts it to my lips.

'Drink!'

When I wake up the next morning I'm trembling. I get up and go into Dirk's room and, seeing the strange, contorted way he's lying there, I know I've come too late. There's nothing I can do any more now but lie down on the bed beside him, and cradle his little, lifeless body in my arms. And I remain there for hours as if I'm dead too.

The autopsy shows Dirk suffered a brain haemorrhage. He must have had a fit in the night while I was asleep. That awful dream was a warning that I didn't heed. I didn't wake up! I'll reproach myself forever for that.

'Could I have prevented his death if I'd been at his side?' I ask the paediatrician. He beats around the bush to avoid giving me a clear answer. I move like a robot through the days that follow, and even at the funeral I'm totally numb. Veronica has stepped in and taken charge. She's made all the arrangements, and she must have informed Karl too because he's there. After the service he comes up to me and says,

'I was devastated when I heard the news, Kathleen. And I'd like to say how truly sorry I am - for everything, I mean - and if there's anything I can do...'

I stare at him blankly without any reaction. I'm catatonic.

My sister Lucy is also at the funeral. I haven't seen her for years - ever since we had our final row. But a death in the family has the power to dissolve feuds and antagonisms, and bring angry people back into their hearts, and I experience a Lucy who is kind and sympathetic. Our mother didn't come. Her health was too bad for her to make the journey, but she sent her condolences. Lucy tells me she's clinically depressed, and drugged up to the eyeballs.

My sister offers to stay with me till I get back on my feet, and I agree. And I must say it's a relief to have her there because, when the funeral is over, all the pain I've been holding in starts to erupt. It's as if a floodgate has opened, and the tears I've been holding back for lives on end come streaming out.

Lucy takes me in her arms, and pats me as if she's comforting a child. 'There, there!' she says. 'Let it all out, Kathy!'

The period of my grieving is long, but at least I grieve thoroughly. And during that time I ask my inner guide some burning questions.

'How can God snatch away the very person you love most, IG? One moment he's there, and the next he's gone! Just an empty bed and an empty wheelchair! It's too brutal!'

'It only appears brutal, Sue, because you're in a body, and your consciousness is confined to a limited time and place. You can't see Dirk with your physical eyes, but he's still with you in spirit.'

'Even if that's true, it's not much comfort if I can't see him or touch him any more. Oh IG! I'll never forgive myself for failing him at the last. I should have been there at his side!'

'Don't beat yourself up about that, Sue. Dirk has an inner guide too, and he wasn't alone when he died. And, although your body was asleep, he felt your love and support right to the end. So let go of your guilt, because guilt is just another way of clinging to the past, while what you need to do now is to accept what's happened and move on.'

'That's a hard one for someone like me.'

'It's an important life lesson - to learn to let go of people we've become emotionally dependent on when the time comes. And sometimes, in order to learn this lesson, we have to suffer the loss of the person we love most in all the world.'

'But why must I suffer this? That's what I want to know. Why must I bear such a heavy blow of fate now, when my life has been hard all along? It seems so unjust!'

'I don't know the answer to that one, Sue, because the part can never know the whole, and there are karmic laws at work beyond our understanding. But I remember that a life-transforming crisis was part of your life-script, though in what form it would come we could not predetermine. So let me give you some advice - harbour love instead of guilt, and then letting go will be easier. Because love has the power to heal every wound, even the deepest and the most painful.'

During the months following Dirk's death, it felt as if my inner walls were crumbling, and the structure of my personality was in meltdown. Then one day the demolition was complete, and I was ready to emerge from the debris. That was like a new birth.

MIDDLE AGE

For a woman of forty-five I'm wearing well. There are lines in my face for sure, and my hair has turned grey, but I've started dyeing it a warm, coppery red - a colour I've always been drawn to. I work at a hospital for women with mental problems, and my work has become my life.

I had to start out as an auxiliary, as I'd had no formal training. But, when they discovered how little could faze me, and saw that the patients trusted me, I was quickly promoted. Soon they were handing the extreme cases over to me - the self-harmers and attempted suicides. I found that I could accompany these women into their craziest psychic spaces, and lead them out again. I was gifted in that way, perhaps because of my childhood as the daughter of a manic depressive mother.

I get a great deal of satisfaction from the knowledge that I'm supporting some of the most vulnerable members of the community, and I'm happy for my private life to take second place. I live alone, having been single for a while now. This is quite a U-turn for someone like me, who used to go in for sex in a big way. I was like an addict craving my regular fix, and, just as users need ever-higher doses of their drug, so I would explore perverse ways of turning the sensuality needle up high. But now I've gone to the opposite extreme and become a puritan. I find my former behaviour morally questionable, and try to dissuade the young girls in my care from being promiscuous like I was.

And so the years pass until at forty-nine I reach the peak in my career with the mental health services when I'm appointed chief of the Health and Social Care Unit. It's my task to supervise the care workers, and ensure that the patients who are out in the community get the support they need. I throw myself into this job with my usual totality and dedication, agreeing to be on call for long hours - often late into the night - and, in the case of an emergency, ready to forego my weekend.

When I took over, I found that some areas of the service were fragmented and dysfunctional. So I immediately started making plans to improve them. However the measures that needed to be taken proved highly unpopular. The word got round that a shake-up was in the pipeline, and redundancies were expected, and the union came out against me. As usual I had rubbed some people up the wrong way and made enemies, for which my caustic tongue is to blame, because, when I'm attacked, it's my nature to counter-attack with greater harshness - although I'm invariably gentle with the patients.

Then one day I received a poisoned pen letter, and that deeply shocked me. I'd been anticipating a stab in the back, and was on my guard, seeing a nigger in every woodpile, but I never expected a cowardly personal attack of this kind. My first reaction was to leave no stone unturned in my determination to discover the culprit. But then I remembered IG's words that I'd committed to memory:

'When you focus on negative thoughts and feelings, you give them energy and they become stronger. But, if you withdraw your attention from them, they weaken and lose their power over you.'

So I decided to burn the letter, and give it no more attention, and I would try to think positively about my staff from now on. Hopefully, in time, they'd come to think positively about me.

They did in the end, but things had to reach a climax first. A patient committed suicide after being discharged from our psychiatric unit. An inquiry was held, and it came to light that she'd been discharged without being examined by a doctor first, and of course I was held responsible. Then the press got hold of the story, and interviewed some members of my staff who treacherously testified against me.

The result was a public outcry, and I was hauled up before the board. My plea that I'd acted within our ruling, as the patient had been discharged for being in possession of illicit drugs, was rejected. My enemies were now jubilant, as they thought I'd have to hand in my resignation. But they rejoiced prematurely, because the board decided to keep me on, although with curtailed powers. A new senior director's post was created to ensure closer supervision of the clinicians, and the man chosen for the job was Dr Paul Moodie - a die-hard conservative who would be certain to oppose my plans for reform.

'This branch of the health service needs a Dr Paul Moodie like a hole in the head!' was my comment, when I heard the news of his appointment. Little did I know that I was speaking of my future husband!

It turned out easier than I expected to win Paul round to my way of thinking. He was going through a rough patch in his private life, and needed someone to talk to, and I've always been a sympathetic listener. We got into the habit of going out for a drink together after work. And there in the pub garden, while he sipped his lager, Paul would pour out his heart to me. His wife had left him for another man, and he'd just gone through an acrimonious divorce. She had received custody of their thirteen-year-old daughter, but Amy didn't get on with her mother's new partner, and wanted to come and live with him.

I find Paul attractive. He's in good nick for a man in his mid fifties, as well as being sensitive and intelligent. And he's also single, which is a big point in his favour. Because I've received more offers from married men in my time than I've had hot dinners, and refused them all. I have my principles. But now, as an understanding develops between us, I decide that I'm open to having an affair with Paul Moodie. However, after we've spent our first night together, Paul pulls a fast one.

'I want to marry you, Kathleen!' he says.

'Good God Paul! Why me for Christ's sake?'

'Because I think you're a wonderful woman - spirited, compassionate and determined. I admire a woman with firm views, and now I've discovered there's icing on the cake too, because you're also good in bed!'

Oh well, I think to myself, then all right!

I'm going to do things differently this time. I blush with shame when I remember the beginnings of my relationship with Karl. That embarrassing pretence about my virginity! How can a relationship ever succeed if it begins with a deceit? I'll always be scrupulously upfront with Paul.

So we are married in the local registry office, and move into the house that we've bought together. Paul turns out to be a kind and considerate husband, ever concerned with my welfare. At first this makes me suspicious. I suspect him of creating an indebtedness, so I'll have to reciprocate by laying on some good sex. But Paul is not Karl. It seems he really does love me in spite of all my faults, and that helps me feel much better about myself.

Things go well until his daughter, Amy, comes to live with us, when it soon becomes clear that she intends to be the thorn in our flesh. Of course she wants her father to herself, and she resents my presence deeply. I do my best to please her. When it's her birthday, I bake her a magnificent cake, only to have it thrown back in my face. And I take her on a trip to the seaside, but she's in such a vile mood that she spoils the day for both of us.

IG has said that other people are like mirrors, and I'm beginning to see my own misery-creating patterns reflected in Amy. I've always mistrusted harmony, and I used to feel compelled to provoke people, stabbing them until I'd brought out the real feelings they were hiding. Like Amy I took sadistic pleasure in administering pain, and fed on emotional strife as a vampire feeds on blood.

But now I'm on the receiving end, because Amy instinctively senses the weak points in my armour and hones in on them. I know that inside she's crying out for someone to love her, but, if we try to show her affection, she bites the hand that feeds her. And I was the same at her age. I wouldn't let anyone come near me.

202

Well before her fifteenth birthday she starts going out in the evenings and coming back late. She's already out of control, although Paul won't admit it. We're reaching the end of our tether, and considering sending her back to her mother. But, when we broach the subject, Amy has hysterics. It seems she detests her stepfather like the plague.

'It's ironical, IG, that I've failed with that girl, because we have so much in common.'

'Perhaps it's because Amy is indirectly telling you something that you don't want to hear.'

'But I can guess what's bugging her. It all boils down to the age-old rivalry between women for the attentions of the man. It's natural for her to be jealous of her stepmother, and see me as a rival.'

'There's more to it than that. Do some self-inquiry, and find out why Amy has the power to stir up your feelings, and make you falter. Is it because she's bringing you in touch with something you've buried inside - something you'd prefer not to look at?'

I do as IG suggests. I retire to my room, after telling Paul not to disturb me, and lie down on the bed and close my eyes. As I lie there, breathing deeply and regularly, I watch the feelings, thoughts and images that arise in my mind. I feel ready to look at my wound at last. I know that, before it can be healed, it has to open so that the pus can flow out.

The first insight I get makes me draw my breath sharply. Amy shows all the signs of being an abused child. Why didn't I see that before? It would explain her hatred of her stepfather, and her rejection of her mother. I realise that we must never put pressure on her to go back and live with them.

Then a memory from long ago begins to emerge into my consciousness. It's something so painful it had to be locked away, banished to my deepest recesses, and a shocking scene assembles itself before my inner eye. I'm just a little girl - four or five years old - and my father is kneeling on the floor in front of me. He's holding me so I can't get away, and putting his tongue in my mouth. I can taste whisky on his saliva, and it makes me feel sick. At the same time he's fondling me between my legs. Suddenly, with a shock of revulsion, I sit bolt upright.

Did that really happen, or have I imagined it? If it happened then, knowing such cases, it was probably the tip of a very nasty iceberg. But it would explain my difficult relationship with my mother, who would have guessed what he was doing and turned a blind eye. Is that why she's always been so inhibited with me - because of guilt? And is that why I've always carried a deep resentment towards her?

'IG! Is it true? Did my father abuse me? I have to know so I can understand what's going on between me and my mother.'

'Yes, you must get to the bottom of it. Just follow your intuition.'

'If it happened, I must have seen it as a betrayal that my mother didn't protect me.'

'But she did protect you from him, Sue. She protected both her daughters by kicking your father out. She was acting for your good.'

'But why did I still love him, in spite of what he'd done? Why did I take his side against her? I don't understand.'

'Because, instead of blaming him for what happened, the five-year-old Kathleen blamed herself.'

'Hmmm... Well that explains why deep down I've always believed I'm no good. The knowledge of my sinfulness was my best-kept secret, though it messed up my relationships with men.'

'Until you met Paul. Now you have a loving relationship, Sue, and that proves you've moved on. You've overcome the effects of your trauma enough to allow intimacy and caring. So I'd say you've come a long way!'

'Yes I have. But there's still the problem of my relationship with my mother. I'd like to talk to her about this, but I'm afraid to. Oh IG! Why must we all suffer these terrible wounds all the time? Why do we have to be so damaged by life?'

'Because we must come to understand that there are treasures hidden in every life experience - even in the most painful and sordid.'

OLD AGE

I'm in my late sixties and I'm sitting in a train. I received the news this morning that my mother is dying, and that she's asking for me. There's something she wants to tell me before she goes, they said. And I'm praying that I'll arrive at the care home in time.

Yes, she hasn't gone yet, they say. A nurse is with her but, when I enter the room, she tactfully withdraws and leaves us alone. My mother is lying on her back with her eyes closed. Perhaps she's asleep. I take her hand.

'Mother, I'm here. It's Kathleen. What did you want to tell me? I'm listening.'

When she hears my voice, she opens her eyes and stares at me, and her pupils have a piercing intensity. Then she starts to speak, but the words that come from her lips are not what I expected to hear. I thought she was going to speak about the incest. As a good catholic, she wouldn't want to die with something like that on her conscience.

She would want to ask my forgiveness, I would have thought. But all she says is, 'My veil, my veil from my first communion. It's in the attic in a box together with the dress I wore. I want you to fetch it for me, Kathleen, so I can wear it when they bury me.'

But the box is no longer in the attic. When my mother left her house ten years ago, everything was cleared out.

'I'll fetch it for you,' I say. 'Don't you fret!'

I'm waiting to see if she'll say something else. Surely she'll find a loving word for me at the last. But my mother just turns her face to the wall and dies without speaking another word. So our relationship ended as it begun - in a deceit.

My sister Lucy arrives, and we arrange the funeral together. I consider telling her about what I think happened with our father, but then I shy away from it. Why open a can of worms? What good would it do now both of them are dead and gone? Let sleeping dogs lie. Neither do I tell Paul, as it would put a slur on my family's name. Better to carry the secret with me to my grave.

Amy lived with us until she left home to go to college, and, after that first difficult year, my relationship with her improved. Paul retired at sixty-five, but I intend to go on working into my seventies. Being old won't prevent me from being a useful member of the community.

Then at seventy-five I suffer a minor stroke, and the doctors discover a faulty valve in my heart. They put me on a drug to thin my blood, so it can pass easily and smoothly through the passages.

People have started dying all round me. I'm always getting out my black coat and hat, and going to funerals. Paul is one of the first to go. One morning I wake up and find him dead in the bed beside me. Dear Paul! He was such a good husband, and I'd come to rely so much on his support. Now I must struggle on alone.

Then my sister Lucy is diagnosed with cancer, and I move into her house to nurse her. I'm privileged to accompany her on her cancer journey through all its depleting phases. And I believe that in her final months we reached an understanding about the past, and there were no more wedges between us. I was with her when she left her body.

So now there's no one left down here to hold me back, and I'm not afraid of dying, because I know death well. I made his acquaintance early, when he snatched Dirk away from me. Yes, I've had plenty of opportunities to learn to let go of the people I love, and now I must let go of myself.

So, when I have put my things in order, and made my preparations, and paid for my funeral, I stop taking the drug I'm being prescribed. I become noticeably weaker in the following days, and on the fourth day my heart stops. Then death in a long black cloak emerges from the bowels of the earth and beckons to me, and I hear IG's voice say,

'Go with him. Your path to the summit, Sue, passes through the abyss. If you entered dark spaces in your life, and moved through fields of destruction, it was because you needed anguish to prepare yourself for future bliss. You were required to embrace the shadow, and you drew it into the light. You suffered the pain of loss, and freed yourself from the fear of loss. And now, because you no longer fear death, you'll no longer fear life.'

I dream that I'm a snake, twisting and writhing in the dust in an effort to shed my skin. Suddenly a great eagle swoops down from the clouds, and carries me away in its beak. And, as we rise into the air, my sheath of old skin falls away, and flutters, wrinkled and shrunken, down to the ground. We soar higher and higher, holding a course towards the east, where the sky is glowing fiery red, and the sun is beginning to rise.

Life 9
SID the SAGITTARIUS

This place is a paradise compared to what it's like down there. It's like sitting in a deckchair on a Caribbean beach, sunning yourself while you sip your cocktail. It's like an eternal holiday, whereas down there you're sweating on the coal seam. You're down a mine drilling coal for three score years and ten! And yet I'm getting restless. I'm bored with bliss, and I can't wait to be off on another adventure!

I joined an incarnation group to be put in the picture, and I'm not the only one who's asking what it's all about, because there are things going on behind the scenes we never get to hear of. So what's the big idea - that's what I'd like to know! There must be a system behind it, and I thought our life coach would know the answers. But, as it turns out, he's only a few steps ahead of us.

When we got round to creating my life script, I said,

'That's not the way I do things. I never plan in advance. I like leaving things open so I get taken by surprise!'

He raised his eyebrows, but agreed to leave the page blank.

So, as I recline my chair in the group room and close my eyes, I haven't the faintest idea what's going to happen, and I'm as excited as a kid on Christmas Eve.

The trip starts with a dream. I'm dreaming that I'm in the cockpit of one of those old, open aeroplanes. I'm chugging up into the night sky, whistling cheerfully, although I know I'm flying into danger. Then, somewhere over the North Sea, an enemy plane shoots out of a cloud and starts firing at me. I keep whistling while I fire back. Then I notice flames coming out of my tail, and a minute later my plane is spiralling out of control. I bale out. My parachute fails to open, and I end up floating face downwards in the water.

Everything goes black as if the film has torn, and when it resumes it must have been spooled back, because it's five minutes earlier. Once more I'm back again in my burning plane, and once again I bale out, but this time my parachute opens.

I'm hanging from its straps, and the wind has blown me back over the land. I can see the outlines of fields and trees below me as I descend, and hear the chuffing of a train and the rattling of wheels. Red sparks are being puffed up towards me, together with clouds of smoke. They come from the funnel of a mighty steam engine, that's snaking its way through the countryside pulling a long line of carriages behind it.

My viewpoint now shifts to inside one them. I see a crowded corridor lit by a line of dim, yellow lights. There are soldiers in uniform with fags in their mouths, people without seats perched on their luggage, mums with kids asleep on their laps. The monotonous jig-jog of the train is making everyone drowsy, but they're suddenly awoken by a commotion in one of the compartments.

A woman starts screaming, and a man goes hurrying off down the train to find the guard. The word soon passes down the corridor that she's having a baby, and a crowd of curious onlookers gather in the compartment doorway. They are just debating whether to pull the emergency cord or not, when the guard appears, all hot and flustered.

'Guard! This lady is about to give birth!' announces a lady in a toque.

'She can't do that - it's against regulations! She must wait till we get to Crewe!'

'And what if she can't? We'll have to do the best we can here!'

At first I thought it all had nothing to do with me, but then I discover it bloody well has, because the next moment the carriage shrinks and becomes a narrow tunnel in which I find myself wedged. I'm struggling with all my might, and for a moment it's like I'm back in the burning plane, trying to get free of the straps, and knowing I have to vacate or I'm done for.

Then I hear a familiar voice say, 'Relax, old man! You'll survive your birth - most people do.' That was IG, and a few minutes later I come shooting out of the tunnel to land in the hands of the terrified guard.

'Don't you worry, madam,' he pants, 'I've got 'im safe and sound!'

The lady takes me from him and wraps me in her shawl. Then she holds me up so the crowd outside can see.

'It's a boy - a bonny, bouncing boy!' she announces, and they all cheer.

Someone passes round a bottle of whisky, and they drink a toast to me and my mum. So my new life gets off to a flying start. As I tell people later, I was born on the *Flying Scotsman* somewhere between London and Crewe on the evening of December 14th 1944. I was four weeks premature, and took my poor mother by surprise, being, as usual, too impatient to wait. They are calling me Edward Unwin Archer.

THE KID

I'm on my mother's lap in the sidecar. My father's beside us, astride his Harley Davidson. He's wearing goggles, and his great leather gloves make his hands look like elephants' feet. The wind is whistling past my ears. Mum has put a scarf round them so they won't freeze off. My father's in the RAF, and we've been on the move since the end of the war, as he's had a series of postings at stations up and down the country. I'm three years old, and I'm clutching my favourite toy. It's Dinky, my miniature Spitfire.

As I'm half asleep, I hardly notice the bike coming to a halt, and being carried though a door into a brightly lit building that smells of carbolic soap.

'Which flat is ours?' asks dad.

'The empty one on the fourth floor.'

'So many stairs to climb!' groans mum.

My mother has popped out for a moment, and left the front door ajar. I seize my chance and, in a flash, I'm down the stairs and out into the street. I set off purposefully, as if I know where I'm going, but, when I reach the end of the street and turn the corner, I find myself in another street stretching far away into the distance. I'm looking for the house where we used to live. I want to go back because it had a view over the airfield, and I could watch the planes taking off and landing.

I break into a run and, just when I've got a pain in my chest and I can run no more, I hear a motorbike coming up behind, and my dad skids to a halt beside me at the curb.

'Where do you think you're going, old chap?'

'To over there,' I reply, pointing to the distant horizon.

'Like a lift?'

I nod, so he picks me up and puts me in the sidecar.

I'm growing up fast, in fact I'm seven now. They call me Mister Crashbang, because I'm full of berserk exuberance, and I keep on crashing into things. Oh crikey! Now I've gone and made my little sister cry!

'Eddie! You're too rough with her! If you have to romp about like that, go outside!' and she pushes me out the door.

I'm running down the street, slashing at the bushes with my stick to frighten the wild beasts that are hiding in them. I'm making for the edge of town, where the streets peter out into woods and open fields. It's where I like playing best, because it's where I feel free.

As it's Saturday, there's no school - hooray - because school is a bore. I'm so quick at doing the exercises teacher sets that I always finish long before the rest. Then, instead of being rewarded for this, I'm punished, because I have to sit still and do nothing, while we wait for the rest of the class to finish.

All I want from life is to have adventures. I need them to lighten the long hours that can drag by at a snail's pace when you're only seven. So, as I slash a path through the nettles with my stick, I'm making up a story in my head. I imagine I'm on an expedition into the jungle, where there are wild animals and hostile tribes to contend with at every turn.

To see if the coast is clear, I skim up a tree. It's a blustery day, and each foothold is precarious, as the wind is rocking the branches. On the way up the story changes, and the tree becomes the mast of a galleon that's floundering in a storm. I'm scaling its dizzy heights to make fast a sail rope that's broken loose. The best adventures are spiced with danger, and on my way up I slip. Now I'm hanging from my hands over a fifteen-foot drop, and there's a moment of suspense before I find a new foothold. Of course I succeed in my mission. I secure the rope, thus saving the ship and the lives of the two hundred souls aboard her. Then I notice that I'm hungry and cold, and I want my tea!

TEENS

I've shot up so suddenly I've grown out of all my clothes, and my voice box sticks out as if my collar's too tight for me. The khaki shorts I'm wearing, however, are still on the long side, and reach all the way down to my nobly knees!

I've got bags of energy, and I'm always on the go. On Mondays I do cross-country running, archery on Tuesdays, astronomy on Wednesdays, rugger on Thursdays and on Fridays there's scouts. I'm very keen on scouting. The tracking and camping and night hikes are right up my street. And my mother is always having to sew new badges onto my uniform.

Our troop is run with soldierly rigour, which I take in my stride. We salute with three fingers in front of a hoisted union jack - I promise to do my best, to do my duty to God and the Queen - which is a bit retro! But to my mind it would do the shirkers and loafers in our school good to be scouts, which is why I go around promoting it as the best thing since canned tomatoes!

As long as I can remember, I've been mad about planes. When I was a kid, my father would take me to the hangars, and I'd be allowed to sit in the cockpits and try the controls. I suppose it's in my blood, because grandfather Archer was a pilot in the First World War. He was shot down over the North Sea, where they found him floating in the water.

But there's another reason why I want to be a pilot. It's because you get to see foreign countries, and it's my ambition to visit every country in the world. I've made a list of them, so I can cross them off when I've been there. At present only France is crossed off!

My other grandfather is also an influence on me. He's just come home from India, where he was a Baptist missionary all his life. I listen open-mouthed while he describes preaching to crowds of five thousand natives, and being invited to maharajas' palaces. The tales he tells of cholera epidemics, and cobra bites, and treks through perilous passes to remote hill stations accompanied by coolies, make me wonder if I have a calling too. I could be a missionary instead of a pilot, and devote my life to converting the heathen. But there's only one snag, and that is I don't believe in God!

TWENTIES

My sole purpose in life as an undergraduate is to have a good time. I've gone up to university on an army scholarship to study electrical engineering - a subject that leaves me cold. I'll never be passionate about electric dynamos and circuits and voltage regulation. So they don't know my face in the engineering department, but I'm a familiar figure at all the parties and social events on the student calendar. There's so much going on here every night that it's hard to decide what to do. And, wherever I go, I always get the feeling that I'm in the wrong place and missing out - that the real action is happening elsewhere! Ha ha!

I've just arrived at the bar where I'm meeting my friends, and I'm late as usual. I've never been good at time keeping, though no one seems to hold this against me. I've made so many friends since I came up. My jocular, hail-fellow-well-met manner goes down well, and I'm quick to offer to pay for rounds of drinks, which always ensures popularity. However, the downside is that my grant is fast disappearing through the holes in my pockets - but I don't care. It's only money after all. Ha ha!

I've just spent all the money my father gave me for books on a second-hand motorbike. Now I'm free to whiz off to the Welsh mountains, or down to the coast whenever I feel like it. And I've discovered that owning a bike upgrades you with the women. They're queuing up to ride pillion. This time yesterday I was roaring along the high ridge of the downs at seventy miles an hour with a girl called Wendy on the back. The track was bumpy and full of potholes, but what's the point in owning a motorbike if you can't get up some velocity?

Wendy was clinging to my waist, squealing with delight - or was it fear? - when I decided to do my stunt. Steering with one hand only, I twisted round to face her, and kissed her on the lips. So we were riding blind for some seconds, and at that break-neck speed, which I thought would be sure to impress her. But, when I screeched to a halt, Wendy burst into tears, and said she never wanted to go on a motorbike again. Give me a break! Unless you live dangerously, life's a dead bore!

I'm in my usual high spirits tonight, and everyone present is soon infected by my mood. I tend to dominate the conversation, having something to say on every subject under the sun, whether I know about it or not. And every now and then my loud, baying laugh rings out. But the observer inside me says, 'Come off it Ed! What you're spouting is a lot of hot air. You're talking out of the top of your hat!' Ha ha!

Rumour has it that there's a party on tonight, but it's a third-year do so we're not invited. Undeterred we decide to gatecrash it. So, when the pub closes, we go round to the tiny, terraced house where it's being held, and jostle our way in through the front door. It's packed inside. The sweaty, humid air is thick with cigarette smoke. There's modern jazz playing on the record player, and couples are dancing or lying entwined in a heap on the floor.

By midnight I'm totally boozed-up. I had quite a few beers and a double whisky in the pub, and now I've drunk most of the bottle of wine I brought with me. So, when Wendy appears before me, she's all blurred.

'Come on Ed, you lazy sloth! Get up and dance!'

It's not a good idea, as I feel like throwing up, but I stagger to my feet all the same, and we begin to gyrate. My head is lolling onto her bare shoulder now, so I can smell her skin, which is very clean and perfumed, when suddenly, without a 'Do you mind?' or a 'Pardon me!' I vomit all down the back of her dress.

When I wake up, I'm back home in bed with no notion of how I got there. Did they bundle me into a taxi? Did Wendy come back and clean me up, and put me to bed? In which case she must be totally disgusted with me. I'm totally disgusted with myself!

'Time to touch base, Sid,' says that voice in my head.

'Now let's get this straight - who are you and why do you call me Sid?'

'I'm IG, your inner guide, and I prefer to talk to Sid because he's the wiser of you two. Sid's the one you call the observer.'

'Then who am I really - Ed or Sid?'

'You're both of them. At present you're mainly identified with Ed, but your consciousness can switch over to Sid any time you like.'

'Gosh that's interesting! So you're saying we're not one person - we're two! That's what Plato believed. He'd call Sid my daemon and Ed my eidolon. And, if I remember rightly, C.G. Jung had a doppelgänger too, who he called Philemon. He used to have inner dialogues with him.'

'That's right. Ed is only as old as your present life, but you were Sid before you were born.'

'Crikey! And what's your status then?'

'I'm your life coach - IG stands for inner guide - but I'm not exclusive to you. I function as inner guide to the whole group. All twelve of you have me in common.'

'All twelve! You mean there are eleven others out there belonging to the same group as me! Who are they?'

'Knowing that wouldn't further the growth of your consciousness, Sid. It's more important at present to get yourself sorted out.'

'You're right. I'm in a mess, I'm ashamed to say.'

'Ever since you came up, it's been continuous partying and boozing. You've gone over the top with it.'

'Yes, I thought I was celebrating the euphoria of life, but now I see drunkenness and riotous living as an insult to human dignity. So I've vowed from this day forth to abjure hedonism.'

'A good move! But why did you go astray in the first place? Could it be that you're studying the wrong subject?'

'That's it! I've never been able to see myself as an engineer, but it's what my parents wanted. My father got me to apply for that army scholarship. 'You could do worse than choose the armed forces for a career,' he said. 'You'll see the world and they'll make a man of you!''

'Like they made a man of you!' I retorted cheekily.'

'When you let other people choose your path for you, you're likely to end up where you don't want to be. But that can happen at your age, because everyone is stuck with their parents' values until they've discovered their own.'

'So what can I do about it?'

'Find a subject to study that you're passionate about.'

'That has to be philosophy. I was reading Nietzsche's Thus Spake Zarathustra the other day - very strong stuff! Yes, I can truly say that I'm passionate about philosophy. So I'll go round to the philosophy department right away, and ask if they'll have me.'

'But break the news gently to your father.'

'Huh! That's not the way I do things. I believe in straight talking with no bullshit!'

The philosophy department welcomed me with open arms. They rejoice over every student they can get. And in my usual happy-go-lucky fashion I relied on the financial side of switching courses to take care of itself. And it did, as I found I was eligible for a county grant. My father was shattered, and my mother was distraught that her social ambitions for me had been shot down, but that's their problem, ha ha!

I now know why my father wanted me to go into the services - to have the career there that he never had, because he stayed a humble member of the ground staff right up until he left the RAF four years ago. I reckon he hadn't the gumption to become a flyer. Now he's unemployed, and spends his time hanging out in bars, playing poker with a bunch of other down-at-heel ex-servicemen. Sometimes he makes a buck or two, which has given him the idea that he can play poker for a living! Mum is worried he's going to the dogs!

When I was little, and he used to take me with him to the airfield, I was proud to call him dad, but now I despise him. In my eyes he's a coward. He hasn't made anything of his life, although he's got brains, and he showed a lot of promise when he was young. But he frittered away his opportunities.

'Hold on Sid! Do you have a right to take the moral high ground, and pass judgement on your father like that? You were on a slippery slope yourself a short while ago.'

'Yes, but I'm a reformed character now. All I needed was the right motivation, which I found in G.E.Moore. His book on ethics has persuaded me to embrace the higher things of life. Now, when I think about parties and pubs, and all that enforced fun, I break out in a cold sweat!'

'So what do you aspire to instead?'

'I'm going to create the final, definitive system of philosophical thought to explain the workings of the universe, and the general laws of human life - in other words a grand theory of everything!'

'Then you've got a lot on your plate! But I'm pleased you've found a goal, although that's only the first step. You're going to need plenty of conviction and sticking power to reach it, because you'll encounter distractions at every turn.'

'But that's life!'

I've been sitting in this hot train all day, fighting off the flies as they alight on my nose. It's the long vacation, and I'm travelling to Greece

214

with Mike Parker. He's writing a thesis on the pre-Socratic philosophers, and wants to absorb some local colour. I said I'd go with him - my appetite for travel being as insatiable as ever. No sooner am I back from one trip but I start planning the next.

It takes us two days and nights to get to Athens by train, but at least we see something of Europe on the way. Athens is baking hot in August, and, after I've dragged Mike round the Acropolis, the Parthenon, the temple of Athena Nike, and the theatre of Herod Atticus, he goes on strike.

'Have mercy!' he gasps. 'Not the archaeological museum as well. It's too much to take in in one day!'

So I go there alone, and I get round much faster without him panting behind me, and shouting that he can't keep up. Then we leave Athens and make for the Peloponnese, hoping it will be cooler on the islands.

'It's awesome to think that these ancient sites spawned some of the greatest minds in human history,' I say, as we revere the sun-baked stones in yet another ruined temple.

Mike doesn't reply. He's too busy with his sunburn and his insect bites. To be honest I'm looking for a chance to dump him, because he's turned out to be a dead loss as a traveling companion.

We're planning to cross to one of the smaller islands, famous for its temple of Venus, and Mike wants to book the boat tickets in advance.

'Nah! Not worth the bother of queuing,' I say. 'We'll just roll up. We're sure to get on.'

But Mike looks dubious. He'd prefer not to risk it.

'I'll try to find out if there's a hostel on the island,' he says.

'We don't need one. What are our sleeping bags for?'

'But it's dangerous to sleep rough - people get mugged.'

'Or raped!' I add.

Mike turns pale.

'Ha ha! It could be just what you need, Mike old buddy!'

The difference between us is that he's a pessimist, while I'm an optimist. He worries about the future, while I always believe things will turn out okay. And they do! Whereas, when you expect the worst, the worst is what you get - that's my experience. And this thought leads to an interesting conclusion, because it implies that our expectations have an influence on future events, so the human mind and the universe are not as separate as science makes out!

When we reach the island, Mike and I part company, and it's a huge relief to be on my own. At nightfall, I find a place on the beach to crash out, only to be awoken by someone shaking me. I open my eyes and there, kneeling beside me in the sand, is a beautiful girl.

215

'Some bugger's walked off with my sleeping bag,' she complains. 'Can I share yours?'

The temperature has dropped sharply, and she's standing there shivering in a skimpy little dress.

'Normally I wouldn't recommend it,' I reply, 'because I thrash around a lot in my sleep, so I need plenty of space. But, as I'm a gentleman, I can't refuse to help a damsel in distress.'

And I undo the zip far enough for her to slip inside.

'By the way, I'm Nancy from Santa Barbara,' she says, as she snuggles up to me.

'I thought you were Venus from the temple.'

And that's how I came to lose my virginity - more or less by chance, ha ha! I hoped she wouldn't notice how nervous I was. My heart was thumping, and I was stiff in all the wrong places. But I managed to perform, though it left me with the impression that sex is not all it's made out to be!

Afterwards we fell asleep, and the next thing I know it's morning, and I'm blinking in bright sunlight. Nancy is no longer in my sleeping bag. She's disappeared, and so has my wallet. Shit! It had my passport in it, as well as my train ticket and all my money.

'Nancy, you little whore!' I shout, 'Where are you?'

I search the beach, but it's deserted. I spend the day combing the island in vain. Venus has vanished.

'Now I'm in a right fix,' I think, 'but I know things will work out!'

And they do, because who should I come across at the landing stage but Akela - the guy who used to run our cub pack! He looks like a Jesus freak now, with his long, unkempt beard, and his dishevelled hair, but I recognise him immediately.

'Edward Archer? You were one of my cubs, weren't you? Of course!' and he gives me a hug. 'I dropped out,' he explains, as if to excuse his appearance. 'I've been in Greece all the summer, hanging out on the beach - meditating. But, now autumn is coming, I'm thinking of moving on.'

'Where are you going?'

'I don't know yet - wherever the wind blows me!'

I envied him. He was the kind of free spirit I'd like to be - moving around with no set route and no return date, taking each day as it comes, and never putting down roots.

When he hears of my predicament, he lends me the money to get to the consulate in Athens.

'They'll issue you with a replacement passport, and see you get home,' he says reassuringly.

And that's what happens. I get home safely, and thereafter I never tire of recounting this anecdote as an example of my incredible luck.

THIRTIES

I've reached thirty, and my career is coming together nicely. This evening I'm attending a reception at the British embassy in Berlin. I've smartened myself up considerably for the occasion by putting on a suit and tie, instead of my usual scruffy jeans and open-necked shirt.

I'm surrounded by a group of venerable patricians, who are listening while I hold forth on the merits of the Common Market. They include Sir Adrian Ward, the British ambassador, and flight commodore Butler from the top echelons of the British forces stationed in the area. So how, you may ask, did Ed Archer a down-at-heel philosophy student come to be hobnobbing with these bigwigs?

I'll tell you. After I'd got my degree - and I got a first - I went on to do a PhD. My thesis was on Wittgenstein's influence on G.E. Moore, and I was as happy as a sand boy doing post-graduate research. I'd work in the British Museum reading room, or travel up to Oxford to the Bodleian. I even flew across the Atlantic once to interview a Wittgenstein expert at the University of Chicago!

I had set my sights on an academic career in philosophy, and knew a lecturer's post would soon fall vacant in the department. In my usual way, I was bumptiously confident that I'd get it. But Mike Parker, the devious sod, pipped me to the post. My hubris was that I'm too outspoken. I tend to say things straight in people's faces with no regard for social niceties, and the prof couldn't take it. So the day came when I put my foot in it once and for all. Mike, the Machiavellian, used the situation for his own ends and, to cut a long story short, he was taken onto the staff while I was shown the door.

However, I'm not one to be deterred by defeat, and I walked away from the philosophy department with my head held high, and with my integrity intact. 'When one door closes another always opens!' I said to myself. I was only twenty-nine, and at that age the world's your oyster.

Then grandfather Unwin conveniently died, and left me a legacy, which I decided to use to buy time to write a book. The idea had been brewing in my mind for a while. It would be about the zeitgeist. I was fascinated by the upsurge of energy from the mid-sixties onwards in swinging London, and the vibrancy of contemporary youth culture.

So I set to work with bags of enthusiasm and a sense of mission, because this was an idea whose time had come. This book was asking to be written, and I was sure it would be a bestseller. However, when it was finally finished, it failed to find a publisher. Although I sent the manuscript round to dozens of publishing houses, it always came back with a rejection slip.

Some commented that the subject I'd chosen was too vast, and others complained that I hadn't researched my facts at all thoroughly. 'Be more circumspect in what you assert,' was one comment. 'Avoid broad-sweeping statements. Inflation erodes the credibility of what you say.' This brought me down to earth with a bump, because I'd been high as a kite. And, in the belief that my book would make me a lot of money, I'd also spent all my savings, and was sliding into debt.

'I need to earn some serious money quick - preferably abroad,' I confided to a friend,

'Why not try the British Council,' he suggested. 'They're expanding at present, and I've heard there are jobs going overseas.'

He was right. There was one up for grabs in Berlin, so I applied for it immediately, and the following week I flew out for an interview. They told me they were looking for someone who was positive and outgoing, and I said that *has* to be me. I must have made the right impression, because they offered me the job on the spot. I would have the title of cultural secretary, and be responsible for running their programme of cultural events, and teaching English language courses.

And that's how I come to be living in one of the world's political hotspots, a mere stone's throw from the notorious wall, and enjoying every minute of it. I've made a lot of friends since I arrived - most of them German. To be honest I find the natives more broad-minded and culturally aware than the British expats, who are a staid and inbred bunch of fogies. Ha ha!

Back to the embassy! I make for the cold buffet where I find myself standing elbow to elbow with flight commodore Butler. He's attacking a bowl of sauerkraut, but it's getting the better of him.

'You're the new fellow at the Council, aren't you?' he says. 'Sorry - I didn't catch your name?'

'Archer,' I splutter, my mouth full of smoked eel.

'Any relation to Humphrey Archer who was at Biggin Hill?'

'He's my father.'

'Is he, by Jove, then you must be very proud of him!'

Proud? A picture comes into my mind of my dad staggering home the worse for drink, and swearing when he can't get his key in the lock, and I shrug in disbelief. But, before any questions can be asked, a big, bustling woman appears, and carts the flight commodore off to the other side of the room.

After lunch I manage to corner Waltraud Hasenbein. I've admired her from afar since my first visit to the embassy where she works, but never dared approach her. Strange how shy I become when I find a woman attractive! You'd never expect it from a big, hulking bloke like me. But contained in this ultra male body is a gentle soul that's sensitive and a bit squeamish.

'I started learning German as a student,' I tell her. 'I wanted to read the German philosophers in the original, you see. So I learned to speak it from writers like Kant and Leibniz, and now, when I try to order a bratwurst, no one understands me. Ha ha!'

Waltraud is not amused. She's looking at me sternly over her glasses. Drat it! I still haven't grasped the German sense of humour - if they have one! So I have a go at impressing her by talking about politics, and she lets me go on for a good ten minutes before she interrupts.

'A lot of people who go abroad are running away from something at home. What are you running away from, Mr Archer?'

As I don't know what to say to this rather personal question, I ignore it and go on talking about Willy Brandt. I thought she couldn't get away, because she's pinned to the wall, but, just as I'm about to ask for her phone number, she says, 'Please excuse me, there's someone with whom I must speak,' and she escapes.

God damn it! Why can't I get my act together with women! There must be something about me that frightens them off. I wish I could put my finger on it. Perhaps my inner guide can enlighten me.

'Where are you, IG, you old rascal?'

'At my post, Sid.'

'Good, because I've got a problem. People would say I'm pretty male in a gung-ho sort of way, and I'm intelligent and interesting to talk to, so why don't I cut much ice with the women?'

'Well, what happened with Waltraud just then? You pinned her to the wall, and talked about subjects she wasn't interested in without giving her a chance to say anything.'

'Hmmm... In other words she found me too much. I was over the top!'

'Yes, you have a strong, dominant energy, and you're not always aware of the other person.'

'When I think back, the only relationship I've had that worked was with Hilda. That lasted two years.'

'But only because Hilda lived in Norway - hundreds of miles away - and you did most of your relating over the phone.'

'It worked because we each had our space, and I kept my freedom. Any closer would have been too close for comfort!'

'But a close emotional and physical relationship with a woman is just what you need, Sid, to bring you out of your mind and into your body. It would ground you.'

'Like a plane that's grounded and been left in the hangar! Ha ha!'

'But, if you haven't found a girlfriend in Berlin, it only proves that on a deeper level you don't want one. You value your freedom higher than having a relationship.'

IG's right there because, since I arrived in Berlin, I'm like a horse who's had his blinkers taken off. I gallop tirelessly round the streets in a state of perpetual excitement. I'm like a pioneer opening up new territory, and laying claim to it. So, having to drag a woman round with me, would only cramp my style.

I keep returning to the ominous wall that slices the city in two, and I picture the Soviet bloc beyond it, stretching eastwards as far as icy Siberia. I have a strong urge to cross over into East Berlin, and from there to cross all the other borders.

When you pass through Checkpoint Charlie, you enter a parallel universe. There's an eerie silence in the streets because of the lack of traffic. Weeds grow out of the crevices in the dilapidated buildings, some pitted with gunshot holes from the street fighting in the war. The air is pungent with the smell of coke burning on thousands of stoves, and you feel you're being watched continuously. The contrast to West Berlin's libidinous consumer paradise couldn't be starker!

Here's a good example, I think, of how different forms of socio-political conditioning create different mind sets. I can see the effect of the oppressive, totalitarian regime here in the bowed heads of the women queuing outside the shops, and in the people I pass in the street who always look away. They know I'm from the West, and they're afraid to be seen fraternizing.

So, when you live in a place like Berlin, where two political systems are in stark contrast with one another, you get a direct experience of cultural relativity. And this helps you to think outside the box - which is why I believe everyone should have an opportunity to live abroad sometime in their lives. Because, until we get a distance to our social backgrounds, we don't realise the extent to which we're the products of them. And we have to detach mentally from our conditioning, before we can find our own values and standards.

I'm leaping up the stairs two at a time. The room where the lesson is held is on the top floor, and I'm late as usual. I apologize to the class, who are waiting patiently. I take the folder out of my briefcase with 'Britain Today' written across it in felt-tip, and begin.

The course I'm teaching is designed to present an overview of the history, geography, religion, politics and culture of the British Isles. When I started, I knew precious little about these subjects, but - as the saying goes - the best way to learn is to teach. And what I don't know I can look up in the book of the same title, published by the British Council. It's so blatantly biased it's downright embarrassing! However, I see that the Council has a political as well as an educational function, and its mission is to present British democratic institutions in the most favourable light.

When the lesson is over, it's our habit to adjourn to a bar round the corner. There I sit, enthroned like a guru surrounded by his disciples, while we sip our lagers and nibble our pretzels. As usual I throw in a free lecture, and my subject tonight is the breakdown of values in western society. They are all listening spellbound - or are they just showing respect to their teacher in a German sort of way?

'I can see the genes of grandfather Unwin coming out in you, Sid, because you're proselytising again.'

'Oh go and boil your head!'

'Getting identified with the role of teacher does dangerous things to the ego, because you're always in the position of the one who knows, while the students, who receive the pearls of wisdom dropping from your lips, don't know!'

'Well, it's much more edifying for them to sit here listening to me than to stay at home watching telly - which is what they do the rest of the week!'

'But always remember, when you hold forth on themes you know very little about, that empty drums make the most noise!'

'What's that supposed to imply?'

'That you're good at making a big impression but, when the chickens come home to roost, your knowledge may be broad but it's often shallow.'

'Okay, there's some truth in that. But I see it as my task, as their teacher, to broaden their minds. That's more helpful to them than correcting their English grammar mistakes.'

'As long as you realise that the ideas you're imparting are not yours - they are all borrowed!'

'What do you mean?'

'You repeat things you've read about but haven't experienced yourself. If you spoke from your own experience, Sid, your words would have more substance, and you'd also be more succint!'

'Then I hope you take your own advice, IG! Because I've noticed how fond you are of lecturing me! Ha ha! What's sauce for the goose is sauce for the gander!'

'I'm only doing my job. And here's one last piece of advice - never forget, when you're wearing your teacher's hat, that the wisest of all wise men is he who knows himself!'

I don't go to football matches often, but England's playing Germany tonight in the European Cup, and it's happening in Berlin, so this is one I can't miss. All the tickets were sold out long ago, but I've managed to get one through the embassy. I arrive at the stadium to discover that my seat is bang in the middle of a solid block of German fans.

England makes a strong start by forming an attacking line-up, but somehow they can't get the ball in the net. Then, just before the end of the first half, Germany scores, which doesn't help England's morale. I'm very fired up, and keep shouting 'Come on England!' while everyone around me is singing 'Deutschland ueber Alle'. And the passion of my feelings surprises me, because I thought I despised patriotism, and I saw myself as a European rather than as an Englishman.

The match ends one-nil to Germany amidst loud boos from the English fans. It takes me a while to realise what's happening, because nothing in the build-up to the match suggested that hooliganism would be problem. So when something hard and heavy comes crashing down from above, hitting the man beside me on the head, I'm taken by surprise. Then I see that the English fans in the top tier are ripping out seats and throwing them down onto the German fans below. It's like a continuation of World War II, and I'm behind enemy lines.

There's a stampede for the exit, and me and my elderly neighbour - who was chatting to me in the interval - are carried along by the crowd. I notice he's bleeding from a gash to his head, and then I see him stumble and fall. The crowd take no notice. They just trample over him, and, instead of going to his aid, I look away.

Afterwards I'm heartily ashamed of myself, and this incident forces me to revise my self-image. I'd always seen myself as a man of courageous principle, but now I know that, when the shit hits the fan, I'm a coward after all. And although I'll never breathe a word about it, I've let myself down in my own eyes, and that's what counts.

Uncle Joe, who's visiting Berlin, drops in on me, and sleeps two nights on my floor. As he emigrated to America in 1946, I hardly know him. He left war-torn Britain to seek a better life across the Atlantic, but now he's pushing sixty his American dream is over. He's divorced, alcoholic and broke, and he's hoping that the British social security net will catch him.

We're sitting in a pavement café on the Friedrichstrasse. 'What!' he says. 'Didn't you know your dad was in the Battle of Britain? He shot down tons of German planes. What's up, Ed? You look as if you've swallowed a canary!'

It takes me a moment to find my tongue.

'If that's true, why did no one ever talk about it?' I say at last.

'Because the stuff about the mental hospital would have come out, and your mother didn't want that!'

'What mental hospital?'

'You'd better go and ask her yourself.'

I decide that it's high time I visited my aged parents, so I surprise them by turning up at their house in Wallington. I haven't been home for three years, and they welcome me with open arms. In fact they're so pleased to see me that I find myself coming over all soppy and tearful.

As soon as I can get my mother alone, I ask her the question that's bugging me.

'Is it true that dad was a pilot, and fought in the Battle of Britain?'

'Oh Joe told you that, did he?'

'Is it true or not?'

'It's true.'

'Then for crying out loud, why keep it from me? Surely I've a right to know something like that about my own father!'

'Well you see, dear, we had to protect him because he'd had a nervous breakdown - that was in 1941. They put him in a mental hospital. When he came out again he'd lost his nerve, and never wanted to fly again. He'd get upset at the very mention of it, so we made a family pact to keep off the subject. And I hope you're not going to rake it up with him now, Edward, because it could still unhinge his mind, even after all these years.'

I promise that I won't.

'This is so much like the plot of a film, IG, that I've started wondering whether my whole life is fiction. I mean Edward has got totally lost in the story, but if I jump out of him, as I'm doing now, into the character you call Sid, then it's just like watching a soap on telly.'

'You're getting warmer.'

'So it's true then - there's something like a cine projector in my head that's projecting the film of my life around me?'

'What you see is not what's really out there, that's for sure. Perception is a very tricky thing, Sid, as science is discovering. You're

223

viewing an internally generated facsimile of reality, and it's more like a recording than first-hand experience. But that's not the point. The point is that Edward is made to engage with it.'

'But why must he do that - for what reason?'

'It's necessary for the growth of consciousness. But you're leaping ahead as usual. Wait till the end of the story before you draw your conclusions, because there's plenty to get on with in the mean time. You haven't cracked Edward's code yet, or sussed out the programme that's running his life.'

'Oh I'm so bored with self-inquiry! Why can't you just tell me the answers?'

'Because wisdom is the fruit of experience. It's never second-hand. So set to work, Sid. You have to investigate the source and inner motivation of all your thoughts, feelings and deeds - why you want to do this and not that, why you're happy or unhappy, why you say what you say - which means you must remain the observer of yourself at all times, even in the thick of action.'

'I don't think I have the patience for that!'

'It's the only way to discover the meaning of life.'

MIDDLE AGE

I'm arriving at Heathrow on a flight from Canada. I'm still with the British Council, but I've moved around a bit since Berlin. Like the ancient mariner, something is propelling me forever onwards. So, when I left Germany I got a job in Mexico City, which was followed by a posting to Thailand. From there I went to Montreal, but I'm getting fed up with it already. I know every nook and cranny of the city, so I'm casting envious glances at the grass on the other side of the fence. Weird how it always looks greener!

When I leave the airport, I go to Victoria station and catch a train to Wallington. The country is celebrating the fiftieth anniversary of the Battle of Britain, and my father is being treated like a superstar. The TV came to interview him! On camera he came over as a burly, blustering RAF type - sociable and even witty. My mother reports that he's surviving the fuss without showing signs of a relapse, which proves she's been too over-protective all these years.

The country is having a ball celebrating its war heroes, but no mention is being made of the price they paid for serving it. I see my father now as war-damaged. And, like thousands of others who fought for their country, and had to carry the scars for the rest of their lives, he never received compensation.

My mother has made a scrapbook of cuttings and old photographs to honour him, which we look at together.

'He helped Britain win the war!' she says with shining eyes.

'He helped me become a pacifist,' I say. 'If there's a third world war, you won't catch me fighting in it. I'll be conscientiously objecting.'

'Don't let your father hear you say that!'

He only survived one more year - his liver was shot to pieces by all the booze. And now my mother's gone too, so I'm crossing the Atlantic again, this time to help my sister sort out their affairs. We're going to sell the house in Wallington, and halve the proceeds. So, for the first time in my life, I'll have money in the bank. And I'm wondering what to do with it, when Don, one of my colleagues in Montreal, comes up with an idea. He says he's thinking of moving back to England and starting a language school there.

'There's money in it,' he says, 'because it's not only the continentals now. There are plenty of rich Japanese coming to Britain to learn English. But we'll need some starting capital.'

I'm ready for pastures new, and there's a streak of recklessness in me that leads me to throw caution to the winds, so I say, 'Count me in!'

And that's how my inheritance came to be used as the down payment on a crumbling Victorian house in Tollgate. Converting it required further investment, and Barclays gave us a loan. Then, in our early entrepreneurial enthusiasm, we splashed out lavishly on furniture and fittings, only to discover that we'd vastly exceeded our budget. I stewed with impatience while the contractors took longer than planned to finish the work, but finally the *Get a Head Language School* was opened with champagne corks flying, and the first students arrived.

When I came to my senses, I couldn't understand what I was doing in a comatose place like Tollgate. How did I strand myself in a small town, full of narrow-minded people, chained to a massive mortgage and bank loan, when it's my nature to be footloose and fancy-free? I decided to ask my inner guide.

'IG, I feel as if I'm going round and round the plughole and never going down! How did I get into this mess?'

'You bought into Don's vision because you lacked a vision of your own.'

'Well, it was a wrong turn - I see that now. When I was young and hungry for experience, I'd take as many bites from life as possible, and swallow them all without chewing. But, now I'm older, and my energy is declining, I need to discriminate, and only do things that are worth doing.'

'And that's not running a language school.'

'No, because I have no business acumen, and no interest in acquiring any - and neither has Don come to that!'

'Your problem, Sid, is that this kind of work doesn't inspire you. You're someone who needs conviction. You have to know where you're going and why. So find an aim you can be passionate about, and then stick with it.'

'The trouble is I'm interested in so many different things.'

'Then you must create a focus of interest and avoid scattering, because you're going to need singleness of purpose to get anywhere in your life.'

'Hmmm... What I need is some sign or omen to point me in the right direction.'

It's always been my principle to avoid love affairs with female students - though sometimes it's hard to resist them. However, when Mercedes arrived from Buenos Aires to do a month-long *Brush up your English* course, she swept me off my feet. To begin with she's very good looking - a real stunner - and she radiates a lusty enjoyment of life in the body that is so un-English it's irresistible.

On the day she arrived she turned my head. During the first week, she bowled me off my feet, and within a fortnight we were in bed together. In the past I was often disappointed by the yawning gap between my inflated expectations, and what I actually experienced with women, but sex with Mercedes is like a dream come true. And it's so effortless - you just light the blue touch paper and the rocket goes up.

As the end of her course approaches, I become more and more agitated. I have to do something to prevent Mercedes from leaving, so I ask her to marry me. This is quite a turn up for the books, because I've been running away from marriage all my life. Every time I fell into the clutches of a woman, and it got close and intimate, a voice inside me would shout 'Run!' and I was off before she knew what had hit her. But, now I'm more mature, I feel I'm ready to stick with a relationship, and make a go of it. Mercedes, however, won't give me a clear answer.

'I have to go home to Argentina,' she says, 'but next year I come back.'

'Scout's honour?'

'What is scout, please?'

'Look it up in the dictionary!'

In the months that follow I spend a fortune on phone calls, which all go onto our business account, and contribute to the alarming figures our accountant produces at the end of the year. Apparently we're ten thousand in the red! The next blow comes when the Inland Revenue decides to target us, resulting in a huge bill for unpaid taxes. There was no fraudulent intention on my part. I'd just been careless as usual, and made mistakes in my sums.

When we're unable to pay, we're threatened with bailiffs and legal action, so we have no other option but to cease trading, and declare ourselves bankrupt. The building, which is seen as a business asset, has to be sold to pay our debts, and, as the property market has slumped in the meantime, we have negative equity. In the end it's auctioned off at a price considerably below what we paid for it.

That leaves me with just enough money to buy a plane ticket to Buenos Aires. I was feeling rather low, but the moment I board the plane my old jaunty self returns. I'm moving into the future again, and, although I don't know what's going to happen, I'm feeling upbeat and confident. Who needs property? You travel lighter without baggage, and the less weight a mountaineer carries, the higher he's going to climb!

'Off on another wild goose chase, Sid?'

'I'm chasing a woman not a goose, IG. Do I look like a gander? Ha ha! I'm going to marry her and start a new life in Argentina.'

'And never look back?'

'Nope! I took a gamble and it didn't pay off, but I've no regrets. I've never regretted anything I've done in my life.'

'That's the right attitude, Sid! We can use all our experiences - especially our experiences of failure - as opportunities to learn and to grow.'

'Which is what we're here for, isn't it, IG? Life is a school. We're all here to learn different lessons, and, if we fail our exams, we don't go up into the next class. Ha ha!'

'You're on the right track.'

.

When I land in Buenos Aires, I land on opportunity's doorstep, because it turns out that Mercedes is an heiress, and belongs to the high society. She gets me plenty of work by recommending me as a private tutor to her rich friends. She also ensconces me in a swish apartment, and lends me the money for the deposit. But some of the impressions I got of Mercedes while she was in England need to be corrected now. She's not thirty - she's forty. And she's not single - she has a husband who she forgot to mention. So, instead of getting married, I find myself embroiled in a clandestine relationship, conducted mainly when her husband is away on business, and he's away a lot!

However, what disturbs me more than the cloak and dagger nature of our love making, is the fact that, after a night of erotic pleasure, Mercedes always goes to confession, her head modestly covered with a black lace shawl. In my eyes that's morally unhealthy! And I'm disturbed by the strong presence of the Catholic Church, which is as pervasive in this land as a bad smell. I've kept organized religion at arm's length since I rejected the Baptist faith in which my mother raised me. And at university I was an atheist of the humanist ilk, fond of making long speeches in which I attacked religion as the opium of the people.

'Don't you believe in God?' Mercedes asks me, looking concerned.

'Not if you mean a patriarchal creator, whose will we have to discover and follow, or else we go to hell! Those are primitive ideas from the Bronze Age. But I'm open to a divine principle immanent in the universe.'

She looks shocked. I wonder how those damned priests have managed to hypnotise such a fiercely headstrong woman as Mercedes. The irony however is that, according to Catholic practice, adultery is okay as long as you confess it to the priest the day after, and receive his absolution. But it takes a while for me to realise the full extent of Mercedes' adultery.

Two other men come and go in her apartment - Sebastian, a rich industrialist who always brings flowers, and Miguel, the music student who teaches her the piano, and I've caught her flirting with both of them. Well, if there's one thing I can't stand it's being embroiled in a romantic intrigue, so I call her bluff.

'Be straight with me, Mercedes,' I say. 'What exactly is your relationship with Sebastian?'

'He's like a father to me,' she says blushing. And then it comes out that he's been her lover in the past.

'And Miguel?'

'Ah that boy is so cute - such a sweetie! I must confess I've fallen a leetle bit in love with him.'

Then it's adios, aufwiedersehen, adieu! Because I must confess that I've fallen out of love with you, Mercedes!

'Hi there IG! I'm planning on leaving Buenos Aires, and I fancy something different - something wild and snowy for a change. I've been dreaming of a log cabin amidst vast tracts of ancient forest and pristine mountains, where I can live a simple life in communion with nature.'

'Real life always happens in the present, Sid. While you sit there dreaming of the future, you are missing what is.'

'But I have to look ahead to decide on my direction.'

'That's not necessary when you live the present moment totally. Because, once you do that, you'll find your future evolving out of it quite naturally.'

'But you always said it's important to have an aim, and now you're saying go with the flow. There's a contradiction there somewhere.'

'When you follow your own deepest conviction and act accordingly, you set your direction. Then you have clarity of vision and a sense of vocation. You know that you're on the right path, and you're realising your potential.'

So I've decided to return to England with the intention of doing something useful with my remaining years. Perhaps I'll become a modern version of Baden Powell, and create a movement that enriches people's lives, and inspires generations of young people with high-minded values.

OLD AGE

I'm sixty-five and bald as a coot - though that's unfair on the bird, because a coot has a splendid head of feathers! Ha ha! I was trying to decide what to do after Buenos Aires, when Don got in touch again. He told me he was now the principal of a London language school. They'd been let down by some staff at the start of the summer term, and urgently needed a good teacher. Was I free? Well, this seemed to be my future taking care of itself, so I said, 'Okay, I'll come.'

I was given a part-time teaching contract, which ensured I had enough to live on, while allowing me space to pursue my latest interest. I'd bought a bike, and had become so passionate about cycling I was trying to persuade everyone else to take it up too. London, however, is anything but cyclist friendly, so I founded a charity to promote cycling as the most environmentally friendly form of transport, and the most healthy leisure activity.

Our vision is of a network of cycle routes running throughout the city. We are pressurizing urban planners to change their priorities, and consider the needs of cyclists and pedestrians before those of motorists. If safe and pleasant cycle routes were available, people would use them, and kids would go to school by bike again. Instead of being battery kids, they'd be free-range like we used to be, and this would cut down on the school run, and reduce carbon emissions, and help to save the planet.

My sister is worried about me because I've made no provision for my old age. So I'll have to manage on a meagre state pension when I retire. At present I'm occupying the caretaker's flat at the top of the building that houses the language school, and doing caretaking duties in lieu of rent. But this will soon come to an end.

'Something will turn up,' I tell her. 'You wait and see!'

Retirement, however, comes quicker than I expected. I'd been having some arthritic pain in my hip, and now the joint has collapsed, leaving me limping around on two sticks like a bloody cripple. My doctor tells me there's a long waiting list for hip operations on the National Health.

'Can't you do something, old boy, like move me to the top of the list?' I say to him. 'I've never been a patient, you see. I've always been an impatient! Ha ha!'

Climbing the stairs to my flat is like climbing Everest, and I'm in dire straights, but at that point Eunice jumps in. Eunice is a friend of mine - one of my fellow-teachers - and we've always got on well.

'Come and live in my bungalow in Hendon,' she suggests. 'There'll be no stairs to climb, and I've got a spare room for you.'

'Eunice, you're a brick!' I reply. 'I'll come tomorrow.'

She says she won't ask me for rent, because she's tired of living alone. She'd enjoy my companionship, as I'm always so cheerful and such a good sport. So I move to Hendon, and, although some of our colleagues make pointed remarks, our relationship is happily platonic and stays that way.

Six months pass, and I still haven't heard from the hospital about my hip operation. I feel like a plane with its engine running, and all ready to take off, that's been wheel-clamped.

'You said I needed grounding, IG. Well, I'm grounded now.'

'Yes, the departure gate is closed for you, Sid. You'll have to go on inner journeys instead.'

'You mean learn to meditate?'

'Exactly. All your life you've been rushing round in search of something outside yourself. But now the time has come to go inside and seek the seeker, because, if life is your oyster, then the seeker is the pearl inside it.'

'Well, there's no way to escape, because this ruddy hip won't let me. So there's nothing else for it, I suppose. I'll just have to become a buddha.'

'Practising meditation would be the best use of your time, Sid, and the way out of your prison. Because the more conscious you become, the more free you are and, when you've become pure consciousness, you're totally free.'

My hip has been replaced, and the operation was successful, so I'm celebrating recovering my mobility with a trip to Egypt. I have to see the pyramids before I die. But the crowds of tourists there soon get on my nerves, so I book a safari into the desert, accompanied only by a Nubian guide.

The donkeys are picking their way over the rough and rock-strewn terrain, and I'm scratching the insect bite on my leg that's refusing to heal. The next time I look down I see that my leg is red and swollen. Is it turning septic? Perhaps that's why I feel so light-headed.

By nightfall I have a raging fever, and my thigh is the size of a baseball. My Nubian friend is very sympathetic, and offers to amputate my leg with his penknife, but I decline. How I regret not bringing my mobile phone, but I wanted some respite from the damned thing.

'I need a doctor urgently,' I say, my teeth chattering.

'I fetch one,' he says, and disappears into the night, leaving me in the tent with only two bottles of water, when I could drink a whole crateful. The silence of the desert is unbroken now, except for the shuffling noises made by my tethered donkey.

I've crawled out of the tent to get some fresh air, and I'm lying on the sand, looking up at the sky that's ablaze with stars. There are myriads of them - stars behind stars behind stars. That one there is Sirius - it's brighter than the rest - and there's Orion. They look so peaceful. I'd like to be peaceful too, I think, and why shouldn't I be, because I've reached my goal? I've been travelling all my life to arrive at this very place - here in this vast starlit desert, under this infinite sky.

Everything goes black and there's a long silence. And when the lights come on again the film is over. I yawn in my reclining chair and stretch my legs.

'That's a joke,' I think. 'A big strong chap like Edward Archer finished off by a tiny mosquito! Ha ha!'

'Be grateful to the little creature for getting the job done,' IG says, 'because you had to get out of your body somehow.'

So that's it - I thought something felt different. I'm out of my body, and Edward has vanished, but he was only a fictitious character anyway. Now I'm left with Sid.

It was a quick and easy way to die, I think, so once again I've been lucky. And, looking back on my life, I have to say that I had a good run for my money. Yes, as lives go, it was great. It was a wow!

Life 10
PAT the CAPRICORN

When I discovered I'd picked the Capricorn medallion, I groaned. Not again! Not another life of hardship, adversity and relentless slog! Because I'd been there before - back in the seventeenth century when I sailed with *The Mayflower* to the new world. The land we built on was marshy and malaria-infested. Our numbers were decimated by attacks from hostile Indians, and the long, terrible winters known as the starving time, but our settlement endured.

So I politely suggested that someone else should have a go at Capricorn - someone like Mab, perhaps, who needed toughening up. But IG said there was a side to the archetype I still had to discover, and spoke of Capricorn's sardonic humour. I must learn to see the comic in everything, he said. Well, I thought, it'll take more than a humorous life-script to make the old, grave-faced Puritan in me smile. But I accepted the challenge, and that's why I'm here, relaxing in my reclining chair, ready to be amused.

The voices of the carol singers echo down the hospital corridor. 'God rest you merry gentlemen!' Merry! There's not much to be merry about with a war on, and me arriving in the thick of it, like a Christmas present to mum and dad from Santa Claus. That's a joke, because I wasn't planned or budgeted for, and they're not going to rejoice when they open the package.

The wards have been decked with twigs of holly and homemade paper chains. I move purposefully through them till I reach the labour ward, where I find my future mother giving birth. I've timed my arrival perfectly to slip into my new body at the moment of my first breath. That's the most efficient way to conduct this operation.

They have put me in one of the cribs in the baby room. It's separated off from the ward where the mothers lie by a glass partition. The other brats are bawling their heads off, but I lie there silently conserving my strength, which I'm soon going to need, because suddenly the air is split by the whooping sound of the siren sounding an air-raid warning. A nurse comes hurrying in.

'Come on you lot, get cracking! Grab your babes and go down to the air-raid shelter. Step on it now before Jerry gets you!'

The ward empties swiftly leaving my mother lying alone. The doctor has ordered her to stay in bed for forty-eight hours, and she never disobeys a doctor's order. And one solitary baby is left behind the glass partition - me! I'm just an hour old and in grave danger, and there's no one here to look after me.

'Well, there's nothing else for it, Pat,' I think. 'You'll just have to grow up this minute and take care of yourself!'

A whining sound passes overhead like the hum of a giant mosquito. Then I hear the muffled roar of an explosion, followed by a deep and bottomless silence. This is finally broken by the all-clear signal. I've made a mental note of my date and time of birth - 23rd December 1944, at 10.30pm. And my new name will be Carol Joyce Armstrong - Joyce after my mother, and Carol because it's Christmas!

THE KID

There's cold comfort at home during my first months of life. The house is unheated due to wartime fuel shortages, and, as my mother's milk dried up before it started flowing, there's no breast either. I'm fed with a bottle every four hours on the dot, and in between I'm left to sleep or cry. I have a cough and a runny nose, but I survive those first dangerous and bitterly cold months of life, which, instead of weakening me, serve to strengthen my system.

Time passes and I grow into a sturdy toddler. My mother and father are elderly parents, and treat me like an elderly child. Most of the time I'm left to my own devices. I've just climbed out of my playpen, and from there onto a chair, and from there onto the table, and from there onto the dresser, which is the highest piece of furniture. I do this purposefully, as if I'm carrying out a plan, and there I perch until I'm discovered and scolded.

My father owns a business selling building materials. It's a family concern, founded by my great-grandfather in 1840. My mother helps in the office, and every morning they take me with them, and put me in a playpen in the corner. I see myself sitting there on my potty. They are submitting me to a rigorous potty training, and know I must sit still and not move until I've done my business. But although I stretch and strain nothing comes. There's an aggrieved expression on mother's face. If I don't perform, it will make extra work for her, as she has to wash all my nappies by hand.

My father wears his glasses on the end of his nose, which makes him look more severe than he is, and goes around with a permanently worried expression on his face.

'Another customer defaulted on payment,' I hear him say. 'There's not much cash around these days and a lot of bad debt!'

After the war our finances went from bad to worse, and in November 1950 my father was forced into bankruptcy. A short time later he met with an accident - at least that's how my mother put it. When I asked her where daddy was, she said she didn't want to talk about it.

His demise left my mother and me to soldier on alone. We were very hard up, as all he had left us were debts, and there were lean dinner times with only potatoes, turnips and powdered egg to eat, while pudding was custard with a teaspoonful of jam on top. My mother got work where she could, and I became a latchkey kid while still at infants' school. But she's a spirited woman, my mother, determined to rise above her circumstances, and the following year she applied for a job as manager of a small seaside hotel. When she came back from the interview she said,

'I got the job, Carol, but I can't take you with me. There's no children allowed, the owner says. So we'll have to find a boarding school that can take you.'

She finds one with a vacancy that's run by the council. So, at the start of the autumn term, we travel there by Green Line bus, me lugging my trunk with my name painted on it in big, bold letters. We arrive at a tall, grey building looking more like a prison than a school, and matron comes down the steps to receive us. I have to shake hands with her. Then I stand there staring at my feet, while mother tells her all about me. Now the time has come to say goodbye and I shy away, as I'm on the brink of bursting into tears, and then what would matron think of me? My mother notices my lower lip trembling, and says briskly,

'Come on Carol, no sniveling! You're a big girl now!'

And she plants a formal kiss on my forehead, and gives me some good advice.

'Always do as you're told, and work hard at your lessons so you'll be a credit to the family!'

If I have to, I can be very brave. So I stifle my tears and follow matron down the corridor to the laundry to collect my bedding. But later on that night in the dorm, after lights are out, the tears I've been holding in start coming out. And on that first night at boarding school I cry myself to sleep - but very quietly so no one can hear. I don't want them thinking I'm a crybaby!

I soon realise that the first thing to do is to memorise all the rules, so I don't break any by mistake. I see other children being ticked off in front of the class for quite minor transgressions, and want to avoid that humiliation. So I start as I mean to go on, staying out of trouble by keeping the rules, and aligning with those in power - the teachers, the prefects and, of course, matron. This keeps me safe, and I not only survive my time at boarding school, I even profit from it, as I develop stamina and grow a thick skin.

In the middle of my fourth term, I get a letter from my mother announcing that she's got married to her boss, the hotel owner. I'll be going home for Christmas to a different home, she writes. Well, it can't be a step down the social ladder, because we're at the bottom already, so it must be a step up. I'm right. Home is now a detached house in a leafy suburb, full of heavy wooden furniture and the smell of boys. We've come up in the world it seems.

'This is Carol!'

My new stepfather peers at me over his newspaper and sniffs.

'The child's all skin and bone! Don't they give them enough to eat at that school?'

'It's her natural build, Henry. I was as thin as a flagpole too at her age.'

He returns to his paper with a grunt, leaving me standing there not knowing what to do. Then I spot an old friend. It's our piano that my mother has brought with her. It looks as stiffly upright and out of place as me. I run to it and open the lid, and play a scale gingerly. My stepfather looks up.

'I hear you'd like piano lessons?' he says.

'Yes please!'

'Then, if you show willing, and make yourself useful in the hotel, we'll find a teacher for you.'

'Oh she'll be useful all right,' my mother butts in. 'She knows there's no free lunches in this world!'

So it seems I'm not going back to boarding school, and that's correct, because after Christmas I start at the local primary down the road.

My stepfather is a widower who's been left with two boys to bring up. John and Brian are older than me - twelve and ten respectively. He's one of those traditionally minded fathers who see the family as a feudal hierarchy, where everyone must keep their place. And I soon discover that I'm last in the pecking order, below John and Brian who treat me with due disdain. If they invite me to play with them, it's only for the pleasure of beating me, because they're very competitive. They're always racing each other at things or doing arm wrestling, and I don't stand a chance against them.

But play doesn't figure large in my life anyway, as I'm burdened by a whole load of after-school duties. I work out ways of getting through them quickly and efficiently, so I have time for my piano practice. And, every evening before bedtime, you'll find me sitting at the piano, practicing my scales and arpeggios with gritty determination. It's not a chore. It's what I like best. I've discovered in music a gateway that leads into a parallel universe full of beauty and harmony.

My mother never forgets to be grateful to my stepfather for enabling her to rise in the world. She turns into his good, obedient donkey, patiently carrying the load of the hotel on her back from morn to night. The only time she takes any notice of me is when I offend her strict sense of propriety.

'You look a fright, Carol!' she'll say, while I'm scrubbing the floor. 'Go and make yourself respectable before one of the guests sees you!'

In deference to my stepfather, she's ever concerned with protecting the hotel's good name, which means she's always worried about what people might think of us.

'When you own a hotel, you're in the public eye,' she says, 'so you have to keep up appearances!'

TEENS

I've grown into a big-boned, gangly teenager. I go to the local grammar school, where I'm an example of the untruth of the proverb that all work and no play makes Jack a dull boy, because, in spite of my hotel duties, I consistently come top of the class. I have a talent for passing exams. Mental application and well-organized notes, together with a good memory, have helped me score over John and Brian at last. Their annual reports are full of 'could do betters' while mine are aglow with 'excellents'.

I've been allowed to stay on into the sixth form because I show exceptional promise, and that makes me realise how much the freedom to choose my path depends on my academic achievements. If I'd failed my O-Levels, I'd be working full-time in the hotel by now - a grim prospect!

My stepfather says he can't afford to send me to university, but I'm determined to go all the same. I have my sights set on Oxford, and my head teacher says I stand a good chance of passing the entrance exam and getting there. After making some enquiries, I discover I'd be eligible for a county grant, which would cover most of my expenses, and I'd earn the rest by working on the side. As it's my free choice to go to university, I want to be financially independent when I get there. And, after I receive the letter confirming that I've been awarded a place, I confront my parents with fait accompli.

If I'd followed my heart's desire, I'd have studied music, but I listen to the voice of reason instead and take a degree in economics. It's a subject I'm cut out for, and I continue to do well, coming top in all the tests. However, when I learn that the other students have christened me 'Carol Swot', I realize there's a downside to being a high achiever - your peer popularity suffers!

A crowd has gathered in front of the department notice board, where the results of our first university examinations have been posted. As I approach, I overhear one of them say,

'There's Carol Swot at the top of the list again. I wish I had her brains!'

'She's a pain in the neck,' says another. 'If she follows you through a revolving door, she'll still manage to come out ahead of you.'

They all laugh and I blush painfully.

When I was a fresher, I used to get invited to the coffee crushes, but I never felt comfortable there. I lack the skill of making small talk, which is a big disadvantage socially. I've never understood how people can go on chatting for hours on end about nothing in particular, and be witty and amusing to boot. So I'd sit bunched up in the corner like a stuffed parrot, till they decided I wasn't much fun and stopped inviting me - not that I care! Having friends takes up your time, and I don't have any to spare.

'Hallo, Pat!' says a voice in my head.

'Nobody has called me Pat for ages.'

'I'm IG, your life coach, contracted to accompany you during this incarnation. It's my role to support your self-inquiry by giving you advice when you ask for it.'

'I probably won't!'

'That's a pity because it was your vowed intention to live more consciously, and I could help you inquire into your patterns.'

'I can do that by myself, thankyou, and anyway everything's fine.'

'Your outer life may be fine, Pat, but what about your emotional state - is that fine too?'

'Not always! Sometimes I feel despondent.'

'Perhaps it's because you don't allow yourself any time to relax and enjoy life. You put yourself under too much achievement pressure.'

'Work before pleasure is my motto!'

'And yet, deep inside, you feel hard done by. I wonder what lies behind this compulsion to work so hard. Do you feel guilty when you're not being productive?'

'No, I just like using my time profitably. When I buy a Sunday paper, for example, I never allow myself the luxury of reading the magazine section, but I limit myself to news items that have a bearing on my subject.'

'It's the puritan work ethic from your past life coming out in you.'

'Then there's not much I can do about it!'

'Oh I wouldn't say that! Just by becoming aware of a pattern you change it. And, when you're aware, you can choose whether or not to strengthen it by repeating it.'

'I see.'

'If you feel depressed, Pat, maybe it's because you're lonely. You don't seem to have made any friends yet.'

'That's true.'

'I was watching you enter the common room the other day and, instead of joining the group of students from your course, you went and sat alone in a corner.'

'I wanted to get on with my book. All right, I admit I have social inhibitions. Actually I'm a deeply shy and very private person.'

'You certainly come over as reserved, and you tend to be formal with people in a rather old-fashioned way.'

'Yes, because formality is a shield I can hide behind.'

'Do you find it hard to trust people?'

'I'm suspicious of outer shows of friendliness when I know that inside people are critical. Those students you saw in the common room have a lot of judgements about me.'

'When criticism comes at us from the outside, it mirrors a critical attitude within us. For example, I've heard you being judgemental, Pat, about how the students spend their free time.'

'Well, I've a problem with all their partying and hanging out together. I mean it's not what they're at university for, and most of them are on grants, so they're wasting the tax payers' money!'

'That's the old, straight-laced puritan in you speaking, Pat. You'd better keep an eye on her, or she'll throw a wet blanket over everything, and never allow you to have any fun.'

'Fun! I thought we were here to work!'

'You're here to see the joke.'

Then I remember that, when we wrote my life script together, IG told me that what I needed most was to learn to look on the bright side. And dawn does follow night and, after the nadir of the winter solstice, the light is always born again. But to arrive at that point we have to pass through the darkest hours of the night, and the shortest and bleakest days of the year.

TWENTIES

On my twenty-first birthday, on December 23rd 1965, I receive an envelope from my mother containing an unopened letter with my name on it. In her accompanying note she wishes me a happy birthday, and then goes on:

'When your father died he left two letters - one for me and one for you. His instructions were to give you yours on your twenty-first birthday, which has now arrived.'

I'd have preferred a bunch of flowers or a box of chocolates! But I know I can expect some sort of present in two days time. My mother has the habit of combining my birthday with Christmas in her usual thrifty way.

The day ahead is going to be a busy one. There are the last lectures of term to attend, followed by a shift in the café where I have a part-time job. When I finally get home, with a bottle of wine under my arm to celebrate, it's past eight o'clock. The envelope with my name on it is sitting on the kitchen table, and I have to drink half the bottle of wine before I have the courage to open it.

'My darling Carol,' it reads. 'I hope you will never know depression, or feel the utter hopelessness that I feel now. Since I lost the business, I've become prey to the black dog of despair. If I had a reason to stay, it would be for you, my dearest daughter, but I know I'd only blight your life. Therefore I am leaving you in the land of the living, while I cross over to the land of the dead. May your life be more successful and happier far than my poor life has ever been. I pray for your understanding and forgiveness. Your ever-loving father, Charles.'

I can't get down to my reading after that, so I put on my hat and coat and go out. After wandering aimlessly up and down the streets for a while, I go into a pub to warm up. There's a Christmas tree inside the door twinkling with coloured lights, and a log fire in the grate, and a crowd of revellers stoked up on beer and Christmas cheer.

And it's in that unlikely place that I meet Charlie, who by some strange twist of fate has the same name as my father. He tells me he's lonely and he needs someone to talk to, and I say 'Snap!' So I listen to his story, and he listens to mine, and my customary inhibitions are melted away by his kindness and gentleness. He's a true gentleman, I think, in all senses of the word.

When it's closing time and we have to leave, Charlie offers to walk me home.

'You don't have to,' I say. 'I'm used to looking after myself.'

'Oh but I insist!' he replies.

We get a surprise when we step outside the door. The dark, dingy streets have been transformed into a white wonderland. And, as we walk down the road, we leave behind us two pairs of intertwining footprints - the very first imprints on the pristine sheet of snow. We part after making arrangements to meet again, and then I find myself back again in my room. The half drunk bottle of wine and the open envelope are still on the table. Everything's as it was before I went out, yet now it all looks different. And, while I'm trying to make sense of what's happened, I hear IG's voice.

'Hallo, Pat!'

'IG! There must be a connection between my father and Charlie, as they both have the same name. Did my father somehow bring us together?'

'There's life beyond death and love beyond despair, as your father would have discovered if he'd waited, instead of ending his life as he did.'

'How did he end it?'

'He hung himself from a beam in the attic.'

'Good grief! I remember the attic. I used to play there!'

'He was only forty-two when it happened - young enough to make a fresh start and build up his business again.'

'Then why did he kill himself?'

'His values were purely material. His only aims were to earn more money and achieve more status. So when his money and his reputation were lost, he saw no more sense in living.'

'I can understand him there, because you have to add up to something in this world or else you get trodden on. But abandoning us like that made it extra hard for me and mother.'

'It had some advantages though. You learned to stand on your own feet, and to take responsibility for yourself from an early age. These skills will stand you in good stead when you go out into the world.'

'Hmmm... I intend to carry on where my father left off, and have the successful career he didn't have. But tell me, IG, is getting married written into my life script?'

'We left that open. You thought you might prefer to be a career girl.'

'I'm asking because I think I've found somebody. It felt so natural and familiar with Charlie right from the start - as if we two belong together.'

'Life is very mysterious, Pat, and there are deeper processes at work which we can only guess at. So my advice to you is to remain open and in a state of wonder, like a small child. Allow yourself to be surprised by what life serves up.'

241

Charlie has become my steady boyfriend. He says he likes being with me because I know what I'm doing, and where I'm going, whereas he doesn't. We complement each other perfectly. I ensure that our life together is well organized - in order in the quantitative sense - while he contributes quality to it.

When I left university, and it was with a first-class degree, I applied for a job with a large multi-national company, where I'd have the scope to expand my wings. I knew I had it in me to go far. I was capable and competent, self-disciplined and self-motivated, and under the illusion that I could bend the world to my will.

They were very keen to have me, and put me on their business management training course. While the course was running, I was given clerical work and moved around the departments, so I'd gain experience of the different sections. I discovered that the company, with its pyramid structure, resembled a huge ant heap in which every employee had a pre-ordained slot. Most of them stayed in their slots and grew old in them, but I classed myself as belonging to the young and upwardly mobile minority.

I soon learned the ropes. To get anywhere, you had to establish yourself as part of the system on the company's terms. You must profess the same opinions as your superiors, and dress and behave in the same way. Individualism was frowned upon, and if you declined to be part of the collective corporate mindset, you were shown the door. To rise through the ranks, you set your sights on the job of the person immediately above you and maneuvered for it, while defending your position from similar attacks from below.

I showed willing from the start, and performed every task I was given to the best of my ability. I've always believed that, if a job is worth doing, it's worth doing well, and I took great pride in being efficient. My bosses were amazed at how much I could get done. I told them it was because I always work out the best way of tackling a job before I start, and I can keep my mind on what I'm doing, unlike the other office girls. Judging from their conversations, their minds are on their boyfriends or their hair-do's most of the time. I notice them surreptiously extending their lunch breaks to go shopping in the West End, and watch them disappear into the cloakroom to try out a new lipstick. I wouldn't tolerate such goings-on if I were in charge.

As time management has always interested me, I chose it for my course project. I've had a thing about economy of effort ever since I was small, and had to get my chores done before I could play the piano. So I carried out some time-motion studies, and produced a paper in which I recommended a number of labour-saving practices. Not only was it awarded a high grade, but my tutor thought it worth passing on to his superiors, which is why I'm in the lift now, travelling up to the tenth floor.

It's the first time I've been as high as this in the building, and I'm impressed by the luxury I find. The floors are thickly carpeted, the walls are hung with tasteful modern art, and the windows have spectacular views over the Thames. I find Sir Gerald Harkins, the senior manager I've been invited to meet, sitting at his desk, comfortably inflated by a business lunch.

'I'm delighted to meet you, Miss Armstrong,' he says. 'I was most impressed by your paper. Not only is it well researched, but you have come to some conclusions that are of value to the company.'

He says they are planning to produce it as a booklet to distribute to the staff, with a little editing of course. A chap from finance will be getting in touch with me to discuss the copyright question and, of course, my remuneration.

'You've got a wise head on your young shoulders, my dear,' he says, when the interview is over. 'So carry on the good work!'

As I walk down the corridor to the lift, glowing with pride, I'm imagining myself in a few years time, sitting pretty in one of these tenth-floor offices with my name on the door in bold upper case type.

'And what would be in it for you, Pat?' IG interrupts.

'Money would be in it and power!' I reply. 'I know I've got what it takes, IG, and I want to see how far it will take me.'

'Well I'm surprised you've become ambitious in a worldly sense. In your Puritan days you embraced poverty and service.'

'I'm aiming higher this time. It's the people with money and status who have the say in society, and I want to be up there with them, making the decisions that count.'

'Then it's not for personal gain. You want your work to benefit the community?'

'Yes, I've always had the feeling that I'm here to perform an important task.'

'That's true, but important in a different sense. I admire your dedication, Pat, but where does your ambition come from?'

'From my childhood I suppose. Maybe I'm still competing with John and Brian. When they kept beating me, I thought to myself, 'I'll show you! One day you'll all have to sit up and take notice of me!'

'But you're going to discover that, however much you achieve, it will never be enough to win their approval much less their love.'

'So I'm doomed to remain despondent!'

'Not if you raise your consciousness to a higher level. Then you'll see that there's no need to achieve in order to prove yourself worthy. The very fact that you've been born shows you're worthy of life, and everything worthy of life is worthy of love and happiness.'

I've been up since seven working, and now it's ten and Charlie's still snoring in bed. 'Wakey wakey!' I shout in his ear, but he doesn't stir. So I pull all the bedclothes off, and push him out of bed. He lands with a bump on the floor, his eyes still closed, and lunges at my leg in a vain attempt to pull me down beside him.

'No horseplay this morning, Charlie - we've got work to do!'

'Oh don't be such a horrid spoilsport, pussikins!'

But he sees I'm in a no-nonsense frame of mind, so he groans and staggers off to the bathroom. Duty before pleasure is my motto, and I'm determined to see that Charlie finishes his degree. However it's not easy to get him to toe the line, because he's as carefree and irresponsible as a small child - though that's the attraction. From the moment I first saw him, that innocent, childlike quality of his touched me to the core.

Charlie and I are a case of opposites attract, as we're as different as chalk from cheese. When I point this out, he says,

'Then I'm the chalk because I'm easy to rub out, and you're the cheese, because you're the type who matures with age, and you taste best when you're mouldy!'

I have to laugh. His whimsical sense of humour always has the power to melt my gravity.

When I told my mother I'd met someone, she said,

'And about time too! We thought you were a blue stocking and on the shelf! But you say he's twenty-six and still a student? At that age he should be out earning his living!'

Her worst fear is that I'll take up with some good-for-nothing layabout, and then my stepfather would lose all respect for me. So I tell her about Charlie's family, which makes her change her tune. He veritably soars in her estimation when she knows he's upper crust.

'Guess what,' she says to my stepfather. 'This new boyfriend of Carol's comes from very good stock!'

I must admit I'm also dazzled by the glamour of Charlie's aristocratic lineage. He's the youngest son of a lord, and his pedigree shines through in his exquisite and impeccable manners. He's got such an elegant way of bowing a lady through a door in front of him. It makes one feel like a queen. But there's a downside to going out with a toff - you become painfully aware of your social inferiority, which is why I dread meeting his family.

This, however, can't be postponed indefinitely, and my first encounter with his mother takes place at the *Chelsea Flower Show*. I buy a new two-piece suit for the occasion, but her extravagant broad-brimmed hat, and flowing Christian Dior robe put me in the shade. She's tall and statuesque and overweening, and she immediately sets about establishing my credentials.

'And what does your father do, Carol?'

'He was a businessman,' I reply, 'but he died when I was six.'

'And what did he trade in?'

'Building materials.'

Her fixed smile thinly covers her disdain. And, when she asks about my mother, and I tell her about the hotel in Broadstairs, her disapproval becomes as long and sharp and cold as an icicle.

'She thinks I'm common,' I say to Charlie afterwards.

'That's her problem,' he laughs. 'Poor mumsie still lives in the Middle Ages. She hasn't registered yet that post-war society is a meritocracy in which gifted people from the lower orders are acquiring rank and privilege.'

'She thinks I'm a social climber and after your money.'

'She's just got to face the fact that the class system is defunct.'

'But Charlie, everywhere you look class rules. This country is a long way from being egalitarian!'

Charlie likes spouting liberal ideas, and he often complains about the unfair distribution of wealth, but he accepts the monthly cheque from his father, that drops through our letterbox, without a qualm.

I'm the one who wants to get married because I'm old fashioned in that way. Now that we're sharing a flat, I'm dogged by the fear that co-habiting without a marriage licence will put a slur on my character. I'd prefer our relationship to be put on a respectable footing, and be ratified by society.

'A marriage license is only a bit of paper,' Charlie says.

'In other words you don't mind one way or another?'

'I don't care, but mumsie will,' and a mischievous gleam comes into his eye. 'It's going to serve her right!' he laughs.

So our union is formalised at the local registry office, with two of Charlie's hippy friends as witnesses. My secret hope is that marriage will change Charlie for the better - make him grow up and shoulder his responsibilities. But he just goes on in his old sweet way. There's only one change - his parents are so piqued that they stop his allowance. But I'm earning enough for the two of us, so it's not the end of the world. In fact I prefer it that way, as I'd hate to be financially dependent on his family.

We move to a house in Fairbanks, a pleasant commuter suburb with easy rail travel into town. Charlie has a legacy from his grandmother, which we use as the down payment, and I sign the mortgage document, as I'm the salaried partner. Charlie is revising for his exams, so he stays at home and does the shopping and cooking while I go to work. At first there's a hot meal on the table every night when I get home from work, but then Charlie starts to lapse.

I've just alighted at Fairbanks station from the 6.30 train. I'm smartly turned out in a well-tailored suit, and I'm wearing a pair of expensive but comfortably flat shoes. I've never set much value on what I wear beyond ensuring that my clothes are practical and appropriate. But, now I've been promoted to a job where I'm more in the public eye, my appearance must be consistently smart and well groomed.

As I pass the row of shops lining the station approach, I'm irritated as usual by all the litter blowing about on the pavement. It was such an effort to get the council to install those litter bins, and now they're not being used! Punitive measures are needed to concentrate people's minds. There's nothing else for it - we will have to introduce fines!

In the distance I see a group of young people lounging on the patch of grass in front of the war memorial. Judging from their fluttering shawls and long hair, they are a bunch of hippies. One is strumming a guitar. And, when I draw closer, I'm horrified to see Charlie amongst them. He's stripped off his shirt, and he's sunbathing on the grass in full view of passers by! I cross to the other side of the road hurriedly.

When he finally arrives home, I give him a ticking off.

'But pussikins what are you upset about?'

'Do you think I like seeing my husband make a public spectacle of himself?'

'But what have you got against my friends?'

'They smoke pot! And they're not productive members of society - most of them are living off benefit!'

Charlie laughs. 'You should take a leaf out of their book, and put the pleasure principle before the work ethic! I enjoy their company. They're the only people left alive in this one-horse town!'

I bridle at this criticism of Fairbanks, which I consider a desirable place to live, but fall back on the hope that Charlie's attitudes will change when he leaves university. He'll have to pull his socks up then, as he'll be forced to measure up to the real world.

'The more you try to control him,' IG says, 'the more irresponsible he'll become. Although Charlie *is* responsible in the true sense of the word, as he has the capacity to respond.'

'I know, and I admire his responsiveness but, if I didn't keep him in order, IG, he'd never make anything of himself.'

'What makes you so sure *you* know what's best for him? He has his life agenda, and no doubt he's achieving what he set out to do.'

'But don't hold your breath!'

'Concentrate on yourself instead, Pat, and inquire into why you got so upset this evening.'

'He was letting the side down. Now that he's my husband, I can't stand there and watch him disgrace both himself and me.'

'And why do you value your public standing so highly?'

'I have my pride like everyone else.'

'There's more to it than that. You're so sensitive about what people think of you that you'll go to any lengths to maintain a respectable public façade and hide your dirty washing.'

'I've got a reputation to keep up. That goes with my position. It was advantageous for me to marry the son of a lord, which counts for a lot in the company's eyes. But a public scandal involving your spouse can jeopardise your career chances. And last week I discovered a little screw of silver foil in Charlie's jacket pocket, and identified its contents by the pungent smell. So I have a reason to clamp down on him.'

THIRTIES

I've been climbing steadily through the ranks and have reached a managerial position. According to my calculations, I should have been identified as senior management material by now, because I've proved I have the confidence to make major business decisions, and shown I have the stamina to sustain long-term projects. But the mind-set of the company is prejudiced against females, as demonstrated by the noticeable absence of women from the higher echelons of power. The directors who grace the top floor penthouse suites are without exception male, and I've had to overcome gender-related obstacles on every step of my path. It's clear that, if I am going to fulfil my ambitions, I'll have to crash through the glass ceiling, which is firmly in place and located between the ninth and tenth floors.

The same applies to our society as a whole. My first class Oxford degree can't compensate for the fact that I'm a woman. And I have to face the inconvenient truth that John and Brian, always so much duller and less talented, are getting the career opportunities denied to me because of my gender.

However, as a manager, I'm enjoying a certain amount of power and prestige. And I'm a good boss - strict but just - though I expect high standards of performance from my staff, and I'm a stickler for discipline. When I'm around they mind their P's and Q's! Well, I work hard myself, so I expect others to do likewise, and this has made me unpopular with the old hands, who are used to a more laid-back regime. I have no patience with these inveterate slackers, and malingers get my goat. I've never missed a day's work myself through sickness, so it's understandable that, when people take time off for the slightest cold (which they always call flu) they fall foul of me.

I still suffer from a certain amount shyness and inhibition in social situations, and I find office parties grueling. But in my professional capacity I'm able to meet people and converse with them confidently, protected by the formality of a set code of behaviour. What floors me, however, is criticism of a personal nature. I once overheard a typist say, 'Her and her airs and graces - just because her old man is a lord!' and that upset me very much.

'Why do I react so sensitively to criticism, IG?'

'Well, do you remember how your mother was always criticizing you? When you were young, her criticisms felt like a threat to your life-support system. You were so afraid of being thrown out of the nest.'

'Yes, she kept me in a state of fear with the threat that, if I didn't measure up, I'd be sent back to boarding-school!'

'It's how she controlled you. You see, criticism can be used to dominate people by making them feel small. You use it yourself to keep the upper hand in the office, so be more aware. A good boss never disempowers her staff - she doesn't need to, because she's centred enough in herself, and rests in her natural authority.'

As the years passed, the playfulness that characterised my relationship with Charlie ebbed and I grew more and more resentful. He had disappointed me. In spite of all my efforts, he'd dropped out of his course and left Oxford without a degree to go off travelling. Perhaps he needed to get away because I nagged him so much.

'Pull yourself together Charlie-boy,' I'd say. 'If you go on like this, you'll never amount to anything!'

When he'd gone, I missed him sorely, and worried constantly that he was getting into bad company and picking up bad habits. Then, when his money ran out, he came home - skinny and scruffy and in debt. I paid his debts and fattened him up, and then discovered he was in no hurry to find work.

'I can't just take any old job, pussikins,' he said. 'My heart has to be in it!'

248

So I gritted my teeth and continued to support him. I was in the role of parent and he was the dependent child, which inside I resented. I've never taken kindly to grown-ups wanting to be babied. I believe we should all stand on our own feet and provide for ourselves financially. It was a shock when I discovered I was pregnant. I was an elderly thirty-seven, and not used to unplanned events happening to me. By then Charlie and I had separated. I'd accepted the fact that he was never going to get his nose anywhere near a grindstone, that he was a non-starter. It was his pattern to take short-term jobs to earn some cash, and then spend it by going traveling. I would pine for him during his absences and, though we were supposed to be separated, I always took him in when he returned. It was weak of me I know, but I was a lonely woman and craved a man in my bed.

Now I had to face the consequences of my laxness. An abortion was out of the question, and I had no illusions about what lay ahead, after years of seeing frazzled women colleagues tying themselves in knots trying to be both mothers and career women at the same time. But I've always enjoyed a hard challenge.

Charlie said he was blissed out by the prospect of becoming a dad.

'You can go to work, pussikins, and I'll look after the baby!' he volunteered.

'Get your facts right first, Charlie-boy!' I said. 'Caring for a baby is relentless. It's fourteen hours a day and seven days a week pure drudgery.'

'You can rely on me, pussikins!'

But of course I couldn't, because Charlie was a letter-downer.

It was a boy and we called him Sam. Charlie's nerves, as I had foreseen, were severely challenged by having to take care of a howling infant, who quickly morphed into a hyperactive toddler. Instead of rising to the challenge, he sank to it, and disappeared off to Thailand for the winter, leaving me to soldier on alone.

I expected no help from Charlie's family, who continued to maintain a haughty distance, and neither did I ask for it. And my mother no longer lived close enough to lend a hand. She'd sold the hotel and moved to Penzance after my stepfather died. It's where she originally came from. So I had to hire a professional child-minder. But I was confident I had the self-discipline and focus that would be needed to stay on top of my workload, and to be a good enough mother to Sam. So, when Sir Gerald Harkins (now my boss) dared to question this, I replied,

'If a woman is the mother of a two-year-old and she still wants to work, that proves she's highly motivated, and she's going to be damn capable at her job!'

When Charlie re-appears, he's lost a lot of weight and his hair is falling out. I guess the reason immediately, and my suspicions are confirmed when I see the scars on his arms left by the needle. 'That's it!' I think, and I make the decision to ditch him without further ado.

'You can't stay here, Charlie. I'm not having you injecting in my house. There's Sam to think of.'

'But I've nowhere else to go,' he says pitifully.

He pleads with me to take him in. He goes down on his bended knees. He weeps, but I remain adamant. The barriers are up now, and behind them there's a total emotional freeze.

'You don't know what you're doing, Carol,' he says. 'Without you and Sam I'll go under! You've always been a tower of strength to me!'

But there are no more chinks in my armour. I stay hard as flint. So he takes Sam in his arms to embrace him one last time, and sobs all over him, and then calls a taxi.

After he's gone, there are tears in my eyes too. The house feels darker and colder now Charlie has departed for good. The rays of sunshine he always brought with him are gone now. Sam is in the kitchen howling inconsolably, and next Sunday the clocks go back, and the long, dark winter nights are coming, and I'm all alone.

I suppose it's my fault that there's no one around to comfort me. I've always valued my privacy and my self-sufficiency. It's never been a habit of mine to talk about my problems with others, just as I have little sympathy when people come to me with their sob stories. Everyone can feel hard done by, but our bruises belong to the knocks of life. Because, when it's been stripped of its frills, life is blood, sweat and tears, and we have to face up to that fact.

I've become increasingly uncomfortable that, in the eyes of the world, I'm still Charlie's wife. Being married to him puts me in a vulnerable position, especially now he's become a drug addict. I could be held legally and financially responsible for his actions, and that must be rectified. However, before I go to my solicitor and start divorce proceedings, it crosses my mind that, through divorcing him, I'd be robbing him of last support. It could lead to Charlie ending it all and taking an overdose. But I'm not in a position to be able to afford such considerations.

MIDDLE AGE

I've just got home from work after collecting Sam from the child-minder. Now I have to feed him, bath him and read him a bedtime story. By nine o'clock he'll be asleep, if I'm lucky, and I'll be able to

250

pour myself a glass of whisky, and collapse in front of the TV. I'm feeling worn out and depressed.

When Charlie exited from my life, my job became my shelter and my solace. It's been like a steady, dependable companion to me all these years. But we've been going through a hard time with a general reshuffle taking place in the company. Time-tested procedures have been ditched or modernised, and I've had to work as hard as is humanly possible to prevent my department from falling into chaos. However, the new job descriptions are in place now, and the records have been updated, and we're slowly getting back on to our feet. But it's been crunch time concerning my role as Sam's mother. He's started having problems at school, and now it's come to light that he's been playing truant. His teacher says he needs a firm hand.

In this dire situation, a letter arrives out of the blue from Charlie's parents. They want to do something for Sam, who they say is now of prep school age. They would like to see he gets a good education, and want him brought up in the family tradition, which means sending him to prep school first and then to Eton.

Eton! What a wonderful chance for my son! I know how much such a privileged start in life counts in our society. But this means Sam will go to boarding school, where he'll probably be miserable like I was. However it's likely he'll emerge with his backbone strengthened, because he's also a survivor - like me. So, assuring myself that it's in Sam's best interest, I reply to Charlie's parents saying I'd like to accept their offer.

Being proficient at my job used to fulfil me, and planning my career gave me a purpose in life. But now I find myself clinging to the underside of the glass ceiling with little prospect of clambering over it and becoming a senior executive. Have I risen as high as I'm going to get? Although my competence is beyond question, and I've made no errors that can be held against me, Sir Gerald seems bent on opposing my further promotion. The fact that I'm a woman disqualifies me in his eyes for a top, high-visibility job. And this has left me angry and bitter.

'What you can't change you must accept, Pat.'

'That's easier said than done, IG. Looking back on my career, I see it as one long obstacle race. I was proud of the fact that I'd cleared all the hurdles. So it's hard for me to accept that this final one could knock me out of the race.'

'Perhaps that's the very thing that needs to happen. All your life you've been driven by a stern inner taskmaster, and he's brought you a long way through never being satisfied with what you've achieved, and goading you on to achieve more.'

'And I know I'm capable of more now! I want to be up in the boardroom. I want to contribute to the agendas, and have the power to make a difference on issues that count.'

'But life, with perfect timing, always presents you with the very challenges you need for your growth. And this time it's a new kind of challenge, Pat. You are required to accept defeat, and to move on.'

'You mean leave the company? Well, perhaps it's time, because I'm becoming disenchanted with them. And I've started to question the purpose of my work. As I see it now, I've been expending my energy merely to increase the company's profits and fill the shareholders' coffers!'

'Then you're no longer identified with the company's aims and values?'

'Hmmm... I can't say this out loud, IG, but I'm becoming increasingly concerned about what they are doing to the planet. I see the company's policies regarding the environment as short-sighted and unethical.'

'Then look for job where you're not required to compromise your principles.'

'But I'm forty-five! At my age that would be as risky as changing boats mid-stream. And I'd lose everything I've laboriously built up over the years - my whole investment.'

'Then you don't trust life to see you land on your foot?'

'No, I'm the eternal pessimist, IG. I know that the fates have it in for me, and the only way I can defend myself against them is to have my life well under control.'

'That negative belief is your greatest obstacle, Pat, and your present challenge is to cross that hurdle. Then, as soon as you're over it, you'll realize that it wasn't real - it was only an idea in your mind!'

But my cautious nature prevents me from acting on this advice, and then my back starts to play up. It begins with a dull, nagging pain in the lower back, which turns into a sharp, stabbing pain that runs up my spine whenever I move. So I don't move - I stay in bed. For the first time in my life I'm off sick. My doctor prescribes me a muscle relaxant, which doesn't help. So I have to drag myself to the hospital to be x-rayed, and to see an orthopedic consultant, who can't find anything wrong with me. He prescribes painkillers, and tells me to stay at home and rest until it's better.

But it doesn't get better and, after I've been off work for eight weeks, I get a telephone call informing me that the colleague who's been standing in for me has officially been given my job. This is a terrible blow.

'Come on girl, get a grip!' I tell myself, 'There's nothing to worry about. The company will find another job for you when you get back.' But I know this thinking is out of step with the times, because things have changed. The company has started buying into modern-day business values, and is adopting an American culture of hire and fire. Long-serving employees are being shown the door, and a hard-nosed, hard-hitting younger generation are taking over.

When I finally go back to work, drugged with painkillers and leaning on a walking stick, Sir Gerald says,

'Welcome back Carol! I've just noticed that your contract is coming up for renewal, so you'll be required to take part in an assessment.'

And then I know my hide is on the line. They'll either sack me, or give me some menial job without prospects, and I start imagining how it will feel to be buried alive in some dusty corner of the archives.

I return home and take to my bed again. I've reached the nadir point now. I'm down to bedrock. Depression kicks in, deep and debilitating, and my life appears as a bottomless pit of suffering. I know that the deeper I allow myself to sink, the less power I'll have to pull myself out again, but there's a part of me that wants to die and surrender to the abyss.

'Pat - just a moment.'

'Go away, IG, and leave me alone.'

'No wait! I've got your father with me, and there's something he wants to say to you.'

I freeze.

'Are you listening, Pat? His message is that he understands how you feel, because he's been there himself. And he's asking you not to make the same choice that he did. 'Don't let history repeat itself,' he says. 'Stay in the game, and move to the next square on the chess board!' And he's right, Pat. If you threw in the sponge now, you'd lose your chance of evolving out of the level of consciousness that focuses on suffering.'

I have no doubt that my father is really there, because I can smell the familiar tobacco smell from his pipe.

'Can I ask him what he means by the next square?'

'He says the chessboard contains two kinds of squares, and you're free to choose whether to move on the black ones or on the white. He says, 'If a house is dark bring in more light. Let more love into your life, and the darkness will disappear.'

'But I'm all alone,' I say. 'There's no one here for me to love,' and tears spring to my eyes.

'He says, 'Change that!''

The next morning I feel almost cheerful. I know I won't go under now. Instead I'll learn the lesson life is trying to teach me, and look for the next square.

OLD AGE

I left the company and took a job managing one of the charities that promotes fair trade. I felt I could identify with their aims, as my work was now helping to support the rights of marginalized producers and workers in the poorest developing countries.

My back problem cleared up as soon as I changed jobs, so I had no more cause to complain. Sam was at Eton and doing well. He would come to me during his school holidays, and I'd take time off work to go on outings with him. I had no other close family to love - my mother had died in the meantime - but the warm-hearted, idealistic people I worked with became my surrogate family, and the friendships I made at that time still mean a lot to me.

In my mid fifties I trained to be magistrate, and I sat on the bench for twelve years, while continuing to work part-time for the fair trade charity. This gave me an opportunity to do some good, and to make a contribution to the community. Thus I led a busy and productive life right up to my retirement, when I sold the house in Fairbanks, and bought a cottage in the Welsh hills. Sam couldn't understand this move.

'Why bury yourself away, mother? You're not old yet!' he said.

But there were financial reasons that I never told him about. After I left the company, I started contributing to a private pension fund, which later went bust. So it was necessary to release some capital, because my small pension was not enough to live on.

I see myself sitting at the piano practicing my scales and arpeggios. I'm determined to recover my lost mastery of the keyboard, and become a proficient pianist again. Sam rang yesterday and announced that he's coming down to lunch today, and bringing his partner, Julie, and baby Pippa with him. Yes, I have a granddaughter! She was born last year on December 23rd - my birthday - and she takes after me. She's got bright, alert eyes and my strong forehead.

I break off in the middle of the Bach prelude I'm playing, because I hear the doorbell ring. I go into the hall, and through the frosted glass I can see three figures standing outside instead of two. I open the front door, ready to embrace Sam and Julie, and to take baby Pippa in my arms, and then I freeze, because behind them, grinning sheepishly, is Charlie!

Some snippets of news about him have reached me over the years. I knew he'd kicked his drug habit, and he'd settled down in Thailand, where he'd married a Thai girl and they'd had two boys. He was earning a living teaching English. Now he tells me that he's back in England for good. His children are grown up, and his wife has divorced him, so he's returned to his roots. I am reserved with him and my manner remains cool, but this is to hide the fact that I can still feel the strong affinity between us.

I'm in my late eighties now, and still managing to look after myself. I get through my chores by following a well thought out plan. I've been stripping myself of my worldly goods, and have given away everything I own beyond the bare necessities. In doing so I felt the kind of relief that trees must feel when they shed their foliage before the winter storms arrive to batter their branches.

My cottage is cold and damp in winter, as old buildings tend to be, and, together with my reduced mobility, this makes my life an endurance test. It seems I'm still competing in the hardship and deprivation stakes! But I'd never consider moving because, living here in the unspoilt wilderness of the Welsh hills, I'm nourished by the living presence of nature all around me.

It's twenty years since Charlie died. He didn't survive long after returning to this country. His earlier lifestyle had weakened his liver and he died of hepatitis, but not before we'd had a reconciliation. Now he's one of the friends who are waiting for me on the other side.

'How are you, Pat?'

'Oh bearing up, IG, bearing up! Sam wants me to ask for help from social services, but I'm determined to soldier on alone.'

'Yes, you're very valiant, Pat. But the reason you won't ask is that you're afraid to show your vulnerability.'

'That's true. Being helpless is bad, but it's even worse when you have to admit that you're helpless to others.'

'You've always had a lot of pride, but perhaps it's time now to practice some humility.'

'Yes, I've been proudly upright all my life, but old age and decrepitude are bringing me to my knees!'

And a few days later I fall and injure my right knee. I have to go into hospital for an operation and, when I come out, what I feared most - helplessness and dependency - come to pass. I need a live-in nurse, and I'm obliged to ask her to do all kinds of intimate things. At first I find this humiliating, but then I learn to ask for help, and to receive the help I'm given gratefully, and this makes me more open to love.

My angle of vision has shifted, and I see myself from above. I'm looking down at the face on the pillow, and it's the face of a ninety-five year old, with balding scalp, tear sacks under her eyes, toothless gums, skin like a shrivelled peach. And beneath the blankets her shrunken body has curled itself into a foetal position. We end where we began.

I'm seeing scenes from my life in a series of flashbacks, and each one strikes me as funny. I laugh at the austere figure I cut in the office - always comporting myself with decorum, taking myself so very seriously. Ha ha! And I see Charlie and me when we were young and in love. Charlie was a joker, and I laugh again at his antics. Then I see myself in my role of magistrate - spectacles on the end of my nose, full of self-importance. Ha ha! And finally I laugh at myself for taking it all so seriously when none of it was real, when my whole life was nothing but virtual reality! Ha ha ha!

A north wind is blowing and we're in for more snow. When big, soft flakes start falling from the sky, I float out of the window and over the white fields. All the hard lines of manmade things - the lanes and the barns, and everything built by human hands - have been covered by a winding sheet of unbroken snow. And the world is pure and utterly silent again.

Life 11
JIM the AQUARIUS

'We have to move with the times,' I told IG.

I was showing him my latest invention - a wireless router that you wear attached to a headband. 'It connects your mind directly with the akashic field,' I explain. 'So you can download your virtual life even faster.'

He said I could give it a try. So, when we're sitting in our reclining chairs, all ready to start, I put on my headband, adjust the router so it sits comfortably on my third eye, and switch on.

The pixels of my mind, that were buzzing about chaotically before, arrange themselves into the neat image of a keyboard. All I need to do now is activate START to run the programme. But I must have got my mental wires crossed, because I activate END by mistake, and, before I can delete, I plunge straight into the end of the story.

A small, stocky man in combat trousers is trudging down a winding road, his shoulders bent under the weight of a heavy backpack. Zooming in on his face, we see he has a sallow skin, thick black hair and bushy eyebrows that meet above his nose. We hear the rumble of a motorbike in the distance, and the man turns. He's hoping to cadge a lift. And, as the heavy machine roars round the corner, with its rider - an elderly Hell's Angel - clad all in black leather, he raises his thumb. The biker skids to a halt and grins, showing a line of rotten teeth.

'Climb on mate!'

Five minutes later I'm lying smashed on the road following a head-on collision with a lorry. In a flurry of rain, the bugger skids while going into a curve, and bang - that's it! I watch him get to his feet and brush himself down, right as rain, while I lie lifeless in the gutter. I'm pissed off, and you would be too, if you'd been snatched from life unprepared and against your will, at the age of forty-four! Then I hear IG's exasperated voice say,

'What are you messing about for, Jim? You're not supposed to know the ending! Rewind at once and return to start.'

So I press REWIND, and my whole life flashes in reverse at a speed of 10,000 frames per second before my inner eye. The knowledge of my tragic ending is going be hard to live with. My only hope is that the amnesia will blot it out.

I get it right the second time round. My new life starts with a view of black and puce clouds gathering overhead. The sun's rays are piercing them like laser beams. Then the storm breaks with a streak of jagged lightning and a massive thunderclap, and the rain buckets down, whipped into furious eddies by the wind. I move my mental cursor upwards, lifting the point of my awareness into the very heart of the thundercloud, and it's phenomenal! The electricity being released up here sets me fizzing and sparking like a broken power cable!

'Carter's Ballbearings' it says in bold letters over the factory gate. But, instead of entering through it like a normal person, I glide through the wall with all the ease of belonging to another dimension, and move towards a door leading into an office. There a dramatic incident is taking place. A woman from the shop floor has gone into labour. A doctor's been called and is preparing to deliver the baby, as she's too far gone to be got to hospital. And I recognise the woman immediately as my future mum.

'God Almighty!' exclaims the harried overseer. 'She said she still had six weeks to go, and we're rushed off our feet. Trust Beale to have a baby on the wrong day!'

But it must be the right day, I think. Otherwise I'd be Fay the Pisces not Jim the Aquarius!

My field of vision has split now, and it's as if I can look through the lenses of two differently positioned cameras. I switch to the second one, which is like a micro-camera planted inside my mother's body, and find I'm looking through the eyes of the baby about to be born. But there's a disadvantage to this vantage point - it's accompanied by a horrible sensation of compression and restriction.

The problem seems to be that I'm the wrong way round. My head should be down and my feet up! That means a breech birth is on the cards, which will severely challenge the doctor. But he's a pompous prick, and I like being difficult, so I stick in that position. It takes time until the birth canal is wide enough for my backside to be born, but at last it sees the light. I feel a pair of strong hands gripping me, and they pull until my shoulders emerge and finally my head.

'You came out butt first! The first thing you showed us was your arse!' my mum said later.

I'm proud of that. It was an act of defiance - like saying 'Fuck you!' - because I'd been born outside the rulebook. I'd broken and entered where I wasn't welcome, and don't think I didn't notice the look grandma gave me!

258

'There's a touch of the tar-brush there alright,' she said ominously.

And, when she went down to the registry office to do the necessary, she let everyone know that it wasn't her idea to call me Emanuel Ghastly. There I discover that my new name is going to be Emanuel Garcia Beale, and my date of birth is January 30th 1945.

THE KID

My dad came from Colombia. He was an illegal immigrant who my mother, moved by his tale of cruel persecution, had adopted. They must have looked an ill-matched pair - he small, dark and swarthy, and she a blonde and buxom English working-class girl. Grandma says he only took up with her because she'd agreed to shelter him. But it was my father who nursed me during my first year of life. He gave me my bottle and changed my nappies, while lying low in our flat in fear of his pursuers. He'd warned us to keep away from the letterbox, in case a bomb had been planted there. Mum never discovered who they were - whether it was the drugs trade or something political. And one day he disappeared into the blue, and the rent money from the cracked teapot disappeared with him, and we never saw him again.

When the rent-collector called and we couldn't pay, we were ordered out. And, when we didn't go, the landlord sent his thugs round. I was three at the time, and clung to mum's knees while they threw all our belongings out onto the street. Mum yelled, 'Not the radio set! Not the radio set!' But they took no notice, and my earliest memory is of our wireless flying through the window and shattering on the pavement. It wasn't the last time things would spiral out of control in my disjointed childhood.

A social worker appears, and I'm taken away in a big, black car. As it drives off, I press my face to the window, watching my mother waving to me from the pavement. She gets smaller and smaller. Then we turn a corner and she's gone. The social worker says she's going to live in a hostel.

'And you're going to go to a nice new mummy and daddy, where you'll have a room of your own and a garden to play in,' she explains.

And that's how I came to be fostered by a middle-aged, middle-class couple living in a bungalow. When they heard which pocket of the town I'd come from, they were horrified.

'Good Lord!' they exclaimed. 'That's the pits!'

By the age of four I'm swearing like a trooper, and nicking coins from foster-mother's purse. They punish me by putting me in the coalhouse to cool my heels. Then, when I'm five, I'm sent to the infant school, which is just another bigger, darker coalhouse. There I join a gang of bullies, whose idea of fun is to torture poor snivellers. And, though this offends my sense of justice, I side with them to save my skin. So I'm given an early experience of the bully's mentality, and afterwards I can see through them. I know all bullies are cry-babies inside.

When foster-mum gets cancer I'm ejected from that home, and land back on birth-mum's doorstep together with the social worker. Mum says it's inconvenient as she's up to her ears with union work, and grandma can't have me because of her arthritis. But in the end she's persuaded to take me back, because then she'd be eligible for a council flat.

Mum goes straight round to the council offices, and bullies them to put us at the top of the list. So, not long after, we move into a new flat in a high-rise block. It may be a socially inspired solution, erected by Birmingham city council in the throes of post-war slum clearance, but it's a culture shock for me. Life in those flats is rough and raw compared to the cushy life my foster-parents led with their middle-class comforts. But the people there are real, and they live real lives. The last thing I ever want to aspire to is to the middle-class!

TEENS

As mum was always out, the neighbours became my family. It was early days for tower blocks, and the share-and-share-alike lifestyle of the slum street prevailed. Wives would gossip while they strung up their washing on the communal balcony, just as they'd done over the garden fence. And the kids living on the same floor were like siblings, and held together when attacked by the kids from above or below. That gave me my first experience of solidarity.

I avoided going to school whenever I could. Because, when someone tries to force me to do something, it's my nature to do the opposite. So, if the law says I have to go to school, I'll play truant. That's why you'll find me hanging round the shops all hours of the day, together with a couple of other young dissidents. The shopkeepers view us with suspicion.

'Bugger off you lot or I'll call the police!' one shouts.

Well, if they expect you to cause trouble, then that's what you do. So, before moving on, I pee in his doorway, which drives him stark raving mad. Well it's society's fault, isn't it? What else is there for us to aspire to in post-war Britain?

My mum's a political animal. Not only is she a trades union rep, but she's also one of the original, hardcore members of the CND. And in

1959 she takes me with her on a march to Aldermaston. She's drummed up a bunch of women and children, all eager to protest against the government's nuclear agenda. We're carrying placards saying 'Ban the Bomb!' And as we march along we shout, 'Think of the kids! Don't destroy their world!'

There's a holiday feel to it all. During the breaks we picnic by the roadside, sharing the food we've brought with us, but later on it starts to rain. Then the macs come out and the wellies, and we slosh along through the mud regardless, mile after weary mile.

Finally we arrive, wet and bedraggled, outside a tall, barbed-wired gate, where we're intercepted by a couple of policemen. Mum wants to be let inside, so she can read out our demands to the authorities, but it's not allowed - they're adamant about that. She argues with them for nearly an hour before accepting defeat. Then, as there's nothing else for it, she reads out our demands to the two policemen instead, after which we agree to disperse peacefully, and catch the train home.

It's two years later and a lot has changed since old Metcalf, the science teacher, started taking an interest in me. We used to make fun of him and call him the nutty professor, but that was before the explosion. One fine day he blew up the science lab while demonstrating the buoyancy of gases, which made us sit up and take notice.

He's persuaded me to go to the after-school science club that he runs for latchkey kids. There we learn to make crystal sets by connecting electronic circuits to amplifiers attached to earphones And we look at pond water and slime mould under a microscope - and sperm when he isn't looking. And all this gets me so fired up that I start going to the school library to read the science books.

'You're a bright kid, Mani,' he says one day (no one ever calls me Emanuel) 'and you've got brains in your head, so you should think about taking O-Levels.'

Well, I don't want to end up working in a factory like my mum. Workers' conditions are slavish at Carter's Ballbearings. So I decide to get some GCEs, and I do better than expected - six O-Levels with grades good enough for the sixth form! But mum wants me to start earning.

'It's time you pulled your weight, Mani,' she says. 'That's only fair. I was out earning my keep at your age.'

Old Metcalfe suggests I become a lab trainee, and helps me write my applications. But every time I go for an interview it's the same old thing.

'You'll have to clean up your act if you want to work here, young man. Our regulations require white overalls to be worn in the lab at all times, and jackets and ties in the office. And normal hair cuts are required, meaning short back and sides!'

That kind of stone-age attitude is a total turn-off. I refuse point blank to give up wearing my black leather coat or to cut my hair, which reaches down to my shoulders, so I don't get the job. However I expected that sort of hassle. In my last year at school we had to do a week's work experience, and they sent me to the council offices. From the start I stuck out there like a sore thumb. I was wearing my hair tied back with an embroidered band at the time, and looked like an Aztec. When I made a fuss about filling in a form, because it involved disclosing personal information, the bloke in charge got shirty and said,

'For Christ's sake! Then go back to your wigwam, Hiawatha, and leave us in peace!' and everyone laughed.

After that, whenever I came into the room, they started singing 'Down among the red men,' and drumming on their desks like they were tom-toms, which I saw as a clear case of racial abuse. And before the week was up I'd walked out. I wasn't going to work in a place that tolerated racial discrimination!

When six months have passed, and I still haven't got a job, mum gets shirty.

'If you don't want to work then clear out. You're old enough to fend for yourself now, Mani!'

So, at the age of seventeen, I leave home and go to London. At first I sleep on park benches, but then I meet this bloke who lives in a squat. He says they've got some space and, if I like, I can doss down there. So when it's dark he takes me round to the house. The ground floor windows are all boarded up, but the lock on the back door is broken, and that's where we enter. It's pitch black inside, and I keep stumbling over sleepers spread eagled on the floor, before I find a place to put down my sleeping bag and crash out.

The next morning I discover it's more like a platform on Victoria station than home sweet home! Spike (the bloke who found the place, and was the first to move in) is welcoming all-comers, because of the work that's got to be done. The cement has to be hacked out of the toilet bowl, and the pool of raw sewage in the bathroom cleaned up, and the rats have to be poisoned. Then, once the electricity and water are restored, it won't be a bad place to live, if you don't mind noise, Because there's always some ruckus going on, though I'm used to that from the tower block, where things went from bad to worse, and by the time I left there was more domestic violence in those flats than hot dinners!

262

I've discovered I can't go on the dole or claim relief until I'm eighteen. It's fuckin' unfair to exclude under-age persons from the welfare of the welfare state! I'm not work-shy. It's just that I refuse to sell out to the capitalists, and become a dupe of the system. So I have a series of temporary jobs - temporary because in each case I walk out, or I get fired, within the first three months.

The worst one was making up boxes at a slaughterhouse. Seeing the panic of the animals, who knew they were going to die, turned me into a vegetarian. Another time I worked in a car breaker's yard, until I had a near-lethal accident. I was cutting up a car with an acetylene torch, when it ignited some vapour left in the tank and caused an explosion. The blast threw me twenty yards, and set my hair on fire. I had the presence of mind to roll on the ground to put the flames out, and they took me in an ambulance to A&E, where they bandaged my whole head, leaving only a few small holes for my eyes and mouth. I looked like a bank robber in a balaclava!

Sometimes I think it would make my life easier if I always went round like that. Because I keep meeting people who take offence at the way I look. I was in a bar this evening, quietly drinking my beer, when a geek at the counter flicks a beer coaster in my face.

'I don't need this,' I think and take no notice.

Then he flicks another, so I ask him politely what his problem is.

'I don't like your fuckin' face!' he says.

'Well, I don't like yours neither - it's like the back of a bus!'

I say this knowing he'll bash the shit out of me, and he does. By the time the barkeeper intervenes it's too late. He's broken my nose, which doesn't make me look any the prettier! So here I am, back in A&E, waiting to be stitched up, and it's taking hours. And, having nothing better to do, I listen to that voice in my head I've been ignoring - the one that goes on and on.

'How are you doing, Jim?' it asks.

'Who's Jim when he's at home?'

'You're Jim, though you think you're Mani. The amnesia's to blame for that, and I'm IG your inner guide.'

'I thought hearing voices in my head meant I was going cuckoo!'

'Well, you shouldn't listen to all of them, but I'm your life coach. So, if you have any questions, come to me.'

'I have one - why do people always pick on me?'

'Aha! To find the answer to that, you must inquire into how you provoke them.'

'I didn't provoke anyone tonight. I was just sitting there, minding my own business.'

'But what were you feeling inside? Because it's not what you do or say, Jim, it's the energy around you that people pick up, and that depends on your emotional state.'

'I've never paid much attention to that.'

'You should. For example, what happens when you're at work, and they try to make you do something you don't want to do? You feel mutinous, don't you? And the people in charge pick that up right away.'

'Hmmm.... One gaffer said he didn't like the glint in my eye. I was wondering what he meant.'

'Yes, your defiance will be read as insolence, which doesn't make you popular with authority figures. So you see, when you get the sack, you're also responsible.'

'That's a new way of seeing it.'

'What we experience in the outer world always corresponds to what's going on inside us. So people who have a violent streak in them are more likely to become victims of violence than others.'

'Well, this is the second time in a fortnight I've been to A&E, so that must mean I've a violent streak.'

'It can be changed like everything else if you bring in more awareness. Start doing your self-inquiry exercises again, Jim.'

'Remind me what self-inquiry is.'

'It's questioning your ideas and attitudes. You're always questioning society, but you should also take time to question yourself. And try to take better care of your body because you need it, Jim. In fact you can't do without it down here!'

Spike's started behaving like the great dictator. Just because he was the first to move in, that doesn't give him the right to order us about! We had this vision of making our squat a free space, where everyone can do as they like, providing they don't hurt other people. Though it's been difficult to implement, because where do you set the boundaries?

Last night, for instance, I came home tired and hungry to discover that one of the housemates had rifled my shopping bag. He'd found my fish fingers and was frying them up! I totally lost it. Afterwards, when I was sane again, I realised that the only solution was to abolish private property, because, as long as people are allowed to own things, there'll never be any equality in the world or any peace.

We're sitting round in a circle on the carpet having a meeting. A bottle of Cinzano is being passed round, and everyone is smoking. It's times like these when we come closest to the community spirit, and I decide that it's the right moment to put out my ideas. So I explain to them the principle of shared property, and suggest we adopt it from now on in the squat. My speech is greeted by hoots of derisive laughter.

'Mani,' says Spike, 'you've only got two problems mate - everything you fuckin' do and everything you fuckin' say!'

So that was end of story as far as my contribution to the squat was concerned, and a few weeks later it got busted anyway. The police arrived in the middle of the night, giving us only enough time to grab a few things before we were thrown out onto the street. There, after some cursory goodbyes, we went our separate ways. I made for the station to catch the train to Birmingham.

Mum's surprised to see me when she opens the door.

'You look a right old scruff,' she says.

She cooks me some dinner, and then starts quizzing me.

'You working?'

'No.'

'I don't understand it, Mani. Why don't you do something with your life instead of sitting around on your backside?'

But she lets me stay, though in return I have to listen to her going on about Fidel Castro and nuclear holocausts till it's coming out of my ears. I know what she wants - she wants me to join the CND. She'd like to see me wearing one of those little badges. But, because I'm me, I refuse to agree with her views and give contra.

'The Russians have as much right as the Americans to put their rockets in other people's countries,' I say, which immediately winds her up.

But I'm proud of my mum really, because she's passionate about what she believes in. But she still believes you can change the world by going on marches and signing petitions, whereas I'm a cynic who sees the world as hopelessly fucked!

'I can't understand why you don't have proper job, Mani,' she says the next morning while we're eating our cornflakes. 'Someone with your brains should have no trouble there.'

'I don't know neither,' I reply. 'I'll do some self-inquiry about it with my inner guide, then get back to you.'

And the look she gives me says it all!

'Why haven't I got a proper job, IG?'

'You haven't found your place in society yet.'

'That's true. I'm like a square peg going round looking for a round hole.'

'But your shape is determined by your beliefs. So you could change it by making adjustments to the way you think.'

'I'd rather make adjustments to the way my employers think! For example I have a big problem when they object to me wearing my earring!'

'That's such a little thing, Jim. Why make a stand on it?'

'It's a matter of principle! Dictating to people about their clothes and hairstyles is pure fascism. I see it as a basic human right that people should be allowed to dress any way they like!'

'But, when you refuse to compromise, your employers interpret this as a sign that you see yourself as someone special, and the rules don't apply to you.'

'Just because I refuse to say 'baa' with the rest of the sheep! But the ponces are going to find that they can't buy me off. I'll not kiss the establishment's arse in exchange for a TV set and a washing machine!'

'You're a rebel, Jim, but a rebel without a cause, because you are opting out of the system without having an alternative to offer.'

'Protest is my alternative, IG. Through refusing to toe the line, I'm making a protest against capitalism and the way this country is being run.'

'Then you're always going to have a problem with authority.'

'Or authority is going to have a problem with me!'

After living for a while in my mother's flat, I start missing the buzz you get when you live somewhere illegally. So, when I hear about this squat in Croydon, I go down to check it out. It's a different kettle of fish from the last one. Instead of a bunch of down-and-outs, I find a group of academically accredited intellectuals. They're not squatting because they're poor and destitute, but in protest against the capitalist monopoly of the housing market.

It's in my favour that I'm genuine working-class, because they need a figurehead. So they allow me to move in, on condition that I agree to keep the rules, which include attending their compulsory weekly meetings. Compulsory! That word always gets my hackles up. But, when they explain that the meetings are essential, because the squat is run on a cooperative basis, and all the decisions are taken by consensus, I calm down.

Living with them, I discover, is the equivalent of a university education, because they've all studied subjects like politics, economics or sociology, and are politicised up to the eyeballs. They communicate with each other in long words I never knew existed. So, to get the gist of what's going on, I start reading the books they leave lying around the house, and the clarity and logic of the ideas I meet in them impresses me. I realise I've never thought things properly through before. Ideas just rushed in and out of my head like express trains through a country station, but now I'm in the picture. I've sussed out the master plan behind society.

I always go to our weekly meetings with an agenda - for example abolishing private property. I'm like a dog with a bone with that one - gnawing it, burying it and digging it up again. But it's never easy to get a word in edgeways, and even when I get a chance to say something, someone will always interrupt. In the end I lodge a formal complaint.

'You're always going on about how the capitalist oppressors are gagging the working class,' I say. 'Well, that's what's happening here - you're gagging me!'

That hit home, and they finally agree to hear me out.

So I present my case for sharing what we have, and I go so far as to suggest that our incomes should be shared too. That would be socialism in the true sense of the word, I say. When I've finished my speech, there's a pause and then Nathan says,

'We agree with you in theory, Mani, but you know what happened when that was tried out in the post-revolutionary communes in Russia, and in the early Isreali kibbuz, don't you?'

I don't.

'Then go away and read the literature, Mani-man, because, unless you're properly informed, whatever you say will just be some old rant!'

I'm thoroughly pissed off with Nathan. In theory we're all supposed to have an equal voice at the meetings, but Nathan's got the biggest mouth so he dominates. And I'm getting fed up with consensus decision-making too, because it means our meetings drag on late into the night, and I need my sleep now that I've got a job. Yes, I've found something I like at last! It's in the record department of a local store called *Home Electronics*, and I've even submitted to wearing a jacket and tie because there are perks. After closing time I'm allowed to stay and listen to records! I can play anything I like. So that's how I spend my evenings - in a booth with my headphones on, singing along with the stars of rock and roll, and jigging up and down like a cat on a hot tin roof!

Sometimes I'll bring a new release home to share it with the housemates. Then invariably a voice will shout, 'For Christ's sake, Mani, give us a break! Turn the bloody volume down!' which I take as my cue to turn it up. Because this place urgently needs a wake-up call. They need to get up off their fat arses and dance, but I'm the only one who thinks like that.

The other day I tried to dye my hair red, but it turned out bright orange, making me look like someone on a space odyssey. I've also started dressing in tight pants and bright glitzy jackets, which goes down like a lead balloon in the squat, where the dress code for men is chunky sweaters and baggy cord trousers.

Croydon is a dump. I feel suffocated by its suburban mentality. There's hardly anyone here who's hip, not even the customers who buy rock 'n roll. So in desperation I catch a train to London and make for Soho, where I prowl the streets in search of kindred spirits. I find plenty of cats in rocker gear, and even more who dress as mods, but scratch the surface and you uncover the same dreary bourgeois mentality. When you talk to them, they turn out to be bank clerks from Surbiton, or office workers from Finchley Wood out on a Saturday night spree.

Later, when I'm sitting discouraged in the train on my way home, I have the following conversation with IG.

'What's your problem, Jim?' he asks.

'I don't fit in anywhere,' I say. 'Perhaps I don't belong on this planet at all. Perhaps I'm an alien from outer space - some fuckin' extra-terrestrial, who's been abducted and put here as an experiment!'

IG laughs. 'That's closer to the truth than you think, Jim! But why do you feel like an outsider?

'People reject me.'

'Or perhaps you reject people - for being too bourgeois, for example.'

'So what must I do? Become a vegetable like them, adopt their vegetable mindset?'

'No, just be yourself, and allow other people to be themselves. You demand a lot of tolerance from others, Jim, but I haven't noticed you being very tolerant yourself.'

'It's because I can't stand complacency! It winds me up.'

'So you feel compelled to shock and provoke them out of it?'

'I have to be provocative to get their attention. Otherwise I wouldn't be seen.'

'That's an important insight, Jim. Well done!'

'It's not that I'm attention seeking, IG. I'm just trying to wake people up to get them to listen to me.'

'If you want them to listen, then you must change the way you communicate, because your present manner alienates them. When you feel strongly about a subject, you become strident and you over-egg the pudding, and then they close down.'

'If I overdo it, it's because I haven't much confidence in my rhetorical power. The others in the squat are so articulate, and what comes out of their mouths is always so clear and logical.'

268

'You're learning from them, Jim, and your verbal skills are improving. But there's something else you should be aware of. You're always complaining that people don't listen to you, but do you listen to them? I've seen you refusing to entertain views that go against your own.'

'That's exactly my problem with Nathan. He's so convinced he's right, that he'll never listen to any arguments that contradict his opinions.'

'And the same applies to you, Jim!'

I'm fed up with the squat. All their talk about democratic procedures is bullshit, because anyone can see that a heirarchy has formed with Nathan on top. We can discuss things at the meetings till we're blue in the face, but in the end it's Nathan who makes all the decisions. That talk about consensus decision making is just a front to hide the fact that the squat is a full-blown dictatorship!

I've discovered that people can know it all intellectually, and have high ideals, and still create a system as repressive as the one they are rejecting. It's a small step from equality to conformity, and from fraternity to exploitation, when you have a leader who abuses his power. Nathan is a bully, and I'm committed to fighting a bully when I find one, so one day I'm going to have to have a show-down with him.

It's turned out that what Nathan understands under liberation from bourgeois constraints is free love, because I've discovered that he's having it off with some of the women housemates. He seems to assume this is his right, because he's the dominant male now, and these are his perks. And there are women here who go along with it, although they say they're committed feminists. It's like it's an honour for them!

Nathan goes on about how the sexual revolution is liberating us from our bourgeois conditioning, but the partners of the women he's seduced are not bought off as easily as that. So the weekly meetings have deteriorated into roundelays of insult-trading, and, listening to this going on, I can't believe these are the same people who advocated civilised debate. They came over at first as so cool and cerebral, and now here they are freaking out, and throwing verbal abuse at each other!

When one of the jealous husbands can't take it any longer, and announces that he's moving out, Nathan pronounces judgement on him. He says he is unsuitable material for our experiment in alternative living, because he has failed to overcome his bourgeois conditioning. And then I know that the moment of my showdown with Nathan has arrived.

'You're bourgeois too,' I shout, 'all of you! You think that, because you live in a squat, this makes you part of some great revolutionary sub-culture. But all you are is a bunch of over-educated, middle-class gits. What do you know about the working class? You call yourselves socialists, and talk about social equality, but you make fuckin' sure you hang on to your privileged bourgeois lifestyle!'

My outburst is followed by a silence, which Nathan is the first to break. He says I've just demonstrated why they've had a problem integrating me in the group. I have a borderline personality disorder, he says. And that explains why what I say is off the wall.

'Fuckin' hell!' I yell. 'If you don't march to Nathan's drum you're labelled a nutcase now! It's like in Russia where the dissidents are sent to the mental hospital!'

And, after that outburst, I walk out of the meeting and out of the squat.

'So what conclusions did you draw from your experience there?' asks IG.

'They were the wrong people for me, because they didn't accept me as I am.'

'That's right Jim. You don't belong where you're not accepted, but you must accept yourself first. I've noticed that you react very sensitively to criticism. Perhaps you have a chip on your shoulder?'

'You mean because of my background? But I'm proud of being working class, IG, and I'm proud of being mixed race!'

'But you felt you didn't belong with the workers in your mother's factory.'

'No, and I wasn't at home with those tramps in the first squat either, or with that bunch of politicised intellectuals. So I'm still a singleton!'

'Is it because you're afraid that other people could rob you of your freedom?'

'Something like that! In every group I've been in, starting from school, I've always felt downtrodden and oppressed.'

'Mani is born free yet everywhere he's in chains!'

'Ha ha! That's Rousseau! See, at least I gleaned a bit of education from the last lot!'

'You'd like to belong to a group, Jim, but at the same time you want to stay completely free. That's like having your cake and eating it.'

'Then there's nothing else for it. I'll just have to go through life as a group of one!'

'Your problem is that you're unwilling to make compromises. You don't co-operate easily.'

'Yes, that's where things comes unstuck. I'm too absolute and uncompromising where my principles are concerned.'

'But life is melting you, Jim. Be more in your heart and less in your head, and then you won't see things so rigidly.'

TWENTIES

Now I have a steady job I can afford to pay rent. So I say goodbye to squats, and move up the social scale by renting a room down the road. The house is owned by a dippy artist, and he's hung his weird pictures all over the place - even in the loo. They don't do anything for your sanity, especially first thing in the morning when you're hung over from the night before!

Other people rent rooms here too, and next door there's an elderly hippy called Avril, who sees herself as a San Francisco flower-power child although she's pushing forty. She goes around in a transparent silk caftan with no underwear underneath, and trails an odour of incense sticks.

It seems that this woman has taken a fancy to me, because she's always trying to waylay me on the landing. At first I'm friendly, because I like talking to people and finding out what they think. But, when she invites me into her room to share a joint, I take a step backwards. The truth is I find her hippy-dippiness pathetic.

However, rejection seems to spur some women on. The more aloof you are, the more their curiosity is aroused, and they can't rest till they've found out what makes you tick, and Avril is one of them. So one Saturday night, when I'm feeling a bit lonely, I end up on the rug in front of her gas fire sharing a joint, while she plays her favourite records to me. As I expected, there's nothing with any oomph in her collection - only touchy-feely stuff. Soon she's edging away from her corner of the rug towards mine. And, when Joan Baez starts to sing one of her heart-rending ballads, she takes this as her cue to wrap her arms tightly around me. I freeze.

'What's up Mani - you a Virgo?'

'No, an Aquarius.'

'Then you should be into sex, albeit in a cerebral way. But perhaps you're Virgo rising. Do you know your time of birth?'

'Look Avril, I'm not into astrology. In fact I disapprove of it. In my view it's just another form of bourgeois escapism!'

'Like sex? Is that a form of bourgeois escapism too?'

'Yes, because in our society sex has become an extension of consumer gratification.'

She chuckles. 'What a very Aquarian thing to say! But why shield yourself behind political ideas, Mani? Why not come out in the open and admit that you're a virgin?'

'Because I'm not!'

Which is not a lie, because one night, back in that first squat, I lost my virginity to a girl who was passing through. She had chipped black nail polish - that's all I can remember - and she was the sort of girl who belonged to no one and everyone. I stayed awake the following night, hoping that she'd come back to my bed, but she never came - the bitch! She was off with another cat, which left me feeling like shit. Since then, with the sexual revolution going hammer and tongs all round me, I've maintained an aloof detachment.

'That's a good subject for self-inquiry,' interrupts IG. 'Why have you never had a girlfriend, Jim?'

'Because I don't want one! I'd feel fenced in. I'd hate it if someone wanted to know where I was going, and when I'd be back, every time I went out!'

'So you're afraid of losing your freedom. Is that why you keep women at arm's length?'

'Yes, because no matter how emancipated they appear, they've all been duped by the same capitalist fairy-tale. They have the same familial and societal expectations around marriage as their mothers had.'

'But having a girlfriend doesn't necessarily mean getting married.'

'I know, but I'd want a committed relationship, and then the same demands and pressures would be there. It would be just like marriage but without a certificate.'

'Wait till you fall passionately in love.'

'To tell you the truth, IG, I don't know what that means. I can get passionate about causes, but I can't imagine myself ever getting passionate about an individual. No, I prefer to relate to women as friends.'

'So how many women friends do you have, Jim?'

'Not many, because women only interest me if they have something original about them. I don't mean girls who are kooky for the sake of it, but Asian girls for example. I went out with a Japanese once, and I found her attractive, though we never got past the language barrier. After her I decided that the most important thing was to be able to talk to a woman.'

'Relating through the head is safer than relating through the feelings. Well, you've managed to avoid intimacy so far, Jim, but life won't let you get away with it. There's a romance written into your life-script, but I'm not telling you when it's coming!'

272

Avril has grasped the full depth of my indifference towards her, and has lost interest in me. She's taken up with a moth-eaten guitar player instead, and he's moved into her room. He keeps me awake at night practising his chords, so I move into another house down the street that has a more anonymous atmosphere.

I'm coming round to see that mum is right - I need a cause to give my life a meaning. So I join a local Marxist group, as a sense of purpose is always part of the package when you become a Marxist. We listen to rousing talks by balding commies, who fought in the Spanish civil war. And I enjoy standing up and singing *The Red Flag* in chorus, and sharing their feeling of moral superiority, but inside I remain cynical about our chances of abolishing capitalism, and creating a workers' paradise in this land.

After the talks are over, mugs of tea are served, and we mingle with each other to discuss current issues. I was hoping to find people here who would listen to my views, but it seems that most of the comrades have come to talk rather than to listen. And, as they all say pretty much the same thing, I conclude that this is nothing but a talking shop, where people meet to reinforce each other's prejudices. And as always, conformity arouses the renegade in me, so I start taking up extreme positions like siding with the Irish terrorists, which earns me the reputation of being ideologically unsound. And, in our next dialogue, IG takes me to task on this.

'When you take up an extreme position like that, do you really believe in it, or are you just reacting to the norm?' he asks.

'I'm reacting, IG. I'm being awkward on purpose, because I see myself as a mould breaker. The comrades here are so entrenched in their communist ideology, it's like their minds are set in concrete!'

'They've invested their whole lives in it, Jim, so trying to reform their thinking won't make you popular.'

'That's unimportant. When ideas have passed their sell-by date they have to be ditched. We must look to the future not to the past.'

'That's true. A rigid attachment to a set of beliefs is always a barrier to progress. But what you say of them also applies to you, because you're stuck in your attitudes too, although they're unconventional ones. You march out of step, and then accuse everyone else of being out of step with you!'

'I'm doing them a good turn.'

'But why do you feel compelled to persuade other people to your way of thinking?'

'Because I'm right!'

'Are you sure? Perhaps deep inside you're uncertain about that, and you're trying to get people to agree with you for reassurance!'

'Hmmm.... Then is that why I hate losing an argument, and I always have to have the last word?'

'Perhaps, and if it's more important for you to prove you're right than to know the truth, that's a sure sign your ego is involved. Our political and religious beliefs become the pillars on which our egos rest - be aware of that. And who would you be if you were stripped of your opinions?'

'I don't know.'

'Then do some self-inquiry, Jim, and find out.'

THIRTIES

Ten years have passed without much changing in my life. I still live in the same anonymous rented room and work at *Home Electronics*. But I'm no longer a Marxist. I've joined the Greens instead. There's a big demonstration being held today outside the building where the conservative party conference is taking place. Scargill's defiance of Thatcher has enflamed leftist passions, which explains the large turnout. He's threatening to bring the miners out on strike, and then the lights will go out all over the country!

I'm at the front of the crowd, immediately behind the police cordon, and I'm chanting 'Down with Thatcher!' with everyone else. A conservative MP comes out to be interviewed by a TV reporter, and I'm close enough to hear what he says.

'The power of the unions is crippling the economy, and their restrictive practices are stirring up discontent and causing social disunity, which is why they must be restricted.'

Then the reporter turns to the crowd, and picks a woman to interview standing a few yards away from me. I've already noticed her. She stood out in that crowd as if she'd been ringed by a marker pen. The interviewer is asking her what she thinks of the Prime Minister's stance.

'Thatcher is a bully,' she proclaims loudly and clearly, 'and I'm committed to fighting a bully when I find one, which is why I'm demonstrating here today!'

Those could have been my words! Afterwards, in the general rush for the station, I elbow my way through the crowd until I'm beside her, and strike up a conversation. I tell her that I share her attitude towards bullies, and enquire about her political affiliations.

'I'm a soldier of fortune,' she replies. 'I'll support any minority group that's fighting for its rights. Though I used to be a signed-up member of the communist party, until I became disillusioned, that is.'

'I've been through Marxism too,' I say.

'It's a lost cause,' she continues. 'The workers have deserted the communist party. They've been bought off by big business and have embraced consumerism. We have to concede victory to the capitalists.'

'That's how I see it too,' I say. 'Marxism has lost its popular support, and that's why the Eastern European countries are dictatorships. The communist states have got to be totalitarian systems of one-party rule or they couldn't stay communist.'

Not only do we share the same political views, it turns out that we're also bound for the same train. And soon we're sitting opposite each other in the crowded compartment, and I can get a proper look at her. She'd be about forty I'd say - so a few years older than me. She's got lovely grey eyes, and her figure unites a feminine curviness with a masculine strength of muscle, which is very attractive.

'And what about you,' I ask, 'what's your name?'

'My name's Ruth,' she replies, 'and I'm a lesbian, so end of story.'

If she expected me to be fazed, I'm not. On the contrary, I admire the honest way she came out with it.

'But end of story is not what I want,' I say, when we arrive at her station and she's getting up to leave, 'because I'd like to see you again.'

She smiles and jots down a telephone number.

It turns out that Ruth is a social worker, and someone who believes in what she's doing. She's committed to the welfare of the underprivileged and deprived in our society - not intellectually but in a hands-on way. We become friends, and she meets me in her lunch hour when she can, and we have a sandwich or a pizza together. I start wondering whether this is love, because I think about her all the time. I'm fascinated by her mix of serious thinker and funky oddball, and when we talk it's like we both share the same brain, because we agree on practically everything. I'm also more relaxed around Ruth than I am around most other women.

However, I get a surprise when she tells me about Ivan and Dimitri, her two little boys. How does having kids square with being a lesbian, I wonder? But I ask no questions there, as I don't want to appear naive in these matters.

She's invited me round to see where she lives. I've heard a lot about the house already. She and a group of other women bought it together five years ago to turn into a kids' and parents' commune.

'Our aim was to create a viable alternative to the nuclear family,' she explains.

Ruth sees the conventional family set-up as a leftover remnant of the patriarchy, so she's choosing to bring up her boys in an alternative extended family for their own good.

'I don't want them becoming chauvinist pigs!' she explains.

When we arrive at the house, we find Ivan and Dimitri running round naked in the garden covered in body paint. It seems they are being politicised from an early age, because their favourite term of abuse is 'Fascist bastard'! I'm also introduced to Tracy, Ruth's girlfriend, although Ruth tries to avoid that appelation. She hates all forms of sexual stereotyping, and she also hates what she calls 'the couple assumption'.

'Exclusive one-to-one relationships soon get claustrophobic,' she says. 'Love must be free or else it isn't love. You agree there, don't you, Mani?'

When lunch is ready, it turns out to be a bean feast served out of an enormous pot. We sit round a table in the garden - five or six mothers and an indeterminate number of kids, who never stay still long enough to be counted. I'm immediately accepted as one of the family, and, as I look round at these friendly, smiling faces, I dare to start hoping that I've found my people at last. Their opinions concerning child rearing may be wacky, but in the end it's not people's beliefs that count. What matters is that you feel at home with them, and you know they are your friends.

A few days later we're lying on the lawn sunbathing - Ruth, Tracy and me - and Ruth is telling me about her traumatic experiences with the macho-male culture that led to her switching to women partners.

'Now that I'm together with Tracy,' she concludes, 'my relationships with men are working much better. In fact some of my best friends are men.'

And that's the moment when I realise that I'm hoping for something more than friendship from Ruth.

Then Tracy, who's a psychotherapist, starts asking me questions about my family. She wants to analyse my emotional dynamics, she says.

'Well, there's not much to tell,' I reply. 'My dad buggered off - did a runner - and my mum works in a factory. She's a committed member of the CND, but the joke is that, although she's spent her life protesting against war, she's at war with her whole family. She quarrelled with her siblings early on, and broke off contact with them. So I grew up not knowing any of my relatives except my grandma, and she died when I was seven.'

'It sounds as if your mum needs to deal with her shit!' comments Tracy.

'But growing up like that had the advantage that I missed out on the briefing kids usually get from their families. So I avoided absorbing society's values and being assimilated. I stayed free and independent.'

'But you never experienced emotional closeness,' Ruth says sympathetically. 'Admit it, Mani, you've never been close to anyone your whole life!'

And she's right.

I soon discover that Tracy doesn't live in the house all the time, but goes home regularly to her husband and children. And on these nights I'm allowed to stay over. I look forward to them enormously because, lying together with Ruth in her double bed after we've had sex, I feel more nourished and complete than ever before. It feels as if I'm loved.

Ruth is encouraging me to set my sights higher than *Home Electronics*, and maybe I could achieve more, because I'm more self-confident now. It's as if Ruth is shoring me up so I can begin to hit my stride. As I'm interested in computers, I decide to study computing at the adult education college. I find I have a natural talent for it. My gift for thinking laterally, and spotting solutions as if out of the corner of my eye, comes in useful now, and learning to programme brings me into my creativity.

There's a picture of mum in the paper. I recognise her as one of the women on Greenham Common who have chained themselves to the perimeter fence outside the cruise missile base. I show it to Ruth with some pride.

'My mum's not all talk like some. She acts on her convictions,' I say. 'But why didn't she tell me she was going when we spoke on the phone the other day?'

'Perhaps she didn't want to worry you.'

'That's not like her. She's always been more concerned about humanity and the future of the planet than about me!'

'Well, at least you can show her that *you* care. Go up to Greenham Common and give her some support, and take her some provisions.'

Ruth's advice is always good advice, so I look out my old penny-sized ban the bomb badge and pin it to my coat, and then I drive up to Greenham Common. It's freezing there, and the women have already been chained to the fence for three days and nights! Hats off to them!

Mum's face lights up when I appear, which proves she must be pleased to see me.

'You cold, mum?'

'No, because I'm wearing four layers of clothing and sitting on a waterproof groundsheet, but I could do with a hot bath!'

'Sorry I can't lay that on for you, but I've brought you some Cornish pasties and a packet of crisps.'

She invites me to share them with her, so I sit down and, while we eat, she puts me in the picture about what's been happening.

'On the first day a base commander came out to us and said, 'As far as we're concerned, ladies, you can sit there till the cows come home. It won't have any effect!' But he didn't reckon with all the media coverage we've attracted. We've been shown on world-wide television, Mani. It's the most talked-of political event of the decade!'

'That's great, mum,' I say. 'You and the other mums are doing a phenomenal job!'

I stay sitting beside her all day, because it's a great opportunity to talk. Mum has to listen to me now because she's chained to the fence. She's a captive audience. So I pass on to her what Tracy has told me about the damaging psychological effects of an emotionally deprived childhood, and mum agrees that she neglected me.

'I'm sorry about that now, Mani, but your life's not your own once you volunteer. The cause always comes first before your personal obligations. Besides, when humanity is being threatened with extinction, you haven't time to stop and do child care!'

I see her point, because I've got her political genes in me too, and I also need a cause higher than myself to devote my life to.

'You take after your dad,' she says, and at that I prick up my ears, because normally she never mentions him. I've always idealised my father. In my eyes he's someone like Che Guavera. It's my belief that he left us to return to South America, where he's been fighting against American imperialism ever since. He's probably in Nicaragua now supporting the Sandinistas.

So I tell this to her, but I'm disappointed by her reply.

'Your dad was never a hero' she says, 'just a drunken sod. Though, when you was newly born, he tended you very lovingly - I'll say that for him.'

So I did get a bit of nurturing after all! But then it would have been all the more of an emotional shock when he abandoned me.

'He must be dead,' mum concludes, 'otherwise we'd have heard something from him by now.'

'What do you think happens to us after we die, mum?'

'Nothing happens to us except we rot!' she says.

MIDDLE AGE

My life has changed radically and without warning. Ruth broke off with Tracy last year because she'd fallen for Sharon, and after that nothing was the same again. For example, Ruth went out and got her arms tattooed and all her hair shaved off. I suppose it was to impress Sharon, who is twenty years her junior.

'I don't know if I'm jealous of Sharon or not,' I said cagily.

'If you were jealous, Mani, you'd know about it!'

When the proportion of nights I spent in Ruth's bed began to shrink, I realised that Sharon presented a serious threat to our relationship. I disliked her from the start, because I saw her as underhand and manipulative. But, if I said anything against her, Ruth would always take her side. Soon she started accusing me of being possessive, which is a cardinal sin in her book. This led to a massive ruckus in which I went bananas and threw an iron at her, and that was that. Ruth has a thing about domestic violence because of her traumatic past, so I got my cards on the spot.

'I'm still in shock, IG.'

'Shocks are good, Jim, because they create gaps in which something new can grow.'

'So what am I supposed to be learning?'

'Your present lesson has to do with your feelings. You've been unaware of them most of your life, and you've also been unaware of other people's feelings, which has led you into this crisis.'

'But Ruth and I often discussed our emotional patterns!'

'It's one thing to talk about feelings, and another to actually feel them. A lot of what you do and say is emotionally driven without you realising it, Jim. So the time has come now to be more aware of your feelings.'

'Which ones?'

'Your jealousy to start with! You've never seen yourself as a jealous person. You thought you were too rational and tolerant for that. But the jealousy Sharon has triggered in you contradicts this previous self-image. Now it seems your emotional aloofness was just a shield to protect you from feeling things like jealousy.'

'Tracy said it was anomie. I was alienated from my feelings because I'd been abandoned by my father and my mother, and this messed up my socialisation process.'

'Yes, it's true that you dissociated from your feelings as a coping mechanism.'

'Then that can't be changed. The past is archive footage!'

'That's not true, Jim. When you become aware of a pattern, it changes immediately. But it's time to drop your emotional dependency on Ruth now. Allow that to be archive footage, because the relationship is over. Be grateful for what it has given you and move on.'

'Hmmm... Perhaps it has helped me believe that I'm worthy of love, because, if Ruth found me lovable, then other people could too. It's also helped me find a job where I can be creative. Yes, now that I've got the mates at work, losing Ruth is not so bad. They are my friends, you see, and they're a great bunch of people, although others might see them as nerds!'

Computer specialists are now in high demand, so it was easy to get a job once I'd qualified. And it's no Mickey Mouse job either! The team I work with are breaking bold new ground in programming. It's so exciting that I'm able to resist the temptation to throw spanners in the works, and I even get on with the boss!

My colleagues are all male, so the atmosphere is blokish and our talk is mostly about techie stuff. But there's no one-upmanship amongst us, as there is in other male circles. We see ourselves as collaborators rather than rivals, and share our resources and help each other out. In fact it's the kind of human interaction I've always dreamed was possible. We have a brand new project - to create a computer game. It's very exciting and they were keen for me to be part of the team.

'We need your input, Mani,' they said, 'because you always have such far-out ideas!'

I also have a circle of friends now in addition to my work mates. There are some interesting characters amongst them - people who study UFO's, for example. I've been interested in extra terrestrials ever since I was a kid, and, when crop circles started appearing, I knew they were created by visitors from parallel universes. So I joined a group that had formed to investigate them.

Over the years, I've come to realise that people are more important than theories and ideologies. They are what matter in life, and everyone is interesting and valuable in his own way. I have this vision of us all forming one common field of being in which individuals are the foci. Because if it's true that we're all connected by one consciousness, this would imply that others are not other in the sense of being separate from us. But that we're all part of a greater whole - one humanity!

Our computer game is finished and has been published under the title of *Virtual Lives*. It's revolutionary in that it goes beyond the limitations of pre-programmed imagery, and creates an interface between the software and the mind of the game player. In this way the player becomes a co-creator of the action. And, instead of using a monitor, the scenes are projected straight into his mind, which becomes then like a screen. We believe that *Virtual Lives* will be hailed worldwide as a wonder of nano-technology.

And this starts me thinking - supposing that my life, that I've always believed to be real, was also virtual? Supposing all the things I experience are computer simulations, and I'm living in a digitally generated dream world in which my thoughts are creating a virtual universe? Well, it's possible, isn't it? Quantum physics says that, in the end, all that exists are waves and particles, and the quantum flow itself is like one great universal mind.

I'm down in Wiltshire on a short break. I thought some country air would do me good, so I put my tent in my backpack and made for crop circle country. Last night I camped out on Salisbury plain, and this morning, when I crawled out of my tent as it was getting light, I had an amazing experience.

As I sat there, I watched a great circle being traced around me by an invisible hand. It happened in slow motion and in silence, and it was as if I'd slipped into an altered state of consciousness. The corn was bent until it formed a perfect geometrical pattern with me sitting bang in the centre. I lost all sense of time and, when I came to, it was finished. I walked once round it meditatively to absorb the energy, and then, high as a kite, I packed up my tent and set off down the road.

And the rest you know, but I'd forgotten the end of the story myself - the amnesia saw to that. Otherwise I'd never have thumbed that lift!

When I get up from the mess in the road that used to be me, I'm indignant.

'Why have I been bumped off prematurely?' I ask IG.

'It's because you would only commit to forty-four years when we wrote your life-script. You couldn't be persuaded to stay longer, because you'd got very involved in some interesting new technology that was being developed up here. But your mates in the interlife were helpful when you were creating that computer game. They are more advanced up here where nano-technology is concerned, so they were able to channel some original ideas down to you.'

'Then those brain-waves I had weren't even mine!'

'No, our ideas are never our ideas, Jim. They all come from the collective mind. We are just vehicles for them.'

'And was my life a useful one?'

'Oh yes! You contributed to the development of human consciousness. You worked on yourself, and important changes were made to your template, which meant the human holon evolved further. Because individuals are fractals of the whole, Jim, and if we develop ourselves, we develop humanity as a whole.'

My mental keyboard reappears, and I press LOG OFF at which a pop-up pops up on the screen of my mind.

'Changes have been made to the global template,' it reads, 'save changes?'

And I click YES.

Life 12
FAY the PISCES

This is the moment I've been waiting for. Now I'm free to fly. It's like IG has blown the dandelion puffball and loosened the seeds from its stalk, so each wafts away in its own direction. With nothing solid under my feet any more, I float gently upwards swooning with joy, to be carried away by the solar wind through the vast, black reaches of the quantum vacuum.

When IG asked, 'Who would you like for your mother?' I replied, 'What will be will be,' because I never like to plan. I follow my intuition moment to moment. I think it likely that my mother will be a dear friend from a past life, because, once two souls have related on a deep level, they remain linked through all eternity. In my last incarnation, around two hundred years ago, I fell in love with a Lakeland poet. He was a blackguard, of course, who seduced and abandoned me, but I kept on loving him in spite of the pain, which is a sure sign he'll reappear in this coming incarnation.

I'm flying over the surface of the earth now just above cloud level, and laughing as I trail my feet in the lake of white mistiness. The vault of heaven is a pale crystal blue, and the sun, sinking on the Western horizon, is tingeing the tips of the cloudscape pink, orange and gold. Suddenly, with an ear-splitting roar, an aircraft shoots up from below, blowing my etheric body to smithereens.

Ouch! That was a shock, though I know the sky in the twentieth century is no longer a safe place to be. However, in my present state I'm as indestructible as a stem cell, which is a comfort, and, sure enough, my particles soon rearrange themselves.

I descend through a bank of cloud to emerge above a landscape shrouded in mist. I can make out a river estuary on whose salty flood plains a group of houses huddle as if for shelter. The law of attraction has me in its grip, and I'm carried straight into one of them. I know it's the right place when I discover a long-lost friend lying in one of the bedrooms. It's Pamela, my chaperone from my life in the seventeenth century. But I'm dismayed to find her in great pain. She's already been in labour for twelve long hours, and complications have set in.

'Never fear, my dear, I'm here,' I whisper as I enter into her. The joy I feel at discovering Pamela is going to be my mother is dampened by the worried look on the midwife's face. She's young and inexperienced, and the doctor she sent for hours ago hasn't turned up. What she doesn't know is that his car has broken down, stranding him miles from nowhere, but I can see this clairvoyantly.

I radiate love to Pamela with all my might, which gives her the stamina to keep going through the final stages of labour. Then, with her last ounce of her strength and a loud cry of despair, she casts me out into the world, and departs from it herself. Lying there, newly born, I'm horrified to see her soul rising up out of her body, and floating away through the ceiling.

'The child will live,' pronounces the doctor when he arrives, 'but tragically you've lost the mother!'

At which the midwife, overwhelmed by her first experience of the close proximity of birth and death, bursts into tears. And that's the story of my re-entry into the world on the evening of March 13th 1945. Later I was given the name my mother had chosen for me - Ruth Bernadette Waters.

THE KID

I'm illegitimate it seems. When her pregnancy could no longer be concealed, my mother ran away from home and had me anonymously. So, until my family can be traced and my identity established, Mrs Brown - a good woman of the parish - takes me in. The authorities manage to find my maternal grandparents, who want nothing to do with me. And, as the identity of my father remains a mystery, Mrs Brown adopts me. She already has Hazel and Tony to look after, and a few months later Mr Brown comes home, scarred in body and soul from his stint in a German prisoner-of-war camp.

It's Christmas and we're going to the fancy dress party in the church hall - me as a fairy and Hazel and Tony as pirates. It's brightly decked with balloons and paper chains, and a table's been erected down the centre, and laden with plates of sandwiches, iced cakes, and bowls of jelly and blancmange. I stand there shivering in my thin, white nightdress, a tiara of tinsel in my hair. I'm clutching my magic wand, but it's not a real one - only a wooden spoon topped with a tinfoil star. Around me a broil of children are chasing balloons and screaming when they pop them. I cringe at each explosion, and soon I've slipped away to find somewhere quiet.

I take shelter in the folds of the big, musty curtain that hangs at the side of the stage. From there I can observe the goings-on without being seen. There's a group of mothers sitting over there drinking cups of tea, and suddenly I notice Pamela in their midst. She looks up and waves to me. It's not the first time she's appeared like that, and disappeared just as suddenly.

In January 1953 our village was hit by the great flood. I'd seen it coming and tried to warn them. In a dream I saw the coast being battered, and enormous waves crumbling the sea defences and flooding the land. But no one would listen to me. Then a few nights later, while we were having our tea, we heard a neighbour shout, 'The sea is coming down the lane!' And soon the carpet was bubbling up around our feet, and all the lights went out.

When the water reached our knees, we had to climb into the loft, as we live in a bungalow. There was just enough time to fetch bedding and candles and some warm clothes before the ground floor submerged. No one got any sleep that night. We could hear the furniture floating about below and crashing against the walls, and we prayed that the next tide wouldn't come up any higher, but it did. So Mr Brown hacked a hole in the roof, and we climbed out through the rafters. By then it was getting light, and we were able to look around. Far and wide on every side all we could see was sea. We perched on the roof until the army arrived to rescue us, and we were housed in a prefab until the bungalow was fit for habitation again.

In the scene I'm seeing now it's one of those winter evenings when all the family huddle in the kitchen for warmth. Hazel and Tony go on squabbling until Mr Brown loses it and bashes their heads together. When I look inside him, I can see a turmoil of desperate feelings ready to erupt. Mum dares to say something and he shouts abuse at her, while I cower in the corner not moving a muscle. You could poke me with a stick and I wouldn't stand up for myself.

At the first opportunity, I slip out through the back door. The patch of garden is like another world - dark and silent and dripping wet. And I sit there in the rain, trying to work things out. Why is there so much suffering in the world? Why must people be full of anger and hatred, and make every one around them miserable, when they could be gentle and loving? If a fairy appeared and offered me a wish, I'd say, 'Wave your magic wand and make everybody in the world happy.' Then I hear mum calling,

'Ruth, you little ninny! Come inside at once or you'll catch your death!'

TEENS

My teacher is looking at me sternly. I've been telling a long rigmarole of a story to explain why I haven't done my homework.

'It's time you came down from the clouds, Ruth Waters, and started living in the real world!'

But I don't like the real world very much. It's too dark and gloomy. The worlds I inhabit in my fantasies are far more beautiful.

'I understand how you feel, Fay,' says IG, my inner guide.

He always calls me Fay, and that's funny because it was my fairy name when I was a little girl.

'I know it's a struggle for you to feel at home on this planet,' he goes on, 'and you'd much rather be back in the interlife, but you came here of your own accord.'

'I wish I could remember the interlife!'

'You joined my incarnation group there - I was your life coach. Like the other eleven in your group, your intention was to use this incarnation to grow in consciousness.'

'Hmmm.... and how do I do that?'

'Self-inquiry is the way. So, whenever you meet a problem, inquire into it.'

'Then I'd like to ask why I'm always being misunderstood. Most people down here don't know what to make of me.'

'Well you don't make it easy for them, Fay. You're difficult to pin down, and you're too subtle to be straightforward and direct.'

'People say I never answer a straight question, and I've been called devious and evasive. But I find, when you put a thing into words, you always distort its meaning.'

'Which is why you prefer to stay silent, and not say anything.'

'Yes, and anyway it's impossible to tell the truth, because the truth is too complicated to be told. Things never seem to be black or white. They're always a grey shade in between.'

'It's your nature to see things more subtly than other people.'

'Yes, and I find it hard to tell the difference between what happened, and what I thought happened. I suppose I've got too much imagination.'

'Your imagination is your greatest strength, Fay, but you must learn how to use it as a creative tool.'

'There's a difference between imagination and fantasy then. I live in a fantasy world most of the time. I'm always getting told off in class for looking out the window, and going off into a dream. And another problem at school is I keep getting teased. It seems that whenever my friends want someone to tease, they always pick on me. I don't know why.'

'Then inquire into your part in it. For instance, what do you do when they tease you?'

'Just put up with it. I know they'll soon get tired, and go off and do something else.'

'Then that's the answer to your question - you get teased because you allow it. Your friends know you won't hold it against them.'

'Yes, they're still my friends, whatever they do.'

'Which makes you an ideal victim.'

'And it's almost as if I'm doing them a service, because I know they need to tease somebody.'

'But you're not doing yourself a service, Fay. You must look after yourself better than that.'

It's true that I don't say much. I'm known as the quiet one in my circle of friends. 'Still Ruth Waters run deep,' they say of me. It's because I find it hard to put the things I feel inside into words - unless I write a poem. I've copied all the poems I've written into a little book, which I keep hidden in my secret hiding place. Tony and Hazel would laugh my poems to scorn if they found them, which would be like a desecration.

'Here in the world I must make,
Vague contortions to make,
The people who pass mistake,
What's hidden behind my eyes.
Because in this world feelings are despised!'

When I'm not in my school uniform, I like dressing in green and turquoise blue. I also have a collection of coloured stockings - pink, blue and mauve - and some green fishnet tights that make my legs look like a mermaid's tail when I put my feet together. My hair's so long I can sit on it, and, when I go out, I put black mascara round my eyes to make my face look wan and waif-like. It's a camouflage.

Other people are only allowed to see my surface. I must keep them out of my inner life, with its sensitive layers of multifarious feeling. They'd crash about in there like bulls in a china shop! And I've discovered that my interiority has hidden depths. It goes down so deep that I can't see the bottom - perhaps it's as deep as the universe!

I've been up to London for the day, wandering through the boutiques and coffee bars looking for something miraculous. I don't find any miracles in the West End, but I find one on the train on the way home, when a group of teenagers - one with a guitar - get into my compartment. They move down the aisle singing a happy song about Jesus and handing out leaflets, and the miracle is that they change the whole energy in the train. When they reach where I'm sitting, the guitar player, who's blonde and beautiful, leans across and says to me,

'Take Jesus into your heart, little sister, and your life will be transformed. It's a thousand times stronger than falling in love!' and he hands me a leaflet.

'Come along on Friday,' he says, 'and you'll meet a real live prophet!

'Surely you're not going up to town again!' mum complains. 'That's the second time in a week! You're so selfish, Ruth. You only think of yourself!'

That's unfair! I help mum more than Tony or Hazel ever do, and I'm always ready to lend an ear and be sympathetic when she needs a moan about dad. So why do I feel guilty? Perhaps it's because I'm sorry for her. Things are going from bad to worse with dad. He doesn't sleep any more at night, and I'll often lie awake, listening to him wandering round the house, and crashing the pots and pans in the kitchen. Mum's afraid he's going out of his mind.

The address on the leaflet is in Finchley Road. And, when I get there, I know it's the right house because the door's wide open. So I walk in, and the first person I meet is the blonde guitar player.

'Hi there,' he says, 'I'm Seth.'

'I'm Ruth '

'Hi Ruth! Great that you've come!' and he leads me into a room that's crowded with people sitting in rows on the floor.

'You're just in time,' he says. 'Ezra hasn't started.'

I find a space at the end of one of the rows, and sit down cross-legged. If I crane my neck, I can see the podium at the far end, where a large black man, dressed immaculately all in white, is adjusting the microphone. When he starts to speak I listen spellbound.

'To be born again is not to change your outer self. It's to leave your old self behind completely, and to receive a new self from Jesus. It's to be pure and clean and virgin again. It's to die to your past and be reborn.'

His voice is as deep and rich as treacle, and I sit there hardly remembering to breathe I'm so enthralled. When he's finished, he invites people to come up for a blessing. And I get to my feet without hesitation, and join the line shuffling towards him. The moment arrives when I'm kneeling at his feet, as open and sensitive as a sea urchin. I'm aware of his hands descending through the aura round my head and coming to rest on my scalp. The effect is electrifying! I can feel the energy zinging all the way down through my body.

'Jesus, sweet Jesus,' he prays, 'make of her heart your habitation, that she may see your light and be twice born.'

And the next thing I know is I'm hit by a lightening bolt so powerful it knocks me over backwards. I fall helplessly to the floor, and thrash about screaming. But kind hands soon appear and hold me tight. And they caress my face and stroke me until I'm back in my body again.

'That one would make a good medium,' I hear Ezra say, as his assistants help me back to my place.

I don't go home that night. It feels right to stay here in this community of gentle, loving people. They say I can use the phone to inform my parents, and I get Tony on the line. Lucky it's not mum! He says he'll pass on the message, but I still worry how she'll take it. Then I tell myself that the Browns were never my real family, and Mrs Brown is not my blood mother - although she did her best to be a good mum to me, I grant her that. And thinking these thoughts helps me feel better.

We're all in love with Ezra - the boys as much as the girls. They say he's a reincarnation of the Old Testament prophet of that name. Now he's gone back to the States we're grief-stricken, but we can tune into his energy whenever we need it, because there are photos of him all round the house. And I submit to the strict routine here out of my love for him, though normally there's nothing I hate more than being organised and pressed into a structure.

They wake us up at six, as we have to do our chores before we go out. We clean the house, see to the laundry and chop the vegetables for supper. Then we pile into our old converted bus, and we're driven to some place in London - it's always somewhere different. There we fan out in small groups, and wander the streets all day, singing songs and collecting money.

We tell the passersby that Jesus loves them, and quote the Bible to them. I've had to learn twenty Bible quotes by heart, but not from the Book of Ezra, which is all fire and brimstone. During these first weeks I feel elated, as if I'm walking on air. Because this is how the early Christians lived - moving about, spreading the word and possessing no worldly goods. Ezra calls us *Children of Light*, and it's as if there's a light shining out of me now. I feel so blessed to be given the task of spreading love and hope amongst all the benighted people in the shopping precincts.

289

Most of the money we collect goes to America to finance the temple that Ezra is building. It's going to be a copy of the temple of Solomon, whose walls and floor were overlaid with gold, and which contained two cherubim of olive-wood, each ten cubits high, with outspread wings that touched the walls on either side and met in the middle. When it's finished, we're all going to go and live there.

We don't even get any pocket money, but I don't feel hard done by because all our needs are taken care of. And it's a relief not to have to worry about meals any more, or what to wear. We all dress in the same sort of T-shirts and jeans, which makes it simple, and all that's required of us in return is our chastity and obedience.

Ezra sets high value on chastity, which is why the boys and girls must sleep in separate dormitories, and personal relationships are frowned upon. After I'd been there a few weeks, Seth came with a pledge for me to sign, in which I must promise to remain a virgin until I'm married. When I read it I burst into tears.

'What's the matter, Ruth?'

'I can't sign,' I sob. 'It wouldn't be right because - because I'm not a virgin - though it wasn't my fault - I was forced!'

And, when I explain the sorry circumstances, Seth is very kind and promises to pray for me. But I feel wretched for the rest of the day, because everyone knows it's easier to get reborn when you're a virgin. However I've found that, when black clouds come, they soon blow away again, and by the next morning I've got over it.

After I've been in the house for a while - I don't know how long because I've lost all sense of time - mum turns up together with Tony and Hazel. When she's told that she can't see me, she gets angry and starts making a fuss. I'm upstairs hiding, but I can hear every word of what's going on below, and it makes me cringe. Then Seth comes to find me, and says I have to go down and speak to them.

'Tell them that you don't want to go home,' he says. 'Tell them that you're happy here.'

'I can't do that,' I say. 'I'd get so upset I'd start crying, and then I wouldn't be able to get the words out.'

'Then take a deep breath and think of Ezra, and he'll give you the strength to do it.'

So I breathe deeply and, keeping the image of Ezra steadily before my mind's eye, I go downstairs to confront them.

'There you are Ruthie! You all right? We've come to take you home.'

290

'I'm not coming, mum,' I say. 'This is my home now.'

'But you're in a cult, Ruthie. The vicar has warned us about these people. They're dangerous!'

'Sorry, mum, but I'm happier here than I've ever been in my life before.'

'You've been brainwashed, but you're too bird-brained to see it,' says Tony.

'You're putty in their hands!' says Hazel.

But I remain firm, 'You can say what you like and it won't make any difference, because I'm not coming back!'

I can see how upset mum is getting.

'You've never used that tone to us before, Ruthie,' she cries. 'It just proves how much they've changed you.'

Then she turns to Seth, and starts shouting that I'm under-age, and she's going to report them to the police for kidnapping. I know what I've got to do now, and it will take some courage, so I think of Ezra as hard as I can.

'If you do that,' I say. 'I'll tell the police what dad did to me!'

There's a shocked silence, and then mum says,

'You always were a liar, Ruth! He didn't do nothing to you. You imagined it. Just get that into your head!'

But now I know the difference between imaginary and real, and I reply, 'He sexually abused me and you know it!'

At that mum starts to cry. 'You ungrateful girl!' she sobs. 'After all we've done for you!'

Seeing her so distraught melts me to jelly. I can feel the tears pricking my eyes now, and I know that, once I've started, I'll never be able to stop. So I escape upstairs, and Seth bars the way to prevent them following me. Then, when I'm safely under the bed covers, I cry and cry until all my tears are out. IG is at my side.

'How could I be so cruel - after she'd taken me in, and fed me and brought me up?'

'It was well done, Fay. The conspiracy of silence needed to be broken.'

'But it happened on a night when dad wasn't in his right mind, and mum was asleep so it wasn't her fault.'

'It was sensitive of you to spare their feelings, but now the time has come to stand up for yourself. You said what needed to be said, and it's to your credit that you showed no vindictiveness. What you felt was not anger but compassion.'

'Thank you IG! That makes me feel better. And is it the right thing then for me to be a *Child of Light*?'

'Yes, because there are important lessons for you to learn here. But be discerning, Fay. Keep a clear head and clear eyes, and let love lead the way. Trust nothing that is not love.'

We're overjoyed that Ezra is back again in London. The lecture room is packed with people who've come to hear him speak. And once again I'm uplifted and inspired by his words. Then afterwards I get a surprise when one of the helpers takes me aside, and says I can sleep in the upstairs flat tonight instead of the dorm, which is a great honour as it's usually out of bounds. As I climb the stairs, carrying my toothbrush and my nightdress, my heart is beating with joyful anticipation.

I gave myself to Ezra that night. I surrendered my body in love, and threw in my heart and soul as well - a willing sacrifice. But it wasn't like in my dreams. I'd imagined sleeping with Ezra as a spiritual experience - like having sex with an archangel. But, once we were in bed together and he'd got down to it, there wasn't much difference between Ezra and poor old dad. They were both mad and bad.

I woke up very early - the first light of dawn was just filtering through the curtains. Ezra was sprawled across the bed snoring. He'd left me only a thin strip of mattress to sleep on. I dressed very quietly so as not to wake him, and slipped out of the house without meeting anyone. Then, when I'm down in the street, I realise I've got no money and nowhere to go. So I turn to my inner guide.

'What shall I do now, IG?' I ask.

'Just follow your nose,' he replies, 'and it will point you in the right direction.'

TWENTIES

I'm in charge of the blue group. It's my job to get them out of bed in the morning, and see they wash and dress and eat their breakfast. I have to know which drugs each one is on, and make sure they get taken. Then we go to the shed to collect the tools, and I supervise them all day while they work in the garden. Not much gardening gets done because they're all over the place most of the time.

I've discovered that the mentally disabled can pull you into some very weird psychic spaces. And, as I've always been so vulnerable to other people's feelings, I find them draining. That's why I need to give them the slip, and go off on my own to recuperate every now and again - though I always feel guilty about leaving them unsupervised.

The mansion we live in has seen better days. It's chipped and battered inside but it has extensive grounds. There's a walled vegetable garden, and a pond with a Japanese bridge, and there's my hideaway - a miniature pagoda surrounded by a thicket of rhododendron bushes. When I sit there, I lose all sense of time, and my imagination runs riot like the maze of creepers and tree roots around me. And that keeps me sane.

They say the garden is haunted, and I've seen a few apparitions there. Once a cross-eyed dwarf appeared from nowhere and leered at me, and another time a squirrel, sitting on a branch, had the pinched face of an old woman. And I saw Pamela there once. She walked past in a long white dress, carrying a parasol. This time she took no notice of me. But I wasn't sad because she looked so peaceful and at rest - not at all like a hungry ghost!

The other mental nurses think I'm anti-social, because I don't sit together with them in their cigarette breaks. One day I overhear one say,

'She's a cold fish that one. She always looks right through you when you pass her.'

I was probably miles away and didn't notice her. But I'm hurt that they see me as cold, so I talk to IG about it.

'You think people can tune into you like you tune into them,' he says, 'but that's not the case.'

'Yes, I always thought people would know what I'm feeling without me saying it. So I couldn't understand how they could be so cruel. But now I know they weren't trampling on my feelings intentionally. They didn't know they were doing it!'

'That's right. You must remember, Fay, that most people down here can't communicate telepathically with each other like in the interlife. You come over as cold because you often retreat into a world of your own, and then you're unavailable.'

'It's my survival mechanism, IG. Because, when I'm with other people, I can't help picking up on all that's going on inside them, and it soon gets too much. So I have to withdraw to recuperate.'

'It's not a good idea to indiscriminately absorb all the energies in your surroundings, especially the unhealthy ones. It's time you learned to protect your psychic space, Fay.'

'How do I do that?'

'Put up a boundary. Imagine a circle drawn around you on the ground, and a flashing light moving round it. And give yourself the suggestion that it's a magic circle, and no one can cross the line without your permission.'

'That's a good idea!'

I'm being waylaid by an inmate in a wheelchair, who seizes my arm and holds it in a vice-like grip. He's under a compulsion to relate his experiences as a mercenary in the Congo, where he blew up a train carrying refugees - mainly women and children. A week later he stepped on a landmine and lost both his legs, which he sees as a punishment from God. And I have to listen to his gruesome story again and again.

Although these terrible events happened far away on another continent, and to people I don't know personally, hearing about them is excruciating. I have so much empathy with the victims of atrocities that I try to avoid watching the television news and reading newspapers, because the piteous images of human suffering they show can go on haunting me for days.

I've befriended another inmate - a troubled young woman called Rita. She'll tap on my door late at night, and I always let her in, though I know it means I won't get to bed for hours. Rita believes that everyone around her is conspiring to make her miserable except me. And her long tales of woe always come to the same conclusion.

'No one loves me,' she'll say.

'And what about your mum and dad?'

'Those arse-holes! They're why I went off the rails in the first place.'

'But deep down they must love you,' I reply, 'even if it's in their way and not in yours.'

'They don't care a shit about me!' she growls.

'But I love you Rita,' I say earnestly. 'I'm sending you lots of love this very minute. Can't you feel it?'

She can't. Rita could be surrounded by love and not feel it, because she doesn't believe it's there. Perhaps that applies to all of us to some extent. Perhaps we're surrounded by a universe of love, like fishes surrounded by the ocean, but we're unable to tune into it, because we don't believe the universe has a soul.

One night Rita steals the key to the drugs cupboard and takes an overdose. I'm horrified when I hear what's happened. I've often heard her say that she wished she was dead, and I ignored these cries for help. Full of remorse, I rush to the hospital.

'How are you feeling, Rita?'

'Bad! I'm such a dud. I couldn't even get that right!'

And she starts complaining that no one is taking any notice of her. They haven't even come to clean up the vomit. I've brought her a bunch of pink roses, but she hardly looks at them. And that's the way she goes through life - seeing the thorns and never the flowers.

'Life is very precious - even right now,' I say.

'What! When you're sitting in a pool of vomit?'

'Yes, not in spite of the vomit but because of it,' I explain, but she doesn't understand what I mean.

'I know what they'll do to me now,' she says gloomily. 'They'll increase my drug dose and make me into a zombie.'

I'm beginning to understand why there's so much suffering in the world, and it has to do with the way we select what we see. But my hospital visit drains me, and I go home exhausted.

'You forgot to draw the magic circle, Fay,' says IG. 'You allowed your mind to be taken over by another person, and made her problems your own.'

'I just wanted to help her.'

'And why did you feel the need to do that?'

'Well, as I see it, the only thing wrong with Rita is the way she sees the world. And I thought, if that could be changed, she'd be healed of her condition.'

'But what if she wants to be miserable? Perhaps she needs her problems, because she believes they're the only identity she has.'

'But, if she saw things differently, that would change.'

'As I see it, preoccupying yourself with other people's problems is a way of avoiding your own. You've been trying to fix Rita instead of fixing yourself, Fay, but you can't be of real help to others unless you've helped yourself first.'

'I'm okay. I'm happy.'

'Only on the surface! Underneath both you and Rita have similar wounds. You are both wounded children, and you sensed that subconsciously, Fay, which is why you wanted to help her. You were indirectly trying to heal your own wounds.'

'I thought that, if I could change the way she saw things, I could make her happy.'

'You can't make people happy if they don't want to be. But you can make yourself happy - truly happy I mean. And, if you do that, you'll spread more happiness in the world.'

THIRTIES

I'm dancing in a disco with my long hair flying. My dress of turquoise silk is swirling around me like seaweed in the waves. Tonight's DJ is a celebrity - it's Freddie Manik - and I've fallen under the spell of his hypnotic mix of rhythm and blues. My normal self, as sensitive as a branch of mimosa, has been spirited away, and I'm dancing in wild abandonment tonight like one possessed.

I'm close to the rostrum where Freddie stands manipulating the turntables. I know that, if I stare at him hard enough, he'll look up. And he does. Our eyes meet, there's an electric energy exchange, and I know him immediately. It's my Lakeland poet - the man I loved so much in my last life I was ready to die for him.

I wait until he takes a break and then go and look for him. I find him sitting on the floor behind the rostrum, swigging a bottle of whisky.

'Hi there darlin',' he says.

'You remember me, don't you?'

'Sure!'

'Nether Stowey 1812,' I say. 'We walked hand in hand over the Quantock hills, and lay in the heather and looked at the stars.'

'And did I fuck you, darlin'?'

'Yes, and I've never forgotten it.'

'You wouldn't!' he laughs.

Then he grabs me and gives me one of his long, hard kisses that always made me swoon.

'Be my girl for tonight,' he whispers. 'Hang around till we've packed up, and I'll take you home with me!'

The taxi drops us outside one of those big houses that overlook Hyde Park. Freddie's flat is like a mansion, but the rooms are all empty except for the moulding on the ceilings and some left-behind paraphenalia. There's a bathtub in the entrance hall shaped like a swan, and a chandelier in the kitchen. The ballroom is empty except for a four poster bed, and that's where we sleep.

When we've lit some candles, and pulled the curtains around it so it's cosy, it's like in the old days back in Nether Stowey. I mention this to Freddie but he looks blank. He says he can't remember his past lives. He can't even remember what he did yesterday, but, never mind, he'll take my word for it!

Making love to Freddie was always a mystical experience. And once again I feel the kundalini energy rushing up through my chakras and out through the crown chakra on my head, and I enter a state of ecstasy.

Now that I've found him again after all these years, I want to be by his side. So I follow on his heels like Mary's little lamb on his trajectory through the London clubs and discos. In addition to his DJ work, Freddie plays bass guitar in a band. And I never miss one of their gigs, although it's impossible to get near him. There are always security guards round the stage, and every free minute he's surrounded by a bevy of girls.

'Getting mobbed by the chicks is one of the perks of being a musician!' he explains.

So I'm always alone, dancing in the crowd yet with him in spirit. And afterwards I wait around to see whether I'm going home with him or not. Sometimes he's too hammered to give me a clear answer. He fell flat on the pavement last week while I was flagging down a taxi. It's not laudanum like last time - it's whisky plus some nasty drug I don't even want to know about.

Yes, the life he leads today is quite a comedown for a man who, in his time, was one of the greatest geniuses to grace the planet. Though, when he was young in this life, he did enjoy a brief period of success. He wrote the lyrics for a number of hits that were sung by world-famous groups, and rich businessmen would engage him to DJ at their private parties. But, as he got more shambolic, all that fell apart. Now the poems written by the great bard who once penned *Frost at Midnight* consist in the main of four letter expletives.

MIDDLE AGE

I've been Freddie's girlfriend for more than three years, and the strain is beginning to tell. Not only does he drag me to all his gigs, but he also drags me through the thornbushes of his emotional life. And no magic circle with flashing lights can save me, because Freddie and I share a soul. His pain is my pain, and his demons are my demons, and when he falls apart I fall apart too.

I accompany him through his inner hells gladly, knowing I'm his support. But, when he turns on me afterwards, that's hard to bear. If he's in a destructive mood, whatever his problem is he'll see it as my fault. Then he'll stab me with verbal abuse till he's got it out of his system. And I offer myself up for this purpose like a sacrificial lamb.

I never expected Freddie to be faithful to me, because he's not the faithful type. The background to our love affair at Nether Stowey was that he was a married man doing the dirty on his wife. And he'd regularly betray both me and Sarah by having a fling on the side. Freddie was and still is a bastard, and I know that, through loving him, I'm throwing myself away. Yet I put up with it every time he takes another girl home with him instead of me, and go back to my room in Islington and cry myself to sleep.

One evening, when the gig has gone especially well, and Freddie's in a good mood, he invites the band to come back with us. We all pile into a taxi, and pick up some pizzas and some bottles of booze on the way. Then, when we've finished eating and we're sitting around smoking pot, the conversation turns to sex.

'The boys played well tonight,' says Freddie. 'They deserve a reward - don't you agree, Ruth? I've told them what a great shag you are, so what about you giving it to them? Go on - do it for me!'

When I'm smoking marijuana, I'm not in my body any more - I'm floating some inches above it. And in this state it seems no big deal to do as Freddie says and give it to them. So I remove my clothes, and lie down on the rug with my eyes closed, and my arms stretched out as if I'm on the cross. And the drums, the keyboard, the lead guitar, and the double bass take me in turn, while Freddie brings up the rear. And that's the night when my daughter, Samantha, is conceived, but I don't find that out till later.

When I awake the next morning I feel like a gutted fish. I'm heading for the trash heap, I think. I'm as near a whore now as makes no difference! And I wonder where the other Ruth has gone - the quiet, contemplative girl who loved the stars. How long is it since I gazed at a starry night sky and went into raptures? I have to get out of here quick, I think. So I dress without waking the boys, and go back to my room in Islington.

The place where I live when I'm not at Freddie's is a slum. The house has damp walls and eternally dripping taps, and the women I share it with are sluts. I arrive to find left over food moulding in the kitchen, and a sink full of dirty dishes partly submerged in cold, greasy water. My room is a shambles too. The floor is littered with yellowing newspapers and orange peel, and there are dirty knickers under the bed. I admit I've neglected the place since becoming involved with Freddie, but I feel a strong urge to rectify this now. So I start cleaning like a maniac, and, while I work, I have the following conversation with IG.

'How do you feel, Fay?'

'Not good! I'm ashamed of what I did last night, but I was totally surrendered to Freddie. I had no will of my own any more.'

'How come he's got all that power over you?'

'Fishes get hooked, and Freddie's caught me hook, line and sinker. I'm addicted to him, IG. I need my regular shot of lurid feelings like an addict needs his fix.'

'Well done Fay for seeing that. Now it will be easier for you to get off the hook.'

'But without Freddie and his roller-coaster moods, my life would be empty.'

'You've become dependent on him because you forgot to draw your magic circle.'

298

'I didn't want to draw it, IG. When you love someone, you don't want barriers of any kind. You want to fuse and become one with the person you love.'

'There's fusion between souls in the higher dimension, Fay, but down here, where you're confronting difficult personality traits in yourself and others, distance is required. You need distance to distinguish between energies that are harmful, and those that are good for you.'

'Then my ideal of giving myself body and soul to the man I love was just a silly romantic notion?'

'Yes, and it blinded you to the fact that Freddie was exploiting you. He never respected you or valued your love.'

'Fool that I am!'

'So never allow your love and devotion to be exploited, Fay. And never give your heart to someone who's unable to value it, because then it's sure to get broken.'

'I always believed my love was strong enough to reform Freddie, but I don't believe that any more.'

'Then let go of him and move on. And you need have no regrets, because your love was not in vain. It's better to love an undeserving object with all your heart than not to love at all.'

That evening I go to a disco on the other side of town, where I know I won't run into Freddie, and there I meet Sanjay. We dance a few numbers together, and then we sit out and talk. He tells me he grew up in Bombay, and has come to London to study medicine. He's twenty-six, so fourteen years younger than me. When I mention that I'm hungry, he says he knows how to make a very delicious curry - his mother's own recipe. Would I like to accompany him to his home to try it? I agree because I like his energy.

Sanjay treats me as an honoured guest. He's polite and respectful, and his curry is fantastic. It's the first home-cooked meal I've eaten for months. My life's been too chaotic to shop and cook. When we've finished eating, he asks me if he can give me a foot massage. I say 'yes', and lie back in a chair while he kneels before me and rubs the soles of my feet with sweet-smelling oils. His gentle touch touches me. It feels as if my emotional soul is being massaged too and I start to weep. When Sanjay notices my tears he says,

'Indian foot massage very good for releasing repressed emotions. So go ahead, Ruth - have a good cry!'

We stay up all night talking, and I tell him about Freddie.

'I have to get away,' I say. 'I have to escape from him, but I don't know where to go.'

'Come to India with me! By chance only this morning I bought an air ticket to Bombay, leaving on Sunday. I could get second ticket for you.'

'Okay,' I say, 'I'll come.'

I have a thousand pounds on my Post Office savings account - backpay from when I was made redundant from my last job - so that should be enough. I've only just met this quietly spoken young Indian, and I know nothing about him, but my intuition tells me he's come into my life to rescue me.

Freddie and I are sitting at a table in a café. It's the following night, and I've just broken the news to him that I'm flying to Bombay on Sunday with Sanjay. His reaction comes as a complete surprise. He bursts into tears - big, choking man's tears that melt my heart. So I put my arms round him and hold him close, and we weep together like two little kids, oblivious of the people around us.

'I know I've treated you like shit,' he says, 'but you let me get away with it. It was your fault, Ruth. Why must you always be so fuckin' compassionate?' And he begs me not to go to India. 'Stay with me, Ruth! I'll go under if you leave me!'

I know I'm on the cliff-edge now, and one more twist of my heartstrings could pull me over. So I get to my feet saying, 'I need some time to think this over,' and before he can stop me I've disappeared out the door.

'You have the choice now, Fay,' says IG. 'Are you going over the cliff with him, or will you climb to safety?'

'I'm climbing to safety, IG. Freddie's a lost cause - I see that now. And I know he's got even further to fall before he hits the bottom, and my love can't save him.'

'Good Fay! A lot of trust is needed to let go of someone you love when they are on a slippery slope. But you can't take away another person's right to suffer.'

'I always saw the angel in him, IG, that was my undoing. There was always a halo of light round his demon-filled darkness.'

'The angel was Freddie's spiritual self, which will always be bright and clear. You must distinguish it from the self-destructive madman he's become in this incarnation.'

'There are always some lunatics around me, IG. I seem to attract them.'

'It's because you're in the purgative phase of your spiritual path.'

'What does that mean?'

'You've taken on the task of integrating some elements of human nature that you've rejected up to now. That has meant coming down from the higher chakras that are all sweetness and light, where you'd prefer to be, and dealing with some mess in the lower ones.'

'Then there's a purpose behind it.That's consoling!'

We're travelling round India by train. Holding Sanjay's hand, I watch mile after mile of red and brown desert slide past the barred window. We pass mountains, rounded and hairy like elephants' backs, where monkeys appear from the bushes and hold out their hands for fruit. I see women in luminous saris gliding down hillside tracks with water pots on their heads, and enormous black crows flying into orange sunsets.

When I throw up my breakfast for the third time, I realise I'm pregnant. I tell Sanjay, who looks at me wide-eyed and asks, 'Is it my child?'

'Don't be silly, Sanjay. We haven't slept together properly yet!'

Considering he's a medical student, he's not very clued up about the facts of life! So I start thinking back and come to the conclusion that the only time I could have conceived was on the night when the band shagged me. So any of them could be the father. I take out the tarot pack that I always carry around with me and select five cards - one for each musician. Then I shuffle the pack and, concentrating on my question, pick a card. It's *The Hanged Man* of course!

'Freddie is the father,' I tell Sanjay.

In India you see abandoned children everywhere - homeless children who have lost their mothers, children whose fathers are unknown. They live together in gangs, and go begging on the streets, and still they smile. Some have smiles so radiant they seem to come from the beyond. These children belong to no one and everyone. Existence takes care of them, so it seems no big deal to bear an illegitimate child in India.

When our money runs out, we go back to Sanjay's family in Bombay. I'm given a room at the far end of the house - well away from Sanjay's bedroom. His mother tells me that Sanjay is engaged to be married. The astrologer has found a very beautiful girl for him from a good Hindu family and what is more with a generous dowry. The wedding is planned for next summer, after Sanjay has finished his degree.

This comes as a shock to me, because Sanjay has never breathed a word about it. So I ask him to explain. First he begs for my forgiveness, and then confesses that he's in a terrible dilemma.

'I can't see any way out,' he says. 'You're the woman I love, Ruth, and I want to be with you. But I owe obedience to my mother and father!'

'You'll just have to make up your mind one way or the other!' I say peeved.

When I'm unable to eat any breakfast, his mother guesses why.

'You must go back to your husband,' she says.

'I don't have a husband - only Sanjay.'

Now she looks worried. I can see she's afraid it's Sanjay's child, though she doesn't dare say so. And Sanjay is in favour of keeping her in the dark.

'It's in our interest,' he says, 'because, if my parents believe I am the father, they possibly come round and agree to me marrying you.'

'I think that's very unlikely.'

And I realise it's the last thing I want - to be married to Sanjay, and to live in this house under the beady eye of his mother. However I don't say this out loud as it would hurt Sanjay's feelings. Besides, I'm dependent on their hospitality as I have no money left. So I allow both Sanjay and his mother to go on misunderstanding the situation. And IG picks me up on this.

'You're being ambiguous intentionally, Fay. You're letting misunderstandings run on without making an attempt to clarify them. I've seen you do that before.'

'Yes, I like leaving things vague.'

'And why?'

'I suppose it's the way I keep my options open. I try to avoid being definite, because that would tie me down.'

'But you've no need to protect your freedom like that any more. You're strong enough now, Fay, to be open and direct with people. Try it and see!'

'When will your family send money?' Sanjay's mother asks.

We're seated round the table, eating one of her delicious curries.

'I don't have a family,' I reply.

She looks incredulous. So I explain how I was adopted and brought up by the Browns, who don't want to know me any more. That puts the cat amongst the pigeons. She says something in Hindi to Sanjay's father, who turns to me with a stern look on his face.

'But you must have some family somewhere, Ruth. Who then supports you financially?'

'Nobody. I live like the sparrows of the air, and existence always provides.'

There follows an angry exchange between Sanjay and his father. I can't understand what they're saying, but I can feel the vibe and it isn't good. So I excuse myself and go to my room.

When Sanjay comes to seek me out, he's looking upset.

'They want you to leave first thing in the morning, Ruth,' he says. 'And I've decided I come with you. We'll go to the ashram.'

As soon as we step inside the gate, I feel the powerful spiritual energy of the place. The tropical garden in which the ashram is situated is bathed in it. The plants are lusher and greener here, and the blossoms brighter than I've ever seen before. And everywhere there's water - little ponds and running streams and splashing waterfalls.

'We've found the earthly paradise! Let's stay here forever,' I say to Sanjay with shining eyes.

'Alright, because the food is delicious,' says Sanjay. 'All vegetarian and organic and cooked with love!'

The meditators, dressed in maroon robes, glide along the white marble paths between the different buildings. I soon join their number, and merge into the wave of maroon filling the meditation hall. As ashram workers, we get our board and lodging free in return for six hours' work a day, which leaves us plenty of time to learn to meditate. My job is to check in the new arrivals at the welcome desk together with Swami Jivan, a tall blonde German.

'As soon as people enter the gate their vibe is raised,' I say to him. 'It's like a magic wand is waved and they're transformed.'

'Yes, if I had not experienced it myself, I would never believe it possible,' he replies.

'It's how I've always imagined people should be with each other - not violent and competitive, but peaceful and loving.'

'And it's scientific,' he goes on. 'The meditation techniques we do here raise the resonance of our subtle body, and move us onto a higher level of consciousness.'

'That's what it feels like!'

'Yes indeed! Our resonance is being lifted higher all the time. Soon we'll become pure light, and be invisible to ordinary eyes like the Mayans.'

'Why the Mayans?'

'Because they did not die out as we are told! What occurred was their shamans raised their collective vibration to the point where they all became light-bodies, and they crossed the threshold together into invisibility.'

Jivan's mind is full of wacky ideas, and it's tempting to speculate on them. But I'm trying to empty my head of thoughts in order to go deeper into meditation. And slowly I'm getting the knack of it. Then one day, while I'm sitting in the meditation hall that's open to the garden, and listening to the birds and the rustle of the bamboo while I watch my thoughts come and go, I feel my baby kick. And the reality of my situation kicks in immediately. What on earth am I going to do?

Sanjay has started spending time with a group of young Indians of his own age. He's no longer there for me, and I haven't a rupee to my name. I realise that I got into this situation because I was avoiding taking responsibility for myself. But now there's someone else to think of. I'm responsible for the baby growing in my womb. So, although I know I've found my spiritual home here, and I don't want to leave it ever, I decide to return to England.

I borrow some money from Swami Jivan, and buy an air ticket from Bombay to London. When I step out of the plane at Heathrow into the grey air of a chilly April morning, it's like a reality shift. Compared to India this country is harsh and cold and rough! Will I be able to hold on to the state I've reached through meditation when I'm immersed in the collective unconscious of the West?

I'm sitting in a train bound for Sheerness. I'm returning to the village where I was born - the village where Pamela sought shelter forty years ago. Like me she was pregnant and like me she was alone. I wonder why she no longer appears to me. If I ever needed a mother it's now!

When I arrive, I find Mrs Brown in a wheelchair. She had a stroke last year and lost the use of her legs.

'I never see Hazel and Tony for weeks on end,' she grumbles. 'They've just left me to get on with it! And where have you been all these years, Ruthie?'

'India.'

'Oh yes - what you been doing there?'

'Meditating.'

If I'd said fornicating she couldn't have looked more disapproving. I see that she's staring at my protruding belly.

'Your poor mother arrived in that condition,' she says. 'Took a room down the road, she did - I knew the landlady. Such a tragedy that poor young thing dying in childbirth! I hope history is not going to repeat itself.'

When I ask after Mr Brown, I hear that he passed away ten years ago. Then I ask if I can stay with her till after the baby's born, and she looks pleased. She says she can do with some help. The woman from social services is so unreliable.

Samantha was born on September 16th making her a Virgo, my complementary sign. And history did repeat itself - I died, but not in childbirth. I died afterwards when I fell into a post-natal depression. It was like a total eclipse of the sun. It threw me into a limbo in which I was disconnected from everything - even from the baby at my breast. I hadn't the energy to meditate any more, so I lost that rapturous inner state I'd found in India. IG tried to comfort me.

'It was bound to happen because the higher you rise the lower you always fall. However, now you know that state of consciousness exists, you'll be able to reach it again.'

'But I still don't understand why I've got this depression, IG. It doesn't make sense when I have a beautiful baby daughter to love now.'

'It does makes sense, because giving birth to her triggered your repressed pain. You had buried it away and forgotten all about it, but the time has come to engage with it now.'

'Is that why I've come back to Sheppey - because there's unfinished business here for me to complete?'

'Yes, your wounds are associated with this place.'

'Does it have to do with losing my mother?'

'That's right. You're carrying the grief of the motherless child and also the guilt, because deep down you've always believed that you killed Pamela. The way Mrs Brown used to speak of her death when you were small gave you the impression that you had killed her.'

'That would explain why I've always felt guilty and never knew why. And it also explains why I try to do so much for others - to assuage my guilt.'

'But it's not true that you killed your mother, Ruth. She had to leave when she did. It was in her life-script. And, if you can accept that it was in your life-script too, and therefore it had a purpose, you'll be able to let go of your guilt and move on.'

And those years that I spent caring for Mrs Brown, and walking along the sea defences looking out over the waves, reconciled me with my past.

OLD AGE

A client gets up to leave, fishing in her handbag for her handkerchief. My sessions always bring people into their feelings.

After Sam was born, I started giving tarot readings. It was just the right thing for me, as it didn't tie me down, and it gave me the scope to use my intuitive skills and my imagination creatively. I found I could use the tarot cards as a tool to help people understand their lives. But I always kept my magic circle in place, and so I avoided losing myself in the helper role.

We managed financially while Sam was growing up thanks to the generosity of Mrs Brown. I often wonder why she left the house to me. Perhaps she was grateful that I stayed and cared for her during her final years. Or perhaps she was sorry for what Mr Brown did, and wanted to make it up to me. Either way I was grateful to her, as it meant I didn't have to pay rent and, through letting a room to a lodger, I even got a small income.

Freddie never saw his daughter. I intended to get in touch with him after Sam was born, but then I heard from a past member of the band that he had no fixed address - he'd become a rough sleeper. And the next time I inquired he was already dead. I grieved for him but not for long, as I have a new life now to be getting on with. And the angel I saw in Freddie lives on in Sam. She has his eyes.

Samantha is twenty-one now, and studying to be a social worker. When she started asking about her father, I told her he'd been a great poet, but that was in another life. In this incarnation he was a musician and songwriter, and he'd died very young. I kept quiet about his addictions, and the fact that he'd lived on the streets at the end. But the irony was that, when she left college, Samantha took a job with a charity that supports street people. And now she's devoting her life to vagrants and human derilects, and bringing light into the confusion of their days. I think of her passing through the night shelters like Florence Nightingale, the lady with the lamp, and I draw a magic circle round her to keep her safe from harm.

Now that Ruth is eighty-five her body is old and dying, while Fay is as young and as fresh as ever. The care home where Ruth lives is close to the beach, and she can hear the waves pounding on the pebbles through the open window. Because of her weak heart she can't walk far any longer - just down to her seat on the sea front, where she likes sitting and watching the seagulls.

She's glad that she learned to meditate, as it's a great resource now she's so immobile. It gives her back her freedom, because, when she goes into meditation, she merges with everything around her - the sky, the sea and the sun.

The sun is setting over the waves, and the gulls are flying out to sea uttering high-pitched cries. Fay flies with them to where, beyond sight of land, the sea becomes sky and the sky becomes sea, and reality is wave upon wave of energy.

When Fay is gone, Ruth's body lies slumped on the bench on the sea-front, her head sunk onto her chest.

306

I'm aware of a bright light that dazzles me at first and makes me blink. Raising my head, I see throngs of people surrounding me. They are very bright, as if like stars they're all illuminated from within. And some of the faces I recognise. Pamela is the first to come forward and give me a long and loving embrace. She is followed by Mr and Mrs Brown who do likewise. And then comes Freddie, wonderfully restored and a picture of health. He must have been through rehab!

'I'm clean now,' he says happily. 'All the dirt has come out in the wash!'

'My life as Ruth taught me a lot, IG. It opened up depths in me I'd never touched before.'

'And now you know that bliss is attained via suffering. And, if you avoid suffering when you write your life-script, you'll not attain bliss, because they both come in by the same door.'

'Yes, and I've also learned that all you need is love. Because, when you're carrying love in your heart, you'll pass through the killing fields of pain and suffering unscathed.'

'Thus life after life, and death after death, deeper and higher we go!'

EPILOGUE

The shadow of the moon has cleared the earth leaving it gleaming white and azure blue again. The eclipse is over; the worm hole has closed.

One by one the group members awoke from their trance to discover, amazed, that they'd been dreaming. They had been here in the group room the whole time!

I was the last to awake. I yawned and stretched and looked around, and found myself sitting in the centre of a circle of twelve empty chairs.

Well, it's given me plenty to mull over, I think. A veritable gold mine of experience! Integrating those impressions and insights is going to keep me out of mischief for a while!

I love my work - it's a dream job in fact! I feel so blessed to be granted a panoramic view of human life in all its zany diversity, and to experience the nitty-gritty of the twelve divine archetypes in the flesh and in real time. Superlative! Talk about job satisfaction - I'd say you can't beat it!

APPENDIX

Worksheet to Determine Your Dominant Archetypes

If you have no personal birth chart, log in to www.astro.com.

Click 'Free Horoscopes'. Click 'Chart drawing, Ascendant'.

Fill in your details with your time of birth as close as possible, then click 'Continue', and your chart will come up.

On the left-hand side you will find the signs of your sun and your ascendant (your rising sign) in red, and the sign of your moon in blue in the box below.

Check whether you have an outer planet within ten degrees of the sun, or of the ascendant in the first house (see Preface page ii).

The sections of the inner wheel (the houses) are numbered anticlockwise. Note the number of the house of your sun. Each house corresponds to an archetype as follows: 1= Aries, 2= Taurus, 3= Gemini, 4= Cancer, 5= Leo, 6= Virgo, 7= Libra, 8= Scorpio, 9= Sagittarius, 10= Capricorn, 11= Aquarius, 12= Pisces. Determine the sign corresponding to the house of your sun.

Now fill in the zodiac signs representing your main archetypes in the table below. Most people will have three or four, and some may have up to six relevant signs. By clicking 'Add an extra person' on astro.com, you can bring up the charts of your family and friends, and add them to the table too.

Now you know which characters in *Virtual Lives* and their life stories are particularly relevant to yourself and to the people close to you. As an example the following table includes a few famous names.

Other worksheets can be found on the author's website at www.astrophoebe.com.

Dominant Archetypes

Name	Sun sign	Ascendant sign	Moon sign	Sun house sign	Archetype of outer planet conjunct sun	Archetype of outer planet conjunct ascendant
David Cameron	Libra	Libra	Leo	Aries		
Prince Charles	Scorpio	Leo	Taurus	Cancer		
J.K.Rowling	Sagittarius	Cancer	Pisces	Leo	Pisces (Neptune)	
Venus Williams	Gemini	Libra	Leo	Sagittarius		Scorpio (Pluto)
Self						
Friend 1						
Friend 2						
Mother						
Partner						

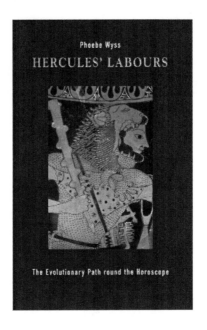

HERCULES' LABOURS

The Evolutionary Path Round The Horoscope by Phoebe Wyss

The myths of Hercules' labours are used as keys in this book to unlock the deeper significance of the twelve houses of the horoscope. These are interpreted archetypally and seen as reflecting the same twelve principles as the signs. Its light and playful style makes Hercules' Labours very accessible – also to readers unversed in astrology. You hear the ancient myths speak to you personally, and are led to uncover your personal agenda of labours.

'Simply written, though never simplistic, this insightful archetypal tour of the astrological houses provides rich food for thought for the novice and experienced astrologer alike. Highly recommended as an addition to any astrologer's library.' *Jane Ridder-Patrick (Principal of the Scottish School of Astrology)*

Tree Tongue Publishing, 2007 · ISBN 0-9546099-6-4
Order for £9.99 from **www.astrophoebe.com**

LEBENSRAD – WHEEL OF LIFE

An Astrology Board Game by Phoebe Wyss

Follow in the footsteps of Hercules and perform your twelve labours as you move round horoscope through the houses, each of which stands for an archetypal field of experience. The synchronicities are striking when you play this oracle game. The planets you take with closed eyes, and the sentences on the task-cards the dice leads you to, are likely to be very relevant to your life, and may bring new insights. When the game is played with friends and family, conversations arise about things that really matter. Thus, through playing Lebensrad, you learn more about astrology, more about yourself and more about others.

For more information and to order see
www.astrophoebe.com

Dear in my heart
your memory
is kept

Lightning Source UK Ltd.
Milton Keynes UK

176565UK00001B/18/P